Older
Americans

A CHANGING
MARKET

Older Americans

A CHANGING MARKET

6th EDITION

The American
Generations Series

New Strategist Publications, Inc.
Ithaca, New York

New Strategist Publications, Inc.
P.O. Box 242, Ithaca, New York 14851
800/848-0842; 607/273-0913
www.newstrategist.com

ISBN 978-1-935114-26-0

Printed in the United States of America

Table of Contents

Chapter 9. Spending

Chapter 10. Time Use

Chapter 11. Wealth

Tables

Chapter 4. Housing

Chapter 5. Income

Chapter 6. Labor Force

Illustrations

Introduction

A revolution is underway. In 2008, the oldest members of the Baby-Boom generation turned 62 and became eligible to collect (early) Social Security benefits. The radical transformation of the 55-or-older age group continues with each birthday celebrated by the enormous Baby-Boom generation as it enters old age.

During the next two decades, no segment of the population will change more than older Americans. Not only is the age group expanding greatly, but its priorities are changing rapidly. Many Boomers are approaching their retirement years with dread, their retirement savings decimated, their homes worth less than they paid for them. The concerns of aging Boomers will be paramount for politicians, policymakers, and businesses in the years ahead. They should watch out: Boomers are frightened and angry, their retirement plans suddenly changed. They are looking for solutions to their mounting problems, but they are more cynical than ever before toward those who claim to have the answers.

The sixth edition of *Older Americans: A Changing Market* reveals the characteristics of the older population today and tomorrow. It details the lifestyles, incomes, and spending patterns of people aged 55 and older. *Older Americans: A Changing Market* reveals what lies ahead as struggling Boomers increasingly dominate the older age group. Those who understand their changing wants and needs will be prepared for the future. *Older Americans: A Changing Market* will help you prepare for what lies ahead.

How to use this book

Older Americans: A Changing Market is designed for easy use. It is divided into 11 chapters, organized alphabetically: Attitudes, Education, Health, Housing, Income, Labor Force, Living Arrangements, Population, Spending, Time Use, and Wealth.

The sixth edition of *Older Americans* includes the latest data on the changing demographics of homeownership, based on the Census Bureau's 2008 Housing Vacancies and Homeownership Survey. In the Health chapter, you will find up-to-date statistics on health insurance coverage. The Income chapter, with statistics from the 2008 Current Population Survey, reveals the struggle of so many Americans to stay afloat. *Older Americans* presents labor force data for 2008, which include the government's labor force projections that show rising labor force participation among people aged 55 and older. It contains new data on the health of the population, and includes updated estimates of the overweight and obese. The Census Bureau's latest population projections are also included in the book and show the enormous growth of the older population already in progress. *Older Americans* also presents estimates of household wealth from the Federal Reserve Board's 2007 Survey of Consumer Finances, which reveal the financial status of households just as the housing bubble burst and the recession began. New to this edition is an Attitudes chapter with data from the 2008 General Social Survey that compare and contrast the perspectives of the generations.

Most of the tables in *Older Americans* are based on data collected by the federal government, in particular the Census Bureau, the Bureau of Labor Statistics, the National Center for Education Statistics, the National Center for Health Statistics, and the Federal Reserve Board. The federal government is the best source of up-to-date, reliable information on the changing characteristics of Americans. By having *Older Americans* on your bookshelf, you can get the answers to your questions faster than you can online. Even better, visit www.newstrategist.com and download the PDF version of *Older Americans*, which includes links to an Excel version of every table in the book, which will enable you to do your own analyses, put together a PowerPoint presentation, etc.

Each chapter of *Older Americans* includes the demographic and lifestyle data most important to researchers. Within each chapter, most of the tables are based on data collected by the federal government, but they are not simple reproductions of government spreadsheets—as is the case in many reference books. Instead, each table is individually compiled and created by New Strategist's editors, with calculations designed to reveal the trends. The task of extracting and processing raw data from the government's web sites to create a single table can require hours of effort. New Strategist has done the work for you, with each table telling a story about older Americans—a story explained by the accompanying text and chart, which analyze the data and highlight future trends. If you need more information than the tables and text provide, you can plumb the original source listed at the bottom of each table.

The book contains a comprehensive table list to help you locate the information you need. For a more detailed search, see the index at the back of the book. Also at the back of the book is the glossary, which defines the terms and describes the many surveys referenced in the tables and text.

With *Older Americans: A Changing Market* in hand, you can position your organization to benefit from the revolution occurring in the older market.

CHAPTER 1

Attitudes

■ Older Americans are the most trusting. Forty-one percent of older Americans say most people can be trusted. In contrast, only 24 percent of Millennials say others can be trusted.

■ Generation Xers are least satisfied with their finances, with 36 percent saying they are not at all satisfied.

■ Boomers are most likely to say that their pay has not kept pace with inflation. Forty-five percent of Boomers feel like they are falling behind.

■ Older Americans are by far most likely to think they are much better off than their parents were at the same age (45 percent). Generation Xers are least likely to agree (24 percent).

■ The percentage of people who think two children is ideal ranges from a high of 55 percent among Baby Boomers to a low of 41 percent among Millennials. A larger 44 percent of Millennials think three or more children is ideal.

■ While only 40 percent of older Americans believe in evolution, the share climbs to 48 percent among Boomers, to 52 percent among Gen Xers, and to 62 percent among Millennials.

■ The 52 percent majority of Millennials sees nothing wrong with sexual relations between adults of the same sex. Support shrinks to 45 percent among Gen Xers, 34 percent among Boomers, and to a mere 19 percent among older Americans.

Older Americans Are the Happiest

Most of the married are very happily married.

When asked how happy they are, only about one in three Americans say they are very happy. The 54 percent majority reports feeling only pretty happy. Older people are happier than middle-aged or younger adults. Forty percent of older Americans say they are very happy compared with 31 percent of Baby Boomers and Generation Xers and just 27 percent of Millennials.

The 62 percent majority of married Americans say they are very happily married. Here, too, older Americans are the happiest group, with 67 of them saying they are very happily married. Only 60 percent of Boomers say the same.

Americans are almost evenly split on whether life is exciting (47 percent) or pretty routine (48 percent). Variations by generation are small, but Generation X is slightly more likely than others to find life exciting.

Few believe most people can be trusted. Only 32 percent of the public says that most people can be trusted, down from 37 percent who felt that way 10 years earlier. Younger generations are far less trusting than older Americans, as only 24 percent of Millennials believe most people can be trusted compared with 41 percent of people aged 63 or older.

■ Younger generations of Americans are struggling with a deteriorating economy, which reduces their happiness and increases their distrust.

Few Millennials trust others

(percent of people aged 18 or older who think most people can be trusted, by generation, 2008)

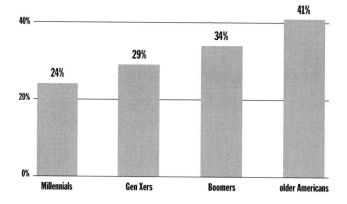

Table 1.1 General Happiness, 2008

"Taken all together, how would you say things are these days—would you say that you are very happy, pretty happy, or not too happy?"

(percent of people aged 18 or older responding by generation, 2008)

	very happy	pretty happy	not too happy
Total people	**31.7%**	**54.4%**	**13.9%**
Millennial generation (aged 18 to 31)	27.4	55.8	16.8
Generation X (aged 32 to 43)	31.0	57.0	12.0
Baby Boom (aged 44 to 62)	30.8	55.6	13.6
Older Americans (aged 63 or older)	39.7	47.2	13.1

Source: Survey Documentation and Analysis, Computer-assisted Survey Methods Program, University of California, Berkeley, General Social Surveys, 1972-2008 Cumulative Data Files, Internet site http://sda.berkeley.edu/cgi-bin32/hsda?harcsda+gss08; calculations by New Strategist

Table 1.2 Happiness of Marriage, 2008

"Taking all things together, how would you describe your marriage?"

(percent of currently married people aged 18 or older responding by generation, 2008)

	very happy	pretty happy	not too happy
Total married people	**62.1%**	**35.3%**	**2.6%**
Millennial generation (aged 18 to 31)	63.7	35.1	1.1
Generation X (aged 32 to 43)	61.5	35.7	2.7
Baby Boom (aged 44 to 62)	60.0	36.7	3.3
Older Americans (aged 63 or older)	66.6	31.7	1.7

Source: Survey Documentation and Analysis, Computer-assisted Survey Methods Program, University of California, Berkeley, General Social Surveys, 1972-2008 Cumulative Data Files, Internet site http://sda.berkeley.edu/cgi-bin32/hsda?harcsda+gss08; calculations by New Strategist

Table 1.3 Is Life Exciting, Routine, or Dull, 2008

"In general, do you find life exciting, pretty routine, or dull?"

(percent of people aged 18 or older responding by generation, 2008)

	exciting	pretty routine	dull
Total people	**47.2%**	**48.1%**	**3.8%**
Millennial generation (aged 18 to 31)	47.4	48.5	3.8
Generation X (aged 32 to 43)	48.6	46.5	3.1
Baby Boom (aged 44 to 62)	46.7	49.0	3.9
Older Americans (aged 63 or older)	46.4	47.7	4.4

Note: Numbers will not sum to total because "don't know" is not shown.
Source: Survey Documentation and Analysis, Computer-assisted Survey Methods Program, University of California, Berkeley, General Social Surveys, 1972-2008 Cumulative Data Files, Internet site http://sda.berkeley.edu/cgi-bin32/hsda?harcsda+gss08; calculations by New Strategist

Table 1.4 Trust in Others, 2008

"Generally speaking, would you say that most people can be trusted or that you can't be too careful in life?"

(percent of people aged 18 or older responding by generation, 2008)

	can trust	cannot trust	depends
Total people	**31.9%**	**63.9%**	**4.3%**
Millennial generation (aged 18 to 31)	24.5	71.1	4.4
Generation X (aged 32 to 43)	29.3	66.7	4.1
Baby Boom (aged 44 to 62)	34.3	61.5	4.2
Older Americans (aged 63 or older)	40.5	55.4	4.1

Source: Survey Documentation and Analysis, Computer-assisted Survey Methods Program, University of California, Berkeley, General Social Surveys, 1972-2008 Cumulative Data Files, Internet site http://sda.berkeley.edu/cgi-bin32/hsda?harcsda+gss08; calculations by New Strategist

Belief in Hard Work Is Strong among Younger Generations

Generation Xers are most likely to own a business.

How do people get ahead? Two-thirds of Americans say it is by hard work. Only 12 percent believe luck alone gets people ahead. Generation Xers (71 percent) and Millennials (70 percent) believe most strongly in hard work to get ahead, whereas Boomers (63 percent) give the least credence to hard work.

Millennials are most likely to live in the same city as they did when they were 16 years old, in part because they have had less time to move than older generations. Boomers are less likely than Gen Xers or older Americans to live in a different state than they did at age 16.

The likelihood of owning a business is greatest among Generation Xers (18 percent) and Boomers (15 percent). Only 8 percent of Millennials own a business, and the share among older Americans is an even smaller 6 percent.

■ The belief in luck as the most important way to get ahead is strongest among older Americans.

Business ownership peaks in middle age

(percent of people aged 18 or older who currently own and help manage a business, by generation, 2008)

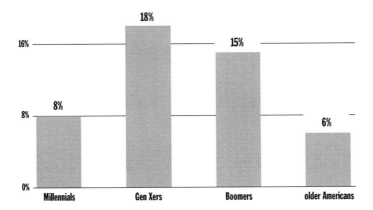

Table 1.5 How People Get Ahead, 2008

"Some people say that people get ahead by their own hard work; others say that lucky breaks or help from other people are more important. Which do you think is most important?"

(percent of people aged 18 or older responding by generation, 2008)

	hard work	both equally	luck
Total people	**67.1%**	**20.8%**	**12.1%**
Millennial generation (aged 18 to 31)	70.2	18.0	11.8
Generation X (aged 32 to 43)	70.7	20.5	8.9
Baby Boom (aged 44 to 62)	63.4	23.7	12.9
Older Americans (aged 63 or older)	66.2	19.2	14.7

Source: Survey Documentation and Analysis, Computer-assisted Survey Methods Program, University of California, Berkeley, General Social Surveys, 1972-2008 Cumulative Data Files, Internet site http://sda.berkeley.edu/cgi-bin32/hsda?harcsda+gss08; calculations by New Strategist

Table 1.6 Geographic Mobility Since Age 16, 2008

"When you were 16 years old, were you living in this same (city/town/county)?"

(percent of people aged 18 or older responding by generation, 2008)

	same city	same state different city	different state
Total people	**40.0%**	**23.2%**	**36.8%**
Millennial generation (aged 18 to 31)	55.4	16.6	28.0
Generation X (aged 32 to 43)	34.1	22.9	43.0
Baby Boom (aged 44 to 62)	37.0	27.1	35.9
Older Americans (aged 63 or older)	32.9	24.5	42.6

Source: Survey Documentation and Analysis, Computer-assisted Survey Methods Program, University of California, Berkeley, General Social Surveys, 1972-2008 Cumulative Data Files, Internet site http://sda.berkeley.edu/cgi-bin32/hsda?harcsda+gss08; calculations by New Strategist

Table 1.7 Business Ownership, 2008

"Are you, alone or with others, currently the owner of a business you help manage, including self-employment or selling any goods or services to others?"

(percent of people aged 18 or older responding by generation, 2008)

	yes	no
Total people	**12.6%**	**87.4%**
Millennial generation (aged 18 to 31)	8.4	91.6
Generation X (aged 32 to 43)	18.1	81.9
Baby Boom (aged 44 to 62)	15.4	84.6
Older Americans (aged 63 or older)	5.8	94.2

Source: Survey Documentation and Analysis, Computer-assisted Survey Methods Program, University of California, Berkeley, General Social Surveys, 1972-2008 Cumulative Data Files, Internet site http://sda.berkeley.edu/cgi-bin32/hsda?harcsda+gss08; calculations by New Strategist

More than One-Third of Gen Xers Are Dissatisfied with Their Finances

Many say that their pay has not kept up with the cost of living.

Few Americans identify with the lower class, but even fewer think they are in the upper class. The 89 percent majority of every generation sees itself as either working class or middle class, but the distribution varies greatly. Whereas Millennials, Xers, and Boomers are more likely to call themselves working class than middle class, the opposite is true for older Americans. The highest share of self-identified lower-class people occurs among Millennials (8 percent). Older Americans are most likely to describe themselves as upper class (5 percent).

A 47 percent plurality of Americans believes their family income is average, while not quite one-third says they make less than average. Baby Boomers are most likely to say they have above average incomes, and they may well be right since they are in their peak earning years.

The share of people who are satisfied with their financial situation stood at 29 percent in 2008, down slightly from the 31 percent of 1998. In parallel, those more or less satisfied with their finances have declined from 44 to 42 percent. Satisfaction with personal finances is greatest among older Americans, only 20 percent of whom are not at all satisfied. The dissatisfied share peaks among Generation Xers at 36 percent, as they juggle college loans, mortgages, and the expenses of growing families.

When asked whether the pay at their current job has kept pace with the cost of living, Boomers are by far most likely to say it has not. The Millennial generation has the largest share of people who say their pay has just about kept pace with inflation. In each generation about one in four say their pay has risen faster than the cost of living.

■ Financial backsliding was common among working Americans even before the current economic disruptions.

Many Boomers and younger adults are dissatisfied with their financial situation

(percent of people aged 18 or older who say they are not at all satisfied with their financial situation, by generation, 2008)

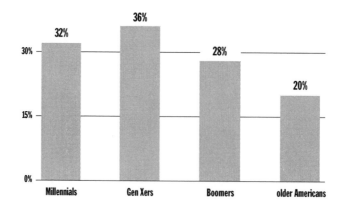

Table 1.8 Social Class Membership, 2008

"If you were asked to use one of four names for your social class, which would you say you belong in: the lower class, the working class, the middle class, or the upper class?"

(percent of people aged 18 or older responding by generation, 2008)

	lower	working	middle	upper
Total people	**7.3%**	**45.7%**	**43.4%**	**3.6%**
Millennial generation (aged 18 to 31)	8.1	49.4	40.1	2.5
Generation X (aged 32 to 43)	6.7	50.5	38.6	4.2
Baby Boom (aged 44 to 62)	7.3	45.5	43.7	3.5
Older Americans (aged 63 or older)	6.6	35.3	53.2	4.8

Source: Survey Documentation and Analysis, Computer-assisted Survey Methods Program, University of California, Berkeley, General Social Surveys, 1972-2008 Cumulative Data Files, Internet site http://sda.berkeley.edu/cgi-bin32/hsda?harcsda+gss08; calculations by New Strategist

Table 1.9 Family Income Relative to Others, 2008

"Compared with American families in general, would you say your family income is far below average, below average, average, above average, or far above average?"

(percent of people aged 18 or older responding by generation, 2008)

	far below average	below average	average	above average	far above average
Total people	**6.3%**	**25.2%**	**46.7%**	**19.8%**	**2.0%**
Millennial generation (aged 18 to 31)	6.6	26.8	49.4	16.5	0.7
Generation X (aged 32 to 43)	7.8	25.5	43.9	20.7	2.2
Baby Boom (aged 44 to 62)	5.6	22.8	46.2	22.4	3.1
Older Americans (aged 63 or older)	5.0	27.8	47.9	17.9	1.4

Source: Survey Documentation and Analysis, Computer-assisted Survey Methods Program, University of California, Berkeley, General Social Surveys, 1972-2008 Cumulative Data Files, Internet site http://sda.berkeley.edu/cgi-bin32/hsda?harcsda+gss08; calculations by New Strategist

Table 1.10 Satisfaction with Financial Situation, 2008

"So far as you and your family are concerned, would you say that you are pretty well satisfied with your present financial situation, more or less satisfied, or not satisfied at all?"

(percent of people aged 18 or older responding by generation, 2008)

	satisfied	more or less satisfied	not at all satisfied
Total people	**28.9%**	**41.7%**	**29.4%**
Millennial generation (aged 18 to 31)	24.8	43.7	31.5
Generation X (aged 32 to 43)	20.5	43.7	35.7
Baby Boom (aged 44 to 62)	27.3	44.2	28.4
Older Americans (aged 63 or older)	48.0	31.6	20.4

Source: Survey Documentation and Analysis, Computer-assisted Survey Methods Program, University of California, Berkeley, General Social Surveys, 1972-2008 Cumulative Data Files, Internet site http://sda.berkeley.edu/cgi-bin32/hsda?harcsda+gss08; calculations by New Strategist

Table 1.11 How Has Pay Changed, 2008

"Thinking about your current employer, how much has your pay changed on your current job since you began? Would you say . . . "

(percent of employed people aged 18 to 62 responding by generation, 2008)

	my pay has gone up more than the cost of living	my pay has stayed about the same as the cost of living	my pay has not kept up with the cost of living
Total people	**23.5%**	**35.6%**	**40.9%**
Millennial generation (aged 18 to 31)	22.7	41.9	35.3
Generation X (aged 32 to 43)	24.9	37.7	37.4
Baby Boom (aged 44 to 62)	22.9	32.3	44.8

Source: Survey Documentation and Analysis, Computer-assisted Survey Methods Program, University of California, Berkeley, General Social Surveys, 1972-2008 Cumulative Data Files, Internet site http://sda.berkeley.edu/cgi-bin32/hsda?harcsda+gss08; calculations by New Strategist

The American Standard of Living May Be Falling

Fewer Americans believe they are better off than their parents.

When comparing their own standard of living now with that of their parents when they were the same age, 63 percent of respondents say they are better off. The figure was 66 percent 10 years earlier. Older Americans are by far most likely to think they are much better off than their parents were at the same age (45 percent). Generation Xers are least likely to agree (24 percent).

When asked whether they think they have a good chance to improve their standard of living, 59 percent of Americans agree. This is down sharply from the 74 percent of a decade earlier. Not surprisingly, younger people—with most of their life ahead of them—are more hopeful than older Americans. Seventy-two percent of Millennials, but only 47 percent of older Americans, believe that their standard of living will improve.

Sixty percent of respondents believe their children will have a better standard of living when they reach the respondent's present age. The share is 67 percent among Millennials, 61 percent among Xers, 57 percent among Boomers, and 53 percent among older Americans. One in four Boomers and older Americans predict their children will be worse off, but fewer Xers (16 percent) and Millennials (13 percent) agree.

■ The Americans who now have the least are most likely to believe things will be better in the future.

Most still believe children will be better off

(percent of people aged 18 or older with children who think their children's standard of living will be somewhat or much better than theirs is now, by generation, 2008)

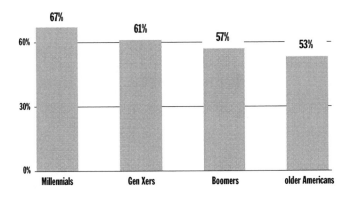

Table 1.12 Parents' Standard of Living, 2008

"Compared to your parents when they were the age you are now, do you think your own standard of living now is much better, somewhat better, about the same, somewhat worse, or much worse than theirs was?"

(percent of people aged 18 or older responding by generation, 2008)

	much better	somewhat better	about the same	somewhat worse	much worse
Total people	**31.6%**	**31.1%**	**21.1%**	**11.5%**	**4.6%**
Millennial generation (aged 18 to 31)	32.9	32.6	20.3	10.5	3.7
Generation X (aged 32 to 43)	24.1	31.6	22.0	16.3	6.1
Baby Boom (aged 44 to 62)	28.9	31.4	22.3	12.4	5.1
Older Americans (aged 63 or older)	45.1	27.9	19.1	5.2	2.7

Source: Survey Documentation and Analysis, Computer-assisted Survey Methods Program, University of California, Berkeley, General Social Surveys, 1972-2008 Cumulative Data Files, Internet site http://sda.berkeley.edu/cgi-bin32/hsda?harcsda+gss08; calculations by New Strategist

Table 1.13 Standard of Living Will Improve, 2008

"The way things are in America, people like me and my family have a good chance of improving our standard of living. Do you agree or disagree?"

(percent of people aged 18 or older responding by generation, 2008)

	strongly agree	agree	neither	disagree	strongly disagree
Total people	**14.7%**	**44.7%**	**13.9%**	**22.9%**	**3.8%**
Millennial generation (aged 18 to 31)	19.6	52.2	11.3	14.0	2.9
Generation X (aged 32 to 43)	15.2	44.7	13.7	21.7	4.6
Baby Boom (aged 44 to 62)	12.0	44.9	11.8	27.9	3.4
Older Americans (aged 63 or older)	13.2	33.6	22.3	26.0	4.9

Source: Survey Documentation and Analysis, Computer-assisted Survey Methods Program, University of California, Berkeley, General Social Surveys, 1972-2008 Cumulative Data Files, Internet site http://sda.berkeley.edu/cgi-bin32/hsda?harcsda+gss08; calculations by New Strategist

Table 1.14 Children's Standard of Living, 2008

"When your children are at the age you are now, do you think their
standard of living will be much better, somewhat better,
about the same, somewhat worse, or much worse than yours is now?"

(percent of people aged 18 or older with children responding by generation, 2008)

	much better	somewhat better	about the same	somewhat worse	much worse
Total people with children	**30.7%**	**29.2%**	**20.0%**	**14.3%**	**5.8%**
Millennial generation (aged 18 to 31)	40.1	27.0	19.3	8.0	5.5
Generation X (aged 32 to 43)	25.5	36.0	22.9	12.4	3.6
Baby Boom (aged 44 to 62)	27.7	29.5	18.4	17.7	6.5
Older Americans (aged 63 or older)	30.3	23.2	21.3	17.5	7.6

Source: Survey Documentation and Analysis, Computer-assisted Survey Methods Program, University of California, Berkeley, General Social Surveys, 1972-2008 Cumulative Data Files, Internet site http://sda.berkeley.edu/cgi-bin32/hsda?harcsda+gss08; calculations by New Strategist

Two Children Are Most Popular

Many Millennials think three children is the ideal number, however.

Across generations a plurality of Americans thinks that two is the ideal number of children. Boomers, who are finished with their childbearing, are most enthusiastic about two—55 percent say two children is ideal and only 29 percent think three or more is best. In contrast, only 41 percent of Millennials think two is ideal and a larger 44 percent say three or more is best. Millennials are more likely than the oldest Americans—who gave birth to the Baby Boom generation—to think three or more children is ideal.

Regardless of their number, most children are subject to a good, hard spanking when they misbehave. Seventy-one percent of Americans believe children sometimes must be spanked, with little difference by generation.

The 52 percent majority of older Americans believes it is better for everyone involved if the man is the achiever outside the home and the woman takes care of the home and family. Only about one-third of the younger generations agree. A similar gap exists with regard to working mothers. Among Boomers and younger generations, about three out of four think a working mother can have just as warm and secure a relationship with her children as a mother who does not work. Only 62 percent of older Americans agree.

Support for the view that government should help people who are sick and in need is strongest among Millennials and declines with age. Twenty-one percent of older Americans—the only age group that is covered by government-provided health insurance—believe people should help themselves. Only 12 percent of Millennials agree.

■ The generation gap in attitudes between Boomers and their parents is greater than the gap between Boomers and their children.

Few among the younger generations think traditional sex roles are best

(percent of people aged 18 or older who think traditional sex roles are best, by generation, 2008)

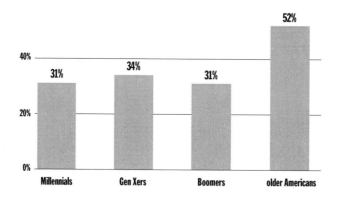

Table 1.15 Ideal Number of Children, 2008

"What do you think is the ideal number of children for a family to have?"

(percent of people aged 18 or older responding by generation, 2008)

	none	one	two	three	four or more	as many as want
Total people	**1.0%**	**2.5%**	**47.7%**	**26.6%**	**10.1%**	**12.1%**
Millennial generation (aged 18 to 31)	0.7	3.9	40.6	34.3	10.1	10.4
Generation X (aged 32 to 43)	0.0	2.5	44.4	29.3	12.0	11.9
Baby Boom (aged 44 to 62)	1.5	1.6	55.2	19.2	9.4	13.2
Older Americans (aged 63 or older)	1.4	2.5	45.5	28.3	9.6	12.6

Source: Survey Documentation and Analysis, Computer-assisted Survey Methods Program, University of California, Berkeley, General Social Surveys, 1972-2008 Cumulative Data Files, Internet site http://sda.berkeley.edu/cgi-bin32/hsda?harcsda+gss08; calculations by New Strategist

Table 1.16 Spanking Children, 2008

"Do you strongly agree, agree, disagree, or strongly disagree that it is sometimes necessary to discipline a child with a good, hard, spanking?"

(percent of people aged 18 or older responding by generation, 2008)

	strongly agree	agree	disagree	strongly disagree
Total people	**24.7%**	**46.2%**	**23.1%**	**6.0%**
Millennial generation (aged 18 to 31)	29.8	41.0	23.0	6.2
Generation X (aged 32 to 43)	19.9	52.3	22.6	5.2
Baby Boom (aged 44 to 62)	24.7	46.1	22.7	6.5
Older Americans (aged 63 or older)	22.9	46.1	25.2	5.7

Source: Survey Documentation and Analysis, Computer-assisted Survey Methods Program, University of California, Berkeley, General Social Surveys, 1972-2008 Cumulative Data Files, Internet site http://sda.berkeley.edu/cgi-bin32/hsda?harcsda+gss08; calculations by New Strategist

Table 1.17 Better for Man to Work, Woman to Tend Home, 2008

"It is much better for everyone involved if the man is the achiever outside
the home and the woman takes care of the home and family."

(percent of people aged 18 or older responding by generation, 2008)

	strongly agree	agree	disagree	strongly disagree
Total people	**8.2%**	**27.0%**	**47.2%**	**17.5%**
Millennial generation (aged 18 to 31)	7.3	24.0	44.5	24.2
Generation X (aged 32 to 43)	8.4	25.2	47.8	18.6
Baby Boom (aged 44 to 62)	7.5	24.0	50.7	17.8
Older Americans (aged 63 or older)	11.3	40.5	42.6	5.5

Source: Survey Documentation and Analysis, Computer-assisted Survey Methods Program, University of California, Berkeley, General Social Surveys, 1972-2008 Cumulative Data Files, Internet site http://sda.berkeley.edu/cgi-bin32/hsda?harcsda+gss08; calculations by New Strategist

Table 1.18 Working Mother's Relationship with Children, 2008

"Do you strongly agree, agree, disagree, or strongly disagree with
the statement: A working mother can establish just as warm and secure
a relationship with her children as a mother who does not work."

(percent of people aged 18 or older responding by generation, 2008)

	strongly agree	agree	disagree	strongly disagree
Total people	**26.3%**	**46.0%**	**22.2%**	**5.4%**
Millennial generation (aged 18 to 31)	26.0	46.1	22.5	5.4
Generation X (aged 32 to 43)	31.4	44.5	20.9	3.2
Baby Boom (aged 44 to 62)	26.3	49.0	19.0	5.6
Older Americans (aged 63 or older)	20.7	41.4	29.9	7.9

Source: Survey Documentation and Analysis, Computer-assisted Survey Methods Program, University of California, Berkeley, General Social Surveys, 1972-2008 Cumulative Data Files, Internet site http://sda.berkeley.edu/cgi-bin32/hsda?harcsda+gss08; calculations by New Strategist

Table 1.19 Should Government Help the Sick, 2008

"Some people think that it is the responsibility of the government in Washington
to see to it that people have help in paying for doctors and hospital bills; they
are at point 1. Others think that these matters are not the responsibility of
the federal government and that people should take care of these things themselves;
they are at point 5. Where would you place yourself on this scale?"

(percent of people aged 18 or older responding by generation, 2008)

	1 government should help	2	3 agree with both	4	5 people should help themselves
Total people	**34.9%**	**18.7%**	**30.0%**	**9.3%**	**7.1%**
Millennial generation (aged 18 to 31)	39.0	23.1	25.9	5.2	6.8
Generation X (aged 32 to 43)	35.0	19.8	30.7	9.4	5.1
Baby Boom (aged 44 to 62)	35.2	18.5	28.0	11.4	7.0
Older Americans (aged 63 or older)	28.7	11.2	39.1	10.0	11.0

*Source: Survey Documentation and Analysis, Computer-assisted Survey Methods Program, University of California, Berkeley,
General Social Surveys, 1972-2008 Cumulative Data Files, Internet site http://sda.berkeley.edu/cgi-bin32/hsda?harcsda+gss08;
calculations by New Strategist*

Religious Diversity Is on the Rise

Share of Protestants dwindles with each successive generation.

Asked whether science makes our way of life change too fast, the 52 percent majority of Americans disagrees with the statement. Each successive generation is a little surer than the previous one. While 51 percent of older Americans think things change too fast, only 45 percent of Millennials hold that opinion.

Americans are almost equally divided between those who believe in evolution (51 percent) and those who do not (49 percent), but there are large differences by generation. While only 40 percent of older Americans believe in evolution, the share climbs to 48 percent among Boomers, to 52 percent among Gen Xers, and to 62 percent among Millennials.

Among older Americans, 60 percent are Protestants. Among Baby Boomers, the figure is 58 percent. Yet only 39 percent of Generation Xers and Millennials call themselves Protestant. Conversely, the share of people with no religious preference climbs from a mere 7 percent among older Americans to a substantial 27 percent among Millennials. Older Americans are twice as likely as members of younger generations to describe themselves as very religious and they are more likely to see the Bible as the word of God.

The majority of Americans disapproves of the Supreme Court decision barring local governments from requiring religious readings in public schools. While the slight majority of Millennials and nearly half the Generation Xers support the decision, only 36 percent of Baby Boomers and just 31 percent of older Americans back the Supreme Court's decision.

■ Along with the growing racial and ethnic diversity of the American, religious preferences are also growing more diverse.

Younger generations are less Protestant

(percent of people aged 18 or older whose religious preference is Protestant, by generation, 2008)

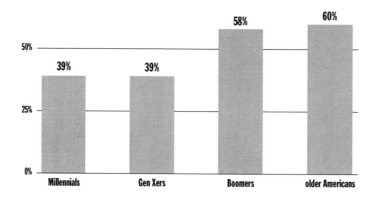

Table 1.20 **Attitude toward Science, 2008**

"Do you strongly agree, agree, disagree, or strongly disagree with the statement:
Science makes our way of life change too fast."

(percent of people aged 18 or older responding by generation, 2008)

	strongly agree	agree	disagree	strongly disagree
Total people	**9.0%**	**38.8%**	**43.9%**	**8.3%**
Millennial generation (aged 18 to 31)	8.3	36.3	46.1	9.3
Generation X (aged 32 to 43)	8.4	39.4	44.9	7.3
Baby Boom (aged 44 to 62)	10.3	38.0	42.2	9.4
Older Americans (aged 63 or older)	7.6	43.4	43.4	5.7

Source: Survey Documentation and Analysis, Computer-assisted Survey Methods Program, University of California, Berkeley, General Social Surveys, 1972-2008 Cumulative Data Files, Internet site http://sda.berkeley.edu/cgi-bin32/hsda?harcsda+gss08; calculations by New Strategist

Table 1.21 **Attitude toward Evolution, 2008**

"True or false: Human beings, as we know them today,
developed from earlier species of animals."

(percent of people aged 18 or older responding by generation, 2008)

	true	false
Total people	**50.9%**	**49.1%**
Millennial generation (aged 18 to 31)	62.1	37.9
Generation X (aged 32 to 43)	51.8	48.2
Baby Boom (aged 44 to 62)	47.8	52.2
Older Americans (aged 63 or older)	39.8	60.2

Source: Survey Documentation and Analysis, Computer-assisted Survey Methods Program, University of California, Berkeley, General Social Surveys, 1972-2008 Cumulative Data Files, Internet site http://sda.berkeley.edu/cgi-bin32/hsda?harcsda+gss08; calculations by New Strategist

Table 1.22 Religious Preference, 2008

"What is your religious preference?"

(percent of people aged 18 or older responding by generation, 2008)

	Protestant	Catholic	Jewish	none
Total people	**49.8%**	**25.1%**	**1.7%**	**16.8%**
Millennial generation (aged 18 to 31)	39.0	26.3	1.2	27.1
Generation X (aged 32 to 43)	39.1	28.1	2.9	18.9
Baby Boom (aged 44 to 62)	58.4	21.1	0.9	13.6
Older Americans (aged 63 or older)	60.1	27.3	2.6	7.2

Note: Figures will not sum to 100 percent because "other religion" is not shown.
Source: Survey Documentation and Analysis, Computer-assisted Survey Methods Program, University of California, Berkeley, General Social Surveys, 1972-2008 Cumulative Data Files, Internet site http://sda.berkeley.edu/cgi-bin32/hsda?harcsda+gss08; calculations by New Strategist

Table 1.23 Degree of Religiosity, 2008

"To what extent do you consider yourself a religious person?"

(percent of people aged 18 or older responding by generation, 2008)

	very religious	moderately religious	slightly religious	not religious
Total people	**18.2%**	**42.2%**	**23.4%**	**16.2%**
Millennial generation (aged 18 to 31)	12.1	33.1	28.1	26.7
Generation X (aged 32 to 43)	13.8	40.6	25.7	19.9
Baby Boom (aged 44 to 62)	20.1	45.9	22.1	11.9
Older Americans (aged 63 or older)	27.7	48.6	17.4	6.3

Source: Survey Documentation and Analysis, Computer-assisted Survey Methods Program, University of California, Berkeley, General Social Surveys, 1972-2008 Cumulative Data Files, Internet site http://sda.berkeley.edu/cgi-bin32/hsda?harcsda+gss08; calculations by New Strategist

Table 1.24 Belief in the Bible, 2008

"Which of these statements comes closest to describing your feelings about the Bible? 1) The Bible is the actual word of God and is to be taken literally, word for word; 2) The Bible is the inspired word of God but not everything in it should be taken literally, word for word; 3) The Bible is an ancient book of fables, legends, history, and moral precepts recorded by men."

(percent of people aged 18 or older responding by generation, 2008)

	word of God	inspired word	book of fables	other
Total people	**32.0%**	**47.0%**	**19.6%**	**1.4%**
Millennial generation (aged 18 to 31)	27.5	50.3	21.0	1.3
Generation X (aged 32 to 43)	30.8	46.3	20.3	2.6
Baby Boom (aged 44 to 62)	33.6	44.9	20.6	1.0
Older Americans (aged 63 or older)	36.0	48.1	15.0	1.0

Source: Survey Documentation and Analysis, Computer-assisted Survey Methods Program, University of California, Berkeley, General Social Surveys, 1972-2008 Cumulative Data Files, Internet site http://sda.berkeley.edu/cgi-bin32/hsda?harcsda+gss08; calculations by New Strategist

Table 1.25 Bible in the Public Schools, 2008

"The United States Supreme Court has ruled that no state or local government may require the reading of the Lord's Prayer or Bible verses in public schools. What are your views on this? Do you approve or disapprove of the court ruling?"

(percent of people aged 18 or older responding by generation, 2008)

	approve	disapprove
Total people	**41.8%**	**58.2%**
Millennial generation (aged 18 to 31)	52.8	47.2
Generation X (aged 32 to 43)	48.0	52.0
Baby Boom (aged 44 to 62)	36.2	63.8
Older Americans (aged 63 or older)	30.7	69.3

Source: Survey Documentation and Analysis, Computer-assisted Survey Methods Program, University of California, Berkeley, General Social Surveys, 1972-2008 Cumulative Data Files, Internet site http://sda.berkeley.edu/cgi-bin32/hsda?harcsda+gss08; calculations by New Strategist

Growing Tolerance of Sexual Behavior

Americans are growing more accepting of premarital sex and homosexuality.

The share of Americans who believe that premarital sex is not wrong at all grew from 43 percent in 1998 to 55 percent in 2008. While the majority of Boomers and younger generations see nothing wrong with premarital sex, the share is just 38 percent among older Americans.

When it comes to sexual relations between adults of the same sex, the trend of growing tolerance is apparent as well. Each successive generation is less likely to condemn homosexuality. The 52 percent majority of Millennials sees nothing wrong with same-sex sexual relations, but support dwindles to 45 percent among Xers, 34 percent among Boomers, and a mere 19 percent among older Americans.

■ Acceptance of gays and lesbians will grow as tolerant Millennials replace older, less tolerant generations in the population.

Most Millennials see nothing wrong with gays and lesbians

(percent of people aged 18 or older who see nothing wrong with sexual relations between two adults of the same sex, by generation, 2008)

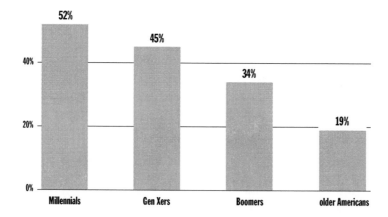

Table 1.26 Premarital Sex, 2008

"If a man and woman have sex relations before marriage, do you think it is always wrong, almost always wrong, wrong only sometimes, or not wrong at all?"

(percent of people aged 18 or older responding by generation, 2008)

	always wrong	almost always wrong	sometimes wrong	not wrong at all
Total people	**22.6%**	**7.2%**	**15.4%**	**54.8%**
Millennial generation (aged 18 to 31)	17.5	6.9	15.8	59.8
Generation X (aged 32 to 43)	21.0	4.9	17.7	56.5
Baby Boom (aged 44 to 62)	23.0	6.5	12.4	58.1
Older Americans (aged 63 or older)	31.0	11.7	18.9	38.4

Source: Survey Documentation and Analysis, Computer-assisted Survey Methods Program, University of California, Berkeley, General Social Surveys, 1972-2008 Cumulative Data Files, Internet site http://sda.berkeley.edu/cgi-bin32/hsda?harcsda+gss08; calculations by New Strategist

Table 1.27 Homosexual Relations, 2008

"What about sexual relations between two adults of the same sex?"

(percent of people aged 18 or older responding by generation, 2008)

	always wrong	almost always wrong	sometimes wrong	not wrong at all
Total people	**52.4%**	**3.1%**	**6.7%**	**37.8%**
Millennial generation (aged 18 to 31)	41.4	1.8	5.3	51.5
Generation X (aged 32 to 43)	47.0	4.3	3.9	44.8
Baby Boom (aged 44 to 62)	53.0	3.3	10.0	33.8
Older Americans (aged 63 or older)	72.6	2.8	5.4	19.2

Source: Survey Documentation and Analysis, Computer-assisted Survey Methods Program, University of California, Berkeley, General Social Surveys, 1972-2008 Cumulative Data Files, Internet site http://sda.berkeley.edu/cgi-bin32/hsda?harcsda+gss08; calculations by New Strategist

Television News Is Most Important

The Internet has jumped into the number two position.

Nearly half of Americans get most of their news from television, 22 percent from the Internet, and 20 percent from the newspaper. Together these three news outlets are the main source of news for 90 percent of the public. But there are big differences by generation. Millennials are far more likely than any other generation to depend on the Internet. Thirty-eight percent of Millennials say the Internet is their most important source of news versus 30 percent of Gen Xers, 15 percent of Boomers and just 5 percent of older Americans. The Millennial attachment to the Internet is so strong that it has boosted the Internet into second place as a news source.

When asked about their political leanings, Americans like to point to the moderate middle (39 percent). A slightly smaller 36 percent say they are conservative, and 26 percent identify themselves as liberal. Millennials are twice as likely as older Americans to hold liberal views. The share of self-described conservatives drops with each successive generation, from 45 percent among older Americans to 28 percent among Millennials. In fact, a larger share of Millennials is liberal than conservative—the only generation in which liberals outnumber conservatives.

■ Millennials depend more on the Internet than on television for the news.

News sources differ dramatically by generation

(percent of people aged 18 or older who turn to each source for the news, by generation, 2008)

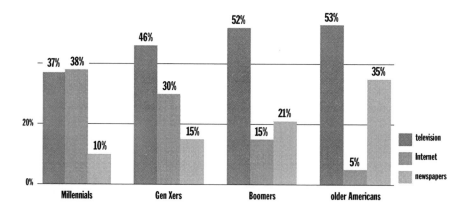

Table 1.28 Main Source of Information about Events in the News, 2008

"We are interested in how people get information about events in the news.
Where do you get most of your information about current news events?"

(percent of people aged 18 or older responding by generation, 2008)

	television	Internet	newspapers	radio	family, friends and colleagues	books, magazines, other
Total people	47.5%	22.0%	19.6%	6.1%	2.8%	2.0%
Millennial generation (aged 18 to 31)	36.8	38.3	9.8	8.4	5.9	0.8
Generation X (aged 32 to 43)	46.3	30.0	15.2	3.1	3.1	2.3
Baby Boom (aged 44 to 62)	52.4	14.8	21.5	7.6	1.5	2.2
Older Americans (aged 63 or older)	53.1	5.0	34.5	3.5	1.0	2.9

Source: Survey Documentation and Analysis, Computer-assisted Survey Methods Program, University of California, Berkeley, General Social Surveys, 1972-2008 Cumulative Data Files, Internet site http://sda.berkeley.edu/cgi-bin32/hsda?harcsda+gss08; calculations by New Strategist

Table 1.29 Political Leanings, 2008

"We hear a lot of talk these days about liberals and conservatives.
On a seven-point scale from extremely liberal (1) to extremely
conservative (7), where would you place yourself?"

(percent of people aged 18 or older responding by generation, 2008)

	1 extremely liberal	2 liberal	3 slightly liberal	4 moderate	5 slightly conservative	6 conservative	7 extremely conservative
Total people	2.9%	12.2%	10.6%	38.6%	15.1%	16.7%	3.9%
Millennial generation (aged 18 to 31)	3.0	16.1	15.3	37.6	13.9	12.2	2.0
Generation X (aged 32 to 43)	3.7	12.9	11.1	39.4	15.6	12.3	5.0
Baby Boom (aged 44 to 62)	2.1	11.1	10.2	38.4	15.9	18.1	4.1
Older Americans (aged 63 or older)	3.2	8.8	4.8	38.4	14.8	25.4	4.6

Source: Survey Documentation and Analysis, Computer-assisted Survey Methods Program, University of California, Berkeley, General Social Surveys, 1972-2008 Cumulative Data Files, Internet site http://sda.berkeley.edu/cgi-bin32/hsda?harcsda+gss08; calculations by New Strategist

Millennials and Gen Xers Are at Odds over Death Penalty

Overall opposition to capital punishment is growing.

Opposition to capital punishment is growing. In 1998, 27 percent of the public opposed the death penalty for persons convicted of murder. In 2008, the figure had increased to 32 percent. In a generational pattern rarely seen, support for the death penalty is strongest among Generation X (71 percent) and weakest among Millennials (63 percent).

The vast majority of Americans favors requiring a permit for gun ownership, and there is little variation by generation. Generation Xers are slightly more likely to favor gun permits than the other generations.

Support for legal abortion under certain circumstances is overwhelming. Nine out of 10 Americans approve of abortion if the women's health is in serious danger, and three-quarters if the pregnancy is the result of rape or there is a chance of serious defect in the baby. Economic and lifestyle reasons garner substantially lower approval ratings of 40 to 44 percent. Generally, there are only small differences in opinion by generation, but there are exceptions. Millennials are sharply less likely than the other generations to allow abortion because of a serious defect in the baby, for example. Boomers are much more accepting than other generations of abortion because a woman does not want more children. Older Americans are more likely than younger generations to want to outlaw abortion for economic and lifestyle reasons, but not for health reasons.

The two-thirds majority of Americans favor the right of the terminally ill to die with a doctor's assistance, but support for this measure has fallen slightly over the last decade. Support is strongest among Boomers, who are at an age when they may well see a terminally ill parent suffer, but it is weakest among older Americans themselves.

■ The generation gap between Boomers and older Americans is readily apparent on the issue of abortion for economic or lifestyle reasons.

Most do not favor allowing abortions for any reason

(percent of people aged 18 or older who favor legal abortion for any reason, by generation, 2008)

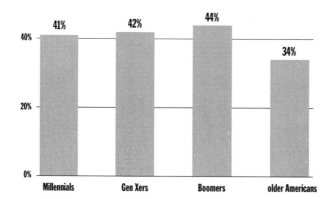

Table 1.30 Favor or Oppose Death Penalty for Murder, 2008

"Do you favor or oppose the death penalty for persons convicted of murder?"

(percent of people aged 18 or older responding by generation, 2008)

	favor	oppose
Total people	**67.6%**	**32.4%**
Millennial generation (aged 18 to 31)	62.8	37.2
Generation X (aged 32 to 43)	71.0	29.0
Baby Boom (aged 44 to 62)	68.0	32.0
Older Americans (aged 63 or older)	69.5	30.5

Source: Survey Documentation and Analysis, Computer-assisted Survey Methods Program, University of California, Berkeley, General Social Surveys, 1972-2008 Cumulative Data Files, Internet site http://sda.berkeley.edu/cgi-bin32/hsda?harcsda+gss08; calculations by New Strategist

Table 1.31 Favor or Oppose Gun Permits, 2008

"Would you favor or oppose a law which would require a person to obtain a police permit before he or she could buy a gun?"

(percent of people aged 18 or older responding by generation, 2008)

	favor	oppose
Total people	**79.1%**	**20.9%**
Millennial generation (aged 18 to 31)	78.3	21.7
Generation X (aged 32 to 43)	81.1	18.8
Baby Boom (aged 44 to 62)	78.4	21.6
Older Americans (aged 63 or older)	78.7	21.3

Source: Survey Documentation and Analysis, Computer-assisted Survey Methods Program, University of California, Berkeley, General Social Surveys, 1972-2008 Cumulative Data Files, Internet site http://sda.berkeley.edu/cgi-bin32/hsda?harcsda+gss08; calculations by New Strategist

Table 1.32 Support for Legal Abortion by Reason, 2008

"Please tell me whether or not you think it should be possible for a
pregnant woman to obtain a legal abortion if . . . "

(percent of people aged 18 or older responding yes by generation, 2008)

	her health is seriously endangered	pregnancy is the result of a rape	there is a serious defect in the baby	she cannot afford more children	she does not want more childen	she is single and does not want to marry the man	she wants it for any reason
Total people	**88.6%**	**75.6%**	**73.7%**	**42.3%**	**43.7%**	**40.3%**	**41.2%**
Millennial generation (aged 18 to 31)	85.5	75.8	64.1	43.9	41.5	38.8	41.2
Generation X (aged 32 to 43)	90.6	76.8	75.6	39.4	41.9	40.3	41.8
Baby Boom (aged 44 to 62)	90.4	74.6	78.1	46.2	50.0	43.3	44.5
Older Americans (aged 63 or older)	86.6	75.4	75.2	35.2	35.4	35.1	33.6

*Source: Survey Documentation and Analysis, Computer-assisted Survey Methods Program, University of California, Berkeley,
General Social Surveys, 1972-2008 Cumulative Data Files, Internet site http://sda.berkeley.edu/cgi-bin32/hsda?harcsda+gss08;
calculations by New Strategist*

Table 1.33 Doctor-Assisted Suicide, 2008

"When a person has a disease that cannot be cured, do you think
doctors should be allowed by law to end the patient's life by
some painless means if the patient and his family request it?"

(percent of people aged 18 or older responding by generation, 2008)

	yes	no
Total people	**66.2%**	**33.8%**
Millennial generation (aged 18 to 31)	63.7	36.3
Generation X (aged 32 to 43)	66.1	33.9
Baby Boom (aged 44 to 62)	69.9	30.1
Older Americans (aged 63 or older)	61.1	38.9

*Source: Survey Documentation and Analysis, Computer-assisted Survey Methods Program, University of California, Berkeley,
General Social Surveys, 1972-2008 Cumulative Data Files, Internet site http://sda.berkeley.edu/cgi-bin32/hsda?harcsda+gss08;
calculations by New Strategist*

2

Education

■ One of the most dramatic changes of the past half-century is the rise in the educational attainment of the older population. As recently as 1970, the solid majority of men and women aged 55 or older had not even graduated from high school. Today, over 80 percent of the age group has a high school diploma.

■ The educational attainment of older men varies greatly by age. Eighty-nine percent of men aged 55 to 64 (an age group almost entirely filled with Baby Boomers) have a high school diploma versus only 74 percent of men aged 75 or older.

■ Older women are also educationally diverse. Among women aged 55 to 59, fully 29 percent have a bachelor's degree. Among women aged 75 or older, only 13 percent have a bachelor's degree.

■ The educational attainment of older Americans also differs greatly by race and Hispanic origin. Among men aged 55 or older, 84 percent of Asians and 87 percent of non-Hispanic whites are high school graduates. This compares with only 71 percent of blacks and 55 percent of Hispanics.

■ Twenty-seven percent of people aged 55 to 64 took part in work-related adult-education courses in 2005.

Big Gains in Educational Attainment

Until 1980, most older men had not completed high school.

Of all the social revolutions that have occurred over the past half-century, one of the most dramatic is the rise in the educational attainment of the nation's older population. Even as recently as 1970, the solid majority of men and women aged 55 or older had not even graduated from high school. Today, over 80 percent of the age group has a high school diploma.

Thirty-one percent of men aged 55 or older have a bachelor's degree today, up from only 5 percent in 1950 and 9 percent in 1970. Among women, the figure has grown from 3 percent in 1950 to 21 percent today. The gap in the educational attainment of men and women will close in the years ahead as better-educated generations of women enter the older age group.

■ The health and wealth of older Americans are improving because of their rising educational attainment. As well-educated Baby Boomers fill the age group, the sophistication of the 55-or-older population will continue to grow.

Educational attainment of older Americans has grown sharply

(percent of people aged 55 or older who are high school graduates, by sex, 1950 and 2008)

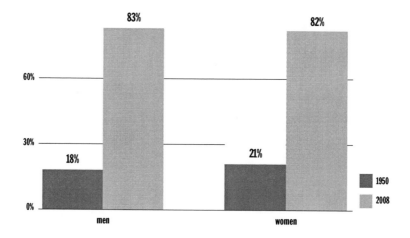

Table 2.1 Educational Attainment of People Aged 55 or Older, 1950 to 2008

(percent of people aged 55 or older by sex and educational attainment, 1950 to 2008)

	total	less than four years of high school	four years of high school or more education	four years of college or more
Men				
2008	100.0%	16.7%	83.3%	30.6%
2000	100.0	24.9	75.1	24.3
1990	100.0	38.5	61.5	18.1
1980	100.0	50.4	49.6	12.6
1970	100.0	65.9	34.1	8.9
1960	100.0	79.2	20.8	5.3
1950	100.0	78.4	17.8	4.6
Women				
2008	100.0	17.6	82.4	21.3
2000	100.0	25.8	74.2	14.6
1990	100.0	38.2	61.8	10.6
1980	100.0	49.4	50.6	7.9
1970	100.0	62.8	37.2	6.3
1960	100.0	75.4	24.6	4.0
1950	100.0	76.4	20.5	3.3

Source: Bureau of the Census, Educational Attainment, Historical Tables, Internet site http://www.census.gov/population/www/ socdemo/educ-attn.html; calculations by New Strategist

Older Americans Are the Least Educated

Generation X is the most highly educated generation.

The percentage of Americans with a bachelor's degree is highest among Generation Xers and Millennials. Thirty-three percent of Generation Xers have a bachelor's degree, the highest level of education among the generations, followed by Millennials with 32 percent. Boomers are not too far behind, at 30 percent. Among Americans aged 65 or older, however, only 20 percent have a bachelor's degree.

By five-year age group, women aged 35 to 39 (members of Generation X) are the best-educated people in the nation. Thirty-seven percent have a bachelor's degree, exceeding the 35 percent with a bachelor's degree among the oldest Boomer men. Men and women aged 75 or older are least likely to have a bachelor's degree, at 23 and 13 percent respectively.

■ The educational attainment of older men and women will rise sharply as Boomers enter the 65-or-older age groups.

Just one in five older Americans has a bachelor's degree

(percent of people aged 25 or older with a bachelor's degree, by generation, 2008)

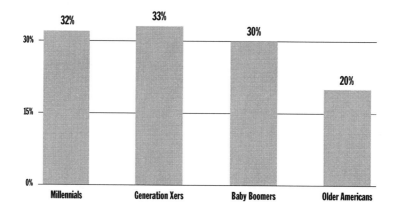

Millennials	32%
Generation Xers	33%
Baby Boomers	30%
Older Americans	20%

Table 2.2 Educational Attainment by Generation, 2008

(number and percent distribution of people aged 25 or older by highest level of education by generation, 2008; numbers in thousands)

	total 25 or older	Millennials (25 to 34)	Generation X (35 to 44)	Boomers (45 to 64)	older Americans (65 or older)
Total people	**196,305**	**40,146**	**42,132**	**77,237**	**36,790**
Not a high school graduate	26,340	4,768	4,792	8,474	8,306
High school graduate	61,183	11,297	12,040	24,290	13,559
Some college, no degree	33,812	7,396	7,199	13,694	5,523
Associate's degree	17,182	3,717	4,158	7,429	1,877
Bachelor's degree	37,559	9,421	9,204	14,527	4,407
Master's degree	14,765	2,792	3,506	6,337	2,129
Professional degree	2,991	490	693	1,356	453
Doctoral degree	2,472	267	538	1,132	536
High school graduate or more	169,964	35,380	37,338	68,765	28,484
Some college or more	108,781	24,083	25,298	44,475	14,925
Associate's degree or more	74,969	16,687	18,099	30,781	9,402
Bachelor's degree or more	57,787	12,970	13,941	23,352	7,525
Total people	**100.0%**	**100.0%**	**100.0%**	**100.0%**	**100.0%**
Not a high school graduate	13.4	11.9	11.4	11.0	22.6
High school graduate	31.2	28.1	28.6	31.4	36.9
Some college, no degree	17.2	18.4	17.1	17.7	15.0
Associate's degree	8.8	9.3	9.9	9.6	5.1
Bachelor's degree	19.1	23.5	21.8	18.8	12.0
Master's degree	7.5	7.0	8.3	8.2	5.8
Professional degree	1.5	1.2	1.6	1.8	1.2
Doctoral degree	1.3	0.7	1.3	1.5	1.5
High school graduate or more	86.6	88.1	88.6	89.0	77.4
Some college or more	55.4	60.0	60.0	57.6	40.6
Associate's degree or more	38.2	41.6	43.0	39.9	25.6
Bachelor's degree or more	29.4	32.3	33.1	30.2	20.5

Source: Bureau of the Census, Educational Attainment in the United States: 2008, detailed tables, Internet site http://www .census.gov/population/www/socdemo/education/cps2008.html; calculations by New Strategist

Table 2.3 Educational Attainment of People Aged 55 or Older, 2008

(number and percent distribution of people aged 25 or older, aged 55 or older, and aged 55 or older in five-year age groups, by highest level of education, 2008; numbers in thousands)

		aged 55 or older						
					aged 65 or older			
	total 25 or older	total	55 to 59	60 to 64	total	65 to 69	70 to 74	75+
Total people	**196,305**	**70,092**	**18,371**	**14,931**	**36,790**	**11,165**	**8,423**	**17,202**
Not a high school graduate	26,340	12,043	1,936	1,801	8,306	1,909	1,810	4,587
High school graduate	61,183	23,780	5,589	4,632	13,559	3,904	3,095	6,560
Some college, no degree	33,812	11,535	3,302	2,710	5,523	1,844	1,262	2,417
Associate's degree	17,182	4,843	1,744	1,222	1,877	714	452	711
Bachelor's degree	37,559	10,503	3,462	2,634	4,407	1,568	1,063	1,776
Master's degree	14,765	5,185	1,679	1,377	2,129	842	514	773
Professional degree	2,991	1,065	344	268	453	155	92	206
Doctoral degree	2,472	1,141	316	289	536	231	133	172
High school graduate or more	169,964	58,052	16,436	13,132	28,484	9,258	6,611	12,615
Some college or more	108,781	34,272	10,847	8,500	14,925	5,354	3,516	6,055
Associate's degree or more	74,969	22,737	7,545	5,790	9,402	3,510	2,254	3,638
Bachelor's degree or more	57,787	17,894	5,801	4,568	7,525	2,796	1,802	2,927
Total people	**100.0%**	**100.0%**	**100.0%**	**100.0%**	**100.0%**	**100.0%**	**100.0%**	**100.0%**
Not a high school graduate	13.4	17.2	10.5	12.1	22.6	17.1	21.5	26.7
High school graduate	31.2	33.9	30.4	31.0	36.9	35.0	36.7	38.1
Some college, no degree	17.2	16.5	18.0	18.2	15.0	16.5	15.0	14.1
Associate's degree	8.8	6.9	9.5	8.2	5.1	6.4	5.4	4.1
Bachelor's degree	19.1	15.0	18.8	17.6	12.0	14.0	12.6	10.3
Master's degree	7.5	7.4	9.1	9.2	5.8	7.5	6.1	4.5
Professional degree	1.5	1.5	1.9	1.8	1.2	1.4	1.1	1.2
Doctoral degree	1.3	1.6	1.7	1.9	1.5	2.1	1.6	1.0
High school graduate or more	86.6	82.8	89.5	88.0	77.4	82.9	78.5	73.3
Some college or more	55.4	48.9	59.0	56.9	40.6	48.0	41.7	35.2
Associate's degree or more	38.2	32.4	41.1	38.8	25.6	31.4	26.8	21.1
Bachelor's degree or more	29.4	25.5	31.6	30.6	20.5	25.0	21.4	17.0

Source: Bureau of the Census, Educational Attainment in the United States: 2008, detailed tables, Internet site http://www .census.gov/population/www/socdemo/education/cps2008.html; calculations by New Strategist

The Oldest Men Are the Least Educated

Men aged 55 to 64 rank among the best educated Americans.

The older population is educationally diverse. At the more youthful end are some of the most educated people in the nation. At the older end are the least educated.

Eighty-nine percent of men aged 55 to 64 (an age group now almost entirely filled with Baby Boomers) have a high school diploma versus only 74 percent of men aged 75 or older. Over 60 percent of men aged 55 to 64 have college experience, and 34 to 35 percent have a bachelor's degree. In contrast, only 40 percent of men aged 75 or older have been to college and just 23 percent have a bachelor's degree. Draft deferments for college students during the Vietnam War are one reason behind the high level of educational attainment among men aged 55 to 64, providing an incentive to stay in school as long as possible.

■ Educational attainment is linked with health status. As better-educated men replace older men with little education, the older population may become increasingly healthy and active.

More than one-third of men aged 55 to 64 have a bachelor's degree

(percent of men aged 55 or older who have a bachelor's degree, 2008)

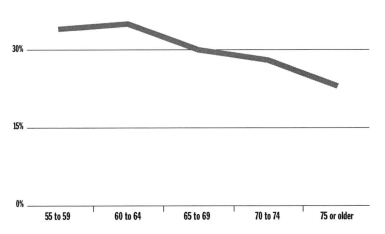

Table 2.4 Educational Attainment of Men Aged 55 or Older, 2008

(number and percent distribution of men aged 25 or older, aged 55 or older, and aged 55 or older in five-year age groups, by highest level of education, 2008; numbers in thousands)

| | | aged 55 or older | | | | | | |
| | | | | | aged 65 or older | | | |
	total 25 or older	total	55 to 59	60 to 64	total	65 to 69	70 to 74	75+
Total men	**94,470**	**31,842**	**8,929**	**7,150**	**15,763**	**5,238**	**3,740**	**6,785**
Not a high school graduate	13,298	5,314	1,003	826	3,485	886	821	1,778
High school graduate	29,491	9,509	2,462	2,002	5,045	1,606	1,156	2,283
Some college, no degree	15,810	5,196	1,609	1,261	2,326	824	537	965
Associate's degree	7,436	2,063	791	576	696	326	190	180
Bachelor's degree	18,042	5,461	1,784	1,398	2,279	841	570	868
Master's degree	6,886	2,698	830	703	1,165	452	291	422
Professional degree	1,877	781	244	186	351	122	74	155
Doctoral degree	1,628	819	206	199	414	180	100	134
High school graduate or more	81,170	26,527	7,926	6,325	12,276	4,351	2,918	5,007
Some college or more	51,679	17,018	5,464	4,323	7,231	2,745	1,762	2,724
Associate's degree or more	35,869	11,822	3,855	3,062	4,905	1,921	1,225	1,759
Bachelor's degree or more	28,433	9,759	3,064	2,486	4,209	1,595	1,035	1,579
Total men	**100.0%**	**100.0%**	**100.0%**	**100.0%**	**100.0%**	**100.0%**	**100.0%**	**100.0%**
Not a high school graduate	14.1	16.7	11.2	11.6	22.1	16.9	22.0	26.2
High school graduate	31.2	29.9	27.6	28.0	32.0	30.7	30.9	33.6
Some college, no degree	16.7	16.3	18.0	17.6	14.8	15.7	14.4	14.2
Associate's degree	7.9	6.5	8.9	8.1	4.4	6.2	5.1	2.7
Bachelor's degree	19.1	17.2	20.0	19.6	14.5	16.1	15.2	12.8
Master's degree	7.3	8.5	9.3	9.8	7.4	8.6	7.8	6.2
Professional degree	2.0	2.5	2.7	2.6	2.2	2.3	2.0	2.3
Doctoral degree	1.7	2.6	2.3	2.8	2.6	3.4	2.7	2.0
High school graduate or more	85.9	83.3	88.8	88.5	77.9	83.1	78.0	73.8
Some college or more	54.7	53.4	61.2	60.5	45.9	52.4	47.1	40.1
Associate's degree or more	38.0	37.1	43.2	42.8	31.1	36.7	32.8	25.9
Bachelor's degree or more	30.1	30.6	34.3	34.8	26.7	30.5	27.7	23.3

Source: Bureau of the Census, Educational Attainment in the United States: 2008, detailed tables, Internet site http://www .census.gov/population/www/socdemo/education/cps2008.html; calculations by New Strategist

The Educational Attainment of Older Women Is Rising

Women aged 55 to 64 are more than twice as likely to be college graduates as those aged 75 or older.

The educational diversity of older women is striking. Women aged 55 to 64 (an age group now mostly filled with Baby Boomers) are much more likely to have finished high school than women aged 75 or older—87 to 90 percent of the younger group versus 73 percent of the older group. While well more than half the women aged 55 to 64 have some college experience, less than one-third of the oldest women do. And while only 13 percent of women aged 75 or older have a bachelor's degree, more than one in four women aged 55 to 64 has graduated from college.

Women constitute the great majority of the older population. As the well-educated Baby-Boom generation fills more of the 55-or-older age group, the educational attainment of older women will climb.

■ The stereotypical image of the elderly could change as more worldly and sophisticated Boomers fill the age group.

More than one in four women aged 55 to 64 has a bachelor's degree

(percent of women aged 55 or older who have a bachelor's degree, 2008)

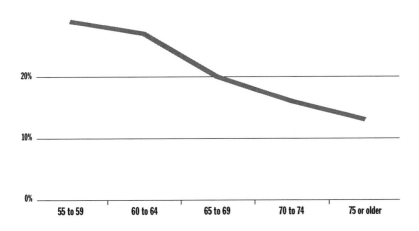

Table 2.5 Educational Attainment of Women Aged 55 or Older, 2008

(number and percent distribution of women aged 25 or older, aged 55 or older, and aged 55 or older in five-year age groups, by highest level of education, 2008; numbers in thousands)

| | | aged 55 or older | | | | | | |
| | | | | | aged 65 or older | | | |
	total 25 or older	total	55 to 59	60 to 64	total	65 to 69	70 to 74	75+
Total women	**101,835**	**38,251**	**9,442**	**7,781**	**21,028**	**5,928**	**4,683**	**10,417**
Not a high school graduate	13,042	6,730	932	975	4,823	1,022	991	2,810
High school graduate	31,692	14,269	3,126	2,630	8,513	2,297	1,939	4,277
Some college, no degree	18,002	6,339	1,693	1,449	3,197	1,020	725	1,452
Associate's degree	9,746	2,780	953	646	1,181	388	262	531
Bachelor's degree	19,517	5,042	1,678	1,236	2,128	727	493	908
Master's degree	7,879	2,486	849	674	963	390	222	351
Professional degree	1,114	284	100	82	102	33	18	51
Doctoral degree	844	322	110	90	122	51	33	38
High school graduate or more	88,794	31,522	8,509	6,807	16,206	4,906	3,692	7,608
Some college or more	57,102	17,253	5,383	4,177	7,693	2,609	1,753	3,331
Associate's degree or more	39,100	10,914	3,690	2,728	4,496	1,589	1,028	1,879
Bachelor's degree or more	29,354	8,134	2,737	2,082	3,315	1,201	766	1,348
Total women	**100.0%**	**100.0%**	**100.0%**	**100.0%**	**100.0%**	**100.0%**	**100.0%**	**100.0%**
Not a high school graduate	12.8	17.6	9.9	12.5	22.9	17.2	21.2	27.0
High school graduate	31.1	37.3	33.1	33.8	40.5	38.7	41.4	41.1
Some college, no degree	17.7	16.6	17.9	18.6	15.2	17.2	15.5	13.9
Associate's degree	9.6	7.3	10.1	8.3	5.6	6.5	5.6	5.1
Bachelor's degree	19.2	13.2	17.8	15.9	10.1	12.3	10.5	8.7
Master's degree	7.7	6.5	9.0	8.7	4.6	6.6	4.7	3.4
Professional degree	1.1	0.7	1.1	1.1	0.5	0.6	0.4	0.5
Doctoral degree	0.8	0.8	1.2	1.2	0.6	0.9	0.7	0.4
High school graduate or more	87.2	82.4	90.1	87.5	77.1	82.8	78.8	73.0
Some college or more	56.1	45.1	57.0	53.7	36.6	44.0	37.4	32.0
Associate's degree or more	38.4	28.5	39.1	35.1	21.4	26.8	22.0	18.0
Bachelor's degree or more	28.8	21.3	29.0	26.8	15.8	20.3	16.4	12.9

Source: Bureau of the Census, Educational Attainment in the United States: 2008, detailed tables, Internet site http://www .census.gov/population/www/socdemo/education/cps2008.html; calculations by New Strategist

Asians Are the Best-Educated Older Americans

Most older Hispanics have not even graduated from high school.

Among people aged 55 or older, Asians, blacks, and non-Hispanic whites are far better educated than Hispanics. Among men aged 55 or older, 84 percent of Asians and 87 percent of non-Hispanic whites are high school graduates. This compares with only 71 percent of blacks and 55 percent of Hispanics. Fully 45 percent of Asian men aged 55 or older have a bachelor's degree versus 33 percent of non-Hispanic whites, 16 percent of blacks, and 13 percent of Hispanics.

Among older women, Asians are less likely than non-Hispanic whites to be high school graduates (75 versus 87 percent). But 32 percent of Asian women aged 55 or older have at least a bachelor's degree compared with a much smaller 23 percent of non-Hispanic whites, 16 percent of blacks, and just 9 percent of Hispanics.

■ The educational attainment of older blacks will continue to rise as Boomers with much more education enter the age group.

Among older men, blacks are better educated than Hispanics

(percent of men aged 55 or older with a high school diploma, by race and Hispanic origin, 2008)

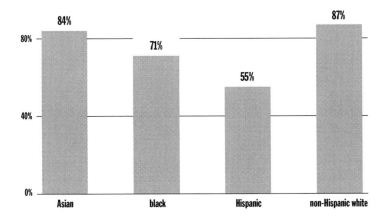

Table 2.6 Educational Attainment of Men Aged 55 or Older by Race and Hispanic Origin, 2008

(number and percent distribution of men aged 55 or older by educational attainment, race, and Hispanic origin, 2008; numbers in thousands)

	total	Asian	black	Hispanic	non-Hispanic white
Total men aged 55 or older	**31,842**	**1,162**	**2,767**	**2,436**	**25,165**
Not a high school graduate	5,314	182	805	1,110	3,172
High school graduate	9,509	289	902	614	7,615
Some college, no degree	5,196	99	427	277	4,325
Associate's degree	2,063	66	193	104	1,667
Bachelor's degree	5,461	306	254	189	4,674
Master's degree	2,698	138	118	96	2,327
Professional degree	781	30	35	34	674
Doctoral degree	819	52	32	16	714
High school graduate or more	26,527	980	1,961	1,330	21,996
Some college or more	17,018	691	1,059	716	14,381
Associate's degree or more	11,822	592	632	439	10,056
Bachelor's degree or more	9,759	526	439	335	8,389
Total men aged 55 or older	**100.0%**	**100.0%**	**100.0%**	**100.0%**	**100.0%**
Not a high school graduate	16.7	15.7	29.1	45.6	12.6
High school graduate	29.9	24.9	32.6	25.2	30.3
Some college, no degree	16.3	8.5	15.4	11.4	17.2
Associate's degree	6.5	5.7	7.0	4.3	6.6
Bachelor's degree	17.2	26.3	9.2	7.8	18.6
Master's degree	8.5	11.9	4.3	3.9	9.2
Professional degree	2.5	2.6	1.3	1.4	2.7
Doctoral degree	2.6	4.5	1.2	0.7	2.8
High school graduate or more	83.3	84.3	70.9	54.6	87.4
Some college or more	53.4	59.5	38.3	29.4	57.1
Associate's degree or more	37.1	50.9	22.8	18.0	40.0
Bachelor's degree or more	30.6	45.3	15.9	13.8	33.3

Note: Asians and blacks are those who identify themselves as being of the race alone and those who identify themselves as being of the race in combination with other races. Non-Hispanic whites are those who identify themselves as being white alone and not Hispanic. Numbers do not add to total because not all races are shown and Hispanics may be of any race.
Source: Bureau of the Census, Educational Attainment in the United States: 2008, detailed tables, Internet site http://www .census.gov/population/www/socdemo/education/cps2008.html; calculations by New Strategist

Table 2.7 Educational Attainment of Women Aged 55 or Older by Race and Hispanic Origin, 2008

(number and percent distribution of women aged 55 or older by educational attainment, race, and Hispanic origin, 2008; numbers in thousands)

	total	Asian	black	Hispanic	non-Hispanic white
Total women aged 55 or older	**38,251**	**1,468**	**3,883**	**2,911**	**29,686**
Not a high school graduate	6,730	363	1,095	1,397	3,813
High school graduate	14,269	399	1,333	803	11,632
Some college, no degree	6,339	137	576	308	5,247
Associate's degree	2,780	97	251	139	2,264
Bachelor's degree	5,042	348	371	176	4,132
Master's degree	2,486	85	225	71	2,095
Professional degree	284	27	17	14	223
Doctoral degree	322	13	17	6	279
High school graduate or more	31,522	1,106	2,790	1,517	25,872
Some college or more	17,253	707	1,457	714	14,240
Associate's degree or more	10,914	570	881	406	8,993
Bachelor's degree or more	8,134	473	630	267	6,729
Total women aged 55 or older	**100.0%**	**100.0%**	**100.0%**	**100.0%**	**100.0%**
Not a high school graduate	17.6	24.7	28.2	48.0	12.8
High school graduate	37.3	27.2	34.3	27.6	39.2
Some college, no degree	16.6	9.3	14.8	10.6	17.7
Associate's degree	7.3	6.6	6.5	4.8	7.6
Bachelor's degree	13.2	23.7	9.6	6.0	13.9
Master's degree	6.5	5.8	5.8	2.4	7.1
Professional degree	0.7	1.8	0.4	0.5	0.8
Doctoral degree	0.8	0.9	0.4	0.2	0.9
High school graduate or more	82.4	75.3	71.9	52.1	87.2
Some college or more	45.1	48.2	37.5	24.5	48.0
Associate's degree or more	28.5	38.8	22.7	13.9	30.3
Bachelor's degree or more	21.3	32.2	16.2	9.2	22.7

Note: Asians and blacks are those who identify themselves as being of the race alone and those who identify themselves as being of the race in combination with other races. Non-Hispanic whites are those who identify themselves as being white alone and not Hispanic. Numbers do not add to total because not all races are shown and Hispanics may be of any race.
Source: Bureau of the Census, Educational Attainment in the United States: 2008, detailed tables, Internet site http://www .census.gov/population/www/socdemo/education/cps2008.html; calculations by New Strategist

Few Older Americans Are in School

Of the nation's 76 million students, only 311,000 are aged 55 or older.

Just 0.4 percent of people aged 55 or older are currently enrolled in school. This figure is much smaller than the proportion of middle-aged Americans in school, but it may grow as the well-educated Baby-Boom generation fills the age group. The more educated a person, the more likely he or she is to return to school to get even more education.

Among older students, women outnumber men 219,000 to 93,000. The big difference results in part because women have a greater propensity to continue their education, but it also reflects the numerical majority of women in the older age groups.

■ As more well-educated Boomers age into their sixties, school enrollment may rise among older Americans.

Older women outnumber older men in school

(number of people aged 55 or older enrolled in school, by sex, 2007)

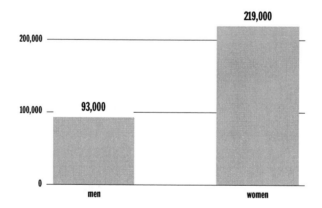

Table 2.8 School Enrollment by Sex and Age, 2007

(total number of people aged 3 or older, and number and percent enrolled in school by sex and age, 2007; numbers in thousands)

		enrolled	
	total	number	percent
Total people	**285,410**	**75,967**	**26.6%**
Under age 55	216,091	75,656	35.0
Aged 55 or older	69,318	311	0.4
Aged 55 to 59	18,250	168	0.9
Aged 60 to 64	14,625	83	0.6
Aged 65 or older	36,443	60	0.2
Total females	**145,806**	**38,398**	**26.3**
Under age 55	107,947	38,179	35.4
Aged 55 or older	37,859	219	0.6
Aged 55 to 59	9,446	127	1.3
Aged 60 to 64	7,605	59	0.8
Aged 65 or older	20,808	32	0.2
Total males	**139,603**	**37,569**	**26.9**
Under age 55	108,145	37,475	34.7
Aged 55 or older	31,459	93	0.3
Aged 55 to 59	8,804	41	0.5
Aged 60 to 64	7,020	24	0.3
Aged 65 or older	15,635	27	0.2

Source: Bureau of the Census, School Enrollment—Social and Economic Characteristics of Students: October 2007, Internet site http://www.census.gov/population/www/socdemo/school/cps2007.html

Few Older Students Attend College

Students aged 55 or older account for less than 2 percent of enrollment.

In 2007, there were just 283,000 college students aged 55 or older. Older students are fairly evenly divided between undergraduate (47 percent) and graduate studies (53 percent). They account for less than 1 percent of undergraduates and 4 percent of graduate students.

■ Only 50,000 people aged 65 or older are in college, but this number will rise as Boomers enter the age group.

Graduate students outnumber undergraduates among older students

(percent distribution of people aged 55 or older enrolled in institutions of higher education by level of enrollment, 2007)

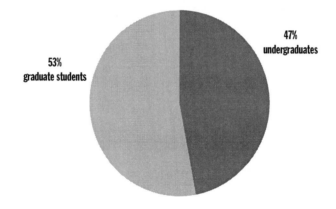

47% undergraduates

53% graduate students

Table 2.9 College Students by Age and Enrollment Level, 2007

(number and percent distribution of people aged 15 or older enrolled in institutions of higher education by age and level of enrollment, 2007; numbers in thousands)

	total	undergraduate	graduate school
Total enrolled	**17,956**	**14,365**	**3,591**
Under age 55	17,672	14,230	3,442
Aged 55 or older	283	133	150
Aged 55 to 59	156	72	84
Aged 60 to 64	77	34	43
Aged 65 or older	50	27	23
PERCENT DISTRIBUTION BY LEVEL OF ENROLLMENT			
Total enrolled	**100.0%**	**80.0%**	**20.0%**
Under age 55	100.0	80.5	19.5
Aged 55 or older	100.0	47.0	53.0
Aged 55 to 59	100.0	46.2	53.8
Aged 60 to 64	100.0	44.2	55.8
Aged 65 or older	100.0	54.0	46.0
PERCENT DISTRIBUTION BY AGE			
Total enrolled	**100.0%**	**100.0%**	**100.0%**
Under age 55	98.4	99.1	95.9
Aged 55 or older	1.6	0.9	4.2
Aged 55 to 59	0.9	0.5	2.3
Aged 60 to 64	0.4	0.2	1.2
Aged 65 or older	0.3	0.2	0.6

Source: Bureau of the Census, School Enrollment—Social and Economic Characteristics of Students: October 2007, Internet site http://www.census.gov/population/www/socdemo/school/cps2007.html; calculations by New Strategist

Many Older Americans Participate in Adult Education for Job-Related Reasons

Life-long learning is becoming a necessity for job security.

As job security dwindles, many workers are turning to the educational system to try to stay on track. Overall, 27 percent of Americans aged 16 or older participated in work-related adult education in 2005 (the latest available data). Not surprisingly, the percentage of older Americans involved in work-related courses falls with age, from 27 percent of people aged 55 to 64 to just 5 percent of those aged 65 or older.

One in five older Americans participates in personal interest courses, but demand for part-time degree or diploma programs is miniscule among people aged 55 or older. In all, 40 percent of people aged 55 to 64, and 23 percent of people aged 65 or older, participated in adult education in 2005.

■ Many Americans who participate in work-related education are retraining themselves to compete in the increasingly global economy.

Work-related training peaks in the 45-to-54 age group

(percent of workers who participated in work-related adult education activities, by age, 2005)

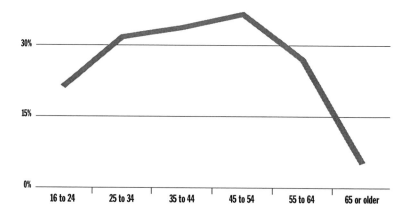

Table 2.10 Participation in Adult Education by Age, 2005

(percent of people aged 16 or older who participate in formal adult education activities, by age and type of adult education activity, 2005)

	total	percent participating in any activity	work-related courses	personal interest courses	part-time degree or diploma programs
Total people	**100.0%**	**44.4%**	**26.9%**	**21.4%**	**5.0%**
Aged 16 to 24	100.0	52.9	21.2	26.6	11.4
Aged 25 to 34	100.0	52.2	31.7	22.1	8.7
Aged 35 to 44	100.0	48.7	33.7	22.1	5.3
Aged 45 to 54	100.0	47.9	36.5	19.7	3.8
Aged 55 to 64	100.0	40.3	27.0	20.7	1.5
Aged 65 or older	100.0	22.9	5.2	18.8	0.3

Source: National Center for Education Statistics, The Condition of Education, Participation in Adult Education, Indicator 10 (2007), Internet site http://nces.ed.gov/programs/coe/2007/section1/indicator10.asp; calculations by New Strategist

Health

■ The percentage of people who rate their health as "very good" or "excellent" declines with age to just 38 percent in the 65-or-older age group.

■ Americans have a weight problem, and older Americans are no exception. The average man aged 50 to 69 weighs nearly 200 pounds. The average woman in the age group weighs more than 170 pounds.

■ Median medical expenses for people aged 65 or older stood at $4,215 in 2006, according to the federal government's Medical Expenditure Panel Survey. Medicare covered 61 percent of that cost.

■ Eighty-seven percent of people aged 65 or older have taken at least one prescription drug in the past month, and 60 percent have taken three or more.

■ The percentage of people with difficulties in physical functioning rises from a low of 5 percent among people aged 18 to 44 to a high of 46 percent among people aged 75 or older.

■ In 2006, Americans visited physicians a total of 902 million times. People aged 65 or older accounted for 25 percent of those visits.

■ In 1950, the average 65-year-old could expect to live only 13.9 more years. In 2006, a 65-year-old could expect to live 19.0 more years.

Fewer than Half of 55-to-64-Year-Olds Say Their Health Is Very Good or Excellent

At every age, however, the percentage saying their health is very good or excellent exceeds the proportion saying it is only fair or poor.

The 55 percent majority of Americans aged 18 or older say their health is "very good" or "excellent. "The figure peaks at 63 percent in the 25-to-34 age group, then declines with age as chronic conditions become more common. The percentage of people who report very good to excellent health falls below 50 percent in the 55-to-64 age group and bottoms out at 38 percent among those aged 65 or older. Even in the oldest age group, however, the proportion of people reporting very good or excellent health surpasses those reporting "fair" or "poor" health (25 percent).

As people age, the number of days per month they experience poor physical health rises. From a low of about 2 days per month among 18-to-34-year-olds, the figure peaks at 6 days among people aged 75 or older. Interestingly, the number of days per month of poor mental health peaks in middle-age at 3.6, than falls to just two days among people aged 65 or older.

■ Medical advances that allow people to manage their chronic conditions should boost the proportion of older Americans who report very good or excellent health.

Nearly half of 55-to-64-year-olds say their health is excellent or very good

(percent of people aged 18 or older who say their health is excellent or very good, by age, 2008)

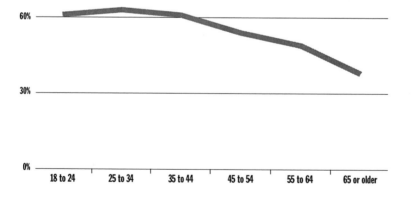

Table 3.1 Health Status by Age, 2008

(percent distribution of people aged 18 or older by self-reported health status, by age, 2008)

	total	excellent	very good	good	fair	poor
Total people	**100.0%**	**20.1%**	**34.9%**	**30.0%**	**10.6%**	**3.8%**
Aged 18 to 24	100.0	25.1	35.7	29.7	6.6	1.0
Aged 25 to 34	100.0	24.8	38.1	28.9	7.3	1.4
Aged 35 to 44	100.0	23.7	37.2	28.3	8.0	2.1
Aged 45 to 54	100.0	19.6	34.5	29.1	10.3	4.2
Aged 55 to 64	100.0	17.3	31.5	30.3	13.8	5.6
Aged 65 or older	100.0	11.4	26.7	34.1	18.0	7.4

Source: Centers for Disease Control and Prevention, Behavioral Risk Factor Surveillance System Prevalence Data, 2008, Internet site http://apps.nccd.cdc.gov/brfss/

Table 3.2 Health Problems in Past 30 Days by Age, 2007

(average number of days during the past 30 days people aged 18 or older reported poor physical or mental health, and average number of days of activity limitation due to poor health, by age, 2007)

	days with poor physical health	days with poor mental health	days with activity limitations due to poor health
Total people	**3.6**	**3.4**	**2.2**
Aged 18 to 24	2.2	4.1	1.4
Aged 25 to 34	2.3	3.6	1.5
Aged 35 to 44	2.9	3.5	1.9
Aged 45 to 54	3.9	3.6	2.5
Aged 55 to 64	4.9	3.4	3.0
Aged 65 to 74	4.9	2.2	2.6
Aged 75 or older	6.0	2.0	2.9

Source: Centers for Disease Control and Prevention, National Center for Chronic Disease Prevention and Health Promotion, Prevalence Data, Internet site http://apps.nccd.cdc.gov/HRQOL/

Table 3.3 Frequent Health Problems in Past 30 Days by Age, 1997 and 2007

(percentage of people aged 18 or older with 14 or more days of poor physical or mental health during the past 30 days, by age, 1997 and 2007; percentage point change, 1997–2007)

	2007	1997	percentage point change
POOR PHYSICAL HEALTH			
Total people	**10.9%**	**9.2%**	**1.7**
Aged 18 to 24	5.1	3.9	1.2
Aged 25 to 34	6.1	5.0	1.1
Aged 35 to 44	8.4	7.6	0.8
Aged 45 to 54	12.0	9.6	2.4
Aged 55 to 64	15.9	13.7	2.2
Aged 65 to 74	15.9	14.8	1.1
Aged 75 or older	19.9	20.0	-0.1
POOR MENTAL HEALTH			
Total people	**10.1**	**9.0**	**1.1**
Aged 18 to 24	11.9	10.4	1.5
Aged 25 to 34	10.6	9.2	1.4
Aged 35 to 44	10.5	10.1	0.4
Aged 45 to 54	10.9	9.8	1.1
Aged 55 to 64	10.7	8.3	2.4
Aged 65 to 74	6.9	5.7	1.2
Aged 75 or older	6.1	6.5	-0.4

Source: Centers for Disease Control and Prevention, National Center for Chronic Disease Prevention and Health Promotion, Prevalence Data, Internet site http://apps.nccd.cdc.gov/HRQOL/

Weight Problems Are the Norm for Older Americans

Few have a healthy weight.

Americans have a weight problem, and older Americans are no exception. The average man aged 50 to 69 weighs nearly 200 pounds. The average woman in the age group weighs more than 170 pounds. The percentage of people aged 55 or older who are overweight ranges from 66 to 80 percent among men and from 63 to 71 percent among women.

Although many people say they exercise, only 31 percent of adults participate in regular leisure-time physical activity, according to government data. The figure ranges from a high of 38 percent among 18-to-24-year-olds to a low of 17 percent among people aged 75 or older. Among 55-to-74-year-olds, only 26 to 27 percent participate in regular leisure-time physical activity.

■ Most Americans lack the willpower to eat less or exercise more—fueling a diet and weight loss industry that never lacks for customers.

Older Americans weigh more than they should

(percent distribution of people aged 55 to 64 by weight status, by sex, 2003–06)

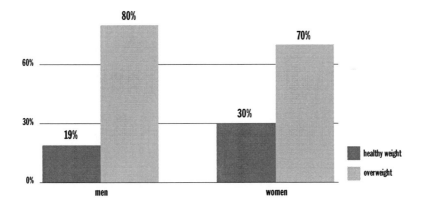

Table 3.4 Average Measured Weight by Age and Sex, 2003–06

(average weight in pounds of people aged 20 or older by age and sex, 2003–06)

	men	women
Total aged 20 or older	194.7	164.7
Aged 20 to 29	188.3	155.9
Aged 30 to 39	194.1	164.7
Aged 40 to 49	202.3	171.3
Aged 50 to 59	198.8	172.1
Aged 60 to 69	198.3	170.5
Aged 70 to 79	187.4	155.6
Aged 80 or older	168.1	142.2

Note: Data are based on measured weight of a sample of the civilian noninstitutionalized population.
Source: National Center for Health Statistics, Anthropometric Reference Data for Children and Adults: United States, 2003–2006, National Health Statistics Reports, Number 10, 2008, Internet site http://www.cdc.gov/nchs/products/pubs/pubd/nhsr/nhsr.htm; calculations by New Strategist

Table 3.5 Weight Status by Sex and Age, 2003–06

(percent distribution of people aged 20 or older by weight status, sex, and age, 2003–06)

			overweight	
	total	healthy weight	total	obese
TOTAL PEOPLE	100.0%	31.4%	66.9%	34.1%
Total men	100.0	26.1	72.6	33.1
Aged 20 to 34	100.0	35.9	61.6	26.2
Aged 35 to 44	100.0	24.1	75.2	37.0
Aged 45 to 54	100.0	20.8	78.5	34.6
Aged 55 to 64	100.0	19.3	79.7	39.3
Aged 65 to 74	100.0	21.2	78.0	33.0
Aged 75 or older	100.0	33.1	65.8	24.0
Total women	100.0	36.6	61.2	35.2
Aged 20 to 34	100.0	45.1	50.9	28.4
Aged 35 to 44	100.0	37.6	60.7	36.1
Aged 45 to 54	100.0	31.1	67.3	40.0
Aged 55 to 64	100.0	29.5	69.6	41.0
Aged 65 to 74	100.0	28.5	70.5	36.4
Aged 75 or older	100.0	35.4	62.6	24.2

Note: Data are based on measured height and weight of a sample of the civilian noninstitutionalized population. Overweight is defined as a body mass index of 25 or higher. Obesity is defined as a body mass index of 30 or higher. Body mass index is calculated by dividing weight in kilograms by height in meters squared.
Source: National Center for Health Statistics, Health, United States, 2008, Internet site http://www.cdc.gov/nchs/hus.htm

Table 3.6 Leisure-Time Physical Activity Level by Sex and Age, 2006

(percent distribution of people aged 18 or older by leisure-time physical activity level, by sex and age, 2006)

	total	physically inactive	at least some physical activity	regular physical activity
TOTAL PEOPLE	100.0%	39.5%	29.6%	30.9%
Aged 18 to 24	100.0	34.8	27.1	38.1
Aged 25 to 44	100.0	35.0	31.6	33.4
Aged 45 to 54	100.0	38.2	30.7	31.1
Aged 55 to 64	100.0	41.9	30.9	27.2
Aged 65 to 74	100.0	48.0	25.8	26.2
Aged 75 or older	100.0	59.6	23.1	17.3
Total men	100.0	38.5	27.4	33.1
Aged 18 to 44	100.0	34.2	28.8	36.9
Aged 45 to 54	100.0	39.0	28.4	32.7
Aged 55 to 64	100.0	41.1	30.6	28.2
Aged 65 to 74	100.0	46.9	25.0	28.2
Aged 75 or older	100.0	52.1	26.6	21.4
Total women	100.0	40.3	30.7	29.0
Aged 18 to 44	100.0	35.6	32.0	32.4
Aged 45 to 54	100.0	37.5	33.0	29.5
Aged 55 to 64	100.0	42.6	31.1	26.3
Aged 65 to 74	100.0	49.0	26.5	24.5
Aged 75 or older	100.0	64.4	20.8	14.7

Note: "Physically inactive" are those with no sessions of light-to-moderate or vigorous leisure-time physical activity of at least 10 minutes duration during past week. "At least some physical activity" includes those with at least one light-to-moderate or vigorous leisure-time physical activity of at least 10 minutes duration during past week, but who did not meet the definition for regular leisure-time activity. "Regular physical activity" includes those who did three or more sessions per week of vigorous activity lasting at least 20 minutes or five or more sessions per week of light-to-moderate activity lasting at least 30 minutes.
Source: National Center for Health Statistics, Health, United States, 2008, Internet site http://www.cdc.gov/nchs/hus.htm

Smoking Declines Sharply with Age

Only 8 percent of people aged 65 or older smoke cigarettes.

The percentage of Americans who smoke cigarettes has declined sharply from what it was a few decades ago. Nevertheless, a substantial 18 percent of people aged 18 or older were current smokers in 2007. The figure peaks among 18-to-34-year-olds at about 23 percent. Among people aged 55 to 64, a smaller 16 percent smoke, and the figure is only half that (8 percent) among people aged 65 or older. Former smokers greatly outnumber current smokers among people aged 45 or older.

Drinking is more popular than smoking among older Americans. Overall, 54 percent of people aged 18 or older have had an alcoholic beverage in the past month. The proportion peaks at 61 percent in the 25-to-44 age group, then declines with age. A 41 percent minority of people aged 65 or older have had a drink in the past month.

A growing share of older Americans has used illicit drugs as the Baby Boom generation—many of whom had experience with marijuana and other illicit drugs—enters the older age groups. The majority of people aged 50 to 59 have used illicit drugs at some time during their lives, a figure that falls to 35 percent among 60-to-64-year-olds and bottoms out at 11 percent among people aged 65 or older.

■ As health problems increase with age, smoking and drinking become less common.

Many older Americans have quit smoking

(percent distribution of people aged 65 or older by cigarette smoking status, 2008)

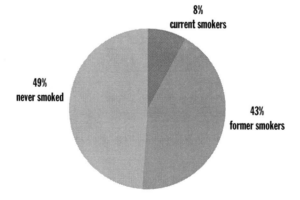

8%
current smokers

49%
never smoked

43%
former smokers

Table 3.7 Cigarette Smoking Status by Age, 2008

(percent distribution of people aged 18 or older by age and cigarette smoking status, 2008)

	total	current smokers			former smoker	never smoked
		total	smoke every day	smoke some days		
Total people	**100.0%**	**18.2%**	**13.4%**	**4.8%**	**25.2%**	**55.3%**
Aged 18 to 24	100.0	23.0	15.8	7.2	7.2	70.0
Aged 25 to 34	100.0	23.5	16.8	6.7	17.6	58.4
Aged 35 to 44	100.0	20.0	14.9	5.1	18.7	60.6
Aged 45 to 54	100.0	20.5	16.0	4.5	25.2	52.4
Aged 55 to 64	100.0	16.4	12.4	4.0	35.0	46.6
Aged 65 or older	100.0	8.0	6.0	2.0	42.9	48.8

Source: Centers for Disease Control and Prevention, Behavioral Risk Factor Surveillance System Prevalence Data, 2008, Internet site http://apps.nccd.cdc.gov/brfss/index.asp; calculations by New Strategist

Table 3.8 Alcohol Use by Age, 2008

(percent distribution of people aged 18 or older by whether they have had at least one drink of alcohol within the past 30 days, by age, 2008)

	total	yes	no
Total people	**100.0%**	**54.4%**	**45.5%**
Aged 18 to 24	100.0	49.9	50.0
Aged 25 to 34	100.0	60.5	39.4
Aged 35 to 44	100.0	60.5	39.4
Aged 45 to 54	100.0	58.4	41.5
Aged 55 to 64	100.0	53.4	46.5
Aged 65 or older	100.0	40.6	59.3

Source: Centers for Disease Control and Prevention, Behavioral Risk Factor Surveillance System Prevalence Data, 2008, Internet site http://apps.nccd.cdc.gov/brfss/index.asp

Table 3.9 Illicit Drug Use by People Aged 12 or Older, 2007

(percent of people aged 12 or older who ever used any illicit drug, who used an illicit drug in the past year, and who used an illicit drug in the past month, by age, 2007)

	ever used	used in past year	used in past month
Total people	**46.1%**	**14.4%**	**8.0%**
Aged 12 to 17	26.2	18.7	9.5
Aged 18 to 25	57.0	34.8	20.7
Aged 26 to 29	57.4	33.2	19.7
Aged 30 to 34	55.5	16.9	9.4
Aged 35 to 39	56.1	13.9	7.3
Aged 40 to 44	58.6	13.1	7.0
Aged 45 to 49	61.0	11.9	7.2
Aged 50 to 54	58.9	10.6	5.7
Aged 55 to 59	51.6	8.0	4.1
Aged 60 to 64	35.0	4.4	1.9
Aged 65 or older	10.7	1.0	0.7

Note: Illicit drugs include marijuana, hashish, cocaine (including crack), heroin, hallucinogens, inhalants, or any prescription-type psychotherapeutic used nonmedically.
Source: SAMHSA, Office of Applied Studies, National Survey on Drug Use and Health, 2007, Internet site http://www.oas .samhsa.gov/nsduh/2k7nsduh/2k7Results.pdf

Many 55-to-64-Year-Olds Lack Health Insurance

Four million 55-to-64-year-olds are uninsured.

Among all Americans, 46 million lacked health insurance in 2007—or 15 percent of the population. While the figure is a smaller 12 percent among 55-to-64-year-olds, the chance of illness in that age group is much greater than average.

Two-thirds of 55-to-64-year-olds have employment-based health insurance coverage, although only half have coverage through their own employer. Another 20 percent have government health insurance. Nearly everyone (94 percent) aged 65 or older is covered by Medicare, the government's health insurance program for the elderly.

■ As Baby Boomers become eligible for Medicare, their entrepreneurial spirit may rise because the need for health insurance will no longer tie them to an employer.

Twelve percent of 55-to-64-year-olds lack health insurance

(percent of people aged 18 or older without health insurance, by age, 2007)

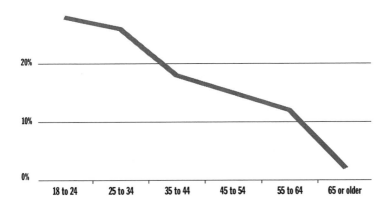

Table 3.10 Health Insurance Coverage by Age, 2007

(number and percent distribution of people by age and health insurance coverage status, 2007; numbers in thousands)

		with health insurance			
	total	total	private	government	not covered
Total people	**299,106**	**253,449**	**201,991**	**83,031**	**45,657**
Under age 18	74,403	66,254	47,750	23,041	8,149
Aged 18 to 24	28,398	20,407	17,074	4,428	7,991
Aged 25 to 34	40,146	29,817	26,430	4,539	10,329
Aged 35 to 44	42,132	34,415	31,067	4,546	7,717
Aged 45 to 54	43,935	37,161	33,350	5,363	6,774
Aged 55 to 64	33,302	29,291	25,114	6,651	4,011
Aged 65 or older	36,790	36,103	21,206	34,464	686

PERCENT DISTRIBUTION BY COVERAGE STATUS

Total people	**100.0%**	**84.7%**	**67.5%**	**27.8%**	**15.3%**
Under age 18	100.0	89.0	64.2	31.0	11.0
Aged 18 to 24	100.0	71.9	60.1	15.6	28.1
Aged 25 to 34	100.0	74.3	65.8	11.3	25.7
Aged 35 to 44	100.0	81.7	73.7	10.8	18.3
Aged 45 to 54	100.0	84.6	75.9	12.2	15.4
Aged 55 to 64	100.0	88.0	75.4	20.0	12.0
Aged 65 or older	100.0	98.1	57.6	93.7	1.9

PERCENT DISTRIBUTION BY AGE

Total people	**100.0%**	**100.0%**	**100.0%**	**100.0%**	**100.0%**
Under age 18	24.9	26.1	23.6	27.7	17.8
Aged 18 to 24	9.5	8.1	8.5	5.3	17.5
Aged 25 to 34	13.4	11.8	13.1	5.5	22.6
Aged 35 to 44	14.1	13.6	15.4	5.5	16.9
Aged 45 to 54	14.7	14.7	16.5	6.5	14.8
Aged 55 to 64	11.1	11.6	12.4	8.0	8.8
Aged 65 or older	12.3	14.2	10.5	41.5	1.5

Note: Numbers may not add to total because some people have more than one type of health insurance coverage.
Source: Bureau of the Census, Health Insurance, Table HI01, Internet site http://pubdb3.census.gov/macro/032008/health/toc .htm; calculations by New Strategist

Table 3.11 Private Health Insurance Coverage by Age, 2007

(number and percent distribution of people by age and private health insurance coverage status, 2007; numbers in thousands)

		with private health insurance			
			employment based		
	total	total	total	own	direct purchase
Total people	**299,106**	**201,991**	**177,446**	**93,774**	**26,673**
Under age 18	74,403	47,750	44,252	227	3,930
Aged 18 to 24	28,398	17,074	13,747	5,386	1,635
Aged 25 to 34	40,146	26,430	24,505	19,005	2,347
Aged 35 to 44	42,132	31,067	29,009	20,616	2,687
Aged 45 to 54	43,935	33,350	30,805	22,486	3,292
Aged 55 to 64	33,302	25,114	22,569	16,612	3,237
Aged 65 or older	36,790	21,206	12,558	9,442	9,546
PERCENT DISTRIBUTION BY COVERAGE STATUS					
Total people	**100.0%**	**67.5%**	**59.3%**	**31.4%**	**8.9%**
Under age 18	100.0	64.2	59.5	0.3	5.3
Aged 18 to 24	100.0	60.1	48.4	19.0	5.8
Aged 25 to 34	100.0	65.8	61.0	47.3	5.8
Aged 35 to 44	100.0	73.7	68.9	48.9	6.4
Aged 45 to 54	100.0	75.9	70.1	51.2	7.5
Aged 55 to 64	100.0	75.4	67.8	49.9	9.7
Aged 65 or older	100.0	57.6	34.1	25.7	25.9
PERCENT DISTRIBUTION BY AGE					
Total people	**100.0%**	**100.0%**	**100.0%**	**100.0%**	**100.0%**
Under age 18	24.9	23.6	24.9	0.2	14.7
Aged 18 to 24	9.5	8.5	7.7	5.7	6.1
Aged 25 to 34	13.4	13.1	13.8	20.3	8.8
Aged 35 to 44	14.1	15.4	16.3	22.0	10.1
Aged 45 to 54	14.7	16.5	17.4	24.0	12.3
Aged 55 to 64	11.1	12.4	12.7	17.7	12.1
Aged 65 or older	12.3	10.5	7.1	10.1	35.8

Note: Numbers may not add to total because some people have more than one type of health insurance coverage.
Source: Bureau of the Census, Health Insurance, Table HI01, Internet site http://pubdb3.census.gov/macro/032008/health/toc
.htm; calculations by New Strategist

Table 3.12 Government Health Insurance Coverage by Age, 2007

(number and percent distribution of people by age and government health insurance coverage status, 2007; numbers in thousands)

	total	with government health insurance total	Medicaid	Medicare	military
Total people	299,106	83,031	39,554	41,375	10,955
Under age 18	74,403	23,041	20,899	518	2,101
Aged 18 to 24	28,398	4,428	3,563	180	823
Aged 25 to 34	40,146	4,539	3,237	501	1,047
Aged 35 to 44	42,132	4,546	3,027	924	1,016
Aged 45 to 54	43,935	5,363	3,103	1,795	1,285
Aged 55 to 64	33,302	6,651	2,462	3,179	2,079
Aged 65 or older	36,790	34,464	3,263	34,278	2,604

PERCENT DISTRIBUTION BY COVERAGE STATUS

Total people	100.0%	27.8%	13.2%	13.8%	3.7%
Under age 18	100.0	31.0	28.1	0.7	2.8
Aged 18 to 24	100.0	15.6	12.5	0.6	2.9
Aged 25 to 34	100.0	11.3	8.1	1.2	2.6
Aged 35 to 44	100.0	10.8	7.2	2.2	2.4
Aged 45 to 54	100.0	12.2	7.1	4.1	2.9
Aged 55 to 64	100.0	20.0	7.4	9.5	6.2
Aged 65 or older	100.0	93.7	8.9	93.2	7.1

PERCENT DISTRIBUTION BY AGE

Total people	100.0%	100.0%	100.0%	100.0%	100.0%
Under age 18	24.9	27.7	52.8	1.3	19.2
Aged 18 to 24	9.5	5.3	9.0	0.4	7.5
Aged 25 to 34	13.4	5.5	8.2	1.2	9.6
Aged 35 to 44	14.1	5.5	7.7	2.2	9.3
Aged 45 to 54	14.7	6.5	7.8	4.3	11.7
Aged 55 to 64	11.1	8.0	6.2	7.7	19.0
Aged 65 or older	12.3	41.5	8.2	82.8	23.8

Note: Numbers may not add to total because some people have more than one type of health insurance coverage.
Source: Bureau of the Census, Health Insurance, Table HI01, Internet site http://pubdb3.census.gov/macro/032008/health/toc .htm; calculations by New Strategist

Older Americans Spend Big on Health Care

Most expenses are covered by Medicare, but many are not.

Medical expenses are the norm for Americans regardless of age. But people aged 65 or older, because they have more medical problems, spend much more than younger adults on medical care. In 2006, median medical expenses for people aged 65 or older stood at a hefty median of $4,215, according to the federal government's Medical Expenditure Panel Survey. Medicare covered 61 percent of the cost.

Among the 81 percent of people aged 55 to 64 with prescription drug expenses, the median expense was a considerable $953 in 2006. Among the 92 percent of people aged 65 or older with prescription drug expenses, the median expense was $1,367. People aged 55 to 64 paid for 37 percent of their prescription drug expenses out-of-pocket. Among people aged 65 or older, 35 percent of prescription drug expenses were paid for out-of-pocket.

■ The Medicare prescription drug plan, which took effect in 2006, lowered out-of-pocket prescription drug expenses for people aged 65 or older.

Medicare pays for the largest share of older Americans' prescription drug expenses

(percent distribution of spending on prescription drugs by people aged 65 or older by source of payment, 2006)

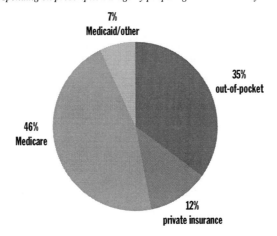

7%
Medicaid/other

35%
out-of-pocket

46%
Medicare

12%
private insurance

Table 3.13 Spending on Health Care by Age, 2006

(percent of people with health care expense, median expense per person, total expenses, and percent distribution of total expenses by source of payment, by age, 2006)

	total (thousands)	percent with expense	median expense per person	total expenses amount (millions)	total expenses percent distribution
Total people	**299,267**	**84.6%**	**$1,185**	**$1,033,056**	**100.0%**
Under age 18	74,106	85.4	462	98,789	9.6
Aged 18 to 29	49,243	73.5	685	79,302	7.7
Aged 30 to 39	39,719	78.5	1,017	94,457	9.1
Aged 40 to 49	44,328	83.8	1,100	129,809	12.6
Aged 50 to 59	39,458	90.0	2,220	207,157	20.1
Aged 60 to 64	14,433	91.8	2,855	90,222	8.7
Aged 65 or older	37,980	96.7	4,215	333,320	32.3

PERCENT DISTRIBUTION BY SOURCE OF PAYMENT

	total	out of pocket	private insurance	Medicare	Medicaid	other
Total people	**100.0%**	**19.0%**	**41.7%**	**23.5%**	**8.7%**	**7.1%**
Under age 18	100.0	20.5	50.7	0.5	23.7	4.6
Aged 18 to 29	100.0	24.8	46.3	0.8	20.0	8.1
Aged 30 to 39	100.0	19.5	62.3	3.0	8.3	6.8
Aged 40 to 49	100.0	20.3	55.3	6.1	10.0	8.3
Aged 50 to 59	100.0	19.6	57.6	8.9	7.0	6.9
Aged 60 to 64	100.0	22.1	52.2	10.7	7.8	7.2
Aged 65 or older	100.0	15.2	14.1	60.9	2.4	7.3

Note: "Other" insurance includes Department of Veterans Affairs (except Tricare), American Indian Health Service, state and local clinics, worker's compensation, homeowner's and automobile insurance, etc.
Source: Agency for Healthcare Research and Quality, Medical Expenditure Panel Survey, 2006, Internet site http://www.meps .ahrq.gov/mepsweb/data_stats/quick_tables_results.jsp?component=1&subcomponent=0&tableSeries=1&year=-1&SearchMet hod=1&Action=Search; calculations by New Strategist

Table 3.14 Health Care Expenditures of People Aged 55 to 64, 2006

(percent of people aged 55 to 64 with health care expense, median amount spent by those with expense, total expenses and percent distribution by type, and percent distribution of expenses by source of payment, 2006; ranked by percent with expense)

| | percent with expense | median amount spent by those with expense | total expenses | | percent distribution of total expenses by source of payment | | | | | |
			(millions)	percent distribution	total	out of pocket	private insurance	Medicare	Medicaid	other
Any health care expense	**91.1%**	**$2,654**	**$198,324**	**100.0%**	**100.0%**	**20.9%**	**55.0%**	**10.7%**	**6.0%**	**7.3%**
Prescription medicine	80.5	953	48,677	24.5	100.0	36.9	44.3	8.9	5.4	4.6
Physician office visits	77.1	434	34,189	17.2	100.0	15.0	59.7	8.4	4.9	12.0
Dental services	46.7	240	9,535	4.8	100.0	49.7	46.4	0.0	2.2	1.7
Hospital outpatient services	27.1	870	22,884	11.5	100.0	12.1	67.8	8.9	3.7	7.5
Vision aids	18.9	285	2,074	1.0	100.0	69.9	24.3	0.2	2.8	2.8
Emergency room services	11.5	708	6,178	3.1	100.0	9.4	61.5	11.3	7.6	10.1
Hospital inpatient services	8.7	11,259	53,143	26.8	100.0	7.5	62.3	16.5	7.2	6.5

Note: "Other" insurance includes Department of Veterans Affairs (except Tricare), American Indian Health Service, state and local clinics, worker's compensation, homeowner's and automobile insurance, etc.
Source: Agency for Healthcare Research and Quality, Medical Expenditure Panel Survey, 2006, Internet site http://www.meps .ahrq.gov/mepsweb/data_stats/quick_tables_results.jsp?component=1&subcomponent=0&tableSeries=1&year=-1&SearchMet hod=1&Action=Search; calculations by New Strategist

Table 3.15 Health Care Expenditures of People Aged 65 or Older, 2006

(percent of people aged 65 or older with health care expense, median amount spent by those with expense, total expenses and percent distribution by type, and percent distribution of expenses by source of payment, 2006; ranked by percent with expense)

| | percent with expense | median amount spent by those with expense | total expenses | | percent distribution of total expenses by source of payment | | | | | |
			(millions)	percent distribution	total	out of pocket	private insurance	Medicare	Medicaid	other
Any health care expense	**96.7%**	**$4,215**	**$333,320**	**100.0%**	**100.0%**	**15.2%**	**14.1%**	**60.9%**	**2.4%**	**7.3%**
Prescription medicine	91.7	1,367	73,422	22.0	100.0	35.3	11.7	46.0	0.5	6.5
Physician office visits	89.4	612	47,599	14.3	100.0	7.7	22.1	59.5	1.7	8.9
Dental services	40.0	243	9,153	2.7	100.0	72.5	18.8	3.3	1.5	3.8
Hospital outpatient services	32.4	722	21,181	6.4	100.0	5.3	20.8	65.3	1.3	7.4
Emergency room services	20.4	455	7,216	2.2	100.0	4.6	18.1	69.6	2.3	5.4
Vision aids	18.9	220	1,956	0.6	100.0	75.3	8.4	6.7	3.9	5.6
Hospital inpatient services	18.1	11,780	123,835	37.2	100.0	1.8	11.2	78.4	1.0	7.6
Home health care	10.7	2,790	22,082	6.6	100.0	11.4	2.2	61.8	18.3	6.3

Note: "Other" insurance includes Department of Veterans Affairs (except Tricare), American Indian Health Service, state and local clinics, worker's compensation, homeowner's and automobile insurance, etc.
Source: Agency for Healthcare Research and Quality, Medical Expenditure Panel Survey, 2006, Internet site http://www.meps .ahrq.gov/mepsweb/data_stats/quick_tables_results.jsp?component=1&subcomponent=0&tableSeries=1&year=-1&SearchMet hod=1&Action=Search; calculations by New Strategist

Health Problems Are Common in the 65-or-Older Age Group

Hypertension and arthritis are the most common health conditions among people aged 65 or older.

Most Americans aged 65 or older have hypertension, making it one of the two most common health conditions in the age group. The other is arthritis, with 43 to 53 percent having been diagnosed with the condition. Thirty to 45 percent of people aged 65 or older have hearing problems, and 20 to 25 percent have had cancer.

The percentage of people experiencing health problems rises steeply with age for most conditions. The percentage of people with hypertension rises from just 8 percent of 18-to-44-year-olds to more than half of those aged 75 or older. Similarly, the percentage with arthritis rises from 7 to 53 percent. Hearing problems increase from just 6 to 45 percent.

As Americans became more aware of the problems associated with high cholesterol over the past few decades, rates have dropped in most age groups. The same cannot be said for high blood pressure. The majority of men aged 65 or older and women aged 55 or older had high blood pressure or were taking antihypertensive medication in 2003–06, a significantly larger share than in 1988–94.

■ As the Baby-Boom generation ages into the 65-or-older age group, the number of people with hypertension, arthritis, and hearing problems will surge.

The percentage of people with arthritis rises with age

(percent of people with arthritis, by age, 2007)

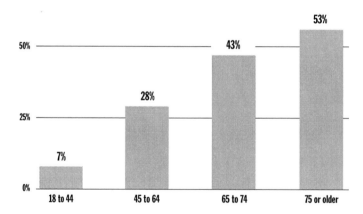

Table 3.16 Number of Adults with Health Conditions by Age, 2007

(number of people aged 18 or older with selected health conditions, by type of condition and age, 2007; numbers in thousands)

				aged 65 or older		
	total	18 to 44	45 to 64	total	65 to 74	75 or older
TOTAL PEOPLE 18 OR OLDER	**223,181**	**110,890**	**76,136**	**36,155**	**19,258**	**16,897**
Selected circulatory diseases						
Heart disease, all types	25,095	4,591	9,266	11,239	5,199	6,040
Coronary	13,674	1,041	5,091	7,542	3,571	3,971
Hypertension	52,920	9,094	24,383	19,442	9,763	9,679
Stroke	5,426	285	2,156	2,985	1,205	1,780
Selected respiratory conditions						
Emphysema	3,736	226	1,765	1,745	861	884
Asthma, ever	24,402	12,996	7,895	3,511	2,030	1,481
Asthma, still	16,177	7,996	5,476	2,704	1,591	1,113
Hay fever	16,882	7,420	7,210	2,252	1,302	950
Sinusitis	25,953	10,261	11,154	4,538	2,589	1,949
Chronic bronchitis	7,604	2,515	3,226	1,863	1,050	813
Selected types of cancer						
Any cancer	16,370	2,085	6,305	7,980	3,757	4,223
Breast cancer	2,630	178	1,028	1,424	626	798
Cervical cancer	1,011	437	417	157	92	65
Prostate cancer	2,037	0	543	1,494	651	843
Other selected diseases and conditions						
Diabetes	17,273	2,432	8,093	6,748	3,840	2,908
Ulcers	14,501	4,616	5,641	4,244	2,119	2,125
Kidney disease	3,343	759	1,226	1,359	593	766
Liver disease	2,649	749	1,374	526	368	158
Arthritis	46,429	7,810	21,428	17,192	8,322	8,870
Chronic joint symptoms	53,945	14,776	24,820	14,350	7,140	7,210
Migraines or severe headaches	27,364	16,427	9,277	1,660	1,075	585
Pain in neck	29,019	11,833	12,073	5,113	2,833	2,280
Pain in lower back	57,070	24,555	21,860	10,655	5,650	5,005
Pain in face or jaw	9,062	4,649	3,455	957	607	350
Selected sensory problems						
Hearing	33,318	6,597	13,400	13,320	5,739	7,581
Vision	22,378	7,596	9,297	5,484	2,472	3,012
Absence of all natural teeth	16,997	2,066	5,606	9,325	4,284	5,041

Note: The conditions shown are those that have ever been diagnosed by a doctor, except as noted. Hay fever, sinusitis, and chronic bronchitis have been diagnosed in the past 12 months. Kidney and liver diseases have been diagnosed in the past 12 months and exclude kidney stones, bladder infections, and incontinence. Chronic joint symptoms are shown if respondent had pain, aching, or stiffness in or around a joint (excluding back and neck) and the condition began more than three months ago. Migraines, and pain in neck, lower back, face, or jaw are shown only if pain lasted a whole day or more.
Source: National Center for Health Statistics, Summary Health Statistics for U.S. Adults: National Health Interview Survey, 2007, Vital and Health Statistics, Series 10, No. 240, 2008, Internet site http://www.cdc.gov/nchs/nhis.htm

Table 3.17 Distribution of Health Conditions among Adults by Age, 2007

(percent distribution of people aged 18 or older with selected health conditions, by type of condition and age, 2007)

	total	18 to 44	45 to 64	aged 65 or older total	65 to 74	75 or older
TOTAL PEOPLE 18 OR OLDER	**100.0%**	**49.7%**	**34.1%**	**16.2%**	**8.6%**	**7.6%**
Selected circulatory diseases						
Heart disease, all types	100.0	18.3	36.9	44.8	20.7	24.1
Coronary	100.0	7.6	37.2	55.2	26.1	29.0
Hypertension	100.0	17.2	46.1	36.7	18.4	18.3
Stroke	100.0	5.3	39.7	55.0	22.2	32.8
Selected respiratory conditions						
Emphysema	100.0	6.0	47.2	46.7	23.0	23.7
Asthma, ever	100.0	53.3	32.4	14.4	8.3	6.1
Asthma, still	100.0	49.4	33.9	16.7	9.8	6.9
Hay fever	100.0	44.0	42.7	13.3	7.7	5.6
Sinusitis	100.0	39.5	43.0	17.5	10.0	7.5
Chronic bronchitis	100.0	33.1	42.4	24.5	13.8	10.7
Selected types of cancer						
Any cancer	100.0	12.7	38.5	48.7	23.0	25.8
Breast cancer	100.0	6.8	39.1	54.1	23.8	30.3
Cervical cancer	100.0	43.2	41.2	15.5	9.1	6.4
Prostate cancer	100.0	0	26.7	73.3	32.0	41.4
Other selected diseases and conditions						
Diabetes	100.0	14.1	46.9	39.1	22.2	16.8
Ulcers	100.0	31.8	38.9	29.3	14.6	14.7
Kidney disease	100.0	22.7	36.7	40.7	17.7	22.9
Liver disease	100.0	28.3	51.9	19.9	13.9	6.0
Arthritis	100.0	16.8	46.2	37.0	17.9	19.1
Chronic joint symptoms	100.0	27.4	46.0	26.6	13.2	13.4
Migraines or severe headaches	100.0	60.0	33.9	6.1	3.9	2.1
Pain in neck	100.0	40.8	41.6	17.6	9.8	7.9
Pain in lower back	100.0	43.0	38.3	18.7	9.9	8.8
Pain in face or jaw	100.0	51.3	38.1	10.6	6.7	3.9
Selected sensory problems						
Hearing	100.0	19.8	40.2	40.0	17.2	22.8
Vision	100.0	33.9	41.5	24.5	11.0	13.5
Absence of all natural teeth	100.0	12.2	33.0	54.9	25.2	29.7

Note: The conditions shown are those that have ever been diagnosed by a doctor, except as noted. Hay fever, sinusitis, and chronic bronchitis have been diagnosed in the past 12 months. Kidney and liver diseases have been diagnosed in the past 12 months and exclude kidney stones, bladder infections, and incontinence. Chronic joint symptoms are shown if respondent had pain, aching, or stiffness in or around a joint (excluding back and neck) and the condition began more than three months ago. Migraines, and pain in neck, lower back, face, or jaw are shown only if pain lasted a whole day or more.
Source: National Center for Health Statistics, Summary Health Statistics for U.S. Adults: National Health Interview Survey, 2007, Vital and Health Statistics, Series 10, No. 240, 2008, Internet site http://www.cdc.gov/nchs/nhis.htm; calculations by New Strategist

Table 3.18 Percent of Adults with Health Conditions by Age, 2007

(percent of people aged 18 or older with selected health conditions, by type of condition and age, 2007)

	total	18 to 44	45 to 64	65 to 74	75 or older
TOTAL PEOPLE 18 OR OLDER	**100.0%**	**100.0%**	**100.0%**	**100.0%**	**100.0%**
Selected circulatory diseases					
Heart disease, all types	11.3	4.1	12.2	27.1	35.8
Coronary	6.1	0.9	6.7	18.6	23.6
Hypertension	23.7	8.2	32.1	50.9	57.4
Stroke	2.4	0.3	2.8	6.3	10.6
Selected respiratory conditions					
Emphysema	1.7	0.2	2.3	4.5	5.2
Asthma, ever	10.9	11.7	10.4	10.6	8.8
Asthma, still	7.3	7.2	7.2	8.3	6.6
Hay fever	7.6	6.7	9.5	6.8	5.6
Sinusitis	11.6	9.3	14.7	13.5	11.6
Chronic bronchitis	3.4	2.3	4.2	5.5	4.8
Selected types of cancer					
Any cancer	7.3	1.9	8.3	19.6	25.0
Breast cancer	1.2	0.2	1.4	3.3	4.7
Cervical cancer	0.9	0.8	1.1	0.9	0.6
Prostate cancer	1.9	0.0	1.5	7.4	12.8
Other selected diseases and conditions					
Diabetes	7.8	2.2	10.7	20.3	17.6
Ulcers	6.5	4.2	7.4	11.0	12.6
Kidney disease	1.5	0.7	1.6	3.1	4.5
Liver disease	1.2	0.7	1.8	1.9	0.9
Arthritis	20.8	7.1	28.2	43.4	52.7
Chronic joint symptoms	24.2	13.3	32.6	37.2	42.9
Migraines or severe headaches	12.3	14.8	12.2	5.6	3.5
Pain in neck	13.0	10.7	15.9	14.7	13.5
Pain in lower back	25.6	22.2	28.7	29.4	29.7
Pain in face or jaw	4.1	4.2	4.5	3.2	2.1
Selected sensory problems					
Hearing	14.9	6.0	17.6	29.8	45.0
Vision	10.0	6.9	12.2	12.9	17.9
Absence of all natural teeth	7.6	1.9	7.4	22.4	30.1

Note: The conditions shown are those that have ever been diagnosed by a doctor, except as noted. Hay fever, sinusitis, and chronic bronchitis have been diagnosed in the past 12 months. Kidney and liver diseases have been diagnosed in the past 12 months and exclude kidney stones, bladder infections, and incontinence. Chronic joint symptoms are shown if respondent had pain, aching, or stiffness in or around a joint (excluding back and neck) and the condition began more than three months ago. Migraines, and pain in neck, lower back, face, or jaw are shown only if pain lasted a whole day or more.
Source: National Center for Health Statistics, Summary Health Statistics for U.S. Adults: National Health Interview Survey, 2007, Vital and Health Statistics, Series 10, No. 240, 2008, Internet site http://www.cdc.gov/nchs/nhis.htm; calculations by New Strategist

Table 3.19 Percent of People Aged 55 or Older with Health Conditions, Problems, and Health Care Contacts by Age, 2000–03

(percent of people aged 55 or older with selected health conditions, difficulties in physical and social functioning, and health care contacts in past 12 months, by age, 2000–03)

	total	55 to 64	65 to 74	75 to 84	85 or older
Conditions					
Hypertension	44.9%	38.0%	47.9%	53.2%	50.5%
Heart disease	25.0	17.0	26.7	35.6	38.5
Diabetes	14.5	12.6	17.0	15.5	11.0
Hearing impairment	31.5	22.3	31.4	43.9	58.0
Vision impairment	14.6	11.0	13.9	19.1	30.3
Loss of all natural teeth	21.6	13.7	24.0	29.5	40.2
Difficulties in functioning					
Walking 1/4 mile	23.8	16.5	22.4	34.2	56.0
Walking up 10 steps	18.6	12.9	17.4	26.2	46.2
Standing for two hours	27.6	20.3	25.7	38.8	59.6
Sitting for two hours	10.5	10.3	9.1	11.3	16.1
Stooping or bending	29.2	22.2	29.2	38.1	52.4
Reaching	10.9	8.7	9.9	14.1	23.3
Grasping	9.4	7.4	8.4	12.3	20.6
Carrying 10 pounds	15.0	10.9	12.9	20.9	38.5
Pushing or pulling large objects	20.5	15.5	19.0	27.7	46.6
Shopping	12.4	9.0	10.5	17.2	35.8
Socializing	9.4	6.5	7.8	13.1	29.2
Relaxing	4.0	3.1	3.1	5.3	11.6
Health care contacts in past 12 months					
Dentist	60.2	64.9	58.9	55.9	46.0
Doctor	91.5	88.6	92.8	94.7	94.9
Emergency room	21.1	18.4	20.6	24.9	31.8
Home care	4.7	2.1	3.9	7.9	17.0

Note: Those with hypertension have been told on at least two health care visits that they had high blood pressure or hypertension. Those with heart disease have been diagnosed with coronary heart disease, angina pectoris, heart attack, or other heart condition. Those with diabetes have been diagnosed by a doctor; borderline cases are excluded. Those with hearing impairments reported having at least a little trouble hearing without a hearing aid. Those with vision impairment have trouble seeing even with glasses or contacts. Those with difficulties in functioning reported finding the activities at least somewhat difficult. Source: National Center for Health Statistics, Health Characteristics of Adults 55 Years of Age and Over: United States, 2000–2003, Advance Data, No. 370, 2006, Internet site http://www.cdc.gov/nchs/nhis.htm

Table 3.20 Hypertension by Sex and Age, 1988–94 and 2003–06

(percent of people aged 20 or older who have hypertension or tak antihypertensive medication, by sex and age, 1988–94 and 2003–06; percentage point change, 1988–94 to 2003–06)

	2003–06	1988–94	percentage point change
TOTAL PEOPLE	**32.1%**	**24.1%**	**8.0**
Total men	**31.3**	**23.8**	**7.5**
Aged 20 to 34	9.2	7.1	2.1
Aged 35 to 44	21.1	17.1	0.0
Aged 45 to 54	36.2	29.2	7.0
Aged 55 to 64	50.2	40.6	9.6
Aged 65 to 74	64.1	54.4	9.7
Aged 75 or older	65.0	60.4	4.6
Total women	**32.9**	**24.4**	**8.5**
Aged 20 to 34	2.2	2.9	–0.7
Aged 35 to 44	12.6	11.2	1.4
Aged 45 to 54	36.2	23.9	12.3
Aged 55 to 64	54.4	42.6	11.8
Aged 65 to 74	70.8	56.2	14.6
Aged 75 or older	80.2	73.6	6.6

Note: A person is defined as having hypertension if he or she has a systolic pressure of at least 140 mmHg, a diastolic pressure of at least 90 mmHg, or takes antihypertensive medication.
Source: National Center for Health Statistics, Health, United States, 2008, Internet site http://www.cdc.gov/nchs/hus.htm; calculations by New Strategist

Table 3.21 High Cholesterol by Sex and Age, 1988–94 and 2003–06

(percent of people aged 20 or older who have high serum cholesterol, by sex and age, 1988–94 and 2003–06; percentage point change, 1988–94 to 2003–06)

	2003–06	1988–94	percentage point change
TOTAL PEOPLE	**16.4%**	**19.6%**	**–3.2**
Total men	**15.2**	**17.7**	**–2.5**
Aged 20 to 34	9.5	8.2	1.3
Aged 35 to 44	20.5	19.4	1.1
Aged 45 to 54	20.8	26.6	–5.8
Aged 55 to 64	16.0	28.0	–12.0
Aged 65 to 74	10.9	21.9	–11.0
Aged 75 or older	9.6	20.4	–10.8
Total women	**17.5**	**21.3**	**–3.8**
Aged 20 to 34	10.3	7.3	3.0
Aged 35 to 44	12.7	12.3	0.4
Aged 45 to 54	19.7	26.7	–7.0
Aged 55 to 64	30.5	40.9	–10.4
Aged 65 to 74	24.2	41.3	–17.1
Aged 75 or older	18.6	38.2	–19.6

Note: High cholesterol is defined as 240 mg/dL or more.
Source: National Center for Health Statistics, Health, United States, 2008, Internet site http://www.cdc.gov/nchs/hus.htm; calculations by New Strategist

Prescription Drug Use Is Increasing

More Americans use a growing number of prescriptions.

The use of prescription drugs to treat a variety of illnesses, particularly chronic conditions, increased substantially between 1988–94 and 2001–04. The percentage of people who take at least one drug in the past month rose from 38 to 47 percent during those years. The percentage who use three or more prescription drugs in the past month climbed from 11 to 20 percent. Eighty-seven percent of people aged 65 or older have taken at least one prescription drug in the past month, and 60 percent have taken three or more.

Regardless of age, most adults have incurred a prescription drug expense during the past year, the proportion rising from a low of 54 percent among 18-to-44-year-olds to a high of 92 percent among people aged 65 or older, according to the federal government's Medical Expenditure Panel Survey. Expenses for prescription drugs rise with age, to more than $1,300 annually for people aged 65 or older.

■ Behind the increase in the use of prescriptions is the introduction and marketing of new drugs to treat chronic health problems.

Most older Americans have prescription drug expenses

(percent of people with prescription drug expenses, by age, 2006)

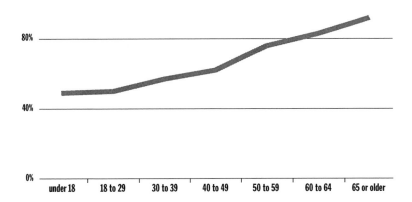

Table 3.22 Prescription Drug Use by Sex and Age, 1988–94 and 2001–04

(percent of people aged 18 or older who take at least one or three or more prescription drugs in the past month, by sex and age, 1988–94 and 2001–04; percentage point change, 1988–94 to 2001–04)

	at least one			three or more		
	2001–04	1988–94	percentage point change	2001–04	1988–94	percentage point change
TOTAL PEOPLE	**46.5%**	**37.8%**	**8.7**	**19.9%**	**11.0%**	**8.9**
Under age 18	23.9	20.5	3.4	4.0	2.4	1.6
Aged 18 to 44	37.6	31.3	6.3	10.2	5.7	4.5
Aged 45 to 64	66.2	54.8	11.4	34.2	20.0	14.2
Aged 65 or older	87.3	73.6	13.7	59.6	35.3	24.3
Total females	**52.2**	**44.6**	**7.6**	**23.3**	**13.6**	**9.7**
Under age 18	22.4	20.6	1.8	3.9	2.3	1.6
Aged 18 to 44	45.9	40.7	5.2	12.3	7.6	4.7
Aged 45 to 64	73.4	62.0	11.4	39.8	24.7	15.1
Aged 65 or older	90.1	78.3	11.8	63.8	38.2	25.6
Total males	**40.5**	**30.6**	**9.9**	**16.3**	**8.3**	**8.0**
Under age 18	25.3	20.4	4.9	4.1	2.6	1.5
Aged 18 to 44	29.2	21.5	7.7	8.0	3.6	4.4
Aged 45 to 64	58.7	47.2	11.5	28.3	15.1	13.2
Aged 65 or older	83.6	67.2	16.4	53.9	31.3	22.6

Source: National Center for Health Statistics, Health, United States, 2008, Internet site http://www.cdc.gov/nchs/hus.htm

Table 3.23 Spending on Prescription Medications by Age, 2006

(percent of people with prescription medication expense, median expense per person, total expenses, and percent distribution of total expenses by source of payment, by age, 2006)

	total (thousands)	percent with expense	median expense per person	total expenses amount (millions)	total expenses percent distribution
Total people	**299,267**	**62.6%**	**$364**	**$223,330**	**100.0%**
Under age 18	74,106	48.9	77	15,180	6.8
Aged 18 to 44	111,078	54.1	191	40,586	18.2
Aged 45 to 54	43,024	69.2	505	45,465	20.4
Aged 55 to 64	33,079	80.5	953	48,677	21.8
Aged 65 or older	37,980	91.7	1,367	73,422	32.9
Aged 65 to 74	19,144	90.2	1,321	37,422	16.8
Aged 75 to 84	13,974	93.7	1,490	27,454	12.3
Aged 85 or older	4,862	92.0	1,229	8,545	3.8

PERCENT DISTRIBUTION BY SOURCE OF PAYMENT	total	out of pocket	private insurance	Medicare	Medicaid	other
Total people	**100.0%**	**34.9%**	**34.0%**	**19.9%**	**7.0%**	**4.3%**
Under age 18	100.0	26.1	47.4	0.7	24.8	0.9
Aged 18 to 44	100.0	40.3	40.4	5.0	11.1	3.2
Aged 45 to 54	100.0	30.2	48.6	9.0	9.6	2.6
Aged 55 to 64	100.0	36.9	44.3	8.9	5.4	4.6
Aged 65 or older	100.0	35.3	11.7	46.0	0.5	6.5
Aged 65 to 74	100.0	33.3	12.2	48.7	0.7	5.0
Aged 75 to 84	100.0	35.9	12.8	42.8	0.3	8.2
Aged 85 or older	100.0	41.8	5.8	44.4	0.4	7.6

Note: "Other" insurance includes Department of Veterans Affairs (except Tricare), American Indian Health Service, state and local clinics, worker's compensation, homeowner's and automobile insurance, etc.
Source: Agency for Healthcare Research and Quality, Medical Expenditure Panel Survey, 2006, Internet site http://www.meps .ahrq.gov/mepsweb/data_stats/quick_tables_results.jsp?component=1&subcomponent=0&tableSeries=1&year=-1&SearchMet hod=1&Action=Search; calculations by New Strategist

Millions of Older Americans Are Disabled

Thirteen million people aged 65 or older have physical difficulties.

Among Americans aged 18 or older in 2007, a substantial 33 million had one or more difficulties in physical functioning, according to a survey by the National Center for Health Statistics. The percentage of people with problems rises from a low of 5 percent among people aged 18 to 44 to a high of 46 percent among people aged 75 or older.

Among people aged 65 or older, 37 percent have physical difficulties. The most common problem is an inability to stand for two hours, mentioned by 23 percent. Twenty-two percent have difficulty walking a quarter mile and 22 percent find it difficult to stoop, bend, or kneel.

■ Although Boomers are supposed to be more health-conscious than older generations of Americans, their weight problems may mean they will have even more physical difficulties in old age.

Disabilities rise in old age

(percent of people with physical difficulties, by age, 2007)

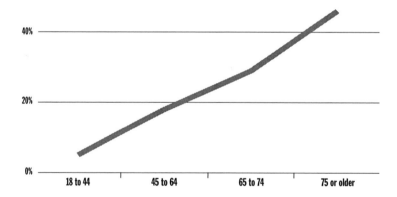

Table 3.24 Difficulties in Physical Functioning among Adults by Age, 2007

(number and percent distribution of people aged 18 or older with difficulties in physical functioning, by type of difficulty and age, 2007; numbers in thousands)

				aged 65 or older		
	total	18 to 44	45 to 64	total	65 to 74	75 or older
Total people aged 18 or older	**223,181**	**110,890**	**76,136**	**36,155**	**19,258**	**16,897**
Total with any physical difficulty	32,977	5,852	13,658	13,467	5,675	7,792
Walk quarter of a mile	16,183	2,000	6,270	7,914	3,142	4,772
Climb 10 steps without resting	12,148	1,469	4,897	5,782	2,128	3,654
Stand for two hours	19,368	2,905	7,971	8,492	3,522	4,970
Sit for two hours	7,220	1,589	3,736	1,895	912	983
Stoop, bend, or kneel	19,943	3,254	8,705	7,983	3,445	4,538
Reach over head	5,543	827	2,517	2,199	861	1,338
Grasp or handle small objects	3,667	482	1,639	1,546	608	938
Lift or carry 10 pounds	8,927	1,237	3,682	4,008	1,574	2,434
Push or pull large objects	14,068	2,333	5,798	5,936	2,465	3,471

PERCENT WITH PHYSICAL DIFFICULTY BY AGE

Total people aged 18 or older	**100.0%**	**100.0%**	**100.0%**	**100.0%**	**100.0%**	**100.0%**
Total with any physical difficulty	14.8	5.3	17.9	37.2	29.5	46.1
Walk quarter of a mile	7.3	1.8	8.2	21.9	16.3	28.2
Climb 10 steps without resting	5.4	1.3	6.4	16.0	11.0	21.6
Stand for two hours	8.7	2.6	10.5	23.5	18.3	29.4
Sit for two hours	3.2	1.4	4.9	5.2	4.7	5.8
Stoop, bend, or kneel	8.9	2.9	11.4	22.1	17.9	26.9
Reach over head	2.5	0.7	3.3	6.1	4.5	7.9
Grasp or handle small objects	1.6	0.4	2.2	4.3	3.2	5.6
Lift or carry 10 pounds	4.0	1.1	4.8	11.1	8.2	14.4
Push or pull large objects	6.3	2.1	7.6	16.4	12.8	20.5

PERCENT DISTRIBUTION OF THOSE WITH PHYSICAL DIFFICULTIES BY AGE

Total people aged 18 or older	**100.0%**	**49.7%**	**34.1%**	**16.2%**	**8.6%**	**7.6%**
Total with any physical difficulty	100.0	17.7	41.4	40.8	17.2	23.6
Walk quarter of a mile	100.0	12.4	38.7	48.9	19.4	29.5
Climb 10 steps without resting	100.0	12.1	40.3	47.6	17.5	30.1
Stand for two hours	100.0	15.0	41.2	43.8	18.2	25.7
Sit for two hours	100.0	22.0	51.7	26.2	12.6	13.6
Stoop, bend, or kneel	100.0	16.3	43.6	40.0	17.3	22.8
Reach over head	100.0	14.9	45.4	39.7	15.5	24.1
Grasp or handle small objects	100.0	13.1	44.7	42.2	16.6	25.6
Lift or carry 10 pounds	100.0	13.9	41.2	44.9	17.6	27.3
Push or pull large objects	100.0	16.6	41.2	42.2	17.5	24.7

Note: Respondents were classified as having difficulties if they responded "very difficult" or "can't do at all."
Source: National Center for Health Statistics, Summary Health Statistics for U.S. Adults: National Health Interview Survey, 2007, Vital and Health Statistics, Series 10, No. 240, 2008, Internet site http://www.cdc.gov/nchs/nhis.htm; calculations by New Strategist

Older Americans Account for One in Four Physician Visits

Most of those in the doctor's office are women.

In 2006, Americans visited physicians a total of 902 million times. People aged 65 or older accounted for 25 percent of those visits. Women account for the 59 percent majority of people aged 65 or older who visited a doctor because women outnumber men in the age group.

People aged 65 or older account for only 16 percent of visits to hospital outpatient departments. Most of the older Americans who visit outpatient departments do so because of chronic problems rather than acute conditions. The 65-or-older age group accounts for 15 percent of visits to emergency rooms. In 2007, 17 percent of people aged 65 or older spent at least one night in a hospital. Among the 35 million people discharged from short-stay hospitals in 2006, 13 million were aged 65 or older. The age group accounted for 62 percent of discharges for heart disease. Although the number of people aged 65 or older who live in nursing homes has increased over the years as the population has grown, the rate at which older Americans are institutionalized has declined sharply thanks to assisted living and more community care.

When people who visit a doctor or health care clinic are asked to rate the care they receive, fewer than half give it the highest rating (a 9 or 10 on a scale of 0 to 10). The proportion rating their experience a 9 or 10 rises with age to a peak of 62 percent among Medicare recipients.

■ As the Baby-Boom generation ages, older Americans will become a larger share of health care consumers, boosting demand for physicians trained in geriatric medicine.

Older Americans are less likely to live in a nursing home

(number of nursing home residents aged 65 or older per 1,000 population in age group, 1973–74 and 2004)

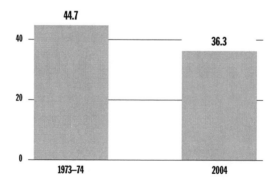

Table 3.25 Physician Office Visits by Sex and Age, 2006

(total number, percent distribution, and number of physician office visits per person per year, by sex and age, 2006; numbers in thousands)

	total	percent distribution	average visits per year
TOTAL VISITS	**901,954**	**100.0%**	**3.1**
Under age 15	157,906	17.5	2.6
Aged 15 to 24	72,411	8.0	1.7
Aged 25 to 44	185,305	20.5	2.3
Aged 45 to 64	256,494	28.4	3.5
Aged 65 to 74	108,063	12.0	5.8
Aged 75 or older	121,774	13.5	7.2
Visits by females	**533,292**	**59.1**	**3.6**
Under age 15	76,300	8.5	2.6
Aged 15 to 24	49,641	5.5	2.4
Aged 25 to 44	122,261	13.6	3.0
Aged 45 to 64	149,778	16.6	3.9
Aged 65 to 74	60,699	6.7	6.0
Aged 75 or older	74,613	8.3	7.3
Visits by males	**368,662**	**40.9**	**2.6**
Under age 15	81,607	9.0	2.6
Aged 15 to 24	22,770	2.5	1.1
Aged 25 to 44	63,044	7.0	1.6
Aged 45 to 64	106,716	11.8	3.0
Aged 65 to 74	47,364	5.3	5.5
Aged 75 or older	47,161	5.2	7.1

Source: National Center for Health Statistics, National Ambulatory Medical Care Survey: 2006 Summary, National Health Statistics Report, No. 3, 2008, Internet site http://www.cdc.gov/nchs/about/major/ahcd/adata.htm

Table 3.26 Hospital Outpatient Department Visits by Age and Reason, 2006

(number and percent distribution of visits to hospital outpatient departments by age and major reason for visit, 2006; numbers in thousands)

	total		major reason for visit					
	number	percent	acute problem	chronic problem, routine	chronic problem, flare-up	pre- or post-surgery	preventive care	unknown
Total visits	102,208	100.0%	36.7%	31.1%	6.8%	4.3%	19.4%	1.7%
Under age 15	19,864	100.0	48.9	17.6	3.7	2.0	24.8	2.8
Aged 15 to 24	12,012	100.0	38.9	16.0	4.7	3.5	34.8	2.1
Aged 25 to 44	25,104	100.0	37.3	27.2	7.0	4.3	22.6	1.5
Aged 45 to 64	28,707	100.0	32.2	41.4	8.4	5.4	11.5	1.1
Aged 65 or older	16,522	100.0	27.4	46.2	8.8	5.9	10.3	1.4
Aged 65 to 74	8,931	100.0	27.5	45.7	8.2	5.8	11.2	1.6
Aged 75 or older	7,591	100.0	27.4	46.8	9.4	5.9	9.2	1.2

Source: National Center for Health Statistics, National Hospital Ambulatory Medical Care Survey: 2006 Outpatient Department Summary, National Health Statistics Reports, No. 4, 2008, Internet site http://www.cdc.gov/nchs/about/major/ahcd/adata .htm; calculations by New Strategist

Table 3.27 Emergency Department Visits by Age and Urgency of Problem, 2006

(number of visits to emergency rooms and percent distribution by urgency of problem, by age, 2006; numbers in thousands)

	total		percent distribution by urgency of problem						
	number	percent distribution	total	immediate	emergent	urgent	semiurgent	nonurgent	unknown
Total visits	119,191	100.0%	100.0%	5.1%	10.8%	36.6%	22.0%	12.1%	13.4%
Under age 15	21,876	18.4	100.0	3.1	7.8	35.0	25.6	14.6	13.9
Aged 15 to 24	19,525	16.4	100.0	4.1	8.4	34.3	24.7	14.3	14.1
Aged 25 to 44	35,034	29.4	100.0	4.3	10.1	36.4	22.7	12.9	13.6
Aged 45 to 64	25,466	21.4	100.0	5.9	12.8	37.1	20.0	11.1	13.2
Aged 65 or older	17,290	14.5	100.0	9.2	15.4	41.3	15.5	6.7	11.9
Aged 65 to 74	7,095	6.0	100.0	9.1	14.2	39.7	17.2	7.5	12.4
Aged 75 or older	10,195	8.6	100.0	9.3	16.2	42.3	14.4	6.1	11.6

Note: "Immediate" is a visit in which the patient should be seen immediately. "Emergent" is a visit in which the patient should be seen within 1 to 14 minutes; "urgent" is a visit in which the patient should be seen within 15 to 60 minutes; "semiurgent" is a visit in which the patient should be seen within 61 to 120 minutes; "nonurgent" is a visit in which the patient should be seen within 121 minutes to 24 hours; "unknown" is a visit with no mention of immediacy or triage or the patient was dead on arrival.
Source: National Center for Health Statistics, National Hospital Ambulatory Medical Care Survey: 2006 Emergency Department Summary, National Health Statistics Reports, No. 7, 2008, Internet site http://www.cdc.gov/nchs/about/major/ahcd/adata .htm

Table 3.28 Number of Overnight Hospital Stays by Age, 2007

(total number of people and percent distribution by experience of an overnight hospital stay in past 12 months, by age, 2007; numbers in thousands)

	total		number of stays	
	number	percent	none	one or more
Total people	**296,905**	**100.0%**	**91.8%**	**8.2%**
Under age 12	48,526	100.0	92.3	7.7
Aged 12 to 17	25,200	100.0	97.5	2.5
Aged 18 to 44	110,889	100.0	93.3	6.7
Aged 45 to 64	76,110	100.0	91.8	8.2
Aged 65 or older	36,180	100.0	82.7	17.3

Source: National Center for Health Statistics, Summary Health Statistics for the U.S. Population: National Health Interview Survey, 2007, Vital and Health Statistics, Series 10, No. 238, 2008, Internet site http://www.cdc.gov/nchs/nhis.htm; calculations by New Strategist

Table 3.29 Hospital Discharges by Diagnosis and Age, 2006

(total number of hospital discharges from nonfederal short-stay hospitals by first-listed diagnosis, and number and percent accounted for by people aged 45 or older, 2006; numbers in thousands)

		aged 45 to 64		aged 65 or older	
	total	number	percent of total	number	percent of total
All conditions	**34,854**	**8,686**	**24.9%**	**13,070**	**37.5%**
Infectious and parasitic diseases	1,088	262	24.1	495	45.5
Neoplasms	1,641	628	38.3	723	44.1
Endocrine, nutritional, and metabolic diseases and immunity disorders	1,663	483	29.0	655	39.4
Diabetes mellitus	584	205	35.1	188	32.2
Diseases of the blood and blood-forming organs	451	102	22.6	196	43.5
Mental disorders	2,419	717	29.6	239	9.9
Diseases of the nervous system and sense organs	615	151	24.6	246	40.0
Diseases of the circulatory system	6,161	1,880	30.5	3,801	61.7
Heart disease	4,202	1,285	30.6	2,624	62.4
Acute myocardial infarction	647	218	33.7	394	60.9
Cerebrovascular disease	889	236	26.5	606	68.2
Diseases of the respiratory system	3,485	804	23.1	1,729	49.6
Diseases of the digestive system	3,517	1,111	31.6	1,329	37.8
Diseases of the genitourinary system	1,974	524	26.5	877	44.4
Diseases of the skin and subcutaneous tissue	780	224	28.7	223	28.6
Diseases of the musculoskeletal system and connective tissue	1,969	720	36.6	911	46.3
Congenital anomalies	193	25	13.0	8	4.1
Symptoms, signs, and ill-defined conditions	189	44	23.3	40	21.2
Injury and poisoning	2,968	764	25.7	1,147	38.6
Supplementary classifications	5,022	246	4.9	453	9.0

Source: National Center for Health Statistics, 2006 National Hospital Discharge Survey, National Health Statistics Report, No. 5, 2008, Internet site http://www.cdc.gov/nchs/about/major/hdasd/listpubs.htm; calculations by New Strategist

Table 3.30 Rating of Health Care Received from Doctor's Office or Clinic, 2006

(number of people aged 18 or older visiting a doctor or health care clinic in past 12 months, and percent distribution by rating for health care received on a scale from 0 (worst) to 10 (best), by age, 2006; people in thousands)

	with health care visit		rating		
	number	percent	9 to 10	7 to 8	0 to 6
Total people	**140,898**	**100.0%**	**49.3%**	**35.8%**	**13.9%**
Aged 18 to 24	14,039	100.0	45.4	38.7	15.1
Aged 25 to 34	21,000	100.0	41.2	41.7	16.3
Aged 35 to 44	25,233	100.0	44.7	39.7	15.0
Aged 45 to 54	27,581	100.0	46.0	37.7	15.7
Aged 55 to 64	24,094	100.0	52.4	34.4	12.5
Aged 65 or older	28,951	100.0	61.9	26.1	10.2

Source: Agency for Healthcare Research and Quality, Medical Expenditure Panel Survey, 2006, Internet site http://www.meps .ahrq.gov/mepsweb/data_stats/quick_tables_results.jsp?component=1&subcomponent=0&tableSeries=3&year=-1&SearchMet hod=1&Action=Search; calculations by New Strategist

---

Table 3.31 Nursing Home Residents Aged 65 or Older, 1973–74 and 2004

(number of nursing home residents aged 65 or older and residents per 1,000 population in age group, 1973–74 and 2004, percent change in number and rate, 1973–74 to 2004, by sex and age; number of residents in thousands)

	number of residents			residents per 1,000 population		
	2004	1973–74	percent change	2004	1973–74	change in rate
Total, aged 65 or older	**13,173**	**9,615**	**37.0%**	**36.3**	**44.7**	**–18.8**
Aged 65 to 74	1,741	1,631	6.7	9.4	12.3	–23.6
Aged 75 to 84	4,687	3,849	21.8	36.1	57.7	–37.4
Aged 85 or older	6,745	4,136	63.1	138.8	257.3	–46.1
Females, aged 65 or older	**9,804**	**6,958**	**40.9**	**46.4**	**54.9**	**–15.5**
Aged 65 to 74	988	980	0.8	9.8	13.1	–25.2
Aged 75 to 84	3,278	2,826	16.0	42.3	68.9	–38.6
Aged 85 or older	5,539	3,153	75.7	165.2	294.9	–44.0
Males, aged 65 or older	**3,369**	**2,657**	**26.8**	**22.2**	**30.0**	**–26.0**
Aged 65 to 74	754	651	15.8	8.9	11.3	–21.2
Aged 75 to 84	1,409	1,023	37.7	27.0	39.9	–32.3
Aged 85 or older	1,206	983	22.7	80.0	182.7	–56.2

Source: National Center for Health Statistics, Health, United States, 2008, Internet site http://www.cdc.gov/nchs/hus.htm

Heart Disease and Cancer Are the Biggest Killers

Cancer is the leading cause of death among people aged 55 to 74.

Among the 2.4 million Americans who died in 2006, 84 percent were aged 55 or older. More than half (56 percent) were aged 75 or older. The 55-or-older age group accounts for 91 percent of deaths due to heart disease, 93 percent of deaths due to influenza and pneumonia, and nearly 100 percent of deaths due to Alzheimer's and Parkinson's diseases. But the age group accounts for only 40 percent of accidental deaths, 30 percent of suicides, and 10 percent of homicides.

While heart disease is the number-one cause of death among people aged 75 or older, cancer is the leading cause of death among 55-to-74-year-olds. Together, the two diseases account for 52 percent of all deaths in the 55-or-older age group. Among the oldest Americans, those aged 85 or older, heart disease causes 34 percent of deaths, while cancer accounts for only 12 percent.

■ With most Americans living to old age, growing numbers must cope with the disabilities of aging. The demands of the disabled drive up health care costs, but they provide opportunities for the health care industry.

Heart disease overtakes cancer as a cause of death in old age

(percent of deaths due to heart disease or cancer, by age, 2006)

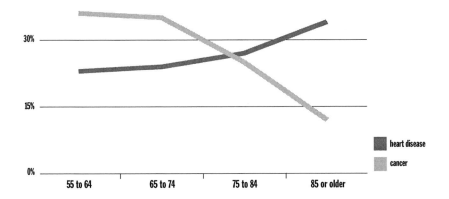

Table 3.32 Deaths from the 15 Leading Causes of Death, 2006: Number of Deaths

(number of deaths from the 15 leading causes of death, by age, 2006; ranked by total number of deaths)

	total	aged 55 or older				
		total	55 to 64	65 to 74	75 to 84	85+
Total deaths	**2,426,264**	**2,040,824**	**281,401**	**390,093**	**667,338**	**701,992**
Diseases of the heart	631,636	576,019	65,477	92,752	180,451	237,339
Malignant neoplasms (cancer)	559,888	488,969	101,454	137,554	164,889	85,072
Cerebrovascular diseases	137,119	127,528	10,518	18,223	43,719	55,068
Chronic lower respiratory disease	124,583	119,220	12,375	28,236	47,406	31,203
Accidents (unintentional injuries)	121,599	48,135	11,446	8,420	13,708	14,561
Diabetes mellitus	72,449	63,783	11,432	15,483	21,763	15,105
Alzheimer's	72,432	72,315	655	3,812	22,915	44,933
Influenza and pneumonia	56,326	52,500	3,154	6,061	16,668	26,617
Nephritis, nephrotic syndrome, and nephrosis	45,344	41,745	4,368	7,453	14,536	15,388
Septicemia	34,234	30,233	4,032	6,064	10,745	9,392
Suicide	33,300	9,882	4,583	2,384	2,075	840
Chronic liver disease and cirrhosis	27,555	16,938	7,217	4,917	3,778	1,026
Essential hypertension	23,855	22,036	2,178	3,174	6,654	10,030
Parkinson's disease	19,566	19,477	397	2,310	9,101	7,669
Homicide	18,573	1,791	1,012	398	279	102

Note: Numbers do not add to total because "age not stated" is not shown.
Source: National Center for Health Statistics, Deaths: Final Data for 2006, National Vital Statistics Reports, Vol. 57, No. 14, 2009, Internet site http://www.cdc.gov/nchs/products/nvsr.htm#vol57; calculations by New Strategist

Table 3.33 Deaths from the 15 Leading Causes of Death, 2006: Distribution by Cause

(percent distribution of deaths by cause for total people and people aged 55 or older, 2006; ranked by total number of deaths)

	total	aged 55 or older				
		total	55 to 64	65 to 74	75 to 84	85+
Total deaths	**100.0%**	**100.0%**	**100.0%**	**100.0%**	**100.0%**	**100.0%**
Diseases of the heart	26.0	28.2	23.3	23.8	27.0	33.8
Malignant neoplasms (cancer)	23.1	24.0	36.1	35.3	24.7	12.1
Cerebrovascular diseases	5.7	6.2	3.7	4.7	6.6	7.8
Chronic lower respiratory disease	5.1	5.8	4.4	7.2	7.1	4.4
Accidents (unintentional injuries)	5.0	2.4	4.1	2.2	2.1	2.1
Diabetes mellitus	3.0	3.1	4.1	4.0	3.3	2.2
Alzheimer's	3.0	3.5	0.2	1.0	3.4	6.4
Influenza and pneumonia	2.3	2.6	1.1	1.6	2.5	3.8
Nephritis, nephrotic syndrome, and nephrosis	1.9	2.0	1.6	1.9	2.2	2.2
Septicemia	1.4	1.5	1.4	1.6	1.6	1.3
Suicide	1.4	0.5	1.6	0.6	0.3	0.1
Chronic liver disease and cirrhosis	1.1	0.8	2.6	1.3	0.6	0.1
Essential hypertension	1.0	1.1	0.8	0.8	1.0	1.4
Parkinson's disease	0.8	1.0	0.1	0.6	1.4	1.1
Homicide	0.8	0.1	0.4	0.1	0.0	0.0

Source: National Center for Health Statistics, Deaths: Final Data for 2006, National Vital Statistics Reports, Vol. 57, No. 14, 2009, Internet site http://www.cdc.gov/nchs/products/nvsr.htm#vol57; calculations by New Strategist

Table 3.34 Deaths from the 15 Leading Causes of Death, 2006: Distribution by Age

(percent distribution of deaths by age for total people and people aged 55 or older, 2006; ranked by total number of deaths)

	total	aged 55 or older				
		total	55 to 64	65 to 74	75 to 84	85+
Total deaths	**100.0%**	**84.1%**	**11.6%**	**16.1%**	**27.5%**	**28.9%**
Heart disease	100.0	91.2	10.4	14.7	28.6	37.6
Malignant neoplasms	100.0	87.3	18.1	24.6	29.5	15.2
Cerebrovascular diseases	100.0	93.0	7.7	13.3	31.9	40.2
Chronic lower respiratory disease	100.0	95.7	9.9	22.7	38.1	25.0
Accidents (unintentional injuries)	100.0	39.6	9.4	6.9	11.3	12.0
Diabetes mellitus	100.0	88.0	15.8	21.4	30.0	20.8
Alzheimer's	100.0	99.8	0.9	5.3	31.6	62.0
Influenza and pneumonia	100.0	93.2	5.6	10.8	29.6	47.3
Nephritis	100.0	92.1	9.6	16.4	32.1	33.9
Septicemia	100.0	88.3	11.8	17.7	31.4	27.4
Suicide	100.0	29.7	13.8	7.2	6.2	2.5
Chronic liver disease	100.0	61.5	26.2	17.8	13.7	3.7
Essential hypertension	100.0	92.4	9.1	13.3	27.9	42.0
Parkinson's disease	100.0	99.5	2.0	11.8	46.5	39.2
Homicide	100.0	9.6	5.4	2.1	1.5	0.5

Source: National Center for Health Statistics, Deaths: Final Data for 2006, National Vital Statistics Reports, Vol. 57, No. 14, 2009, Internet site http://www.cdc.gov/nchs/products/nvsr.htm#vol57; calculations by New Strategist

Table 3.35 Leading Causes of Death for People Aged 55 to 64, 2006

(number and percent distribution of deaths accounted for by the 10 leading causes of death for people aged 55 to 64, 2006)

		number	percent distribution
	All causes	**281,401**	**100.0%**
1.	Malignant neoplasms (cancer) (2)	101,454	36.1
2.	Diseases of heart (1)	65,477	23.3
3.	Chronic lower respiratory disease (4)	12,375	4.4
4.	Accidents (unintentional injuries) (5)	11,446	4.1
5.	Diabetes mellitus (6)	11,432	4.1
6.	Cerebrovascular diseases (3)	10,518	3.7
7.	Chronic liver disease and cirrhosis (12)	7,217	2.6
8.	Suicide (11)	4,583	1.6
9.	Nephritis, nephrotic syndrome, nephrosis (9)	4,368	1.6
10.	Septicemia (10)	4,032	1.4
	All other causes	48,499	17.2

Note: Number in parentheses shows rank for all Americans if the cause of death is among top 15.
Source: National Center for Health Statistics, Deaths: Final Data for 2006, National Vital Statistics Reports, Vol. 57, No. 14, 2009, Internet site http://www.cdc.gov/nchs/products/nvsr.htm#vol57; calculations by New Strategist

Table 3.36 Leading Causes of Death for People Aged 65 to 74, 2006

(number and percent distribution of deaths accounted for by the 10 leading causes of death for people aged 65 to 74, 2006)

		number	percent distribution
	All causes	**390,093**	**100.0%**
1.	Malignant neoplasms (cancer) (2)	137,554	35.3
2.	Diseases of the heart (1)	92,752	23.8
3.	Chronic lower respiratory disease (4)	28,236	7.2
4.	Cerebrovascular diseases (3)	18,223	4.7
5.	Diabetes mellitus (6)	15,483	4.0
6.	Accidents (unintentional injuries) (5)	8,420	2.2
7.	Nephritis, nephrotic syndrome, nephrosis (9)	7,453	1.9
9.	Septicemia (10)	6,064	1.6
8.	Influenza and pneumonia (8)	6,061	1.6
10.	Chronic liver disease and cirrhosis (12)	4,917	1.3
	All other causes	64,930	16.6

Note: Number in parentheses shows rank for all Americans if the cause of death is among top 15.
Source: National Center for Health Statistics, Deaths: Final Data for 2006, National Vital Statistics Reports, Vol. 57, No. 14, 2009, Internet site http://www.cdc.gov/nchs/products/nvsr.htm#vol57; calculations by New Strategist

Table 3.37 Leading Causes of Death for People Aged 75 to 84, 2006

(number and percent distribution of deaths accounted for by the 10 leading causes of death for people aged 75 to 84, 2006)

	number	percent distribution
All causes	**667,338**	**100.0%**
1. Diseases of the heart (1)	180,451	27.0
2. Malignant neoplasms (cancer) (2)	164,889	24.7
3. Chronic lower respiratory disease (4)	47,406	7.1
4. Cerebrovascular diseases (3)	43,719	6.6
5. Alzheimer's disease (7)	22,915	3.4
6. Diabetes mellitus (6)	21,763	3.3
7. Influenza and pneumonia (8)	16,668	2.5
8. Nephritis, nephrotic syndrome, nephrosis (9)	14,536	2.2
9. Accidents (unintentional injuries) (5)	13,708	2.1
10. Septicemia (10)	10,745	1.6
All other causes	130,538	19.6

Note: Number in parentheses shows rank for all Americans if the cause of death is among top 15.
Source: National Center for Health Statistics, Deaths: Final Data for 2006, National Vital Statistics Reports, Vol. 57, No. 14, 2009, Internet site http://www.cdc.gov/nchs/products/nvsr.htm#vol57; calculations by New Strategist

Table 3.38 Leading Causes of Death for People Aged 85 or Older, 2006

(number and percent distribution of deaths accounted for by the 10 leading causes of death for people aged 85 or older, 2006)

	number	percent distribution
All causes	**701,992**	**100.0%**
1. Diseases of the heart (1)	237,339	33.8
2. Malignant neoplasms (cancer) (2)	85,072	12.1
3. Cerebrovascular diseases (3)	55,068	7.8
4. Alzheimer's disease (7)	44,933	6.4
5. Chronic lower respiratory disease (4)	31,203	4.4
6. Influenza and pneumonia (8)	26,617	3.8
7. Nephritis, nephrotic syndrome, nephrosis (9)	15,388	2.2
8. Diabetes mellitus (6)	15,105	2.2
9. Accidents (unintentional injuries) (5)	14,561	2.1
10. Essential hypertension (13)	10,030	1.4
All other causes	166,676	23.7

Note: Number in parentheses shows rank for all Americans if the cause of death is among top 15.
Source: National Center for Health Statistics, Deaths: Final Data for 2006, National Vital Statistics Reports, Vol. 57, No. 14, 2009, Internet site http://www.cdc.gov/nchs/products/nvsr.htm#vol57; calculations by New Strategist

Life Expectancy Has Grown at Older Ages

Older Americans have gained five more years of life since 1950.

In 1950, the average 65-year-old could expect to live 13.9 more years. In 2006, a 65-year-old could expect to live 19.0 more years. The gain in life expectancy is due primarily to the success of medical science at curtailing deaths due to heart disease, the biggest killer of Americans.

Life expectancy at birth stood at 75.1 years for males and 80.2 years for females in 2006. At all ages, the life expectancy of females is greater than that of males. Among people aged 85, men can expect to live another 5.7 years, while women can expect 6.8 more years of life.

■ Medical science has made great strides in lengthening life, but older Americans are now demanding improved quality of life as well.

More years remain at the end of life

(expected number of years of life remaining for people aged 65 or older, 1950 and 2006)

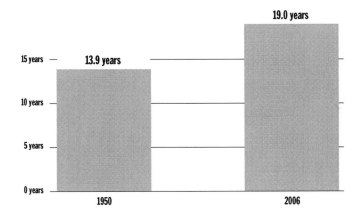

Table 3.39 Life Expectancy by Age, 1950 to 2006

(expected years of life remaining at birth and age 65, 1950 to 2006; change in expected years of life remaining for selected years)

	at birth	age 65
2006	78.1	19.0
2000	77.0	17.9
1990	75.4	17.2
1980	73.7	16.4
1970	70.8	15.2
1960	69.7	14.3
1950	68.2	13.9
Change		
2000 to 2006	1.1	1.1
1950 to 2006	9.9	5.1

Source: National Center for Health Statistics, Deaths: Preliminary Deaths for 2006, National Vital Statistics Report, Vol. 56, No. 16, 2008, Internet site http://www.cdc.gov/nchs/deaths.htm; calculations by New Strategist

Table 3.40 Life Expectancy by Age and Sex, 2006

(years of life remaining at selected ages, by sex, 2006)

	total	females	males
At birth	**77.7**	**80.2**	**75.1**
Aged 1	77.2	79.7	74.7
Aged 5	73.3	75.8	70.8
Aged 10	68.4	70.8	65.8
Aged 15	63.4	65.9	60.9
Aged 20	58.6	61.0	56.1
Aged 25	53.9	56.1	51.5
Aged 30	49.2	51.3	46.9
Aged 35	44.4	46.4	42.2
Aged 40	39.7	41.7	37.6
Aged 45	35.2	37.0	33.1
Aged 50	30.7	32.5	28.8
Aged 55	26.5	28.0	24.7
Aged 60	22.4	23.8	20.7
Aged 65	18.5	19.7	17.0
Aged 70	14.9	15.9	13.6
Aged 75	11.6	12.3	10.5
Aged 80	8.7	9.3	7.8
Aged 85	6.4	6.8	5.7
Aged 90	4.6	4.8	4.1
Aged 95	3.2	3.3	2.9
Aged 100	2.3	2.3	2.0

Source: National Center for Health Statistics, Deaths: Final Data for 2006, National Vital Statistics Reports, Vol. 57, No. 14, 2009, Internet site http://www.cdc.gov/nchs/products/nvsr.htm#vol57; calculations by New Strategist

Housing

■ The homeownership rate in the United States fell by 1.2 percentage points between 2004 and 2008. But the rate continued to rise during those years among householders aged 55 or older.

■ Sixty-nine percent of householders aged 65 or older live in a single-family, detached home. Twenty percent live in an apartment building, and 7 percent in a mobile home.

■ Older Americans are no less likely to have a home outfitted with amenities than is the average household. Fully 85 percent have a porch, deck, balcony, or patio, 63 percent have central air conditioning, and most have a dishwasher.

■ When asked to rate their housing unit on a scale of 1 (worst) to 10 (best), 80 percent of householders aged 65 or older rate their home an 8 or higher. Seventy-seven percent rate their neighborhood an 8 or higher.

■ Housing costs are lowest for homeowners aged 65 or older regardless of household type. Median monthly housing costs for married homeowners aged 65 or older were just $514 in 2007.

■ Older Americans are less likely to move than the average person. Among movers, however, people aged 55 or older are more likely to head to a different state. Thirteen percent of all movers moved to a different state between 2007 and 2008, but the proportion rises as high as 20 percent among movers aged 60 to 64 and 80 to 84.

Homeownership Rate Has Declined

Among older Americans, however, the rate has increased.

The homeownership rate in the United States reached a record high of 69.0 percent in 2004. Since then, the rate has fallen by 1.2 percentage points, to 67.8 percent in 2008, as the housing market collapsed. Homeownership rates continued to rise during those years among householders aged 55 or older, however. In 2008, the nation's homeownership rate set a record high at 83 percent among householders aged 65 to 74.

In 2008, the overall homeownership rate was 0.4 percentage points greater than in 2000. But for older Americans, the gain in homeownership was even greater. The homeownership rate of householders aged 55 to 59 grew by 2.4 percentage points during those years, climbing to 81.2 percent. The rate increase between 2000 and 2008 gets bigger with each succeeding age group. Among householders aged 75 or older, the homeownership rate climbed by 6.5 percentage points between 2000 and 2008, to 78.8 percent.

■ Homeownership among older Americans has continued to grow because few bought homes during the housing bubble, which means that few are at risk of losing their home.

Homeownership rate still rising among householders aged 55 or older

(homeownership rate for householders aged 55 or older, by age, 2004 and 2008)

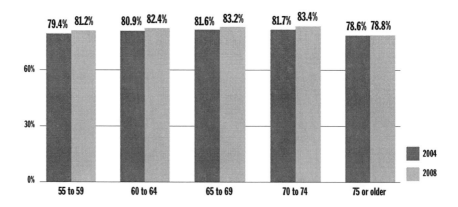

Table 4.1 Homeownership by Age of Householder, 2000 to 2008

(percentage of householders who own their home by age of householder, 2000 to 2008; percentage point change, 2004–08, and 2000–08)

	2008	2004	2000	percentage point change	
				2004–08	2000–08
Total households	**67.8%**	**69.0%**	**67.4%**	**–1.2**	**0.4**
Under age 35	41.0	43.1	40.8	–2.1	0.2
Aged 35 to 44	67.0	69.2	66.3	–2.2	0.7
Aged 45 to 54	75.0	77.2	75.2	–2.2	–0.2
Aged 55 to 59	81.2	79.4	78.8	1.8	2.4
Aged 60 to 64	82.4	80.9	79.8	1.5	2.6
Aged 65 to 69	83.2	81.6	80.0	1.6	3.2
Aged 70 to 74	83.4	81.7	78.4	1.7	5.0
Aged 75 or older	78.8	78.6	72.3	0.2	6.5

Source: Bureau of the Census, Housing Vacancies and Homeownership Survey, Internet site http://www.census.gov/hhes/www/housing/hvs/annual08/ann08ind.html; calculations by New Strategist

Homeownership Rises with Age

About eight of 10 householders aged 55 or older own their home.

The housing bubble was not the only reason for the booming housing industry over the past decade. Another factor was the aging of the population into the lifestage when homeownership peaks. The homeownership rate climbs with age and tops 80 percent among householders ranging in age from 60 to 74. As the large Baby-Boom generation approached the age in which homeownership peaks, it fueled the real estate, construction, and home improvement industries. In fact, Boomer demand for homes helped to create the housing bubble.

Only 18 to 21 percent of householders aged 55 or older are renters. Older adults account for one-third of the nation's homeowners, but only 13 percent of its renters.

■ Although the overall homeownership rate has receded from its peak, the pattern of homeownership—a rising rate as people age—is unchanged.

Homeowners greatly outnumber renters among householders aged 55 or older

(percent distribution of householders aged 55 or older by homeownership status and age, 2008)

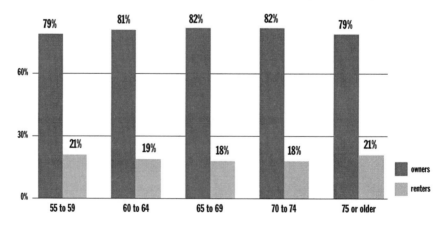

Table 4.2 Owners and Renters by Age of Householder, 2008

(number and percent distribution of householders by homeownership status, and owner and renter share of total, by age of householder, 2008; numbers in thousands)

		owners			renters		
	total	number	percent distribution	share of total	number	percent distribution	share of total
Total households	**111,409**	**75,566**	**100.0%**	**67.8%**	**35,843**	**100.0%**	**32.2%**
Under age 35	24,710	10,120	13.4	41.0	14,589	40.7	59.0
Aged 35 to 44	21,524	14,425	19.1	67.0	7,098	19.8	33.0
Aged 45 to 54	23,382	17,537	23.2	75.0	5,845	16.3	25.0
Aged 55 to 59	10,217	8,107	10.7	79.4	2,109	5.9	20.6
Aged 60 to 64	8,601	6,962	9.2	80.9	1,639	4.6	19.1
Aged 65 or older	22,976	18,414	24.4	80.1	4,562	12.7	19.9
Aged 65 to 69	6,642	5,421	7.2	81.6	1,221	3.4	18.4
Aged 70 to 74	5,114	4,176	5.5	81.7	938	2.6	18.3
Aged 75 or older	11,219	8,816	11.7	78.6	2,403	6.7	21.4

Source: Bureau of the Census, Housing Vacancies and Homeownership Survey, Internet site http://www.census.gov/hhes/www/ housing/hvs/historic/index.html; calculations by New Strategist

Married Couples Are Most Likely to Be Homeowners

Among couples aged 55 or older, homeownership is greater than 90 percent.

The homeownership rate among all married couples stood at 83.4 percent in 2008, much higher than the 67.8 percent rate for all households. Among older couples, the homeownership rate surpasses 90 percent. It peaks at 92.6 percent among couples aged 65 to 69, then falls slightly with advancing age.

Homeownership is also the norm among Americans aged 55 or older who live alone or who head families without a spouse. The homeownership rate ranges from a low of 59.3 percent among men aged 55 to 59 who live alone to a high of 86.9 percent of men aged 75 or older who head families without a spouse.

■ The lax lending standards of the housing bubble did not eliminate differences in homeownership rates by household type.

Even among couples aged 75 or older, more than 90 percent are homeowners

(percent of married-couple householders who own their home, by age, 2008)

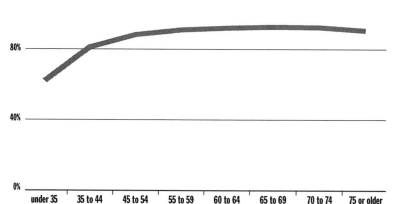

Table 4.3 Homeownership Rate by Age of Householder and Type of Household, 2008

(percent of households that own their home, by age of householder and type of household, 2008)

| | | family households | | | people living alone | |
	total	married couples	female householder, no spouse present	male householder, no spouse present	females	males
Total households	**67.8%**	**83.4%**	**49.5%**	**57.6%**	**58.6%**	**50.6%**
Under age 35	41.0	62.0	26.2	42.0	22.7	28.8
Aged 35 to 44	67.0	81.2	45.2	56.5	47.5	45.6
Aged 45 to 54	75.0	88.2	60.1	69.4	55.0	53.9
Aged 55 to 59	79.4	90.9	66.0	76.7	64.0	59.3
Aged 60 to 64	80.9	92.0	67.7	75.2	68.0	61.2
Aged 65 or older	80.1	91.7	81.2	81.2	69.4	68.2
Aged 65 to 69	81.6	92.6	76.2	74.3	68.3	64.5
Aged 70 to 74	81.7	92.3	77.4	75.3	72.4	63.6
Aged 75 or older	78.6	90.5	85.9	86.9	68.9	72.4

Source: Bureau of the Census, Housing Vacancies and Homeownership Survey, Internet site http://www.census.gov/hhes/www/housing/hvs/annual08/ann08ind.html

Most Older Blacks and Hispanics Are Homeowners

The homeownership rate exceeds 60 percent among blacks and Hispanics aged 55 or older.

The homeownership rate of blacks and Hispanics is well below average. The overall homeownership rate stood at 68.3 percent for all households in 2007 (the latest data available by race, Hispanic origin, and age). Among blacks, the rate was a smaller 46.7 percent. The Hispanic rate was slightly greater at 50.5 percent.

Homeownership surpasses 50 percent among black householders beginning in the 45-to-54 age group. Among Hispanics, the rate surpasses 50 percent in the 35-to-44 age group. Homeownership peaks in the 65-or-older age group for both blacks and Hispanics.

■ Blacks are less likely than Hispanics to be homeowners because married couples head a smaller share of black households.

Most older Americans are homeowners, regardless of race or Hispanic origin

(homeownership rate of total householders and householders aged 55 or older, by race and Hispanic origin, 2007)

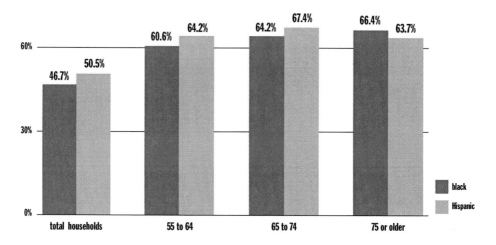

Table 4.4 Black and Hispanic Homeownership Rate by Age, 2007

(percent of total, black, and Hispanic households that own their home, by age of householder, 2007)

	total	black	Hispanic
Total households	**68.3%**	**46.7%**	**50.5%**
Under age 35	42.0	21.8	32.3
Aged 35 to 44	67.9	44.8	53.5
Aged 45 to 54	75.6	55.1	61.1
Aged 55 to 64	80.7	60.6	64.2
Aged 65 to 74	82.2	64.2	67.4
Aged 75 or older	77.5	66.4	63.7

Note: Blacks include only those who identify themselves as being black alone. Hispanics may be of any race.
Source: Bureau of the Census, American Housing Survey for the United States: 2007, Internet site http://www.census.gov/hhes/ www/housing/ahs/ahs07/ahs07.html; calculations by New Strategist

Among Older Americans, Homeownership Is Highest in the South

Their rate of homeownership is lowest in the central cities.

Among householders aged 65 or older, homeownership is highest in the South at 85.0 percent. It is lowest in the Northeast, at 72.8 percent.

Regardless of their metropolitan status, the majority of older householders are homeowners. The figures range from a high of nearly 84 percent for those living in the suburbs or in nonmetropolitan areas to a low of 68.8 percent for those in central cities.

■ Among Americans aged 65 or older who live in a central city, nearly one-third are renters.

Most older Americans own their home, regardless of region

(percent of householders aged 65 or older who own their home, by region, 2007)

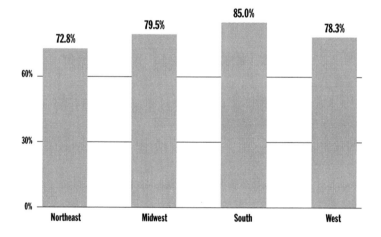

Table 4.5 Households Headed by People Aged 65 or Older by Region and Homeownership Status, 2007

(number of households headed by people aged 65 or older and percent distribution by region and homeownership status, 2007; numbers in thousands)

	total	owner	renter
Total householders aged 65 or older	**22,864**	**18,271**	**4,593**
Northeast	4,628	3,367	1,261
Midwest	5,351	4,256	1,096
South	8,305	7,063	1,243
West	4,580	3,586	994
PERCENT DISTRIBUTION BY HOMEOWNERSHIP STATUS			
Total householders aged 65 or older	**100.0%**	**79.9%**	**20.1%**
Northeast	100.0	72.8	27.2
Midwest	100.0	79.5	20.5
South	100.0	85.0	15.0
West	100.0	78.3	21.7

Source: Bureau of the Census, American Housing Survey for the United States: 2007, Internet site http://www.census.gov/hhes/ www/housing/ahs/ahs07/ahs07.html; calculations by New Strategist

Table 4.6 Households Headed by People Aged 65 or Older by Metropolitan Residence and Homeownership Status, 2007

(number of households headed by people aged 65 or older and percent distribution by metropolitan and homeownership status, 2007; numbers in thousands)

	total	owner	renter
Total householders aged 65 or older	**22,864**	**18,271**	**4,593**
In metropolitan areas	16,399	12,857	3,543
Central cities	5,987	4,121	1,867
Suburbs	10,412	8,736	1,676
In nonmetropolitan areas	6,465	5,415	1,050
PERCENT DISTRIBUTION BY HOMEOWNERSHIP STATUS			
Total householders aged 65 or older	**100.0%**	**79.9%**	**20.1%**
In metropolitan areas	100.0	78.4	21.6
Central cities	100.0	68.8	31.2
Suburbs	100.0	83.9	16.1
In nonmetropolitan areas	100.0	83.8	16.2

Source: Bureau of the Census, American Housing Survey for the United States: 2007, Internet site http://www.census.gov/hhes/ www/housing/ahs/ahs07/ahs07.html; calculations by New Strategist

Most Older Americans Live in a Single-Family Home

The majority of elderly homeowners have three or more bedrooms.

Sixty-nine percent of householders aged 65 or older live in a single-family, detached home. Twenty percent live in an apartment building, and 7 percent in a mobile home. Not surprisingly, older homeowners are much more likely to live in a single-family home than older renters (81 versus 20 percent).

Despite their smaller household size, many older householders have large homes. Seventy-one percent of elderly homeowners have three or more bedrooms, and 54 percent have two or more bathrooms. Thirty-one percent have a room used for business.

■ Many Americans downsize their home as they age. The collapse of the housing market, however, may prevent many older Americans from selling their larger home and moving into something smaller.

Most older homeowners have three or more bedrooms

(percent distribution of homeowners aged 65 or older by number of bedrooms in home, 2007)

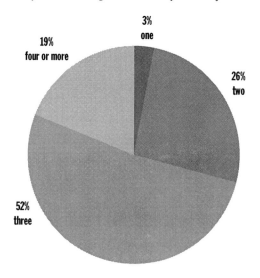

Table 4.7 Number of Units in Structure by Age of Householder, 2007

(number and percent distribution of households by age of householder and number of units in structure, 2007; numbers in thousands)

	total	one, detached	one, attached	multi-unit dwellings total	2 to 4	5 to 9	10 to 19	20 to 49	50 or more	mobile homes
Total households	**110,692**	**71,435**	**6,083**	**26,256**	**8,790**	**5,258**	**4,697**	**3,645**	**3,866**	**6,919**
Under age 35	24,653	11,274	1,594	10,343	3,377	2,389	2,214	1,507	854	1,441
Aged 35 to 54	44,964	31,327	2,299	8,611	3,147	1,746	1,581	1,168	967	2,729
Aged 55 to 64	18,211	13,125	1,033	2,832	1,020	499	440	351	521	1,222
Aged 65 or older	22,865	15,710	1,157	4,470	1,246	622	461	617	1,524	1,528
Aged 65 to 74	11,700	8,359	597	1,863	605	293	236	249	480	881
Aged 75 or older	11,165	7,351	560	2,607	641	329	225	368	1,044	647
Median age	49	51	48	41	41	37	37	40	57	50

PERCENT DISTRIBUTION BY AGE OF HOUSEHOLDER

	total	one, detached	one, attached	multi-unit dwellings total	2 to 4	5 to 9	10 to 19	20 to 49	50 or more	mobile homes
Total households	**100.0%**	**100.0%**	**100.0%**	**100.0%**	**100.0%**	**100.0%**	**100.0%**	**100.0%**	**100.0%**	**100.0%**
Under age 35	22.3	15.8	26.2	39.4	38.4	45.4	47.1	41.3	22.1	20.8
Aged 35 to 54	40.6	43.9	37.8	32.8	35.8	33.2	33.7	32.0	25.0	39.4
Aged 55 to 64	16.5	18.4	17.0	10.8	11.6	9.5	9.4	9.6	13.5	17.7
Aged 65 or older	20.7	22.0	19.0	17.0	14.2	11.8	9.8	16.9	39.4	22.1
Aged 65 to 74	10.6	11.7	9.8	7.1	6.9	5.6	5.0	6.8	12.4	12.7
Aged 75 or older	10.1	10.3	9.2	9.9	7.3	6.3	4.8	10.1	27.0	9.4

PERCENT DISTRIBUTION BY UNITS IN STRUCTURE

	total	one, detached	one, attached	multi-unit dwellings total	2 to 4	5 to 9	10 to 19	20 to 49	50 or more	mobile homes
Total households	**100.0%**	**64.5%**	**5.5%**	**23.7%**	**7.9%**	**4.8%**	**4.2%**	**3.3%**	**3.5%**	**6.3%**
Under age 35	100.0	45.7	6.5	42.0	13.7	9.7	9.0	6.1	3.5	5.8
Aged 35 to 54	100.0	69.7	5.1	19.2	7.0	3.9	3.5	2.6	2.2	6.1
Aged 55 to 64	100.0	72.1	5.7	15.6	5.6	2.7	2.4	1.9	2.9	6.7
Aged 65 or older	100.0	68.7	5.1	19.5	5.4	2.7	2.0	2.7	6.7	6.7
Aged 65 to 74	100.0	71.4	5.1	15.9	5.2	2.5	2.0	2.1	4.1	7.5
Aged 75 or older	100.0	65.8	5.0	23.3	5.7	2.9	2.0	3.3	9.4	5.8

Source: Bureau of the Census, American Housing Survey for the United States: 2007, Internet site http://www.census.gov/hhes/ www/housing/ahs/ahs07/ahs07.html; calculations by New Strategist

Table 4.8 Number of Units in Structures Occupied by Householders Aged 65 or Older, 2007

(number and percent distribution of householders aged 65 or older by number of units in structure and homeownership status, 2007; numbers in thousands)

	total	owner	renter
Total householders aged 65 or older	**22,864**	**18,271**	**4,594**
1, detached	15,710	14,803	907
1, attached	1,157	945	212
Multi-unit dwellings	4,471	1,123	3,346
2 to 4 units	1,246	443	802
5 to 9 units	622	131	491
10 to 19 units	461	126	335
20 to 49 units	618	159	458
50 or more units	1,524	264	1,260
Mobile home	1,528	1,400	128

PERCENT DISTRIBUTION BY HOMEOWNERSHIP STATUS

	total	owner	renter
Total householders aged 65 or older	**100.0%**	**79.9%**	**20.1%**
1, detached	100.0	94.2	5.8
1, attached	100.0	81.7	18.3
Multi-unit dwellings	100.0	25.1	74.8
2 to 4 units	100.0	35.6	64.4
5 to 9 units	100.0	21.1	78.9
10 to 19 units	100.0	27.3	72.7
20 to 49 units	100.0	25.7	74.1
50 or more units	100.0	17.3	82.7
Mobile home	100.0	91.6	8.4

PERCENT DISTRIBUTION BY NUMBER OF UNITS IN STRUCTURE

	total	owner	renter
Total householders aged 65 or older	**100.0%**	**100.0%**	**100.0%**
1, detached	68.7	81.0	19.7
1, attached	5.1	5.2	4.6
Multi-unit dwellings	19.6	6.1	72.8
2 to 4 units	5.4	2.4	17.5
5 to 9 units	2.7	0.7	10.7
10 to 19 units	2.0	0.7	7.3
20 to 49 units	2.7	0.9	10.0
50 or more units	6.7	1.4	27.4
Mobile home	6.7	7.7	2.8

Source: Bureau of the Census, American Housing Survey for the United States: 2007, Internet site http://www.census.gov/hhes/ www/housing/ahs/ahs07/ahs07.html; calculations by New Strategist

Table 4.9 Size of Housing Unit Occupied by Householders Aged 65 or Older, 2007

(number and percent distribution of householders aged 65 or older by size of unit and homeownership status, 2007; numbers in thousands)

	number			percent distribution		
	total	owner	renter	total	owner	renter
TOTAL HOUSEHOLDERS AGED 65 OR OLDER	**22,864**	**18,271**	**4,594**	**100.0%**	**100.0%**	**100.0%**
Number of bedrooms						
None	163	5	158	0.7	0.0	3.4
One	2,710	548	2,162	11.9	3.0	47.1
Two	6,264	4,723	1,541	27.4	25.8	33.5
Three	10,032	9,440	592	43.9	51.7	12.9
Four or more	3,696	3,555	141	16.2	19.5	3.1
Number of bathrooms						
None	94	67	27	0.4	0.4	0.6
One	8,464	4,944	3,520	37.0	27.1	76.6
One-and-one-half	3,781	3,421	360	16.5	18.7	7.8
Two or more	10,525	9,839	687	46.0	53.9	15.0
Rooms used for business						
With room(s) used for business	6,853	5,574	1,280	30.0	30.5	27.9

Source: Bureau of the Census, American Housing Survey for the United States: 2007, Internet site http://www.census.gov/hhes/ www/housing/ahs/ahs07/ahs07.html; calculations by New Strategist

Few Older Homeowners Live in a New Home

Householders under age 35 are most likely to live in a new home.

Overall, only 6 percent of homeowners live in a new home—one built in the past four years. Among homeowners aged 55 to 64, a smaller 4 percent live in a new home. Among those aged 65 or older, the proportion is just 3 percent.

Householders aged 55 or older account for 44 percent of the nation's homeowners, but for only 23 percent of the owners of homes built in the past four years. They account for only 18 percent of renters in new rental units.

■ With many older adults living in an older home, they are a large and growing market for home remodeling and repair services.

Older householders account for a small share of the owners of recently built homes

(percent distribution of homeowners who live in homes built in the past four years, by age of householder, 2007)

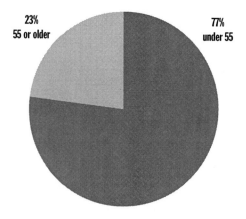

23%
55 or older

77%
under 55

Table 4.10 Owners and Renters of New Homes by Age of Householder, 2007

(number of total occupied housing units, number and percent built in the past four years, and percent distribution of new units by housing tenure and age of householder, 2007; numbers in thousands)

		new homes		
	total	number	percent of total	percent distribution
Total households	**110,692**	**5,747**	**5.2%**	**100.0%**
Under age 35	24,653	1,860	7.5	32.4
Aged 35 to 44	21,756	1,536	7.1	26.7
Aged 45 to 54	23,208	1,056	4.6	18.4
Aged 55 to 64	18,211	683	3.8	11.9
Aged 65 or older	22,865	611	2.7	10.6
Aged 65 to 74	11,700	414	3.5	7.2
Aged 75 or older	11,165	197	1.8	3.4
Total owner households	**75,647**	**4,710**	**6.2**	**100.0**
Under age 35	10,361	1,354	13.1	28.7
Aged 35 to 44	14,781	1,318	8.9	28.0
Aged 45 to 54	17,539	935	5.3	19.9
Aged 55 to 64	14,695	616	4.2	13.1
Aged 65 or older	18,271	487	2.7	10.3
Aged 65 to 74	9,617	361	3.8	7.7
Aged 75 or older	8,654	126	1.5	2.7
Total renter households	**35,045**	**1,036**	**3.0**	**100.0**
Under age 35	14,291	507	3.5	48.9
Aged 35 to 44	6,975	217	3.1	20.9
Aged 45 to 54	5,669	121	2.1	11.7
Aged 55 to 64	3,516	67	1.9	6.5
Aged 65 or older	4,593	124	2.7	12.0
Aged 65 to 74	2,082	53	2.5	5.1
Aged 75 or older	2,511	71	2.8	6.9

Source: Bureau of the Census, American Housing Survey for the United States: 2007, Internet site http://www.census.gov/hhes/www/housing/ahs/ahs07/ahs07.html; calculations by New Strategist

Most Older Americans Depend on Piped Gas for Heat

Renters are more likely than homeowners to heat with electricity.

Among homeowners aged 65 or older, 54 percent depend on piped gas as their main heating fuel. Among renters, the figure is a smaller 40 percent. Electricity is the second most common heating fuel, used by 27 percent of elderly homeowners and 45 percent of renters.

One in 10 older homeowners uses fuel oil as the primary heating fuel. A hardy 2 percent still depend primarily on coal.

■ Households in the South are more likely than those in other regions to use electricity as a primary heating fuel. As the South has grown, electricity has become increasingly important as a heating fuel.

Piped gas is the most widely used heating fuel among older Americans

(percent distribution of homeowners aged 65 or older by primary heating fuel used, 2007)

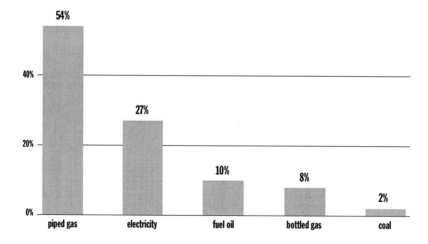

Table 4.11 Main Home Heating Fuel Used by Householders Aged 65 or Older, 2007

(number and percent distribution of housing units occupied by a householder aged 65 or older by main house heating fuel and homeownership status, 2007; numbers in thousands)

	total	owner	renter
Total households headed by people aged 65 or older using heating fuel	**22,786**	**18,215**	**4,571**
Electricity	6,872	4,838	2,035
Piped gas	11,556	9,749	1,808
Bottled gas	1,540	1,394	146
Fuel oil	2,231	1,759	472
Kerosene or other liquid fuel	124	101	23
Wood	19	16	3
Coal or coke	358	308	50
Solar energy	6	3	3
Other	80	49	31

PERCENT DISTRIBUTION BY TYPE OF HEATING FUEL

Total households headed by people aged 65 or older using heating fuel	**100.0%**	**100.0%**	**100.0%**
Electricity	30.2	26.6	44.5
Piped gas	50.7	53.5	39.6
Bottled gas	6.8	7.7	3.2
Fuel oil	9.8	9.7	10.3
Kerosene or other liquid fuel	0.5	0.6	0.5
Wood	0.1	0.1	0.1
Coal or coke	1.6	1.7	1.1
Solar energy	0.0	0.0	0.1
Other	0.4	0.3	0.7

Source: Bureau of the Census, American Housing Survey for the United States: 2007, Internet site http://www.census.gov/hhes/ www/housing/ahs/ahs07/ahs07.html; calculations by New Strategist

Older Americans' Homes Have Many Amenities

Most have a dishwasher, central air conditioning, and a garage or carport.

The homes of older Americans are outfitted with a variety of amenities. Fully 85 percent have a porch, deck, balcony, or patio. Washing machines are also in 85 percent of the homes of older Americans, while clothes dryers are in 81 percent. Seventy-one percent have a garage or carport, and 63 percent have central air conditioning. Fifty-nine percent have a dishwasher.

Older homeowners are much more likely than older renters to have amenities in the home. Sixty-five percent of elderly homeowners have a dishwasher, for example, compared with 32 percent of renters. Thirty-nine percent of elderly homeowners have a useable fireplace versus only 8 percent of renters.

■ Although many older Americans were raised with few amenities, they have outfitted their homes with most of the conveniences.

Most older householders have a home with central air conditioning

(percent of households headed by people aged 65 or older with selected amenities, 2007)

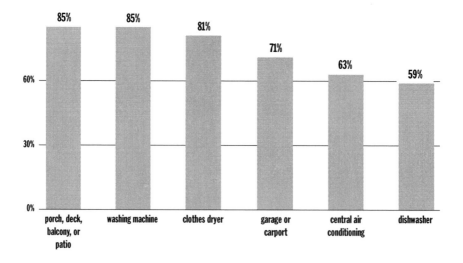

Table 4.12 Amenities of Housing Units Occupied by Householders Aged 65 or Older, 2007

(number and percent distribution of households headed by people aged 65 or older by amenities in unit and homeownership status, 2007; numbers in thousands)

	total	owner	renter
Total households headed by people aged 65 or older	**22,864**	**18,271**	**4,594**
Telephone	22,533	18,054	4,479
Porch, deck, balcony, or patio	19,491	16,706	2,786
Washing machine	19,406	17,470	1,936
Clothes dryer	18,446	16,801	1,645
Garage or carport	16,192	14,745	1,447
Central air conditioning	14,439	12,199	2,240
Dishwasher	13,404	11,916	1,488
Separate dining room	11,243	10,242	1,000
Disposal in kitchen sink	10,292	8,370	1,922
Usable fireplace	7,510	7,164	346
Two or more living/recreation rooms	6,935	6,636	298
PERCENT DISTRIBUTION BY AMENITY			
Total households headed by people aged 65 or older	**100.0%**	**100.0%**	**100.0%**
Telephone	98.6	98.8	97.5
Porch, deck, balcony, or patio	85.2	91.4	60.6
Washing machine	84.9	95.6	42.1
Clothes dryer	80.7	92.0	35.8
Garage or carport	70.8	80.7	31.5
Central air conditioning	63.2	66.8	48.8
Dishwasher	58.6	65.2	32.4
Separate dining room	49.2	56.1	21.8
Disposal in kitchen sink	45.0	45.8	41.8
Usable fireplace	32.8	39.2	7.5
Two or more living/recreation rooms	30.3	36.3	6.5

Source: Bureau of the Census, American Housing Survey for the United States: 2007, Internet site http://www.census.gov/hhes/ www/housing/ahs/ahs07/ahs07.html; calculations by New Strategist

Most of the Elderly Are Satisfied with Their Home and Neighborhood

Homeowners are happier than renters, but few renters are dissatisfied.

When asked to rate their housing unit on a scale of 1 (worst) to 10 (best), 80 percent of householders aged 65 or older rate their home an 8 or higher. Homeowners rate their homes more highly than renters—82 percent of owners and 74 percent of renters give their home at least an 8. Forty-one percent of homeowners and 35 percent of renters give their home the highest rating of 10.

Opinions are almost as positive when older householders are asked to rate their neighborhood. Seventy-seven percent rate their neighborhood an 8 or higher, including 78 percent of homeowners and 73 percent of renters.

■ Older householders rate their home and neighborhood highly because, over the years, those who were unhappy found a new place to live.

Most older householders rate their home and neighborhood highly

(percent of householders aged 65 or older who rate their home and neighborhood an 8 or higher on a scale of 1 to 10, 2007)

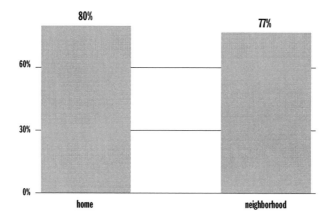

Table 4.13 Opinion of Housing Unit among Householders Aged 65 or Older by Homeownership Status, 2007

(number and percent distribution of housing units occupied by householders aged 65 or older by opinion of housing unit and homeownership status, 2007; numbers in thousands)

	total	owner	renter
Total householders aged 65 or older	**22,864**	**18,271**	**4,594**
1 (worst)	59	37	22
2	32	15	17
3	70	52	19
4	112	76	36
5	806	544	262
6	717	497	220
7	1,791	1,338	453
8	5,492	4,377	1,116
9	3,822	3,140	681
10 (best)	9,087	7,480	1,607

PERCENT DISTRIBUTION BY OPINION OF HOUSING UNIT

Total householders aged 65 or older	**100.0%**	**100.0%**	**100.0%**
1 (worst)	0.3	0.2	0.5
2	0.1	0.1	0.4
3	0.3	0.3	0.4
4	0.5	0.4	0.8
5	3.5	3.0	5.7
6	3.1	2.7	4.8
7	7.8	7.3	9.9
8	24.0	24.0	24.3
9	16.7	17.2	14.8
10 (best)	39.7	40.9	35.0

PERCENT DISTRIBUTION BY HOMEOWNERSHIP STATUS

Total householders aged 65 or older	**100.0%**	**79.9%**	**20.1%**
1 (worst)	100.0	62.7	37.3
2	100.0	46.9	53.1
3	100.0	74.3	27.1
4	100.0	67.9	32.1
5	100.0	67.5	32.5
6	100.0	69.3	30.7
7	100.0	74.7	25.3
8	100.0	79.7	20.3
9	100.0	82.2	17.8
10 (best)	100.0	82.3	17.7

Note: Numbers do not add to total because "not reported" is not shown.
Source: Bureau of the Census, American Housing Survey for the United States: 2007, Internet site http://www.census.gov/hhes/www/housing/ahs/ahs07/ahs07.html; calculations by New Strategist

Table 4.14 Opinion of Neighborhood among Householders Aged 65 or Older by Homeownership Status, 2007

(number and percent distribution of housing units occupied by householders aged 65 or older by opinion of neighborhood and homeownership status, 2007; numbers in thousands)

	total	owner	renter
Total householders aged 65 or older	**22,864**	**18,271**	**4,594**
1 (worst)	103	69	34
2	63	44	19
3	130	101	29
4	208	155	53
5	921	663	259
6	873	672	201
7	2,096	1,636	460
8	5,474	4,460	1,014
9	3,950	3,235	716
10 (best)	8,127	6,492	1,634

PERCENT DISTRIBUTION BY OPINION OF NEIGHBORHOOD

	total	owner	renter
Total householders aged 65 or older	**100.0%**	**100.0%**	**100.0%**
1 (worst)	0.5	0.4	0.7
2	0.3	0.2	0.4
3	0.6	0.6	0.6
4	0.9	0.8	1.2
5	4.0	3.6	5.6
6	3.8	3.7	4.4
7	9.2	9.0	10.0
8	23.9	24.4	22.1
9	17.3	17.7	15.6
10 (best)	35.5	35.5	35.6

PERCENT DISTRIBUTION BY HOMEOWNERSHIP STATUS

	total	owner	renter
Total householders aged 65 or older	**100.0%**	**79.9%**	**20.1%**
1 (worst)	100.0	67.0	33.0
2	100.0	69.8	30.2
3	100.0	77.7	22.3
4	100.0	74.5	25.5
5	100.0	72.0	28.1
6	100.0	77.0	23.0
7	100.0	78.1	21.9
8	100.0	81.5	18.5
9	100.0	81.9	18.1
10 (best)	100.0	79.9	20.1

Note: Numbers do not add to total because "not reported" and "no neighborhood" are not shown.
Source: Bureau of the Census, American Housing Survey for the United States: 2007, Internet site http://www.census.gov/hhes/ www/housing/ahs/ahs07/ahs07.html; calculations by New Strategist

Many Older Americans Live near Open Space, Woodlands

Few are bothered by crime, street noise, or other problems.

Of the 23 million householders aged 65 or older in the United States, 85 percent report having single-family detached houses within 300 feet of their home—88 percent of homeowners and 74 percent of renters. Thirty-nine percent of homeowners and 34 percent of renters report having open space, park, woods, farm, or ranchland close by.

Many older householders have commercial or institutional buildings within 300 feet of their home—19 percent of homeowners and 51 percent of renters. Just 3 to 7 percent report industries or factories nearby, while a larger 14 percent say a four-lane highway, railroad, or airport is within 300 feet.

Few older householders report bothersome neighborhood problems. The biggest problem is street noise or heavy traffic, reported by 21 percent of homeowners and 25 percent of renters. Crime ranks second but only 10 percent of homeowners and 13 percent of renters say serious crime has been a problem in their neighborhood in the past 12 months. Smoke, gas, or bad smells is the third biggest problem, mentioned by 4 percent. People are the fourth biggest neighborhood problem, bothering 3 percent of older householders nationwide.

■ Despite media reports of crime problems in many neighborhoods, few older householders say a serious crime has occurred in their area recently.

The biggest neighborhood problem among the elderly is street noise

(percent of householders aged 65 or older who say they are bothered by selected neighborhood problems, 2007)

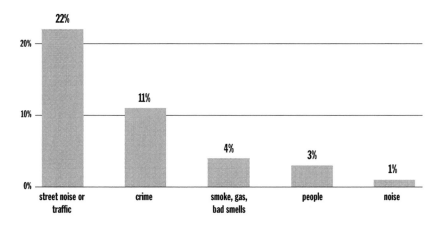

Table 4.15 Characteristics of Neighborhood among Householders Aged 65 or Older by Homeownership Status, 2007

(number and percent distribution of housing units occupied by householders aged 65 or older by description of area within 300 feet, by homeownership status, 2007; numbers in thousands)

	total	owner	renter
Total householders aged 65 or older	**22,864**	**18,271**	**4,594**
Single-family detached houses	19,502	16,125	3,377
Single-family attached structures	3,762	2,465	1,297
Multi-unit residential buildings	5,536	2,619	2,917
1 to 3 story multi-unit	3,818	2,022	1,797
4 to 6 story multi-unit	808	345	463
7 or more story multi-unit	791	227	564
Mobile homes	3,075	2,763	312
Commerical/institutional buildings	5,888	3,533	2,355
Industrial buildings or factories	793	487	306
Open space, park, woods, farm, or ranch	8,711	7,149	1,562
Four or more lane highway, railroad, or airport	3,251	2,201	1,050
Waterfront property	900	791	109

PERCENT DISTRIBUTION BY DESCRIPTION OF NEIGHBORHOOD

Total householders aged 65 or older	**100.0%**	**100.0%**	**100.0%**
Single-family detached houses	85.3	88.3	73.5
Single-family attached structures	16.5	13.5	28.2
Multi-unit residential buildings	24.2	14.3	63.5
1 to 3 story multi-unit	16.7	11.1	39.1
4 to 6 story multi-unit	3.5	1.9	10.1
7 or more story multi-unit	3.5	1.2	12.3
Mobile homes	13.4	15.1	6.8
Commerical/institutional buildings	25.8	19.3	51.3
Industrial buildings or factories	3.5	2.7	6.7
Open space, park, woods, farm, or ranch	38.1	39.1	34.0
Four or more lane highway, railroad, or airport	14.2	12.0	22.9
Waterfront property	3.9	4.3	2.4

PERCENT DISTRIBUTION BY HOMEOWNERSHIP STATUS

Total householders aged 65 or older	**100.0%**	**79.9%**	**20.1%**
Single-family detached houses	100.0	82.7	17.3
Single-family attached structures	100.0	65.5	34.5
Multi-unit residential buildings	100.0	47.3	52.7
1 to 3 story multi-unit	100.0	53.0	47.1
4 to 6 story multi-unit	100.0	42.7	57.3
7 or more story multi-unit	100.0	28.7	71.3
Mobile homes	100.0	89.9	10.1
Commerical/institutional buildings	100.0	60.0	40.0
Industrial buildings or factories	100.0	61.4	38.6
Open space, park, woods, farm, or ranch	100.0	82.1	17.9
Four or more lane highway, railroad, or airport	100.0	67.7	32.3
Waterfront property	100.0	87.9	12.1

Note: Numbers do not add to total because more than one category may apply to unit.
Source: Bureau of the Census, American Housing Survey for the United States: 2007, Internet site http://www.census.gov/hhes/www/housing/ahs/ahs07/ahs07.html; calculations by New Strategist

Table 4.16 Neighborhood Problems Reported by Householders Aged 65 or Older by Homeownership Status, 2007

(number and percent of housing units occupied by householders aged 65 or older by neighborhood conditions considered bothersome by householder, and percent distribution of bothersome conditions by homeownership status, 2007; numbers in thousands)

	total	owner	renter
Total householders aged 65 or older	**22,864**	**18,271**	**4,594**
Street noise or heavy traffic	5,002	3,864	1,137
Serious crime in past 12 months	2,442	1,822	620
Smoke, gas, or bad smells	955	720	235
Noise	339	283	56
Litter or housing deterioration	267	234	33
Poor city or county services	82	74	8
Undesirable commercial/institutional/industrial facility	88	86	2
People	722	585	137
PERCENT WITH PROBLEM			
Total householders aged 65 or older	**100.0%**	**100.0%**	**100.0%**
Street noise or heavy traffic	21.9	21.1	24.7
Serious crime in past 12 months	10.7	10.0	13.5
Smoke, gas, or bad smells	4.2	3.9	5.1
Noise	1.5	1.5	1.2
Litter or housing deterioration	1.2	1.3	0.7
Poor city or county services	0.4	0.4	0.2
Undesirable commercial/institutional/industrial facility	0.4	0.5	0.0
People	3.2	3.2	3.0
PERCENT DISTRIBUTION OF PROBLEMS BY HOMEOWNERSHIP STATUS			
Total householders aged 65 or older	**100.0%**	**79.9%**	**20.1%**
Street noise or heavy traffic	100.0	77.2	22.7
Serious crime in past 12 months	100.0	74.6	25.4
Smoke, gas, or bad smells	100.0	75.4	24.6
Noise	100.0	83.5	16.5
Litter or housing deterioration	100.0	87.6	12.4
Poor city or county services	100.0	90.2	9.8
Undesirable commercial/institutional/industrial facility	100.0	97.7	2.3
People	100.0	81.0	19.0

Source: Bureau of the Census, American Housing Survey for the United States: 2007, Internet site http://www.census.gov/hhes/ www/housing/ahs/ahs07/ahs07.html; calculations by New Strategist

Housing Costs Are Lower for Older Americans

Most elderly homeowners have paid off their mortgage.

Housing costs are lowest for homeowners aged 65 or older regardless of household type. Median monthly housing costs for married homeowners aged 65 or older were just $514 in 2007. For all couples who own a home, median monthly housing costs were a much higher $927.

Among married couples, homeowners have higher monthly housing costs than renters until age 65. Among couples aged 65 or older, renters pay more for housing. The same pattern holds true for elderly men and women who live alone and those who head families without a spouse.

Elderly homeowners have lower housing costs because most have paid off their mortgage. Only 24 percent of homeowners aged 65 or older have a mortgage. Consequently, elderly homeowners devote only 20 percent of their monthly income to housing. Among elderly renters, the figure is a much higher 41 percent.

■ As Boomers enter the 65-or-older age group, the percentage of elderly homeowners with mortgages will rise because many Boomers refinanced their home to cover living expenses.

Housing costs are lowest for the oldest homeowners

(median monthly housing costs for married-couple homeowners, by age of householder, 2007)

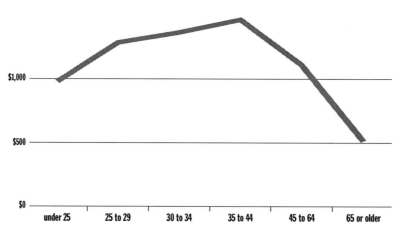

Table 4.17 Median Monthly Housing Costs by Household Type and Age of Householder, 2007

(median monthly housing costs and indexed costs by type of household, age of householder, and housing tenure, 2007)

	median monthly cost			indexed cost		
	total	owners	renters	total	owners	renters
Total households	$843	$927	$755	100	110	90
TWO-OR-MORE-PERSON HOUSEHOLDS						
Married couples	1,026	1,088	878	122	129	104
Under age 25	810	979	716	96	116	85
Aged 25 to 29	1,100	1,286	871	130	153	103
Aged 30 to 34	1,200	1,366	897	142	162	106
Aged 35 to 44	1,349	1,466	937	160	174	111
Aged 45 to 64	1,078	1,113	895	128	132	106
Aged 65 or older	536	514	814	64	61	97
Other male householder	870	960	817	103	114	97
Under age 45	903	1,131	832	107	134	99
Aged 45 to 64	877	951	782	104	113	93
Aged 65 or older	550	505	739	65	60	88
Other female householder	801	867	773	95	103	92
Under age 45	830	1,029	775	98	122	92
Aged 45 to 64	849	935	769	101	111	91
Aged 65 or older	559	496	750	66	59	89
SINGLE-PERSON HOUSEHOLDS						
Male householder	665	681	658	79	81	78
Under age 45	757	996	694	90	118	82
Aged 45 to 64	654	691	631	78	82	75
Aged 65 or older	463	426	524	55	51	62
Female householder	585	523	640	69	62	76
Under age 45	774	991	708	92	118	84
Aged 45 to 64	666	717	616	79	85	73
Aged 65 or older	425	390	528	50	46	63

Note: Housing costs include utilities, mortgages, real estate taxes, property insurance, and regime fees. The index is calculated by dividing median monthly housing costs for each household type by the median cost for total households and multiplying by 100.

Source: Bureau of the Census, American Housing Survey for the United States: 2007, Internet site http://www.census.gov/hhes/www/housing/ahs/ahs07/ahs07.html; calculations by New Strategist

Table 4.18 **Monthly Housing Costs of Householders Aged 65 or Older by Homeownership Status, 2007**

(total median monthly housing costs, monthly housing costs as a percent of current income, and median monthly amount paid for selected services and utilities, for householders aged 65 or older by homeownership status, 2007;

	householders aged 65 or older		
	total	owner	renter
Total median monthly housing cost	**$487**	**$464**	**$607**
Monthly housing cost as a percent of current income	23%	20%	41%
Median monthly cost of electricity	$87	$92	$62
Median monthly cost of piped gas	71	73	46
Median monthly cost of fuel oil	130	132	107
Median monthly cost of property insurance	50	54	20
Median monthly cost of water	35	35	24
Median monthly cost of trash removal	21	21	19
Percent with a mortgage	–	24.4%	–
Median monthly payment for principal and interest	–	$605	–
Median monthly real estate taxes	–	112	–

Note: Median costs are for those with the expense; "–" means not applicable.
Source: Bureau of the Census, American Housing Survey for the United States: 2007, Internet site http://www.census.gov/hhes/ www/housing/ahs/ahs07/ahs07.html; calculations by New Strategist

Value of Homes Owned by Older Americans Is below Average

Home values peak in middle age.

The median value of the homes owned by people aged 65 or older stood at $168,654 in 2007, substantially below the $191,471 value of the average owned home. Behind the lesser value is the fact that elderly homeowners are more likely than the average homeowner to live in an older and smaller home. The homes owned by elderly married couples were valued at a median of $193,584 in 2007—close to the national average. Fourteen percent of married-couple homeowners aged 65 or older owned a home worth $500,000 or more in that year.

Older homeowners have substantial equity in their homes for two reasons. First, most bought their home years ago when housing costs were much lower. The median purchase price of homes owned by the elderly was just $45,191. Second, the great majority of older homeowners have paid off their mortgage. Although housing values have declined sharply over the past few years, the elderly have plenty of equity remaining in their homes.

■ Home values have been falling and are now significantly lower than the 2007 figures shown in these tables.

Home values were close to their peak in 2007

(median value of homes owned by married couples, by age of householder, 2007)

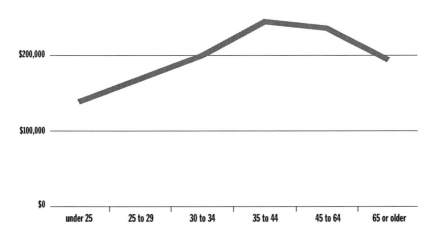

Table 4.19 Value of Owner-Occupied Homes by Type of Household and Age of Householder, 2007

(number of homeowners by value of home, median value of home, and indexed median value, by type of household and age of householder, 2007)

	number (in 000s)	under $100,000	$100,000– $149,999	$150,000– $199,999	$200,000– $299,999	$300,000– $399,999	$400,000– $499,999	$500,000– $749,999	$750,000 or more	median value of home ($)	indexed median value
Total homeowners	75,647	18,779	11,048	9,643	13,132	8,060	4,740	6,234	4,013	191,471	100
TWO-OR-MORE-PERSON HOUSEHOLDS											
Married couples	46,570	9227	6,282	5,992	8,660	5,664	3,348	4,443	2,955	220,607	115
Under age 25	540	176	122	55	66	55	17	37	11	138,617	72
Aged 25 to 29	2,133	494	438	359	415	257	72	89	10	168,736	88
Aged 30 to 34	3,456	709	500	525	739	357	234	264	128	199,431	104
Aged 35 to 44	10,245	1560	1,331	1,334	2,020	1,375	852	1,073	701	244,492	128
Aged 45 to 64	21,119	4048	2,655	2,502	3,795	2,714	1,568	2,274	1,564	235,723	123
Aged 65 or older	9,078	2242	1,237	1,216	1,625	906	605	706	541	193,584	101
Other male householder	4,408	1256	642	597	723	422	205	366	196	175,616	92
Under age 45	2,050	558	349	298	363	174	94	146	67	169,745	89
Aged 45 to 64	1,792	495	245	241	269	174	95	173	102	182,457	95
Aged 65 or older	565	204	48	57	91	75	16	48	27	177,446	93
Other female householder	7,984	2644	1,323	925	1,196	643	427	523	305	151,366	79
Under age 45	3,076	1036	609	406	403	229	138	176	78	141,246	74
Aged 45 to 64	3,349	1037	484	345	543	300	210	250	180	172,275	90
Aged 65 or older	1,558	571	230	173	250	113	79	96	46	145,242	76
SINGLE-PERSON HOUSEHOLDS											
Men living alone	6,930	2321	1,147	935	1,007	563	318	403	235	149,840	78
Under age 45	2,235	663	413	335	392	166	99	122	45	156,298	82
Aged 45 to 64	2,813	991	436	371	385	232	123	161	113	147,605	77
Aged 65 or older	1,882	667	299	229	229	165	96	120	77	145,811	76
Women living alone	9,756	3330	1,653	1,195	1,547	768	442	499	322	146,812	77
Under age 45	1,408	416	225	192	270	138	77	65	25	166,550	87
Aged 45 to 64	3,161	1035	500	453	546	246	157	146	78	155,029	81
Aged 65 or older	5,187	1880	928	550	731	384	208	288	219	138,439	72

Source: Bureau of the Census, American Housing Survey for the United States: 2007, Internet site http://www.census.gov/hhes/www/housing/ahs/ahs07/ahs07.html; calculations by New Strategist

Table 4.20 Housing Value and Purchase Price for Homeowners Aged 65 or Older, 2007

(number and percent distribution of homeowners aged 65 or older by value of home and purchase price, 2007; numbers in thousands)

	number	percent distribution
Total homeowners aged 65 or older	**18,271**	**100.0%**
Value of home		
Under $100,000	5,564	30.5
$100,000 to $149,999	2,742	15.0
$150,000 to $199,999	2,225	12.2
$200,000 to $299,999	2,926	16.0
$300,000 to $399,999	1,642	9.0
$400,000 to $499,999	1,004	5.5
$500,000 to $749,999	1,258	6.9
$750,000 or more	910	5.0
Median value	$168,654	–
Purchase price of homes purchased or built		
Under $50,000	8,019	43.9
$50,000 to $99,999	2,936	16.1
$100,000 to $149,999	1,563	8.6
$150,000 to $199,999	1,024	5.6
$200,000 to $249,999	521	2.9
$250,000 to $299,999	342	1.9
$300,000 or more	764	4.2
Received as inheritance or gift	1,072	5.9
Median purchase price	$45,191	–

Note: Numbers may not add to total because "not reported" is not shown; "–" means not applicable.
Source: Bureau of the Census, American Housing Survey for the United States: 2007, Internet site http://www.census.gov/hhes/www/housing/ahs/ahs07/ahs07.html; calculations by New Strategist

Mobility Rate Is Low in Old Age

Behind the lower mobility of older Americans are high rates of homeownership and strong community ties.

While 12 percent of Americans aged 1 or older moved between March 2007 and March 2008, the proportion was a much smaller 4 percent among people aged 65 or older. Among movers, however, older adults are more likely to move to a different state. Thirteen percent of all movers moved to a different state, but the proportion rises as high as 20 percent among movers aged 60 to 64 and 80 to 84. Many in the younger group are moving to warmer climates in retirement. Many in the older group are moving closer to adult children as they become increasingly frail with age.

Among movers aged 65 to 74, the 38 percent plurality of those who moved between March 2007 and March 2008 did so for housing reasons. Among movers aged 75 or older, however, only 29 percent moved for housing reasons and a larger 33 percent moved for family reasons. Seventeen percent of movers aged 75 or older say they moved for health reasons.

■ Americans are moving less than they once did. Several factors are behind the lower mobility rates including the economic downturn and the aging of the population.

Older Americans are not likely to move

(percent of people aged 1 or older who moved between March 2007 and March 2008, by age)

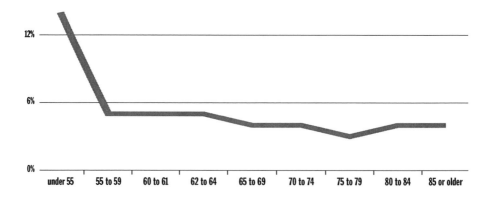

Table 4.21 Geographic Mobility by Age and Type of Move, 2007–08

(total number of people aged 1 or older, and number and percent who moved between March 2007 and March 2008, by age and type of move; numbers in thousands)

	total	total movers	same county	different county, same state	different state total	different state same region	different state different region	movers from abroad
Total, aged 1 or older	**294,851**	**35,166**	**23,013**	**6,282**	**4,727**	**2,248**	**2,479**	**1,145**
Under age 55	224,760	32,107	21,255	5,551	4,241	2,032	2,209	1,055
Aged 55 to 59	18,371	1,006	605	219	166	84	82	16
Aged 60 to 61	6,941	328	184	98	36	10	26	9
Aged 62 to 64	7,990	367	203	90	61	20	41	13
Aged 65 or older	36,789	1,360	767	321	223	104	119	50
Aged 65 to 69	11,165	463	234	104	94	44	50	32
Aged 70 to 74	8,423	301	165	93	36	11	25	7
Aged 75 to 79	7,353	225	139	58	25	5	20	4
Aged 80 to 84	5,559	220	127	43	44	27	17	5
Aged 85 or older	4,289	151	102	23	24	17	7	2

PERCENT DISTRIBUTION BY MOBILITY STATUS

	total	total movers	same county	different county, same state	different state total	different state same region	different state different region	movers from abroad
Total, aged 1 or older	**100.0%**	**11.9%**	**7.8%**	**2.1%**	**1.6%**	**0.8%**	**0.8%**	**0.4%**
Under age 55	100.0	14.3	9.5	2.5	1.9	0.9	1.0	0.5
Aged 55 to 59	100.0	5.5	3.3	1.2	0.9	0.5	0.4	0.1
Aged 60 to 61	100.0	4.7	2.7	1.4	0.5	0.1	0.4	0.1
Aged 62 to 64	100.0	4.6	2.5	1.1	0.8	0.3	0.5	0.2
Aged 65 or older	100.0	3.7	2.1	0.9	0.6	0.3	0.3	0.1
Aged 65 to 69	100.0	4.1	2.1	0.9	0.8	0.4	0.4	0.3
Aged 70 to 74	100.0	3.6	2.0	1.1	0.4	0.1	0.3	0.1
Aged 75 to 79	100.0	3.1	1.9	0.8	0.3	0.1	0.3	0.1
Aged 80 to 84	100.0	4.0	2.3	0.8	0.8	0.5	0.3	0.1
Aged 85 or older	100.0	3.5	2.4	0.5	0.6	0.4	0.2	0.0

PERCENT DISTRIBUTION OF MOVERS BY TYPE OF MOVE

	total	total movers	same county	different county, same state	different state total	different state same region	different state different region	movers from abroad
Total, aged 1 or older	–	**100.0%**	**65.4%**	**17.9%**	**13.4%**	**6.4%**	**7.0%**	**3.3%**
Under age 55	–	100.0	66.2	17.3	13.2	6.3	6.9	3.3
Aged 55 to 59	–	100.0	60.1	21.8	16.5	8.3	8.2	1.6
Aged 60 to 61	–	100.0	56.1	29.9	11.0	3.0	7.9	2.7
Aged 62 to 64	–	100.0	55.3	24.5	16.6	5.4	11.2	3.5
Aged 65 or older	–	100.0	56.4	23.6	16.4	7.6	8.8	3.7
Aged 65 to 69	–	100.0	50.5	22.5	20.3	9.5	10.8	6.9
Aged 70 to 74	–	100.0	54.8	30.9	12.0	3.7	8.3	2.3
Aged 75 to 79	–	100.0	61.8	25.8	11.1	2.2	8.9	1.8
Aged 80 to 84	–	100.0	57.7	19.5	20.0	12.3	7.7	2.3
Aged 85 or older	–	100.0	67.5	15.2	15.9	11.3	4.6	1.3

Note: "–" means not applicable.
Source: Bureau of the Census, Geographic Mobility: 2007 to 2008, Detailed Tables, Internet site http://www.census.gov/population/www/socdemo/migrate/cps2008.html; calculations by New Strategist

Table 4.22 Reason for Moving among People Aged 65 to 74, 2007–08

(number and percent distribution of movers aged 65 to 74 by primary reason for move and share of total movers between March 2007 and March 2008, by age; numbers in thousands)

	total movers	movers aged 65 to 74		
		number	percent distribution	share of total
TOTAL MOVERS	**35,167**	**764**	**100.0%**	**2.2%**
Family reasons	**10,738**	**237**	**31.0**	**2.2**
Change in marital status	1,987	45	5.9	2.3
To establish own household	3,682	27	3.5	0.7
Other family reasons	5,069	165	21.6	3.3
Employment reasons	**7,352**	**155**	**20.3**	**2.1**
New job or job transfer	2,940	30	3.9	1.0
To look for work or lost job	794	12	1.6	1.5
To be closer to work/easier commute	2,183	39	5.1	1.8
Retired	140	32	4.2	22.9
Other job-related reason	1,295	42	5.5	3.2
Housing reasons	**14,098**	**294**	**38.5**	**2.1**
Wanted own home, not rent	2,033	20	2.6	1.0
Wanted better home/apartment	4,866	75	9.8	1.5
Wanted better neighborhood	1,778	40	5.2	2.2
Wanted cheaper housing	2,872	67	8.8	2.3
Other housing reasons	2,549	92	12.0	3.6
Other reasons	**2,106**	**77**	**10.1**	**3.7**
To attend or leave college	872	0	0.0	0.0
Change of climate	212	12	1.6	5.7
Health reasons	460	36	4.7	7.8
Natural disaster	61	3	0.4	4.9
Other reasons	1,373	26	3.4	1.9

Source: Bureau of the Census, Geographic Mobility: 2007 to 2008, Detailed Tables, Internet site http://www.census.gov/population/www/socdemo/migrate/cps2008.html; calculations by New Strategist

Table 4.23 Reason for Moving among People Aged 75 or Older, 2007–08

(number and percent distribution of movers aged 75 or older by primary reason for move and share of total movers between March 2007 and March 2008, by age; numbers in thousands)

| | total movers | movers aged 75 or older | | |
		number	percent distribution	share of total
TOTAL MOVERS	**35,167**	**597**	**100.0%**	**1.7%**
Family reasons	**10,738**	**198**	**33.2**	**1.8**
Change in marital status	1,987	23	3.9	1.2
To establish own household	3,682	12	2.0	0.3
Other family reasons	5,069	163	27.3	3.2
Employment reasons	**7,352**	**99**	**16.6**	**1.3**
New job or job transfer	2,940	2	0.3	0.1
To look for work or lost job	794	8	1.3	1.0
To be closer to work/easier commute	2,183	28	4.7	1.3
Retired	140	25	4.2	17.9
Other job-related reason	1,295	36	6.0	2.8
Housing reasons	**14,098**	**172**	**28.8**	**1.2**
Wanted own home, not rent	2,033	12	2.0	0.6
Wanted better home/apartment	4,866	36	6.0	0.7
Wanted better neighborhood	1,778	40	6.7	2.2
Wanted cheaper housing	2,872	31	5.2	1.1
Other housing reasons	2,549	53	8.9	2.1
Other reasons	**2,106**	**127**	**21.3**	**6.0**
To attend or leave college	872	0	0.0	0.0
Change of climate	212	8	1.3	3.8
Health reasons	460	100	16.8	47.2
Natural disaster	61	2	0.3	0.4
Other reasons	1,373	17	2.8	27.9

Source: Bureau of the Census, Geographic Mobility: 2007 to 2008, Detailed Tables, Internet site http://www.census.gov/ population/www/socdemo/migrate/cps2008.html; calculations by New Strategist

Income

■ Householders aged 55 to 74 saw their median income climb 6 percent between 2000 and 2007, while those aged 75 or older experienced a 3 percent gain. This increase stands in contrast to the decline in median income of all households during those years.

■ Household income falls as people age and retire from the labor force. While the $57,386 median income of householders aged 55 to 64 exceeds that of the average household, the $28,305 median income of householders aged 65 or older is well below average.

■ The most affluent older householders are couples aged 55 to 59 because most are still in the labor force. Their median income was a lofty $84,645 in 2007, and 40 percent had incomes of $100,000 or more.

■ Between 2000 and 2007 younger age groups experienced income reductions, but the median incomes of men and women aged 55 or older grew. Women aged 55 to 64 enjoyed the highest increase in median income, up 24 percent.

■ Among Americans aged 65 or older, 88 percent of men and 90 percent of women received income from Social Security in 2007, making it the most common source of income for the age group.

■ The poverty rate of older Americans is below average. Only 9.2 percent of people aged 55 or older are poor compared with a larger 12.5 percent of all Americans.

Incomes of Older Householders Have Increased

In younger age groups, median income has declined since 2000.

Householders aged 55 to 74 saw their median income climb 6 percent between 2000 and 2007, while those aged 75 or older experienced a 3 percent gain. This increase stands in contrast to the nearly 1 percent decline in the median income of householders of all ages. Measured against the 1990 value, the median income of householders aged 55 or older grew 15 percent versus a 9 percent gain for all households.

The median income of householders aged 55 to 64 is growing because fewer are opting for early retirement. The median income of householders aged 65 or older is growing because a more educated, affluent generation is entering the age group.

■ The incomes of households headed by 55-to-64-year-olds will continue to grow as Boomers entirely fill the age group and early retirement becomes less common.

Older householders have made income gains

(percent change in median income of total households and households headed by people aged 55 or older, by age, 2000–07; in 2007 dollars)

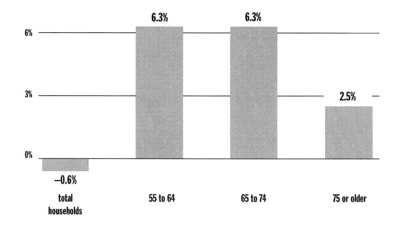

Table 5.1 Median Income of Households Headed by People Aged 55 or Older, 1990 to 2007

(median income of total households and households headed by people aged 55 or older, and index of age group to total, 1990 to 2007; percent change for selected years; in 2007 dollars)

	total households	55 to 64	householders aged 65 or older total	65 to 74	75 or older
2007	$50,233	$57,386	$28,305	$36,032	$23,230
2006	49,568	56,141	28,587	34,916	23,462
2005	49,202	55,505	27,652	33,636	23,198
2004	48,665	55,315	26,911	33,899	22,463
2003	48,835	55,483	26,817	33,415	21,950
2002	48,878	54,403	26,684	32,470	22,244
2001	49,455	53,714	27,075	32,994	22,456
2000	50,557	54,005	27,793	33,895	22,653
1999	50,641	55,579	28,368	34,035	23,832
1998	49,397	54,837	27,603	33,171	22,720
1997	47,665	53,269	26,742	32,578	21,999
1996	46,704	52,393	25,592	30,807	21,048
1995	46,034	51,439	25,797	31,113	20,726
1994	44,636	48,742	25,034	29,637	20,380
1993	44,143	47,299	25,082	30,111	20,245
1992	44,359	49,220	24,810	29,496	19,721
1991	44,726	49,445	25,202	29,786	20,686
1990	46,049	49,773	25,921	31,207	20,223
Percent change					
2000 to 2007	–0.6%	6.3%	1.8%	6.3%	2.5%
1990 to 2007	9.1	15.3	9.2	15.5	14.9
INDEX					
2007	100	114	56	72	46
2006	100	113	58	70	47
2005	100	113	56	68	47
2004	100	114	55	70	46
2003	100	114	55	68	45
2002	100	111	55	66	46
2001	100	109	55	67	45
2000	100	107	55	67	45
1999	100	110	56	67	47
1998	100	111	56	67	46
1997	100	112	56	68	46
1996	100	112	55	66	45
1995	100	112	56	68	45
1994	100	109	56	66	46
1993	100	107	57	68	46
1992	100	111	56	66	44
1991	100	111	56	67	46
1990	100	108	56	68	44

Note: The index is calculated by dividing the median income of the age group by the national median and multiplying by 100.
Source: Bureau of the Census, Current Population Survey Annual Social and Economic Supplements, Internet site http://www
.census.gov/hhes/www/income/histinc/inchhtoc.html; calculations by New Strategist

Many Older Householders Have High Incomes

More than 7 million have incomes of $100,000 or more.

Household income falls as people age because many retire from the labor force and live on savings, pensions, and Social Security benefits. While the $57,386 median income of householders aged 55 to 64 exceeds that of the average household, the $28,305 median income of householders aged 65 or older is well below average. Median income bottoms out at $23,230 among householders aged 75 or older.

Many older householders are affluent, however. Twenty-seven percent of householders aged 55 to 59 have annual incomes of $100,000 or more, as do 9 percent of those aged 65 or older. Among the nation's nearly 24 million households with incomes of $100,000 or more, 31 percent are aged 55 or older.

■ The household incomes of 55-to-64-year-olds will continue to grow as working Boomers completely fill the age group.

Incomes decline with age

(median income of households by age of householder, 2007)

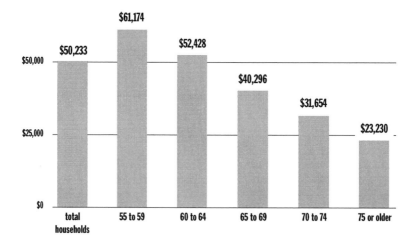

total households	$50,233	
55 to 59	$61,174	
60 to 64	$52,428	
65 to 69	$40,296	
70 to 74	$31,654	
75 or older	$23,230	

Table 5.2 Income of Households Headed by People Aged 55 or Older, 2007: Total Households

(number and percent distribution of total households and households headed by people aged 55 or older, by income, 2007; households in thousands as of 2008)

	total	aged 55 or older								
		total	aged 55 to 64			aged 65 or older				
			total	55–59	60–64	total	aged 65 to 74			75+
							total	65–69	70–74	
Total households	**116,783**	**44,022**	**19,909**	**10,813**	**9,096**	**24,113**	**12,284**	**6,990**	**5,293**	**11,829**
Under $10,000	8,455	3,923	1,483	706	777	2,440	1,079	597	481	1,360
$10,000 to $19,999	13,778	7,799	1,848	855	992	5,951	2,236	1,087	1,151	3,715
$20,000 to $29,999	13,115	6,076	1,793	926	866	4,283	1,914	1,000	914	2,369
$30,000 to $39,999	12,006	4,708	1,849	951	898	2,859	1,448	786	663	1,411
$40,000 to $49,999	10,733	3,751	1,734	947	787	2,017	1,217	711	507	799
$50,000 to $59,999	9,565	3,077	1,628	879	750	1,449	902	548	354	545
$60,000 to $69,999	8,009	2,451	1,429	831	596	1,022	636	392	244	386
$70,000 to $79,999	7,006	2,024	1,232	697	534	792	537	369	169	254
$80,000 to $89,999	5,788	1,558	977	549	428	581	393	229	164	188
$90,000 to $99,999	4,741	1,408	920	521	398	488	350	212	136	138
$100,000 or more	23,586	7,249	5,016	2,950	2,067	2,233	1,570	1,060	509	663
Median income	$50,233	$41,457	$57,386	$61,174	$52,428	$28,305	$36,032	$40,296	$31,654	$23,230
Total households	**100.0%**	**100.0%**	**100.0%**	**100.0%**	**100.0%**	**100.0%**	**100.0%**	**100.0%**	**100.0%**	**100.0%**
Under $10,000	7.2	8.9	7.4	6.5	8.5	10.1	8.8	8.5	9.1	11.5
$10,000 to $19,999	11.8	17.7	9.3	7.9	10.9	24.7	18.2	15.6	21.7	31.4
$20,000 to $29,999	11.2	13.8	9.0	8.6	9.5	17.8	15.6	14.3	17.3	20.0
$30,000 to $39,999	10.3	10.7	9.3	8.8	9.9	11.9	11.8	11.2	12.5	11.9
$40,000 to $49,999	9.2	8.5	8.7	8.8	8.7	8.4	9.9	10.2	9.6	6.8
$50,000 to $59,999	8.2	7.0	8.2	8.1	8.2	6.0	7.3	7.8	6.7	4.6
$60,000 to $69,999	6.9	5.6	7.2	7.7	6.6	4.2	5.2	5.6	4.6	3.3
$70,000 to $79,999	6.0	4.6	6.2	6.4	5.9	3.3	4.4	5.3	3.2	2.1
$80,000 to $89,999	5.0	3.5	4.9	5.1	4.7	2.4	3.2	3.3	3.1	1.6
$90,000 to $99,999	4.1	3.2	4.6	4.8	4.4	2.0	2.8	3.0	2.6	1.2
$100,000 or more	20.2	16.5	25.2	27.3	22.7	9.3	12.8	15.2	9.6	5.6

Source: Bureau of the Census, 2008 Current Population Survey Annual Social and Economic Supplement, Internet site http://www.census.gov/hhes/www/macro/032008/hhinc/new02_001.htm; calculations by New Strategist

Non-Hispanic Whites Have Higher Incomes than Blacks or Hispanics

Among older Americans, Asians have the highest incomes, however.

Households headed by non-Hispanic whites aged 55 to 64 had a median income of $62,449 in 2007, much greater than the $35,987 black median and the $40,541 Hispanic median. Asian householders aged 55 to 64 had a median income of $65,565, surpassing that of non-Hispanic whites. Thirty-one percent of Asian and 28 percent of non-Hispanic white householders aged 55 to 64 had an income of $100,000 or more in 2007. This compares with only 12 percent of blacks and 13 percent of Hispanics.

Income disparities are smaller among householders aged 65 or older. The median income of Asian households headed by people aged 65 or older was $33,759 in 2007 versus a slightly lower $29,617 for non-Hispanic whites. Among their Hispanic counterparts, median household income was just $21,860, while the black median stood at an even lower $19,370. Black householders aged 75 or older have the lowest median income, just $16,633.

■ Income disparities by race and Hispanic origin will persist among older householders because the underlying factors—the scarcity of married couples among blacks and the poor educational level of Hispanics—are also present among younger generations of Americans.

Many Asian householders aged 65 or older have incomes of $100,000 or more

(percent of households headed by people aged 65 or older with incomes of $100,000 or more, by race and Hispanic origin, 2007)

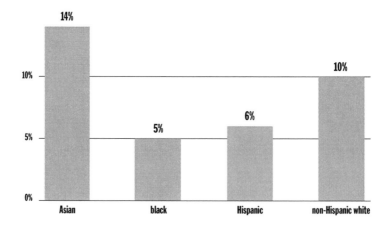

Table 5.3 Income of Households Headed by People Aged 55 or Older, 2007: Asian Households

(number and percent distribution of total Asian households and Asian households headed by people aged 55 or older, by income, 2007; households in thousands as of 2008)

						aged 55 or older				
							aged 65 or older			
			aged 55 to 64					aged 65 to 74		
	total	total	total	55–59	60–64	total	total	65–69	70–74	75+
Total Asian households	**4,715**	**1267**	**663**	**385**	**278**	**604**	**365**	**235**	**129**	**239**
Under $10,000	311	135	49	16	33	86	42	17	23	45
$10,000 to $19,999	365	156	53	18	36	103	52	27	26	50
$20,000 to $29,999	388	139	43	30	13	96	55	40	16	41
$30,000 to $39,999	357	117	59	33	26	58	32	19	13	24
$40,000 to $49,999	372	105	66	38	28	39	34	24	10	4
$50,000 to $59,999	336	82	41	24	16	41	28	22	5	13
$60,000 to $69,999	327	71	31	21	10	40	25	17	8	16
$70,000 to $79,999	307	59	31	19	13	28	20	16	4	8
$80,000 to $89,999	243	56	43	27	15	13	10	7	3	4
$90,000 to $99,999	240	59	40	23	18	19	13	7	5	5
$100,000 or more	1,468	291	207	139	68	84	54	38	16	30
Median income	$65,876	$50,403	$65,565	$76,539	$50,656	$33,759	$40,370	$45,888	$30,793	$25,633
Total Asian households	**100.0%**	**100.0%**	**100.0%**	**100.0%**	**100.0%**	**100.0%**	**100.0%**	**100.0%**	**100.0%**	**100.0%**
Under $10,000	6.6	10.7	7.4	4.2	11.9	14.2	11.5	7.2	17.8	18.8
$10,000 to $19,999	7.7	12.3	8.0	4.7	12.9	17.1	14.2	11.5	20.2	20.9
$20,000 to $29,999	8.2	11.0	6.5	7.8	4.7	15.9	15.1	17.0	12.4	17.2
$30,000 to $39,999	7.6	9.2	8.9	8.6	9.4	9.6	8.8	8.1	10.1	10.0
$40,000 to $49,999	7.9	8.3	10.0	9.9	10.1	6.5	9.3	10.2	7.8	1.7
$50,000 to $59,999	7.1	6.5	6.2	6.2	5.8	6.8	7.7	9.4	3.9	5.4
$60,000 to $69,999	6.9	5.6	4.7	5.5	3.6	6.6	6.8	7.2	6.2	6.7
$70,000 to $79,999	6.5	4.7	4.7	4.9	4.7	4.6	5.5	6.8	3.1	3.3
$80,000 to $89,999	5.2	4.4	6.5	7.0	5.4	2.2	2.7	3.0	2.3	1.7
$90,000 to $99,999	5.1	4.7	6.0	6.0	6.5	3.1	3.6	3.0	3.9	2.1
$100,000 or more	31.1	23.0	31.2	36.1	24.5	13.9	14.8	16.2	12.4	12.6

Note: Asians include those who identify themselves as being of the race alone and those who identify themselves as being of the race in combination with other races.
Source: Bureau of the Census, 2008 Current Population Survey Annual Social and Economic Supplement, Internet site http:// www.census.gov/hhes/www/macro/032008/hhinc/new02_001.htm; calculations by New Strategist

Table 5.4 **Income of Households Headed by People Aged 55 or Older, 2007: Black Households**

(number and percent distribution of total black households and black households headed by people aged 55 or older, by income, 2007; households in thousands as of 2008)

		aged 55 or older								
						aged 65 or older				
			aged 55 to 64					aged 65 to 74		
	total	total	total	55–59	60–64	total	total	65–69	70–74	75+
Total black households	14,976	4,580	2,308	1,344	964	2,272	1,319	736	583	953
Under $10,000	2,256	851	355	209	145	496	272	139	133	224
$10,000 to $19,999	2,444	1,042	375	219	155	667	332	180	152	334
$20,000 to $29,999	1,988	598	270	144	126	328	191	104	89	137
$30,000 to $39,999	1,746	467	240	124	115	227	146	73	73	80
$40,000 to $49,999	1,379	373	214	112	102	159	113	62	51	47
$50,000 to $59,999	1,161	302	199	119	78	103	64	33	31	38
$60,000 to $69,999	867	197	133	83	50	64	40	28	12	22
$70,000 to $79,999	683	151	88	61	27	63	47	35	11	15
$80,000 to $89,999	549	115	84	48	35	31	21	12	7	10
$90,000 to $99,999	403	100	69	37	32	31	24	19	6	7
$100,000 or more	1,500	386	282	186	96	104	68	51	16	36
Median income	$34,091	$27,744	$35,987	$37,447	$3,870	$19,370	$22,733	$24,365	$20,684	$16,633
Total black households	100.0%	100.0%	100.0%	100.0%	100.0%	100.0%	100.0%	100.0%	100.0%	100.0%
Under $10,000	15.1	18.6	15.4	15.6	15.0	21.8	20.6	18.9	22.8	23.5
$10,000 to $19,999	16.3	22.8	16.2	16.3	16.1	29.4	25.2	24.5	26.1	35.0
$20,000 to $29,999	13.3	13.1	11.7	10.7	13.1	14.4	14.5	14.1	15.3	14.4
$30,000 to $39,999	11.7	10.2	10.4	9.2	11.9	10.0	11.1	9.9	12.5	8.4
$40,000 to $49,999	9.2	8.1	9.3	8.3	10.6	7.0	8.6	8.4	8.7	4.9
$50,000 to $59,999	7.8	6.6	8.6	8.9	8.1	4.5	4.9	4.5	5.3	4.0
$60,000 to $69,999	5.8	4.3	5.8	6.2	5.2	2.8	3.0	3.8	2.1	2.3
$70,000 to $79,999	4.6	3.3	3.8	4.5	2.8	2.8	3.6	4.8	1.9	1.6
$80,000 to $89,999	3.7	2.5	3.6	3.6	3.6	1.4	1.6	1.6	1.2	1.0
$90,000 to $99,999	2.7	2.2	3.0	2.8	3.3	1.4	1.8	2.6	1.0	0.7
$100,000 or more	10.0	8.4	12.2	13.8	10.0	4.6	5.2	6.9	2.7	3.8

Note: Blacks include those who identify themselves as being of the race alone and those who identify themselves as being of the race in combination with other races.
Source: Bureau of the Census, 2008 Current Population Survey Annual Social and Economic Supplement, Internet site http://www.census.gov/hhes/www/macro/032008/hhinc/new02_001.htm; calculations by New Strategist

Table 5.5 Income of Households Headed by People Aged 55 or Older, 2007: Hispanic Households

(number and percent distribution of total Hispanic households and Hispanic households headed by people aged 55 or older, by income, 2007; households in thousands as of 2008)

		aged 55 or older								
						aged 65 or older				
			aged 55 to 64				aged 65 to 74			
	total	total	total	55–59	60–64	total	total	65–69	70–74	75+
Total Hispanic households	13,339	2,891	1,497	868	629	1,394	830	499	330	564
Under $10,000	1,184	419	169	89	80	250	132	84	48	117
$10,000 to $19,999	1,901	615	220	102	118	395	217	109	109	177
$20,000 to $29,999	1,961	368	163	90	73	205	109	52	56	96
$30,000 to $39,999	1,787	327	185	116	69	142	94	65	30	45
$40,000 to $49,999	1,387	247	131	79	52	116	83	57	26	32
$50,000 to $59,999	1,119	196	122	76	46	74	53	41	13	20
$60,000 to $69,999	921	149	105	72	33	44	34	19	16	10
$70,000 to $79,999	758	127	88	52	36	39	26	22	6	10
$80,000 to $89,999	534	81	61	35	26	20	12	11	1	7
$90,000 to $99,999	401	84	57	36	21	27	18	5	11	9
$100,000 or more	1,385	278	193	119	74	85	48	34	13	37
Median income	$38,679	$31,533	40,541	$44,338	$35,600	$21,860	$25,361	$30,400	$20,875	$18,965
Total Hispanic households	100.0%	100.0%	100.0%	100.0%	100.0%	100.0%	100.0%	100.0%	100.0%	100.0%
Under $10,000	8.9	14.5	11.3	10.3	12.7	17.9	15.9	16.8	14.5	20.7
$10,000 to $19,999	14.3	21.3	14.7	11.8	18.8	28.3	26.1	21.8	33.0	31.4
$20,000 to $29,999	14.7	12.7	10.9	10.4	11.6	14.7	13.1	10.4	17.0	17.0
$30,000 to $39,999	13.4	11.3	12.4	13.4	11.0	10.2	11.3	13.0	9.1	8.0
$40,000 to $49,999	10.4	8.5	8.8	9.1	8.3	8.3	10.0	11.4	7.9	5.7
$50,000 to $59,999	8.4	6.8	8.1	8.8	7.3	5.3	6.4	8.2	3.9	3.5
$60,000 to $69,999	6.9	5.2	7.0	8.3	5.2	3.2	4.1	3.8	4.8	1.8
$70,000 to $79,999	5.7	4.4	5.9	6.0	5.7	2.8	3.1	4.4	1.8	1.8
$80,000 to $89,999	4.0	2.8	4.1	4.0	4.1	1.4	1.4	2.2	0.3	1.2
$90,000 to $99,999	3.0	2.9	3.8	4.1	3.3	1.9	2.2	1.0	3.3	1.6
$100,000 or more	10.4	9.6	12.9	13.7	11.8	6.1	5.8	6.8	3.9	6.6

Source: Bureau of the Census, 2008 Current Population Survey Annual Social and Economic Supplement, Internet site http://www.census.gov/hhes/www/macro/032008/hhinc/new02_001.htm; calculations by New Strategist

Table 5.6 Income of Households Headed by People Aged 55 or Older, 2007: Non-Hispanic White Households

(number and percent distribution of total non-Hispanic white households and non-Hispanic white households headed by people aged 55 or older, by income, 2007; households in thousands as of 2008)

		aged 55 or older								
							aged 65 or older			
			aged 55 to 64					aged 65 to 74		
	total	total	total	55–59	60–64	total	total	65–69	70–74	75+
Total non-Hispanic white households	82,765	34,863	15,238	8,126	7,112	19,625	9,627	5,446	4,181	9,998
Under $10,000	4,607	2,456	881	387	496	1,575	611	347	265	963
$10,000 to $19,999	8,971	5,925	1,185	508	677	4,740	1,609	760	849	3,131
$20,000 to $29,999	8,639	4,906	1,290	651	639	3,616	1,543	796	748	2,073
$30,000 to $39,999	8,017	3,755	1,352	675	677	2,403	1,155	619	536	1,249
$40,000 to $49,999	7,479	2,993	1,303	711	592	1,690	980	562	417	710
$50,000 to $59,999	6,854	2,455	1,244	655	590	1,211	739	441	301	471
$60,000 to $69,999	5,836	2,009	1,149	646	502	860	526	322	204	337
$70,000 to $79,999	5,213	1,673	1,019	562	458	654	436	292	145	219
$80,000 to $89,999	4,419	1,289	779	432	347	510	343	193	149	167
$90,000 to $99,999	3,664	1,161	748	425	325	413	292	184	108	120
$100,000 or more	19,062	6,239	4,287	2,476	1,810	1,952	1,392	930	462	560
Median income	$54,920	$43,967	$62,449	$66,874	$57,902	$29,617	$38,998	$43,114	$34,524	$24,104
Total non-Hispanic white households	100.0%	100.0%	100.0%	100.0%	100.0%	100.0%	100.0%	100.0%	100.0%	100.0%
Under $10,000	5.6	7.0	5.8	4.8	7.0	8.0	6.3	6.4	6.3	9.6
$10,000 to $19,999	10.8	17.0	7.8	6.3	9.5	24.2	16.7	14.0	20.3	31.3
$20,000 to $29,999	10.4	14.1	8.5	8.0	9.0	18.4	16.0	14.6	17.9	20.7
$30,000 to $39,999	9.7	10.8	8.9	8.3	9.5	12.2	12.0	11.4	12.8	12.5
$40,000 to $49,999	9.0	8.6	8.6	8.7	8.3	8.6	10.2	10.3	10.0	7.1
$50,000 to $59,999	8.3	7.0	8.2	8.1	8.3	6.2	7.7	8.1	7.2	4.7
$60,000 to $69,999	7.1	5.8	7.5	7.9	7.1	4.4	5.5	5.9	4.9	3.4
$70,000 to $79,999	6.3	4.8	6.7	6.9	6.4	3.3	4.5	5.4	3.5	2.2
$80,000 to $89,999	5.3	3.7	5.1	5.3	4.9	2.6	3.6	3.5	3.6	1.7
$90,000 to $99,999	4.4	3.3	4.9	5.2	4.6	2.1	3.0	3.4	2.6	1.2
$100,000 or more	23.0	17.9	28.1	30.5	25.4	9.9	14.5	17.1	11.0	5.6

Note: Non-Hispanic whites are those who identify themselves as being white alone and not Hispanic.
Source: Bureau of the Census, 2008 Current Population Survey Annual Social and Economic Supplement, Internet site http://www.census.gov/hhes/www/macro/032008/hhinc/new02_001.htm; calculations by New Strategist

Many Older Couples Are Comfortably Well Off

Older men and women who live alone have much lower incomes.

Among married-couple householders aged 55 to 59, median income stood at $84,645 in 2007—more than $23,000 greater than the median income of the average household in the age group. The median income of married-couple householders aged 60 to 64 is about $20,000 above the average for the age group. For couples aged 65 or older, median household income was $43,209, also well above the $28,305 average. The most affluent older householders are couples aged 55 to 59 because most are still in the labor force. Forty percent had an income of $100,000 or more.

The median income of male-headed families surpasses that of married couples among householders aged 75 or older. Behind the higher incomes of male-headed families is the likely presence of an additional earner in the household—such as a grown son or daughter in the labor force.

Women who live alone have the lowest incomes. Among householders aged 75 or older, women who live alone had a median income of just $15,424 in 2007, well below the $23,230 median for all households in the age group.

■ The household incomes of older Americans should rise in the years ahead as Boomers fill the 60-to-69 age group and postpone retirement.

Women who live alone have the lowest incomes

(median income of householders aged 65 or older, by household type, 2007)

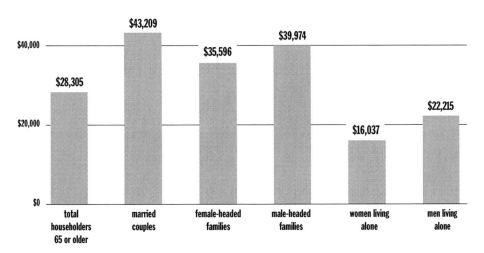

Table 5.7 Income of Households by Household Type, 2007: Aged 55 to 64

(number and percent distribution of households headed by people aged 55 to 64, by income and household type, 2007; households in thousands as of 2008)

| | | family households | | | nonfamily households | | | |
| | | | | | female householder | | male householder | |
	total	married couples	female hh, no spouse present	male hh, no spouse present	total	living alone	total	living alone
Total households headed by 55-to-64-year-olds	**19,909**	**11,144**	**1,562**	**513**	**3,746**	**3,434**	**2,944**	**2,561**
Under $10,000	1,483	236	135	27	648	641	435	417
$10,000 to $19,999	1,848	465	203	53	668	647	460	440
$20,000 to $29,999	1,793	654	195	51	550	510	342	299
$30,000 to $39,999	1,849	808	178	46	453	427	363	333
$40,000 to $49,999	1,734	856	169	53	396	375	260	225
$50,000 to $59,999	1,628	908	147	64	284	252	226	200
$60,000 to $69,999	1,429	861	120	46	228	188	174	142
$70,000 to $79,999	1,232	846	102	30	124	106	131	110
$80,000 to $89,999	977	709	77	28	74	66	89	52
$90,000 to $99,999	920	710	47	15	73	49	76	62
$100,000 or more	5,016	4,091	190	98	247	174	389	279
Median income	$57,386	$79,000	$44,501	$52,137	$30,113	$27,851	$35,678	$32,687
Total households headed by 55-to-64-year-olds	**100.0%**	**100.0%**	**100.0%**	**100.0%**	**100.0%**	**100.0%**	**100.0%**	**100.0%**
Under $10,000	7.4	2.1	8.6	5.3	17.3	18.7	14.8	16.3
$10,000 to $19,999	9.3	4.2	13.0	10.3	17.8	18.8	15.6	17.2
$20,000 to $29,999	9.0	5.9	12.5	9.9	14.7	14.9	11.6	11.7
$30,000 to $39,999	9.3	7.3	11.4	9.0	12.1	12.4	12.3	13.0
$40,000 to $49,999	8.7	7.7	10.8	10.3	10.6	10.9	8.8	8.8
$50,000 to $59,999	8.2	8.1	9.4	12.5	7.6	7.3	7.7	7.8
$60,000 to $69,999	7.2	7.7	7.7	9.0	6.1	5.5	5.9	5.5
$70,000 to $79,999	6.2	7.6	6.5	5.8	3.3	3.1	4.4	4.3
$80,000 to $89,999	4.9	6.4	4.9	5.5	2.0	1.9	3.0	2.0
$90,000 to $99,999	4.6	6.4	3.0	2.9	1.9	1.4	2.6	2.4
$100,000 or more	25.2	36.7	12.2	19.1	6.6	5.1	13.2	10.9

Note: "hh" is short for householder.
Source: Bureau of the Census, 2008 Current Population Survey Annual Social and Economic Supplement, Internet site http:// www.census.gov/hhes/www/macro/032008/hhinc/new02_000.htm; calculations by New Strategist

Table 5.8 Income of Households by Household Type, 2007: Aged 55 to 59

(number and percent distribution of households headed by people aged 55 to 59, by income and household type, 2007; households in thousands as of 2008)

| | | family households | | | nonfamily households | | | |
| | | | | | female householder | | male householder | |
	total	married couples	female hh, no spouse present	male hh, no spouse present	total	living alone	total	living alone
Total households headed by 55-to-59-year-olds	**10,813**	**6,049**	**920**	**301**	**1,878**	**1,703**	**1,666**	**1,448**
Under $10,000	706	81	81	16	271	269	259	246
$10,000 to $19,999	855	201	127	21	265	250	240	231
$20,000 to $29,999	926	305	114	35	301	279	173	151
$30,000 to $39,999	951	368	93	28	244	227	219	206
$40,000 to $49,999	947	441	103	35	221	207	147	125
$50,000 to $59,999	879	460	82	45	160	146	131	113
$60,000 to $69,999	831	489	67	28	137	112	109	91
$70,000 to $79,999	697	469	65	15	68	58	80	68
$80,000 to $89,999	549	409	45	16	32	31	48	27
$90,000 to $99,999	521	411	29	5	42	28	33	26
$100,000 or more	2,950	2,416	112	58	137	96	227	166
Median income	$61,174	$84,645	$44,819	$51,530	$35,057	$32,105	$36,659	$34,205
Total households headed by 55-to-59-year-olds	**100.0%**	**100.0%**	**100.0%**	**100.0%**	**100.0%**	**100.0%**	**100.0%**	**100.0%**
Under $10,000	6.5	1.3	8.8	5.3	14.4	15.8	15.5	17.0
$10,000 to $19,999	7.9	3.3	13.8	7.0	14.1	14.7	14.4	16.0
$20,000 to $29,999	8.6	5.0	12.4	11.6	16.0	16.4	10.4	10.4
$30,000 to $39,999	8.8	6.1	10.1	9.3	13.0	13.3	13.1	14.2
$40,000 to $49,999	8.8	7.3	11.2	11.6	11.8	12.2	8.8	8.6
$50,000 to $59,999	8.1	7.6	8.9	15.0	8.5	8.6	7.9	7.8
$60,000 to $69,999	7.7	8.1	7.3	9.3	7.3	6.6	6.5	6.3
$70,000 to $79,999	6.4	7.8	7.1	5.0	3.6	3.4	4.8	4.7
$80,000 to $89,999	5.1	6.8	4.9	5.3	1.7	1.8	2.9	1.9
$90,000 to $99,999	4.8	6.8	3.2	1.7	2.2	1.6	2.0	1.8
$100,000 or more	27.3	39.9	12.2	19.3	7.3	5.6	13.6	11.5

Note: "hh" is short for householder.
Source: Bureau of the Census, 2008 Current Population Survey Annual Social and Economic Supplement, Internet site http:// www.census.gov/hhes/www/macro/032008/hhinc/new02_000.htm; calculations by New Strategist

Table 5.9 Income of Households by Household Type, 2007: Aged 60 to 64

(number and percent distribution of households headed by people aged 60 to 64, by income and household type, 2007; households in thousands as of 2008)

| | | family households | | | nonfamily households | | | |
| | | | | | female householder | | male householder | |
	total	married couples	female hh, no spouse present	male hh, no spouse present	total	living alone	total	living alone
Total households headed by 60-to-64-year-olds	**9,096**	**5,095**	**642**	**212**	**1,868**	**1,731**	**1,279**	**1,112**
Under $10,000	777	156	54	11	377	372	177	172
$10,000 to $19,999	992	262	76	31	403	397	221	210
$20,000 to $29,999	866	348	82	18	250	231	170	148
$30,000 to $39,999	898	441	83	17	209	200	146	127
$40,000 to $49,999	787	415	65	19	176	168	112	100
$50,000 to $59,999	750	448	66	19	123	106	95	85
$60,000 to $69,999	596	371	52	18	91	77	65	52
$70,000 to $79,999	534	377	35	16	56	49	53	43
$80,000 to $89,999	428	301	32	14	42	34	39	26
$90,000 to $99,999	398	299	17	10	30	19	41	36
$100,000 or more	2,067	1,675	79	40	111	77	162	113
Median income	$52,428	$72,242	$43,784	$55,587	$25,681	$23,508	$33,714	$31,418
Total households headed by 60-to-64-year-olds	**100.0%**	**100.0%**	**100.0%**	**100.0%**	**100.0%**	**100.0%**	**100.0%**	**100.0%**
Under $10,000	8.5	3.1	8.4	5.2	20.2	21.5	13.8	15.5
$10,000 to $19,999	10.9	5.1	11.8	14.6	21.6	22.9	17.3	18.9
$20,000 to $29,999	9.5	6.8	12.8	8.5	13.4	13.3	13.3	13.3
$30,000 to $39,999	9.9	8.7	12.9	8.0	11.2	11.6	11.4	11.4
$40,000 to $49,999	8.7	8.1	10.1	9.0	9.4	9.7	8.8	9.0
$50,000 to $59,999	8.2	8.8	10.3	9.0	6.6	6.1	7.4	7.6
$60,000 to $69,999	6.6	7.3	8.1	8.5	4.9	4.4	5.1	4.7
$70,000 to $79,999	5.9	7.4	5.5	7.5	3.0	2.8	4.1	3.9
$80,000 to $89,999	4.7	5.9	5.0	6.6	2.2	2.0	3.0	2.3
$90,000 to $99,999	4.4	5.9	2.6	4.7	1.6	1.1	3.2	3.2
$100,000 or more	22.7	32.9	12.3	18.9	5.9	4.4	12.7	10.2

Note: "hh" is short for householder.
Source: Bureau of the Census, 2008 Current Population Survey Annual Social and Economic Supplement, Internet site http:// www.census.gov/hhes/www/macro/032008/hhinc/new02_000.htm; calculations by New Stategist

Table 5.10 Income of Households by Household Type, 2007: Aged 65 or Older

(number and percent distribution of households headed by people aged 65 or older, by income and household type, 2007; households in thousands as of 2008)

| | | family households | | | nonfamily households | | | |
| | | | | | female householder | | male householder | |
	total	married couples	female hh, no spouse present	male hh, no spouse present	total	living alone	total	living alone
Total households headed by people 65 or older	**24,113**	**10,178**	**1,866**	**449**	**8,500**	**8,297**	**3,120**	**2,917**
Under $10,000	2,440	247	125	34	1,677	1,660	360	348
$10,000 to $19,999	5,951	1,005	321	54	3,558	3,539	1,011	992
$20,000 to $29,999	4,283	1,888	313	68	1,490	1,448	524	500
$30,000 to $39,999	2,859	1,500	278	68	628	600	388	360
$40,000 to $49,999	2,017	1,135	219	52	365	342	242	222
$50,000 to $59,999	1,449	833	175	36	252	230	151	137
$60,000 to $69,999	1,022	663	99	31	137	126	92	73
$70,000 to $79,999	792	516	91	9	98	88	78	67
$80,000 to $89,999	581	396	64	10	57	55	53	45
$90,000 to $99,999	488	339	43	25	38	29	45	32
$100,000 or more	2,233	1,656	139	60	202	179	176	140
Median income	$28,305	$43,209	$35,596	$39,974	$16,276	$16,037	$23,682	$22,215
Total households headed by people 65 or older	**100.0%**	**100.0%**	**100.0%**	**100.0%**	**100.0%**	**100.0%**	**100.0%**	**100.0%**
Under $10,000	10.1	2.4	6.7	7.6	19.7	20.0	11.5	11.9
$10,000 to $19,999	24.7	9.9	17.2	12.0	41.9	42.7	32.4	34.0
$20,000 to $29,999	17.8	18.5	16.8	15.1	17.5	17.5	16.8	17.1
$30,000 to $39,999	11.9	14.7	14.9	15.1	7.4	7.2	12.4	12.3
$40,000 to $49,999	8.4	11.2	11.7	11.6	4.3	4.1	7.8	7.6
$50,000 to $59,999	6.0	8.2	9.4	8.0	3.0	2.8	4.8	4.7
$60,000 to $69,999	4.2	6.5	5.3	6.9	1.6	1.5	2.9	2.5
$70,000 to $79,999	3.3	5.1	4.9	2.0	1.2	1.1	2.5	2.3
$80,000 to $89,999	2.4	3.9	3.4	2.2	0.7	0.7	1.7	1.5
$90,000 to $99,999	2.0	3.3	2.3	5.6	0.4	0.3	1.4	1.1
$100,000 or more	9.3	16.3	7.4	13.4	2.4	2.2	5.6	4.8

Note: "hh" is short for householder.
Source: Bureau of the Census, 2008 Current Population Survey Annual Social and Economic Supplement, Internet site http://www.census.gov/hhes/www/macro/032008/hhinc/new02_000.htm; calculations by New Strategist

Table 5.11 Income of Households by Household Type, 2007: Aged 65 to 74

(number and percent distribution of households headed by people aged 65 to 74, by income and household type, 2007; households in thousands as of 2008)

| | | family households | | | nonfamily households | | | |
| | | | | | female householder | | male householder | |
	total	married couples	female hh, no spouse present	male hh, no spouse present	total	living alone	total	living alone
Total households headed by 65-to-74-year-olds	**12,284**	**6,365**	**940**	**197**	**3,213**	**3,083**	**1,568**	**1,459**
Under $10,000	1,079	154	75	20	653	637	179	168
$10,000 to $19,999	2,236	511	167	28	1,051	1,041	477	465
$20,000 to $29,999	1,914	955	119	30	564	543	246	232
$30,000 to $39,999	1,448	817	127	20	290	278	194	183
$40,000 to $49,999	1,217	710	121	27	222	206	135	122
$50,000 to $59,999	902	590	101	12	121	102	76	68
$60,000 to $69,999	636	451	43	13	79	74	52	41
$70,000 to $79,999	537	364	57	5	71	64	39	35
$80,000 to $89,999	393	295	38	3	29	26	28	27
$90,000 to $99,999	350	272	16	13	20	12	32	26
$100,000 or more	1,570	1,246	73	27	116	96	109	89
Median income	$36,032	$50,566	$38,138	$40,350	$18,293	$17,499	$25,675	$24,409
Total households headed by 65-to-74-year-olds	**100.0%**	**100.0%**	**100.0%**	**100.0%**	**100.0%**	**100.0%**	**100.0%**	**100.0%**
Under $10,000	8.8	2.4	8.0	10.2	20.3	20.7	11.4	11.5
$10,000 to $19,999	18.2	8.0	17.8	14.2	32.7	33.8	30.4	31.9
$20,000 to $29,999	15.6	15.0	12.7	15.2	17.6	17.6	15.7	15.9
$30,000 to $39,999	11.8	12.8	13.5	10.2	9.0	9.0	12.4	12.5
$40,000 to $49,999	9.9	11.2	12.9	13.7	6.9	6.7	8.6	8.4
$50,000 to $59,999	7.3	9.3	10.7	6.1	3.8	3.3	4.8	4.7
$60,000 to $69,999	5.2	7.1	4.6	6.6	2.5	2.4	3.3	2.8
$70,000 to $79,999	4.4	5.7	6.1	2.5	2.2	2.1	2.5	2.4
$80,000 to $89,999	3.2	4.6	4.0	1.5	0.9	0.8	1.8	1.9
$90,000 to $99,999	2.8	4.3	1.7	6.6	0.6	0.4	2.0	1.8
$100,000 or more	12.8	19.6	7.8	13.7	3.6	3.1	7.0	6.1

Note: "hh" is short for householder.
Source: Bureau of the Census, 2008 Current Population Survey Annual Social and Economic Supplement, Internet site http:// www.census.gov/hhes/www/macro/032008/hhinc/new02_000.htm; calculations by New Strategist

Table 5.12 Income of Households by Household Type, 2007: Aged 65 to 69

(number and percent distribution of households headed by people aged 65 to 69, by income and household type, 2007; households in thousands as of 2008)

| | | family households | | | nonfamily households | | | |
| | | | | | female householder | | male householder | |
	total	married couples	female hh, no spouse present	male hh, no spouse present	total	living alone	total	living alone
Total households headed by 65-to-69-year-olds	**6,990**	**3,726**	**547**	**119**	**1,689**	**1,620**	**908**	**856**
Under $10,000	597	75	42	11	369	362	102	99
$10,000 to $19,999	1,087	238	103	14	471	466	261	255
$20,000 to $29,999	1,000	480	65	17	285	280	154	147
$30,000 to $39,999	786	436	73	14	161	157	101	94
$40,000 to $49,999	711	413	73	13	131	122	81	80
$50,000 to $59,999	548	371	52	9	68	57	47	44
$60,000 to $69,999	392	266	28	10	57	53	31	27
$70,000 to $79,999	369	251	44	5	44	39	24	20
$80,000 to $89,999	229	174	17	1	18	16	17	17
$90,000 to $99,999	212	173	6	8	10	7	18	15
$100,000 or more	1,060	848	47	20	73	60	73	60
Median income	$40,296	$55,695	$38,932	$42,606	$20,123	$19,304	$26,330	$25,317
Total households headed by 65-to-69-year-olds	**100.0%**	**100.0%**	**100.0%**	**100.0%**	**100.0%**	**100.0%**	**100.0%**	**100.0%**
Under $10,000	8.5	2.0	7.7	9.2	21.8	22.3	11.2	11.6
$10,000 to $19,999	15.6	6.4	18.8	11.8	27.9	28.8	28.7	29.8
$20,000 to $29,999	14.3	12.9	11.9	14.3	16.9	17.3	17.0	17.2
$30,000 to $39,999	11.2	11.7	13.3	11.8	9.5	9.7	11.1	11.0
$40,000 to $49,999	10.2	11.1	13.3	10.9	7.8	7.5	8.9	9.3
$50,000 to $59,999	7.8	10.0	9.5	7.6	4.0	3.5	5.2	5.1
$60,000 to $69,999	5.6	7.1	5.1	8.4	3.4	3.3	3.4	3.2
$70,000 to $79,999	5.3	6.7	8.0	4.2	2.6	2.4	2.6	2.3
$80,000 to $89,999	3.3	4.7	3.1	0.8	1.1	1.0	1.9	2.0
$90,000 to $99,999	3.0	4.6	1.1	6.7	0.6	0.4	2.0	1.8
$100,000 or more	15.2	22.8	8.6	16.8	4.3	3.7	8.0	7.0

Note: "hh" is short for householder.
Source: Bureau of the Census, 2008 Current Population Survey Annual Social and Economic Supplement, Internet site http://www.census.gov/hhes/www/macro/032008/hhinc/new02_000.htm; calculations by New Strategist

Table 5.13 Income of Households by Household Type, 2007: Aged 70 to 74

(number and percent distribution of households headed by people aged 70 to 74, by income and household type, 2007; households in thousands as of 2008)

| | | family households | | | nonfamily households | | | |
| | | | | | female householder | | male householder | |
	total	married couples	female hh, no spouse present	male hh, no spouse present	total	living alone	total	living alone
Total households headed by 70-to-74-year-olds	**5,293**	**2,639**	**393**	**78**	**1,524**	**1,463**	**659**	**603**
Under $10,000	481	78	35	9	283	275	77	71
$10,000 to $19,999	1,151	274	64	15	578	574	218	211
$20,000 to $29,999	914	478	55	11	278	263	91	85
$30,000 to $39,999	663	381	54	6	127	121	94	89
$40,000 to $49,999	507	297	50	15	91	84	54	43
$50,000 to $59,999	354	219	50	3	53	45	30	26
$60,000 to $69,999	244	185	14	3	22	21	20	14
$70,000 to $79,999	169	113	15	0	25	24	16	16
$80,000 to $89,999	164	120	20	2	10	10	13	12
$90,000 to $99,999	136	98	10	5	10	5	13	11
$100,000 or more	509	398	26	7	42	36	36	29
Median income	$31,654	$42,661	$36,886	$35,816	$17,094	$16,702	$24,608	$22,948
Total households headed by 70-to-74-year-olds	**100.0%**	**100.0%**	**100.0%**	**100.0%**	**100.0%**	**100.0%**	**100.0%**	**100.0%**
Under $10,000	9.1	3.0	8.9	11.5	18.6	18.8	11.7	11.8
$10,000 to $19,999	21.7	10.4	16.3	19.2	37.9	39.2	33.1	35.0
$20,000 to $29,999	17.3	18.1	14.0	14.1	18.2	18.0	13.8	14.1
$30,000 to $39,999	12.5	14.4	13.7	7.7	8.3	8.3	14.3	14.8
$40,000 to $49,999	9.6	11.3	12.7	19.2	6.0	5.7	8.2	7.1
$50,000 to $59,999	6.7	8.3	12.7	3.8	3.5	3.1	4.6	4.3
$60,000 to $69,999	4.6	7.0	3.6	3.8	1.4	1.4	3.0	2.3
$70,000 to $79,999	3.2	4.3	3.8	0.0	1.6	1.6	2.4	2.7
$80,000 to $89,999	3.1	4.5	5.1	2.6	0.7	0.7	2.0	2.0
$90,000 to $99,999	2.6	3.7	2.5	6.4	0.7	0.3	2.0	1.8
$100,000 or more	9.6	15.1	6.6	9.0	2.8	2.5	5.5	4.8

Note: "hh" is short for householder.
Source: Bureau of the Census, 2008 Current Population Survey Annual Social and Economic Supplement, Internet site http://www.census.gov/hhes/www/macro/032008/hhinc/new02_000.htm; calculations by New Strategist

Table 5.14 Income of Households by Household Type, 2007: Aged 75 or Older

(number and percent distribution of households headed by people aged 75 or older, by income and household type, 2007; households in thousands as of 2008)

| | total | family households | | | nonfamily households | | | |
| | | married couples | female hh, no spouse present | male hh, no spouse present | female householder | | male householder | |
					total	living alone	total	living alone
Total households headed by people 75 or older	**11,829**	**3,813**	**925**	**252**	**5,287**	**5,213**	**1,552**	**1,458**
Under $10,000	1,360	91	50	15	1,023	1,022	181	181
$10,000 to $19,999	3,715	494	154	25	2,508	2,500	535	528
$20,000 to $29,999	2,369	933	193	40	927	905	278	267
$30,000 to $39,999	1,411	683	148	48	338	322	193	176
$40,000 to $49,999	799	426	99	25	144	136	107	100
$50,000 to $59,999	545	243	73	24	130	127	75	68
$60,000 to $69,999	386	212	58	19	57	50	40	32
$70,000 to $79,999	254	151	34	5	27	24	38	31
$80,000 to $89,999	188	103	27	7	27	27	24	17
$90,000 to $99,999	138	68	26	12	18	16	13	6
$100,000 or more	663	410	66	33	87	83	67	51
Median income	$23,230	$35,223	$33,214	$39,640	$15,568	$15,424	$21,812	$20,629
Total households headed by people 75 or older	**100.0%**	**100.0%**	**100.0%**	**100.0%**	**100.0%**	**100.0%**	**100.0%**	**100.0%**
Under $10,000	11.5	2.4	5.4	6.0	19.3	19.6	11.7	12.4
$10,000 to $19,999	31.4	13.0	16.6	9.9	47.4	48.0	34.5	36.2
$20,000 to $29,999	20.0	24.5	20.9	15.9	17.5	17.4	17.9	18.3
$30,000 to $39,999	11.9	17.9	16.0	19.0	6.4	6.2	12.4	12.1
$40,000 to $49,999	6.8	11.2	10.7	9.9	2.7	2.6	6.9	6.9
$50,000 to $59,999	4.6	6.4	7.9	9.5	2.5	2.4	4.8	4.7
$60,000 to $69,999	3.3	5.6	6.3	7.5	1.1	1.0	2.6	2.2
$70,000 to $79,999	2.1	4.0	3.7	2.0	0.5	0.5	2.4	2.1
$80,000 to $89,999	1.6	2.7	2.9	2.8	0.5	0.5	1.5	1.2
$90,000 to $99,999	1.2	1.8	2.8	4.8	0.3	0.3	0.8	0.4
$100,000 or more	5.6	10.8	7.1	13.1	1.6	1.6	4.3	3.5

Note: "hh" is short for householder.
Source: Bureau of the Census, 2008 Current Population Survey Annual Social and Economic Supplement, Internet site http://www.census.gov/hhes/www/macro/032008/hhinc/new02_000.htm; calculations by New Strategist

Older Americans Buck Income Trend

Both men and women aged 55 or older have seen their incomes grow since 2000.

Younger age groups saw their incomes decline between 2000 and 2007, but the median income of men and women aged 55 or older grew. The slowest growth of just 0.5 percent was recorded among men aged 75 or older, while women aged 55 to 64 enjoyed the highest increase in median income, a comforting 24 percent rise. The median income of women aged 65 or older grew 6 percent from 2000 to 2007, while their male counterparts saw a 4 percent increase.

The median income of older Americans was significantly higher in 2007 than in 1990. Among 55-to-64-year-old men, for example, median income rose 10 percent during those years, after adjusting for inflation. This substantial gain is a mere pittance, however, compared with the whopping 75 percent increase for their female counterparts. Among women aged 65 or older, median income rose 13 percent between 1990 and 2007, while the gain was 12 percent among men in the age group.

■ The median income of men and women aged 55 to 64 should continue to climb thanks to rising labor force participation rates in the age group.

Median income has grown since 2000 for older men and women

(percent change in median income of people aged 55 or older, by sex, 2000–07; in 2007 dollars)

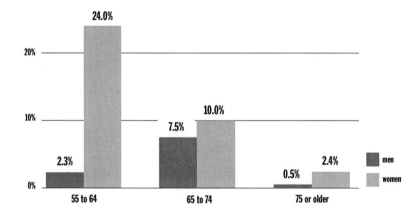

Table 5.15 Median Income of Men Aged 55 or Older, 1990 to 2007

(median income of men aged 15 or older and aged 55 or older, and index of age group to total, 1990 to 2007; percent change for selected years; in 2007 dollars)

	total men	55 to 64	65 or older		
			total	65 to 74	75 or older
2007	$33,196	$42,129	$24,323	$27,786	$20,799
2006	33,180	42,654	24,167	27,018	21,225
2005	33,217	43,178	23,136	25,831	20,649
2004	33,497	43,126	23,195	26,578	20,555
2003	33,743	43,871	22,956	26,111	20,044
2002	33,698	41,811	22,401	24,539	20,179
2001	34,082	41,736	23,058	25,408	20,520
2000	34,126	41,165	23,371	25,846	20,702
1999	33,963	41,668	24,017	26,704	21,126
1998	33,654	41,637	23,077	25,069	20,934
1997	32,475	40,132	22,886	25,312	19,845
1996	31,363	38,853	21,955	24,482	19,073
1995	30,480	39,150	22,269	24,786	19,129
1994	30,049	37,457	21,098	22,964	18,897
1993	29,817	35,521	21,171	23,012	18,965
1992	29,617	37,089	21,135	22,892	18,658
1991	30,389	37,799	21,315	22,767	19,355
1990	31,208	38,146	21,812	24,557	17,964
Percent change					
2000 to 2007	−2.7%	2.3%	4.1%	7.5%	0.5%
1990 to 2007	6.4	10.4	11.5	13.1	15.8
INDEX					
2007	100	127	73	84	63
2006	100	129	73	81	64
2005	100	130	70	78	62
2004	100	129	69	79	61
2003	100	130	68	77	59
2002	100	124	66	73	60
2001	100	122	68	75	60
2000	100	121	68	76	61
1999	100	123	71	79	62
1998	100	124	69	74	62
1997	100	124	70	78	61
1996	100	124	70	78	61
1995	100	128	73	81	63
1994	100	125	70	76	63
1993	100	119	71	77	64
1992	100	125	71	77	63
1991	100	124	70	75	64
1990	100	122	70	79	58

Note: The index is calculated by dividing the median income of the age group by the national median and multiplying by 100.
Source: Bureau of the Census, data from the Current Population Survey Annual Demographic Supplements, Internet site http://www.census.gov/hhes/www/income/histinc/p08AR.html; calculations by New Strategist

Table 5.16 Median Income of Women Aged 55 or Older, 1990 to 2007

(median income of women aged 15 or older and aged 55 or older, and index of age group to total, 1990 to 2007; percent change for selected years; in 2007 dollars)

| | total women | 55 to 64 | 65 or older | | |
			total	65 to 74	75 or older
2007	$20,922	$25,262	$14,021	$14,442	$13,697
2006	20,582	24,872	13,989	14,478	13,679
2005	19,729	23,495	13,271	13,637	13,054
2004	19,393	22,834	13,261	13,487	13,109
2003	19,457	22,962	13,354	13,690	13,116
2002	19,376	22,088	13,146	12,999	13,258
2001	19,458	20,873	13,249	13,118	13,346
2000	19,340	20,372	13,272	13,134	13,377
1999	19,044	19,838	13,636	13,661	13,617
1998	18,331	18,642	13,344	13,279	13,396
1997	17,650	18,517	12,961	13,062	12,876
1996	16,863	17,523	12,667	12,706	12,630
1995	16,387	16,726	12,638	12,533	12,735
1994	15,863	15,034	12,382	12,210	12,537
1993	15,608	15,301	12,009	12,218	11,820
1992	15,513	14,672	11,848	11,895	11,802
1991	15,553	14,701	12,158	12,078	12,235
1990	15,486	14,456	12,371	12,595	12,135

Percent change

2000 to 2007	8.2%	24.0%	5.6%	10.0%	2.4%
1990 to 2007	35.1	74.8	13.3	14.7	12.9

INDEX

2007	100	121	67	69	65
2006	100	121	68	70	66
2005	100	119	67	69	66
2004	100	118	68	70	68
2003	100	118	69	70	67
2002	100	114	68	67	68
2001	100	107	68	67	69
2000	100	105	69	68	69
1999	100	104	72	72	72
1998	100	102	73	72	73
1997	100	105	73	74	73
1996	100	104	75	75	75
1995	100	102	77	76	78
1994	100	95	78	77	79
1993	100	98	77	78	76
1992	100	95	76	77	76
1991	100	95	78	78	79
1990	100	93	80	81	78

Note: The index is calculated by dividing the median income of the age group by the national median and multiplying by 100.
Source: Bureau of the Census, data from the Current Population Survey Annual Demographic Supplements, Internet site http://www.census.gov/hhes/www/income/histinc/p08AR.html; calculations by New Strategist

Older Men Command High Salaries

Income peaks among working men aged 55 to 59.

Among all men, those aged 55 to 59 make the most money, a median of $45,112 in 2007. Among men who work full-time, however, those aged 65 to 69 have the highest incomes, a median of $62,944. Only 23 percent of men in that age group still work full-time.

Median income drops with age not because workers get paid less, but because fewer people work. The proportion of men who work full-time falls from the 66 percent majority of men aged 55 to 59 to a 49 percent minority of men aged 60 to 64. Only 13 percent of men aged 65 or older work full-time, as do 5 percent of those aged 75 or older.

Among men aged 55 or older with income, non-Hispanic whites have the highest median income, $32,741 in 2007. Asian men have a lower median of just $27,098. The median income of black men aged 55 or older stood at $22,458, while that of Hispanics was $22,303.

■ Among older men, those with high earnings may be more likely to stay on the job than those who earn less, driving up the median income of older men who work full-time.

Incomes are high among older men who work full-time

(median income of men who work full-time, by age, 2007)

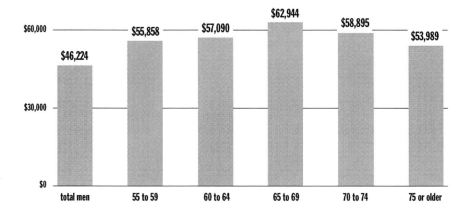

Table 5.17 Income of Men Aged 55 or Older, 2007: Total Men

(number and percent distribution of men aged 15 or older and aged 55 or older by income, 2007; median income by work status, and percent working year-round, full-time; men in thousands as of 2008)

		aged 55 or older					aged 65 or older			
								aged 65 to 74		
			aged 55 to 64							
	total	total	total	55–59	60–64	total	total	65–69	70–74	75+
TOTAL MEN	115,678	31,841	16,079	8,929	7,150	15,762	8,977	5,238	3,740	6,785
Without income	10,889	1,002	557	317	240	445	263	161	104	181
With income	104,789	30,839	15,522	8,612	6,910	15,317	8,714	5,077	3,636	6,604
Under $10,000	13,989	2,903	1,251	664	586	1,652	847	428	420	805
$10,000 to $19,999	16,953	6,784	2,088	1,046	1,042	4,696	2,331	1,227	1,104	2,366
$20,000 to $29,999	15,483	4,690	1,862	960	901	2,828	1,486	871	615	1,341
$30,000 to $39,999	13,877	3,746	1,972	1,100	873	1,774	1,051	609	443	723
$40,000 to $49,999	10,420	2,783	1,678	925	753	1,105	733	469	265	371
$50,000 to $59,999	8,291	2,165	1,370	788	581	795	501	300	201	292
$60,000 to $69,999	5,814	1,637	1,096	641	456	541	349	239	110	192
$70,000 to $79,999	4,677	1,225	836	502	334	389	256	144	112	133
$80,000 to $89,999	3,066	892	628	383	244	264	194	129	64	70
$90,000 to $99,999	2,273	669	440	228	212	229	167	118	51	60
$100,000 or more	9,949	3,345	2,299	1,371	928	1,046	797	544	253	249
Median income of men with income	$33,196	$33,315	$42,129	$45,112	$40,435	$24,323	$27,786	$30,178	$24,577	$20,799
Median income of full-time workers	46,224	57,027	56,262	55,858	57,090	60,589	61,510	62,944	58,895	53,989
Percent working full-time	54.5%	35.7%	58.1%	65.8%	48.6%	12.7%	18.5%	22.9%	12.4%	5.1%
TOTAL MEN	100.0%	100.0%	100.0%	100.0%	100.0%	100.0%	100.0%	100.0%	100.0%	100.0%
Without income	9.4	3.1	3.5	3.6	3.4	2.8	2.9	3.1	2.8	2.7
With income	90.6	96.9	96.5	96.4	96.6	97.2	97.1	96.9	97.2	97.3
Under $10,000	12.1	9.1	7.8	7.4	8.2	10.5	9.4	8.2	11.2	11.9
$10,000 to $19,999	14.7	21.3	13.0	11.7	14.6	29.8	26.0	23.4	29.5	34.9
$20,000 to $29,999	13.4	14.7	11.6	10.8	12.6	17.9	16.6	16.6	16.4	19.8
$30,000 to $39,999	12.0	11.8	12.3	12.3	12.2	11.3	11.7	11.6	11.8	10.7
$40,000 to $49,999	9.0	8.7	10.4	10.4	10.5	7.0	8.2	9.0	7.1	5.5
$50,000 to $59,999	7.2	6.8	8.5	8.8	8.1	5.0	5.6	5.7	5.4	4.3
$60,000 to $69,999	5.0	5.1	6.8	7.2	6.4	3.4	3.9	4.6	2.9	2.8
$70,000 to $79,999	4.0	3.8	5.2	5.6	4.7	2.5	2.9	2.7	3.0	2.0
$80,000 to $89,999	2.7	2.8	3.9	4.3	3.4	1.7	2.2	2.5	1.7	1.0
$90,000 to $99,999	2.0	2.1	2.7	2.6	3.0	1.5	1.9	2.3	1.4	0.9
$100,000 or more	8.6	10.5	14.3	15.4	13.0	6.6	8.9	10.4	6.8	3.7

Source: Bureau of the Census, 2008 Current Population Survey Annual Social and Economic Supplement, Internet site http:// www.census.gov/hhes/www/macro/032008/perinc/new01_000.htm; calculations by New Strategist

Table 5.18 Income of Men Aged 55 or Older, 2007: Asian Men

(number and percent distribution of Asian men aged 15 or older and aged 55 or older by income, 2007; median income by work status, and percent working year-round, full-time; men in thousands as of 2008)

						aged 55 or older				
							aged 65 or older			
			aged 55 to 64					aged 65 to 74		
	total	total	total	55–59	60–64	total	total	65–69	70–74	75+
TOTAL ASIAN MEN	5,414	1,162	604	356	248	558	360	223	138	197
Without income	705	116	41	20	21	75	45	28	18	30
With income	4,709	1,046	563	336	227	483	315	195	120	167
Under $10,000	639	192	70	29	41	122	74	45	30	47
$10,000 to $19,999	645	207	76	32	43	131	86	42	44	44
$20,000 to $29,999	646	151	73	43	29	78	52	38	15	27
$30,000 to $39,999	536	108	62	35	28	46	36	24	12	11
$40,000 to $49,999	426	81	61	39	21	20	13	7	6	6
$50,000 to $59,999	338	55	33	22	10	22	13	12	2	9
$60,000 to $69,999	278	36	26	18	11	10	7	6	0	3
$70,000 to $79,999	276	48	41	31	10	7	2	1	1	4
$80,000 to $89,999	156	39	29	22	7	10	5	5	0	3
$90,000 to $99,999	144	21	17	10	6	4	4	2	3	0
$100,000 or more	625	110	75	53	22	35	20	14	6	14
Median income of men with income	$36,729	$27,098	$39,791	$46,119	$30,056	$18,955	$19,552	$22,173	$16,247	$17,447
Median income of full-time workers	51,001	49,369	51,419	57,386	45,139	41,051	–	–	–	–
Percent working full-time	58.5%	38.3%	59.1%	68.3%	46.0%	15.8%	19.7%	25.1%	10.9%	8.6%
TOTAL ASIAN MEN	100.0%	100.0%	100.0%	100.0%	100.0%	100.0%	100.0%	100.0%	100.0%	100.0%
Without income	13.0	10.0	6.8	5.6	8.5	13.4	12.5	12.6	13.0	15.2
With income	87.0	90.0	93.2	94.4	91.5	86.6	87.5	87.4	87.0	84.8
Under $10,000	11.8	16.5	11.6	8.1	16.5	21.9	20.6	20.2	21.7	23.9
$10,000 to $19,999	11.9	17.8	12.6	9.0	17.3	23.5	23.9	18.8	31.9	22.3
$20,000 to $29,999	11.9	13.0	12.1	12.1	11.7	14.0	14.4	17.0	10.9	13.7
$30,000 to $39,999	9.9	9.3	10.3	9.8	11.3	8.2	10.0	10.8	8.7	5.6
$40,000 to $49,999	7.9	7.0	10.1	11.0	8.5	3.6	3.6	3.1	4.3	3.0
$50,000 to $59,999	6.2	4.7	5.5	6.2	4.0	3.9	3.6	5.4	1.4	4.6
$60,000 to $69,999	5.1	3.1	4.3	5.1	4.4	1.8	1.9	2.7	0.0	1.5
$70,000 to $79,999	5.1	4.1	6.8	8.7	4.0	1.3	0.6	0.4	0.7	2.0
$80,000 to $89,999	2.9	3.4	4.8	6.2	2.8	1.8	1.4	2.2	0.0	1.5
$90,000 to $99,999	2.7	1.8	2.8	2.8	2.4	0.7	1.1	0.9	2.2	0.0
$100,000 or more	11.5	9.5	12.4	14.9	8.9	6.3	5.6	6.3	4.3	7.1

Note: Asians include those who identify themselves as being of the race alone and those who identify themselves as being of the race in combination with other races. "–" means sample is too small to make a reliable estimate.
Source: Bureau of the Census, 2008 Current Population Survey Annual Social and Economic Supplement, Internet site http://www.census.gov/hhes/www/macro/032008/perinc/new01_000.htm; calculations by New Strategist

Table 5.19 Income of Men Aged 55 or Older, 2007: Black Men

(number and percent distribution of black men aged 15 or older and aged 55 or older by income, 2007; median income by work status, and percent working year-round, full-time; men in thousands as of 2008)

		aged 55 or older								
							aged 65 or older			
			aged 55 to 64					aged 65 to 74		
	total	total	total	55–59	60–64	total	total	65–69	70–74	75+
TOTAL BLACK MEN	13,370	2,767	1,509	916	593	1,258	789	466	323	469
Without income	2,389	174	103	79	23	71	44	28	15	27
With income	10,981	2,593	1,406	837	570	1,187	745	438	308	442
Under $10,000	2,307	493	214	117	97	279	180	107	75	98
$10,000 to $19,999	2,145	709	284	163	121	425	237	137	99	189
$20,000 to $29,999	1,691	379	195	117	79	184	121	69	52	62
$30,000 to $39,999	1,559	294	214	126	86	80	57	32	25	24
$40,000 to $49,999	997	213	129	78	52	84	56	27	29	28
$50,000 to $59,999	747	140	92	71	20	48	27	20	7	23
$60,000 to $69,999	482	102	77	33	43	25	22	14	9	3
$70,000 to $79,999	345	78	57	29	27	21	17	13	4	3
$80,000 to $89,999	196	44	40	30	12	4	3	3	0	1
$90,000 to $99,999	122	22	19	14	6	3	3	0	3	0
$100,000 or more	390	118	85	57	28	33	21	15	6	12
Median income of men with income	$25,792	$22,458	$30,238	$30,882	$27,847	$16,051	$16,831	$17,028	$16,475	$14,922
Median income of full-time workers	36,780	41,736	41,104	41,168	40,982	44,991	44,033	43,955	–	–
Percent working full-time	46.1%	31.3%	48.1%	54.1%	38.8%	11.2%	15.2%	18.0%	11.1%	4.5%
TOTAL BLACK MEN	100.0%	100.0%	100.0%	100.0%	100.0%	100.0%	100.0%	100.0%	100.0%	100.0%
Without income	17.9	6.3	6.8	8.6	3.9	5.6	5.6	6.0	4.6	5.8
With income	82.1	93.7	93.2	91.4	96.1	94.4	94.4	94.0	95.4	94.2
Under $10,000	17.3	17.8	14.2	12.8	16.4	22.2	22.8	23.0	23.2	20.9
$10,000 to $19,999	16.0	25.6	18.8	17.8	20.4	33.8	30.0	29.4	30.7	40.3
$20,000 to $29,999	12.6	13.7	12.9	12.8	13.3	14.6	15.3	14.8	16.1	13.2
$30,000 to $39,999	11.7	10.6	14.2	13.8	14.5	6.4	7.2	6.9	7.7	5.1
$40,000 to $49,999	7.5	7.7	8.5	8.5	8.8	6.7	7.1	5.8	9.0	6.0
$50,000 to $59,999	5.6	5.1	6.1	7.8	3.4	3.8	3.4	4.3	2.2	4.9
$60,000 to $69,999	3.6	3.7	5.1	3.6	7.3	2.0	2.8	3.0	2.8	0.6
$70,000 to $79,999	2.6	2.8	3.8	3.2	4.6	1.7	2.2	2.8	1.2	0.6
$80,000 to $89,999	1.5	1.6	2.7	3.3	2.0	0.3	0.4	0.6	0.0	0.2
$90,000 to $99,999	0.9	0.8	1.3	1.5	1.0	0.2	0.4	0.0	0.9	0.0
$100,000 or more	2.9	4.3	5.6	6.2	4.7	2.6	2.7	3.2	1.9	2.6

Note: Blacks include those who identify themselves as being of the race alone and those who identify themselves as being of the race in combination with other races. "–" means sample is too small to make a reliable estimate.
Source: Bureau of the Census, 2008 Current Population Survey Annual Social and Economic Supplement, Internet site http://www.census.gov/hhes/www/macro/032008/perinc/new01_000.htm; calculations by New Strategist

Table 5.20 Income of Men Aged 55 or Older, 2007: Hispanic Men

(number and percent distribution of Hispanic men aged 15 or older and aged 55 or older by income, 2007; median income by work status, and percent working year-round, full-time; men in thousands as of 2008)

						aged 55 or older				
							aged 65 or older			
				aged 55 to 64				aged 65 to 74		
	total	total	total	55–59	60–64	total	total	65–69	70–74	75+
TOTAL HISPANIC MEN	**16,837**	**2,436**	**1,342**	**787**	**555**	**1,094**	**665**	**378**	**287**	**429**
Without income	**2,228**	**167**	**93**	**48**	**45**	**74**	**39**	**18**	**21**	**35**
With income	**14,609**	**2,269**	**1,249**	**739**	**510**	**1,020**	**626**	**360**	**266**	**394**
Under $10,000	2,135	393	145	72	74	248	134	63	68	115
$10,000 to $19,999	3,548	670	276	157	117	394	234	136	100	158
$20,000 to $29,999	3,168	350	215	135	78	135	86	41	45	48
$30,000 to $39,999	2,143	304	207	131	76	97	64	40	24	34
$40,000 to $49,999	1,209	157	116	64	53	41	32	24	8	9
$50,000 to $59,999	809	130	93	52	41	37	24	17	7	12
$60,000 to $69,999	513	68	43	31	13	25	19	16	3	6
$70,000 to $79,999	330	46	40	26	14	6	6	5	1	0
$80,000 to $89,999	201	35	27	14	13	8	8	5	2	0
$90,000 to $99,999	127	25	23	17	8	2	2	0	2	0
$100,000 or more	425	92	65	40	25	27	14	9	5	13
Median income of men with income	$24,451	$22,303	$29,252	$30,180	$27,159	$15,455	$16,392	$17,240	$14,806	$14,005
Median income of full-time workers	30,454	36,064	36,263	35,507	38,061	35,194	35,731	35,762	–	–
Percent working full-time	58.0%	39.4%	58.2%	64.0%	49.9%	16.4%	21.1%	26.7%	13.6%	9.1%
TOTAL HISPANIC MEN	**100.0%**	**100.0%**	**100.0%**	**100.0%**	**100.0%**	**100.0%**	**100.0%**	**100.0%**	**100.0%**	**100.0%**
Without income	**13.2**	**6.9**	**6.9**	**6.1**	**8.1**	**6.8**	**5.9**	**4.8**	**7.3**	**8.2**
With income	**86.8**	**93.1**	**93.1**	**93.9**	**91.9**	**93.2**	**94.1**	**95.2**	**92.7**	**91.8**
Under $10,000	12.7	16.1	10.8	9.1	13.3	22.7	20.2	16.7	23.7	26.8
$10,000 to $19,999	21.1	27.5	20.6	19.9	21.1	36.0	35.2	36.0	34.8	36.8
$20,000 to $29,999	18.8	14.4	16.0	17.2	14.1	12.3	12.9	10.8	15.7	11.2
$30,000 to $39,999	12.7	12.5	15.4	16.6	13.7	8.9	9.6	10.6	8.4	7.9
$40,000 to $49,999	7.2	6.4	8.6	8.1	9.5	3.7	4.8	6.3	2.8	2.1
$50,000 to $59,999	4.8	5.3	6.9	6.6	7.4	3.4	3.6	4.5	2.4	2.8
$60,000 to $69,999	3.0	2.8	3.2	3.9	2.3	2.3	2.9	4.2	1.0	1.4
$70,000 to $79,999	2.0	1.9	3.0	3.3	2.5	0.5	0.9	1.3	0.3	0.0
$80,000 to $89,999	1.2	1.4	2.0	1.8	2.3	0.7	1.2	1.3	0.7	0.0
$90,000 to $99,999	0.8	1.0	1.7	2.2	1.4	0.2	0.3	0.0	0.7	0.0
$100,000 or more	2.5	3.8	4.8	5.1	4.5	2.5	2.1	2.4	1.7	3.0

Note: "–" means sample is too small to make a reliable estimate.
Source: Bureau of the Census, 2008 Current Population Survey Annual Social and Economic Supplement, Internet site http://www.census.gov/hhes/www/macro/032008/perinc/new01_000.htm; calculations by New Strategist

Table 5.21 Income of Men Aged 55 or Older, 2007: Non-Hispanic White Men

(number and percent distribution of non-Hispanic white men aged 15 or older and aged 55 or older by income, 2007; median income by work status, and percent working year-round, full-time; men in thousands as of 2008)

| | | aged 55 or older | | | | aged 65 or older | | | |
| | | | aged 55 to 64 | | | | aged 65 to 74 | | |
	total	total	total	55–59	60–64	total	total	65–69	70–74	75+
TOTAL NON-HISPANIC WHITE MEN	79,100	25,166	12,452	6,763	5,689	12,714	7,062	4,114	2,948	5,651
Without income	5,483	539	312	164	148	227	133	85	48	93
With income	73,617	24,627	12,140	6,599	5,541	12,487	6,929	4,029	2,900	5,558
Under $10,000	8,760	1,794	807	435	371	987	453	212	238	535
$10,000 to $19,999	10,470	5,125	1,425	684	742	3,700	1,746	905	842	1,954
$20,000 to $29,999	9,834	3,757	1,357	648	710	2,400	1,200	701	499	1,200
$30,000 to $39,999	9,518	2,999	1,471	797	675	1,528	877	503	373	652
$40,000 to $49,999	7,703	2,317	1,360	738	621	957	629	408	221	327
$50,000 to $59,999	6,323	1,815	1,131	625	505	684	433	250	184	249
$60,000 to $69,999	4,493	1,414	939	554	385	475	296	199	96	180
$70,000 to $79,999	3,717	1,045	695	412	282	350	226	121	105	125
$80,000 to $89,999	2,491	764	525	309	216	239	175	113	61	65
$90,000 to $99,999	1,871	596	378	185	192	218	158	114	42	60
$100,000 or more	8,438	2,999	2,052	1,209	843	947	738	502	236	209
Median income of men with income	$37,373	$32,741	$46,495	$49,919	$43,067	$26,229	$30,615	$33,743	$27,515	$21,947
Median income of full-time workers	51,465	61,807	60,818	60,570	61,226	66,408	67,213	69,083	61,717	58,676
Percent working full-time	55.0%	35.8%	59.5%	67.6%	49.8%	12.5%	18.7%	23.1%	12.7%	4.8%
TOTAL NON-HISPANIC WHITE MEN	100.0%	100.0%	100.0%	100.0%	100.0%	100.0%	100.0%	100.0%	100.0%	100.0%
Without income	6.9	2.1	2.5	2.4	2.6	1.8	1.9	2.1	1.6	1.6
With income	93.1	97.9	97.5	97.6	97.4	98.2	98.1	97.9	98.4	98.4
Under $10,000	11.1	7.1	6.5	6.4	6.5	7.8	6.4	5.2	8.1	9.5
$10,000 to $19,999	13.2	20.4	11.4	10.1	13.0	29.1	24.7	22.0	28.6	34.6
$20,000 to $29,999	12.4	14.9	10.9	9.6	12.5	18.9	17.0	17.0	16.9	21.2
$30,000 to $39,999	12.0	11.9	11.8	11.8	11.9	12.0	12.4	12.2	12.7	11.5
$40,000 to $49,999	9.7	9.2	10.9	10.9	10.9	7.5	8.9	9.9	7.5	5.8
$50,000 to $59,999	8.0	7.2	9.1	9.2	8.9	5.4	6.1	6.1	6.2	4.4
$60,000 to $69,999	5.7	5.6	7.5	8.2	6.8	3.7	4.2	4.8	3.3	3.2
$70,000 to $79,999	4.7	4.2	5.6	6.1	5.0	2.8	3.2	2.9	3.6	2.2
$80,000 to $89,999	3.1	3.0	4.2	4.6	3.8	1.9	2.5	2.7	2.1	1.2
$90,000 to $99,999	2.4	2.4	3.0	2.7	3.4	1.7	2.2	2.8	1.4	1.1
$100,000 or more	10.7	11.9	16.5	17.9	14.8	7.4	10.5	12.2	8.0	3.7

Note: Non-Hispanic whites are those who identify themselves as being white alone and not Hispanic.
Source: Bureau of the Census, 2008 Current Population Survey Annual Social and Economic Supplement, Internet site http://www.census.gov/hhes/www/macro/032008/perinc/new01_000.htm; calculations by New Strategist

Older Women Have Low Incomes

Those who work are much better off than those who are not in the labor force.

The median income of women aged 55 or older who work full-time stood at $40,251 in 2007, more than double the $15,740 median for all women with income in the age group. Few older women work full-time, however, the proportion ranging from a high of 50 percent among women aged 55 to 59 to just 6 percent among women aged 65 or older.

Because most women aged 65 or older do not work, and because most did not spend much time in the labor force, their incomes are extremely low. Much of their financial support comes from Social Security. The median income of all women aged 65 or older was just $14,021 in 2007. Non-Hispanic white women in the age group have the highest incomes, a median of $14,726. Their Hispanic counterparts have the lowest incomes—a median of just $9,786. For black women the figure is $11,573 and for Asians $12,242.

■ The incomes of older women will rise substantially in the years ahead as the working women of the Baby-Boom generation enter the older age groups.

Among older women, the incomes of full-time workers are more than double the average

(median income of women aged 55 or older by work status, 2007)

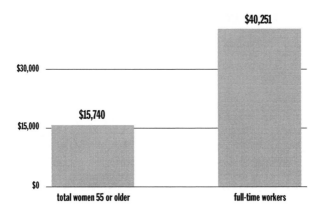

Table 5.22 Income of Women Aged 55 or Older, 2007: Total Women

(number and percent distribution of women aged 15 or older and aged 55 or older by income, 2007; median income by work status, and percent working year-round, full-time; women in thousands as of 2008)

		aged 55 or older								
							aged 65 or older			
			aged 55 to 64				aged 65 to 74			
	total	total	total	55–59	60–64	total	total	65–69	70–74	75+
TOTAL WOMEN	122,470	38,251	17,223	9,442	7,781	21,028	10,611	5,928	4,683	10,417
Without income	17,240	2,483	1,622	928	694	861	469	255	214	392
With income	105,230	35,768	15,601	8,514	7,087	20,167	10,142	5,673	4,469	10,025
Under $10,000	26,931	9,656	3,410	1,603	1,806	6,246	3,217	1,735	1,482	3,029
$10,000 to $19,999	23,616	10,518	3,027	1,495	1,530	7,491	3,187	1,631	1,555	4,304
$20,000 to $29,999	16,710	5,265	2,423	1,373	1,050	2,842	1,421	828	593	1,420
$30,000 to $39,999	12,457	3,273	1,893	1,100	794	1,380	858	491	366	523
$40,000 to $49,999	8,573	2,256	1,537	923	613	719	500	345	156	219
$50,000 to $59,999	5,461	1,547	1,050	611	438	497	294	201	92	204
$60,000 to $69,999	3,589	935	665	427	237	270	184	119	65	88
$70,000 to $79,999	2,317	631	454	286	168	177	127	85	43	48
$80,000 to $89,999	1,371	393	275	170	103	118	83	59	24	35
$90,000 to $99,999	958	276	194	128	66	82	52	43	9	31
$100,000 or more	3,246	1,021	676	395	281	345	220	137	83	125
Median income of women with income	$20,922	$15,740	$25,262	$27,888	$21,462	$14,021	$14,442	$15,301	$13,666	$13,697
Median income of full-time workers	36,167	40,251	40,061	40,433	38,171	41,333	41,487	42,249	39,282	40,165
Percent working full-time	37.3%	22.2%	41.9 %	49.8%	32.3%	6.0%	10.1%	13.9%	5.4%	1.8%
TOTAL WOMEN	100.0%	100.0%	100.0%	100.0%	100.0%	100.0%	100.0%	100.0%	100.0%	100.0%
Without income	14.1	6.5	9.4	9.8	8.9	4.1	4.4	4.3	4.6	3.8
With income	85.9	93.5	90.6	90.2	91.1	95.9	95.6	95.7	95.4	96.2
Under $10,000	22.0	25.2	19.8	17.0	23.2	29.7	30.3	29.3	31.6	29.1
$10,000 to $19,999	19.3	27.5	17.6	15.8	19.7	35.6	30.0	27.5	33.2	41.3
$20,000 to $29,999	13.6	13.8	14.1	14.5	13.5	13.5	13.4	14.0	12.7	13.6
$30,000 to $39,999	10.2	8.6	11.0	11.7	10.2	6.6	8.1	8.3	7.8	5.0
$40,000 to $49,999	7.0	5.9	8.9	9.8	7.9	3.4	4.7	5.8	3.3	2.1
$50,000 to $59,999	4.5	4.0	6.1	6.5	5.6	2.4	2.8	3.4	2.0	2.0
$60,000 to $69,999	2.9	2.4	3.9	4.5	3.0	1.3	1.7	2.0	1.4	0.8
$70,000 to $79,999	1.9	1.6	2.6	3.0	2.2	0.8	1.2	1.4	0.9	0.5
$80,000 to $89,999	1.1	1.0	1.6	1.8	1.3	0.6	0.8	1.0	0.5	0.3
$90,000 to $99,999	0.8	0.7	1.1	1.4	0.8	0.4	0.5	0.7	0.2	0.3
$100,000 or more	2.7	2.7	3.9	4.2	3.6	1.6	2.1	2.3	1.8	1.2

Source: Bureau of the Census, 2008 Current Population Survey Annual Social and Economic Supplement, Internet site http://www.census.gov/hhes/www/macro/032008/perinc/new01_000.htm; calculations by New Strategist

Table 5.23 Income of Women Aged 55 or Older, 2007: Asian Women

(number and percent distribution of Asian women aged 15 or older and aged 55 or older by income, 2007; median income by work status, and percent working year-round, full-time; women in thousands as of 2008)

	total	aged 55 or older total	aged 55 to 64 total	55–59	60–64	aged 65 or older total	aged 65 or older total	aged 65 to 74 65–69	70–74	75+
TOTAL ASIAN WOMEN	6,029	1,467	732	417	316	735	408	249	159	327
Without income	1,243	265	145	76	70	120	72	47	24	48
With income	4,786	1,202	587	341	246	615	336	202	135	279
Under $10,000	1,217	371	121	67	56	250	124	68	57	127
$10,000 to $19,999	866	303	132	75	57	171	97	62	37	74
$20,000 to $29,999	632	158	81	52	27	77	50	36	12	28
$30,000 to $39,999	511	100	68	34	32	32	18	5	12	16
$40,000 to $49,999	426	67	51	33	17	16	8	6	3	7
$50,000 to $59,999	289	56	31	14	17	25	17	16	1	8
$60,000 to $69,999	212	32	22	13	11	10	4	1	2	7
$70,000 to $79,999	171	24	16	10	6	8	6	4	2	3
$80,000 to $89,999	102	15	15	9	6	0	0	0	0	0
$90,000 to $99,999	94	21	12	10	2	9	5	1	4	4
$100,000 or more	265	52	38	25	13	14	8	4	4	5
Median income of women with income	$24,095	$16,707	$23,873	$25,112	$22,259	$12,242	$12,826	$14,080	$11,664	$11,444
Median income of full-time workers	41,254	–	40,086	39,712	40,550	–	–	–	–	–
Percent working full-time	40.4%	25.4%	41.8%	48.7%	32.6%	9.0%	14.0%	15.7%	11.3%	2.8%
TOTAL ASIAN WOMEN	100.0%	100.0%	100.0%	100.0%	100.0%	100.0%	100.0%	100.0%	100.0%	100.0%
Without income	20.6	18.1	19.8	18.2	22.2	16.3	17.6	18.9	15.1	14.7
With income	79.4	81.9	80.2	81.8	77.8	83.7	82.4	81.1	84.9	85.3
Under $10,000	20.2	25.3	16.5	16.1	17.7	34.0	30.4	27.3	35.8	38.8
$10,000 to $19,999	14.4	20.7	18.0	18.0	18.0	23.3	23.8	24.9	23.3	22.6
$20,000 to $29,999	10.5	10.8	11.1	12.5	8.5	10.5	12.3	14.5	7.5	8.6
$30,000 to $39,999	8.5	6.8	9.3	8.2	10.1	4.4	4.4	2.0	7.5	4.9
$40,000 to $49,999	7.1	4.6	7.0	7.9	5.4	2.2	2.0	2.4	1.9	2.1
$50,000 to $59,999	4.8	3.8	4.2	3.4	5.4	3.4	4.2	6.4	0.6	2.4
$60,000 to $69,999	3.5	2.2	3.0	3.1	3.5	1.4	1.0	0.4	1.3	2.1
$70,000 to $79,999	2.8	1.6	2.2	2.4	1.9	1.1	1.5	1.6	1.3	0.9
$80,000 to $89,999	1.7	1.0	2.0	2.2	1.9	0.0	0.0	0.0	0.0	0.0
$90,000 to $99,999	1.6	1.4	1.6	2.4	0.6	1.2	1.2	0.4	2.5	1.2
$100,000 or more	4.4	3.5	5.2	6.0	4.1	1.9	2.0	1.6	2.5	1.5

Note: Asians include those who identify themselves as being of the race alone and those who identify themselves as being of the race in combination with other races. "–" means sample is too small to make a reliable estimate.
Source: Bureau of the Census, 2008 Current Population Survey Annual Social and Economic Supplement, Internet site http:// www.census.gov/hhes/www/macro/032008/perinc/new01_000.htm; calculations by New Strategist

Table 5.24 Income of Women Aged 55 or Older, 2007: Black Women

(number and percent distribution of black women aged 15 or older and aged 55 or older by income, 2007; median income by work status, and percent working year-round, full-time; women in thousands as of 2008)

						aged 55 or older				
							aged 65 or older			
			aged 55 to 64					aged 65 to 74		
	total	total	total	55–59	60–64	total	total	65–69	70–74	75+
TOTAL BLACK WOMEN	16,097	3,883	1,926	1,112	814	1,957	1,085	598	487	872
Without income	2,670	303	180	112	68	123	65	31	33	59
With income	13,427	3,580	1,746	1,000	746	1,834	1,020	567	454	813
Under $10,000	3,628	1,136	391	210	180	745	373	182	190	372
$10,000 to $19,999	3,158	1,076	434	219	215	642	327	167	159	316
$20,000 to $29,999	2,295	497	301	165	135	196	137	87	48	60
$30,000 to $39,999	1,659	306	201	119	83	105	78	51	28	27
$40,000 to $49,999	1,016	202	145	98	48	57	39	24	15	17
$50,000 to $59,999	594	148	117	81	36	31	21	18	3	10
$60,000 to $69,999	435	87	65	41	24	22	18	15	2	4
$70,000 to $79,999	220	42	30	25	5	12	9	6	2	2
$80,000 to $89,999	139	32	26	21	5	6	4	2	2	2
$90,000 to $99,999	63	12	10	7	2	2	1	1	0	1
$100,000 or more	223	43	27	14	13	16	15	13	1	2
Median income of women with income	$19,712	$14,387	$21,208	$22,926	$18,451	$11,573	$12,300	$13,778	$11,376	$10,704
Median income of full-time workers	31,672	33,526	32,490	35,472	31,201	40,943	41,812	41,685	–	–
Percent working full-time	41.2%	24.2%	42.7%	48.0%	35.6%	5.9%	9.3%	14.7%	2.9%	1.5%
TOTAL BLACK WOMEN	100.0%	100.0%	100.0%	100.0%	100.0%	100.0%	100.0%	100.0%	100.0%	100.0%
Without income	16.6	7.8	9.3	10.1	8.4	6.3	6.0	5.2	6.8	6.8
With income	83.4	92.2	90.7	89.9	91.6	93.7	94.0	94.8	93.2	93.2
Under $10,000	22.5	29.3	20.3	18.9	22.1	38.1	34.4	30.4	39.0	42.7
$10,000 to $19,999	19.6	27.7	22.5	19.7	26.4	32.8	30.1	27.9	32.6	36.2
$20,000 to $29,999	14.3	12.8	15.6	14.8	16.6	10.0	12.6	14.5	9.9	6.9
$30,000 to $39,999	10.3	7.9	10.4	10.7	10.2	5.4	7.2	8.5	5.7	3.1
$40,000 to $49,999	6.3	5.2	7.5	8.8	5.9	2.9	3.6	4.0	3.1	1.9
$50,000 to $59,999	3.7	3.8	6.1	7.3	4.4	1.6	1.9	3.0	0.6	1.1
$60,000 to $69,999	2.7	2.2	3.4	3.7	2.9	1.1	1.7	2.5	0.4	0.5
$70,000 to $79,999	1.4	1.1	1.6	2.2	0.6	0.6	0.8	1.0	0.4	0.2
$80,000 to $89,999	0.9	0.8	1.3	1.9	0.6	0.3	0.4	0.3	0.4	0.2
$90,000 to $99,999	0.4	0.3	0.5	0.6	0.2	0.1	0.1	0.2	0.0	0.1
$100,000 or more	1.4	1.1	1.4	1.3	1.6	0.8	1.4	2.2	0.2	0.2

Note: Blacks include those who identify themselves as being of the race alone and those who identify themselves as being of the race in combination with other races. "–" means sample is too small to make a reliable estimate.
Source: Bureau of the Census, 2008 Current Population Survey Annual Social and Economic Supplement, Internet site http:// www.census.gov/hhes/www/macro/032008/perinc/new01_000.htm; calculations by New Strategist

Table 5.25 Income of Women Aged 55 or Older, 2007: Hispanic Women

(number and percent distribution of Hispanic women aged 15 or older and aged 55 or older by income, 2007; median income by work status, and percent working year-round, full-time; women in thousands as of 2008)

| | | aged 55 or older | | | | | aged 65 or older | | | |
| | | | aged 55 to 64 | | | | | aged 65 to 74 | | |
	total	total	total	55–59	60–64	total	total	65–69	70–74	75+
TOTAL HISPANIC WOMEN	**15,853**	**2,911**	**1,450**	**824**	**626**	**1,461**	**865**	**509**	**356**	**596**
Without income	**4,588**	**514**	**311**	**171**	**140**	**203**	**121**	**68**	**53**	**82**
With income	**11,265**	**2,397**	**1,139**	**653**	**486**	**1,258**	**744**	**441**	**303**	**514**
Under $10,000	3,397	1,013	360	184	175	653	398	225	172	257
$10,000 to $19,999	2,967	686	295	162	132	391	203	114	90	186
$20,000 to $29,999	1,973	256	155	91	63	101	62	35	28	38
$30,000 to $39,999	1,284	171	123	85	39	48	33	28	5	14
$40,000 to $49,999	675	99	75	53	22	24	17	13	3	6
$50,000 to $59,999	359	59	44	20	23	15	9	9	0	6
$60,000 to $69,999	202	36	25	17	9	11	8	7	1	3
$70,000 to $79,999	144	24	22	11	12	2	2	2	0	0
$80,000 to $89,999	66	14	9	7	1	5	5	2	3	0
$90,000 to $99,999	51	7	5	3	2	2	0	0	0	2
$100,000 or more	148	33	25	18	7	8	7	7	0	1
Median income of women with income	$16,748	$11,464	$16,788	$18,584	$14,422	$9,786	$9,625	$9,880	$9,315	$10,012
Median income of full-time workers	27,154	31,165	31,206	30,893	31,785	30,914	–	–	–	–
Percent working full-time	34.2%	20.4%	35.2%	42.0%	26.2%	5.7%	8.3%	11.8%	3.4%	2.0%
TOTAL HISPANIC WOMEN	**100.0%**	**100.0%**	**100.0%**	**100.0%**	**100.0%**	**100.0%**	**100.0%**	**100.0%**	**100.0%**	**100.0%**
Without income	**28.9**	**17.7**	**21.4**	**20.8**	**22.4**	**13.9**	**14.0**	**13.4**	**14.9**	**13.8**
With income	**71.1**	**82.3**	**78.6**	**79.2**	**77.6**	**86.1**	**86.0**	**86.6**	**85.1**	**86.2**
Under $10,000	21.4	34.8	24.8	22.3	28.0	44.7	46.0	44.2	48.3	43.1
$10,000 to $19,999	18.7	23.6	20.3	19.7	21.1	26.8	23.5	22.4	25.3	31.2
$20,000 to $29,999	12.4	8.8	10.7	11.0	10.1	6.9	7.2	6.9	7.9	6.4
$30,000 to $39,999	8.1	5.9	8.5	10.3	6.2	3.3	3.8	5.5	1.4	2.3
$40,000 to $49,999	4.3	3.4	5.2	6.4	3.5	1.6	2.0	2.6	0.8	1.0
$50,000 to $59,999	2.3	2.0	3.0	2.4	3.7	1.0	1.0	1.8	0.0	1.0
$60,000 to $69,999	1.3	1.2	1.7	2.1	1.4	0.8	0.9	1.4	0.3	0.5
$70,000 to $79,999	0.9	0.8	1.5	1.3	1.9	0.1	0.2	0.4	0.0	0.0
$80,000 to $89,999	0.4	0.5	0.6	0.8	0.2	0.3	0.6	0.4	0.8	0.0
$90,000 to $99,999	0.3	0.2	0.3	0.4	0.3	0.1	0.0	0.0	0.0	0.3
$100,000 or more	0.9	1.1	1.7	2.2	1.1	0.5	0.8	1.4	0.0	0.2

Note: "–" means sample is too small to make a reliable estimate.
Source: Bureau of the Census, 2008 Current Population Survey Annual Social and Economic Supplement, Internet site http://www.census.gov/hhes/www/macro/032008/perinc/new01_000.htm; calculations by New Strategist

Table 5.26 Income of Women Aged 55 or Older, 2007: Non-Hispanic White Women

(number and percent distribution of non-Hispanic white women aged 15 or older and aged 55 or older by income, 2007; median income by work status, and percent working year-round, full-time; women in thousands as of 2008)

| | | aged 55 or older | | | | | aged 65 or older | | | |
| | | | aged 55 to 64 | | | | aged 65 to 74 | | | |
	total	total	total	55–59	60–64	total	total	65–69	70–74	75+
TOTAL NON-HISPANIC WHITE WOMEN	83,534	29,686	12,957	7,015	5,942	16,729	8,164	4,518	3,646	8,565
Without income	8,632	1,393	980	566	414	413	210	107	104	202
With income	74,902	28,293	11,977	6,449	5,528	16,316	7,954	4,411	3,542	8,363
Under $10,000	18,386	7,012	2,483	1,120	1,360	4,529	2,279	1,237	1,041	2,251
$10,000 to $19,999	16,472	8,389	2,144	1,027	1,116	6,245	2,545	1,280	1,267	3,699
$20,000 to $29,999	11,666	4,312	1,860	1,048	812	2,452	1,166	666	499	1,286
$30,000 to $39,999	8,904	2,678	1,489	858	630	1,189	721	403	319	467
$40,000 to $49,999	6,403	1,867	1,250	731	518	617	427	293	134	188
$50,000 to $59,999	4,185	1,278	854	496	357	424	244	156	88	179
$60,000 to $69,999	2,719	770	544	350	193	226	153	95	59	74
$70,000 to $79,999	1,769	535	383	238	146	152	109	73	35	43
$80,000 to $89,999	1,053	329	224	134	89	105	72	55	18	33
$90,000 to $99,999	746	237	166	108	59	71	46	42	5	25
$100,000 or more	2,596	888	581	336	245	307	190	112	78	117
Median income of women with income	$21,687	$16,226	$26,794	$30,233	$22,636	$14,726	$15,352	$16,491	$14,526	$14,350
Median income of full-time workers	38,678	41,305	41,181	41,489	40,564	41,997	42,215	43,370	40,385	40,723
Percent working full-time	37.0%	21.9%	42.6%	51.1%	32.6%	5.9%	10.2%	14.0%	5.6%	1.8%
TOTAL NON-HISPANIC WHITE WOMEN	100.0%	100.0%	100.0%	100.0%	100.0%	100.0%	100.0%	100.0%	100.0%	100.0%
Without income	10.3	4.7	7.6	8.1	7.0	2.5	2.6	2.4	2.9	2.4
With income	89.7	95.3	92.4	91.9	93.0	97.5	97.4	97.6	97.1	97.6
Under $10,000	22.0	23.6	19.2	16.0	22.9	27.1	27.9	27.4	28.6	26.3
$10,000 to $19,999	19.7	28.3	16.5	14.6	18.8	37.3	31.2	28.3	34.8	43.2
$20,000 to $29,999	14.0	14.5	14.4	14.9	13.7	14.7	14.3	14.7	13.7	15.0
$30,000 to $39,999	10.7	9.0	11.5	12.2	10.6	7.1	8.8	8.9	8.7	5.5
$40,000 to $49,999	7.7	6.3	9.6	10.4	8.7	3.7	5.2	6.5	3.7	2.2
$50,000 to $59,999	5.0	4.3	6.6	7.1	6.0	2.5	3.0	3.5	2.4	2.1
$60,000 to $69,999	3.3	2.6	4.2	5.0	3.2	1.4	1.9	2.1	1.6	0.9
$70,000 to $79,999	2.1	1.8	3.0	3.4	2.5	0.9	1.3	1.6	1.0	0.5
$80,000 to $89,999	1.3	1.1	1.7	1.9	1.5	0.6	0.9	1.2	0.5	0.4
$90,000 to $99,999	0.9	0.8	1.3	1.5	1.0	0.4	0.6	0.9	0.1	0.3
$100,000 or more	3.1	3.0	4.5	4.8	4.1	1.8	2.3	2.5	2.1	1.4

Note: Non-Hispanic whites are only those who identify themselves as being white alone and not Hispanic.
Source: Bureau of the Census, 2008 Current Population Survey Annual Social and Economic Supplement, Internet site http://www.census.gov/hhes/www/macro/032008/perinc/new01_000.htm; calculations by New Strategist

Education Boosts Earnings of Older Americans

Men and women with a college degree earn the most.

College-educated men aged 55 to 64 who work full-time earned a median of $76,155 in 2007. This figure is 47 percent greater than the $51,962 earned by the average full-time worker in the age group. Among women aged 55 to 64 who work full-time, those with a college degree earned a median of $53,239—44 percent more than the $37,042 average.

Getting an education boosts earnings not only because the college-educated command higher salaries, but because they are more likely to work full-time. Among men aged 55 to 64, fully 68 percent of those with a college degree work full-time versus a smaller 54 percent of those with only a high school diploma. Among women aged 55 to 64, 49 percent of the college educated work full-time compared with 39 percent of women with no more than a high school diploma.

Education plays an important role in earnings even among people aged 65 or older. Eighteen percent of men aged 65 or older with a college diploma work full-time, with median earnings of $71,216 in 2007. In contrast, only 11 percent of their high school–educated counterparts work full-time, with median earnings of $36,441. Among women aged 65 or older who work full-time, those with a college degree earn nearly twice as much as those with only a high school diploma.

■ Education has long guaranteed higher earnings, but the warranty may be running out as the Internet allows educated workers in other countries to compete with Americans for the same jobs.

Among older Americans, college graduates earn more

(median earnings of full-time workers aged 55 to 64, by sex and educational attainment, 2007)

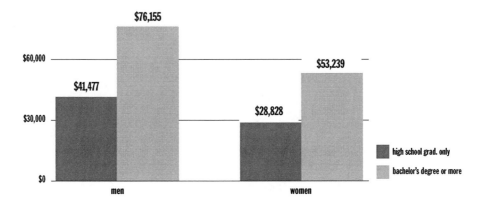

Table 5.27 Earnings of Men by Education, 2007: Aged 55 to 64

(number and percent distribution of men aged 55 to 64 by earnings and education, 2007; men in thousands as of 2008)

	total	less than 9th grade	9th to 12th grade, no degree	high school graduate, incl. GED	some college, no degree	associate's degree	bachelor's degree or more — total	bachelor's degree	master's degree	professional degree	doctoral degree
TOTAL MEN AGED 55 TO 64	16,079	783	1,046	4,464	2,869	1,368	5,549	3,182	1,532	429	405
Without earnings	4,184	374	477	1,356	762	317	898	613	222	28	35
With earnings	11,895	409	569	3,109	2,107	1,050	4,651	2,568	1,311	402	370
Under $10,000	830	52	78	231	154	78	237	159	66	7	5
$10,000 to $19,999	1,050	104	107	355	197	73	212	127	60	17	9
$20,000 to $29,999	1,425	109	107	549	297	94	270	193	60	8	10
$30,000 to $39,999	1,555	78	98	508	372	176	321	193	94	13	21
$40,000 to $49,999	1,392	23	67	494	245	149	415	228	161	13	13
$50,000 to $59,999	1,237	18	46	337	249	142	443	262	140	13	29
$60,000 to $69,999	999	4	19	237	208	98	434	250	116	31	36
$70,000 to $79,999	714	7	15	138	115	69	369	207	101	30	30
$80,000 to $89,999	545	2	10	94	75	65	298	171	80	20	26
$90,000 to $99,999	343	1	3	23	34	17	263	128	97	18	21
$100,000 or more	1,809	11	17	141	162	89	1,388	649	335	232	172
Median earnings of men with earnings	$46,648	$22,225	$29,132	$36,768	$40,680	$46,154	$69,443	$62,094	$64,161	$100,000+	$91,399
Median earnings of full-time workers	51,962	26,468	35,735	41,477	47,061	51,058	76,155	70,776	72,326	100,000+	100,000+
Percent working full-time	58.1%	38.1%	37.3%	54.3%	56.4%	60.9%	68.2%	65.4%	69.3%	78.8%	74.1%
TOTAL MEN AGED 55 TO 64	100.0%	100.0%	100.0%	100.0%	100.0%	100.0%	100.0%	100.0%	100.0%	100.0%	100.0%
Without earnings	26.0	47.8	45.6	30.4	26.6	23.2	16.2	19.3	14.5	6.5	8.6
With earnings	74.0	52.2	54.4	69.6	73.4	76.8	83.8	80.7	85.6	93.7	91.4
Under $10,000	5.2	6.6	7.5	5.2	5.4	5.7	4.3	5.0	4.3	1.6	1.2
$10,000 to $19,999	6.5	13.3	10.2	8.0	6.9	5.3	3.8	4.0	3.9	4.0	2.2
$20,000 to $29,999	8.9	13.9	10.2	12.3	10.4	6.9	4.9	6.1	3.9	1.9	2.5
$30,000 to $39,999	9.7	10.0	9.4	11.4	13.0	12.9	5.8	6.1	6.1	3.0	5.2
$40,000 to $49,999	8.7	2.9	6.4	11.1	8.5	10.9	7.5	7.2	10.5	3.0	3.2
$50,000 to $59,999	7.7	2.3	4.4	7.5	8.7	10.4	8.0	8.2	9.1	3.0	7.2
$60,000 to $69,999	6.2	0.5	1.8	5.3	7.2	7.2	7.8	7.9	7.6	7.2	8.9
$70,000 to $79,999	4.4	0.9	1.4	3.1	4.0	5.0	6.6	6.5	6.6	7.0	7.4
$80,000 to $89,999	3.4	0.3	1.0	2.1	2.6	4.8	5.4	5.4	5.2	4.7	6.4
$90,000 to $99,999	2.1	0.1	0.3	0.5	1.2	1.2	4.7	4.0	6.3	4.2	5.2
$100,000 or more	11.3	1.4	1.6	3.2	5.6	6.5	25.0	20.4	21.9	54.1	42.5

Source: Bureau of the Census, 2008 Current Population Survey Annual Social and Economic Supplement, Internet site http://www.census.gov/hhes/www/macro/032008/perinc/new03_000.htm; calculations by New Strategist

Table 5.28 Earnings of Men by Education, 2007: Aged 65 or Older

(number and percent distribution of men aged 65 or older by earnings and education, 2007; men in thousands as of 2008)

	total	less than 9th grade	9th to 12th grade, no degree	high school graduate, incl. GED	some college, no degree	associate's degree	bachelor's degree or more total	bachelor's degree	master's degree	professional degree	doctoral degree
TOTAL MEN AGED 65 OR OLDER	15,762	1,781	1,705	5,045	2,326	695	4,210	2,279	1,165	351	414
Without earnings	11,826	1,563	1,430	3,927	1,686	464	2,757	1,578	766	196	217
With earnings	3,936	217	275	1,119	640	231	1,453	701	400	155	197
Under $10,000	879	51	84	308	152	49	236	110	87	18	21
$10,000 to $19,999	667	65	48	222	114	22	197	116	46	18	17
$20,000 to $29,999	494	41	43	165	84	22	138	75	32	8	22
$30,000 to $39,999	386	33	36	109	82	21	103	49	28	14	11
$40,000 to $49,999	299	11	17	86	68	37	81	58	17	0	5
$50,000 to $59,999	249	0	18	59	48	27	98	54	28	6	10
$60,000 to $69,999	199	3	6	43	23	16	104	50	34	8	14
$70,000 to $79,999	126	5	10	21	21	9	59	32	20	3	2
$80,000 to $89,999	114	0	2	26	18	13	55	21	16	3	15
$90,000 to $99,999	81	1	0	15	8	6	49	22	5	17	6
$100,000 or more	443	7	9	63	24	7	333	112	87	58	76
Median earnings of men with earnings	$27,454	$18,615	$20,577	$21,537	$26,083	$40,009	$44,211	$39,286	$41,927	$80,001	$75,251
Median earnings of full-time workers	45,340	26,835	31,876	36,441	41,666	51,381	71,216	52,066	77,331	96,996	100,000+
Percent working full-time	12.7%	5.7%	9.1%	10.8%	13.1%	19.1%	18.2%	16.5%	15.8%	25.4%	28.7%
TOTAL MEN AGED 65 OR OLDER	100.0%	100.0%	100.0%	100.0%	100.0%	100.0%	100.0%	100.0%	100.0%	100.0%	100.0%
Without earnings	75.0	87.8	83.9	77.8	72.5	66.8	65.5	69.2	65.8	55.8	52.4
With earnings	25.0	12.2	16.1	22.2	27.5	33.2	34.5	30.8	34.3	44.2	47.6
Under $10,000	5.6	2.9	4.9	6.1	6.5	7.1	5.6	4.8	7.5	5.1	5.1
$10,000 to $19,999	4.2	3.6	2.8	4.4	4.9	3.2	4.7	5.1	3.9	5.1	4.1
$20,000 to $29,999	3.1	2.3	2.5	3.3	3.6	3.2	3.3	3.3	2.7	2.3	5.3
$30,000 to $39,999	2.4	1.9	2.1	2.2	3.5	3.0	2.4	2.2	2.4	4.0	2.7
$40,000 to $49,999	1.9	0.6	1.0	1.7	2.9	5.3	1.9	2.5	1.5	0.0	1.2
$50,000 to $59,999	1.6	0.0	1.1	1.2	2.1	3.9	2.3	2.4	2.4	1.7	2.4
$60,000 to $69,999	1.3	0.2	0.4	0.9	1.0	2.3	2.5	2.2	2.9	2.3	3.4
$70,000 to $79,999	0.8	0.3	0.6	0.4	0.9	1.3	1.4	1.4	1.7	0.9	0.5
$80,000 to $89,999	0.7	0.0	0.1	0.5	0.8	1.9	1.3	0.9	1.4	0.9	3.6
$90,000 to $99,999	0.5	0.1	0.0	0.3	0.3	0.9	1.2	1.0	0.4	4.8	1.4
$100,000 or more	2.8	0.4	0.5	1.2	1.0	1.0	7.9	4.9	7.5	16.5	18.4

Source: Bureau of the Census, 2008 Current Population Survey Annual Social and Economic Supplement, Internet site http://www.census.gov/hhes/www/macro/032008/perinc/new03_000.htm; calculations by New Strategist

Table 5.29 Earnings of Women by Education, 2007: Aged 55 to 64

(number and percent distribution of women aged 55 to 64 by earnings and education, 2007; women in thousands as of 2008)

	total	less than 9th grade	9th to 12th grade, no degree	high school graduate, incl. GED	some college, no degree	associate's degree	bachelor's degree or more				
							total	bachelor's degree	master's degree	professional degree	doctoral degree
TOTAL WOMEN AGED 55 TO 64	17,223	798	1,108	5,756	3,143	1,598	4,819	2,915	1,523	182	200
Without earnings	6,333	532	648	2,354	1,072	449	1,278	845	347	46	39
With earnings	10,890	267	460	3,403	2,070	1,149	3,541	2,069	1,176	136	160
Under $10,000	1,509	104	128	531	269	107	372	234	126	8	3
$10,000 to $19,999	1,868	94	175	818	321	172	288	211	62	6	8
$20,000 to $29,999	1,989	46	69	834	442	222	376	282	74	11	9
$30,000 to $39,999	1,674	10	53	614	347	240	412	277	113	9	10
$40,000 to $49,999	1,287	7	20	297	287	166	508	333	155	9	12
$50,000 to $59,999	895	5	11	141	163	104	470	214	224	10	22
$60,000 to $69,999	537	0	0	63	100	71	302	170	95	6	30
$70,000 to $79,999	387	0	0	44	43	29	271	129	108	15	18
$80,000 to $89,999	230	0	0	21	35	22	152	63	68	13	8
$90,000 to $99,999	121	0	0	21	6	4	89	31	47	5	7
$100,000 or more	394	0	4	17	56	14	303	125	104	43	31
Median earnings of women with earnings	$30,282	$12,859	$15,606	$23,426	$30,039	$31,615	$46,216	$40,602	$51,595	$73,559	$61,887
Median earnings of full-time workers	37,042	19,730	19,440	28,828	36,222	37,159	53,239	48,895	58,249	85,293	67,397
Percent working full-time	41.9%	14.9%	22.9%	39.5%	45.5%	48.0%	49.1%	48.1%	50.2%	52.7%	52.5%
TOTAL WOMEN AGED 55 TO 64	100.0%	100.0%	100.0%	100.0%	100.0%	100.0%	100.0%	100.0%	100.0%	100.0%	100.0%
Without earnings	36.8	66.7	58.5	40.9	34.1	28.1	26.5	29.0	22.8	25.3	19.5
With earnings	63.2	33.5	41.5	59.1	65.9	71.9	73.5	71.0	77.2	74.7	80.0
Under $10,000	8.8	13.0	11.6	9.2	8.6	6.7	7.7	8.0	8.3	4.4	1.5
$10,000 to $19,999	10.8	11.8	15.8	14.2	10.2	10.8	6.0	7.2	4.1	3.3	4.0
$20,000 to $29,999	11.5	5.8	6.2	14.5	14.1	13.9	7.8	9.7	4.9	6.0	4.5
$30,000 to $39,999	9.7	1.3	4.8	10.7	11.0	15.0	8.5	9.5	7.4	4.9	5.0
$40,000 to $49,999	7.5	0.9	1.8	5.2	9.1	10.4	10.5	11.4	10.2	4.9	6.0
$50,000 to $59,999	5.2	0.6	1.0	2.4	5.2	6.5	9.8	7.3	14.7	5.5	11.0
$60,000 to $69,999	3.1	0.0	0.0	1.1	3.2	4.4	6.3	5.8	6.2	3.3	15.0
$70,000 to $79,999	2.2	0.0	0.0	0.8	1.4	1.8	5.6	4.4	7.1	8.2	9.0
$80,000 to $89,999	1.3	0.0	0.0	0.4	1.1	1.4	3.2	2.2	4.5	7.1	4.0
$90,000 to $99,999	0.7	0.0	0.0	0.4	0.2	0.3	1.8	1.1	3.1	2.7	3.5
$100,000 or more	2.3	0.0	0.4	0.3	1.8	0.9	6.3	4.3	6.8	23.6	15.5

Source: Bureau of the Census, 2008 Current Population Survey Annual Social and Economic Supplement, Internet site http://www.census.gov/hhes/www/macro/032008/perinc/new03_000.htm; calculations by New Strategist

Table 5.30 Earnings of Women by Education, 2007: Aged 65 or Older

(number and percent distribution of women aged 65 or older by earnings and education, 2007; women in thousands as of 2008)

	total	less than 9th grade	9th to 12th grade, no degree	high school graduate, incl. GED	some college, no degree	associate's degree	bachelor's degree or more total	bachelor's degree	master's degree	professional degree	doctoral degree
TOTAL WOMEN AGED 65 OR OLDER	21,028	2,343	2,479	8,513	3,197	1,181	3,314	2,127	964	102	121
Without earnings	17,728	2,221	2,218	7,287	2,595	929	2,479	1,636	693	73	77
With earnings	3,300	123	261	1,226	602	252	836	491	271	29	45
Under $10,000	1,148	63	97	460	216	71	243	148	83	5	8
$10,000 to $19,999	729	45	107	301	120	45	111	74	29	0	7
$20,000 to $29,999	497	6	38	219	78	56	100	79	18	0	3
$30,000 to $39,999	299	2	12	114	81	23	66	37	22	0	5
$40,000 to $49,999	210	1	3	68	47	15	76	40	31	1	3
$50,000 to $59,999	161	3	2	31	22	21	82	43	31	6	2
$60,000 to $69,999	86	3	0	19	7	12	45	30	10	2	2
$70,000 to $79,999	58	0	0	4	6	4	42	15	22	1	7
$80,000 to $89,999	35	0	0	4	2	0	30	8	13	4	4
$90,000 to $99,999	12	0	0	2	3	0	6	5	0	1	0
$100,000 or more	65	0	4	5	19	3	33	12	12	7	3
Median earnings of women with earnings	$15,714	$9,713	$11,749	$13,487	$15,949	$21,270	$24,032	$21,488	$30,996	–	–
Median earnings of full-time workers	31,517	–	20,625	26,489	36,403	40,482	50,467	46,367	55,114	–	–
Percent working full-time	6.0%	1.8%	3.1%	5.6%	7.6%	7.3%	10.3%	9.6%	10.4%	16.7%	15.7%
TOTAL WOMEN AGED 65 OR OLDER	100.0%	100.0%	100.0%	100.0%	100.0%	100.0%	100.0%	100.0%	100.0%	100.0%	100.0%
Without earnings	84.3	94.8	89.5	85.6	81.2	78.7	74.8	76.9	71.9	71.6	63.6
With earnings	15.7	5.2	10.5	14.4	18.8	21.3	25.2	23.1	28.1	28.4	37.2
Under $10,000	5.5	2.7	3.9	5.4	6.8	6.0	7.3	7.0	8.6	4.9	6.6
$10,000 to $19,999	3.5	1.9	4.3	3.5	3.8	3.8	3.3	3.5	3.0	0.0	5.8
$20,000 to $29,999	2.4	0.3	1.5	2.6	2.4	4.7	3.0	3.7	1.9	0.0	2.5
$30,000 to $39,999	1.4	0.1	0.5	1.3	2.5	1.9	2.0	1.7	2.3	0.0	4.1
$40,000 to $49,999	1.0	0.0	0.1	0.8	1.5	1.3	2.3	1.9	3.2	1.0	2.5
$50,000 to $59,999	0.8	0.1	0.1	0.4	0.7	1.8	2.5	2.0	3.2	5.9	1.7
$60,000 to $69,999	0.4	0.1	0.0	0.2	0.2	1.0	1.4	1.4	1.0	2.0	1.7
$70,000 to $79,999	0.3	0.0	0.0	0.0	0.2	0.3	1.3	0.7	2.3	1.0	5.8
$80,000 to $89,999	0.2	0.0	0.0	0.0	0.1	0.0	0.9	0.4	1.3	3.9	3.3
$90,000 to $99,999	0.1	0.0	0.0	0.0	0.1	0.0	0.2	0.2	0.0	1.0	0.0
$100,000 or more	0.3	0.0	0.2	0.1	0.6	0.3	1.0	0.6	1.2	6.9	2.5

Note: "–" means sample is too small to make a reliable estimate.
Source: Bureau of the Census, 2008 Current Population Survey Annual Social and Economic Supplement, Internet site http://www.census.gov/hhes/www/macro/032008/perinc/new03_000.htm; calculations by New Strategist

Most Older Americans Receive Social Security

The Social Security income of older Americans exceeds their pension or interest income.

Among Americans aged 65 or older, 88 percent of men and 90 percent of women received income from Social Security in 2007, making it the most common source of income for the age group. The amount of Social Security income received by people aged 65 or older is modest, however, the median ranging from $10,000 for women to $14,054 for men. Among men and women aged 55 to 64, only 17 and 20 percent, respectively, receive Social Security, most collecting it because they opted to retire at age 62.

Besides Social Security, the only other type of income the majority of people aged 65 or older received is interest, with just about half receiving it. But the median amount of interest income older Americans received is small, a median of about $1,860 annually.

Forty percent of men aged 65 or older received pension income in 2007, collecting a median of $12,505. A much smaller 22 percent of women receive pension income, and the amount they collect is also smaller than that of men—a median of just $8,110 in 2007.

■ When Boomers enter the 65-or-older age group, expect the percentage of older Americans with earnings to increase.

Social Security income is modest

(median annual Social Security income received by people aged 65 or older, by sex, 2007)

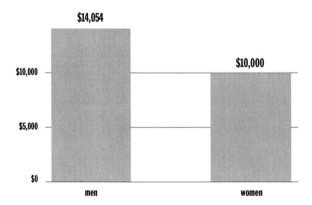

Table 5.31 Sources of Income for Men Aged 55 to 64, 2007

(number and percent distribution of men aged 55 to 64 with income and median income for those with income, by selected sources of income, 2007; men in thousands as of 2008; ranked by percent receiving source)

	number	percent with income	median income
Total men aged 55 to 64 with income	**15,522**	**100.0%**	**$42,129**
Earnings	11,895	76.6	46,648
Wages and salary	10,606	68.3	47,159
Nonfarm self-employment	1,569	10.1	26,142
Farm self-employment	299	1.9	6,024
Property income	8,799	56.7	2,069
Interest	8,256	53.2	1,715
Dividends	3,887	25.0	1,990
Rents, royalties, estates, or trusts	1,285	8.3	2,316
Retirement income	2,888	18.6	18,880
Company or union retirement	1,607	10.4	13,025
State or local government retirement	599	3.9	27,149
Military retirement	307	2.0	20,046
Federal government retirement	236	1.5	25,954
IRA, Keogh, or 401(k)	62	0.4	–
Annuities	42	0.3	–
Railroad retirement	51	0.3	–
Other or don't know	97	0.6	11,291
Social Security	2,577	16.6	13,347
Pension income	2,558	16.5	19,662
Company or union retirement	1,482	9.5	13,693
State or local government retirement	546	3.5	28,273
Military retirement	285	1.8	20,152
Federal government retirement	210	1.4	28,834
Railroad retirement	32	0.2	–
Annuities	19	0.1	–
Veterans' benefits	709	4.6	9,426
Unemployment compensation	483	3.1	3,881
Supplemental Security Income	393	2.5	7,866
Disability benefits	309	2.0	9,330
Workers' compensation	196	1.3	8,195
Survivor benefits	118	0.8	10,163
Educational assistance	55	0.4	–
Financial assistance from other household	40	0.3	–
Public assistance	41	0.3	–
Child support	13	0.1	–
Alimony	0	0.0	–
Other income	90	0.6	1,484

Note: "–" means sample is too small to make a reliable estimate.
Source: Bureau of the Census, 2008 Current Population Survey Annual Social and Economic Supplement, Internet site http://pubdb3.census.gov/macro/032008/perinc/new08_000.htm; calculations by New Strategist

Table 5.32 Sources of Income for Men Aged 65 or Older, 2007

(number and percent distribution of men aged 65 or older with income and median income for those with income, by selected sources of income, 2007; men in thousands as of 2008; ranked by percent receiving source)

	number	percent with income	median income
Total men aged 65 or older with income	**15,317**	**100.0%**	**$24,323**
Social Security	13,428	87.7	14,054
Property income	8,671	56.6	2,323
Interest	8,153	53.2	1,928
Dividends	3,454	22.6	2,093
Rents, royalties, estates, or trusts	1,225	8.0	3,159
Retirement income	6,618	43.2	12,476
Company or union retirement	4,509	29.4	9,440
State or local government retirement	934	6.1	21,757
Federal government retirement	599	3.9	23,661
Military retirement	345	2.3	17,733
IRA, Keogh, or 401(k)	232	1.5	10,644
Annuities	136	0.9	4,718
Railroad retirement	78	0.5	21,058
Other or don't know	162	1.1	9,102
Pension income	6,197	40.5	12,505
Company or union retirement	4,347	28.4	9,495
State or local government retirement	905	5.9	22,180
Federal government retirement	563	3.7	23,834
Military retirement	327	2.1	18,269
Annuities	88	0.6	4,435
Railroad retirement	77	0.5	20,956
Earnings	3,936	25.7	27,454
Wages and salary	3,271	21.4	28,547
Nonfarm self-employment	668	4.4	20,016
Farm self-employment	183	1.2	10,517
Veterans' benefits	837	5.5	7,811
Supplemental Security Income	334	2.2	5,627
Survivor benefits	290	1.9	7,131
Disability benefits	129	0.8	7,728
Unemployment compensation	106	0.7	2,507
Workers' compensation	61	0.4	–
Financial assistance from other household	47	0.3	–
Public assistance	19	0.1	–
Alimony	2	0.0	–
Child support	1	0.0	–
Educational assistance	0	0.0	–
Other income	99	0.6	1,732

Note: "–" means sample is too small to make a reliable estimate.
Source: Bureau of the Census, 2008 Current Population Survey Annual Social and Economic Supplement, Internet site http:// pubdb3.census.gov/macro/032008/perinc/new08_000.htm; calculations by New Strategist

Table 5.33 Sources of Income for Women Aged 55 to 64, 2007

(number and percent distribution of women aged 55 to 64 with income and median income for those with income, by selected sources of income, 2007; women in thousands as of 2008; ranked by percent receiving source)

	number	percent with income	median income
Total women aged 55 to 64 with income	**15,601**	**100.0%**	**$25,262**
Earnings	10,890	69.8	30,282
Wages and salary	10,167	65.2	30,634
Nonfarm self-employment	974	6.2	13,295
Farm self-employment	126	0.8	2,406
Property income	8,846	56.7	1,958
Interest	8,295	53.2	1,688
Dividends	3,581	23.0	1,806
Rents, royalties, estates, or trusts	1,135	7.3	2,218
Social Security	3,032	19.4	9,119
Retirement income	2,058	13.2	13,253
Company or union retirement	924	5.9	10,106
State or local government retirement	751	4.8	18,510
Federal government retirement	161	1.0	19,639
Annuities	68	0.4	–
Military retirement	41	0.3	–
IRA, Keogh, or 401(k)	37	0.2	–
Railroad retirement	10	0.1	–
Other or don't know	154	1.0	7,034
Pension income	1,505	9.6	15,132
Company or union retirement	676	4.3	10,557
State or local government retirement	648	4.2	19,932
Federal government retirement	108	0.7	19,644
Military retirement	24	0.2	–
Annuities	21	0.1	–
Railroad retirement	5	0.0	–
Supplemental Security Income	577	3.7	6,977
Survivor benefits	409	2.6	10,116
Disability benefits	294	1.9	6,999
Unemployment compensation	283	1.8	3,489
Workers' compensation	207	1.3	2,271
Public assistance	113	0.7	2,451
Alimony	109	0.7	9,955
Child support	92	0.6	3,181
Veterans' benefits	82	0.5	6,102
Educational assistance	73	0.5	–
Financial assistance from other household	73	0.5	–
Other income	101	0.6	1,681

Note: "–" means sample is too small to make a reliable estimate.
Source: Bureau of the Census, 2008 Current Population Survey Annual Social and Economic Supplement, Internet site http://pubdb3.census.gov/macro/032008/perinc/new08_000.htm; calculations by New Strategist

Table 5.34 Sources of Income for Women Aged 65 or older, 2007

(number and percent distribution of women aged 65 or older with income and median income for those with income, by selected sources of income, 2007; women in thousands as of 2008; ranked by percent receiving source)

	number	percent with income	median income
Total women 65 or older with income	**20,167**	**100.0%**	**$14,021**
Social Security	18,128	89.9	10,000
Property income	10,119	50.2	2,089
Interest	9,616	47.7	1,801
Dividends	3,329	16.5	2,068
Rents, royalties, estates, or trusts	1,256	6.2	3,178
Retirement income	5,831	28.9	8,152
Company or union retirement	3,331	16.5	5,389
State or local government retirement	1,458	7.2	11,687
Federal government retirement	536	2.7	13,214
IRA, Keogh, or 401(k)	166	0.8	5,296
Annuities	130	0.6	5,392
Military retirement	112	0.6	10,307
Railroad retirement	95	0.5	12,390
Other or don't know	274	1.4	10,386
Pension income	4,472	22.2	8,110
Company or union retirement	2,607	12.9	5,136
State or local government retirement	1,346	6.7	11,729
Federal government retirement	316	1.6	16,290
Annuities	54	0.3	–
Railroad retirement	50	0.2	–
Military retirement	21	0.1	–
Earnings	3,300	16.4	15,714
Wages and salary	2,916	14.5	16,376
Nonfarm self-employment	381	1.9	9,859
Farm self-employment	65	0.3	–
Survivor benefits	1,585	7.9	7,042
Supplemental Security Income	803	4.0	4,328
Veterans' benefits	153	0.8	11,023
Financial assistance from other household	112	0.6	3,789
Unemployment compensation	98	0.5	3,621
Disability benefits	68	0.3	–
Public assistance	61	0.3	–
Workers' compensation	52	0.3	–
Alimony	47	0.2	–
Child support	29	0.1	–
Educational assistance	4	0.0	–
Other income	114	0.6	1,560

Note: "–" means sample is too small to make a reliable estimate.
Source: Bureau of the Census, 2008 Current Population Survey Annual Social and Economic Supplement, Internet site http:// pubdb3.census.gov/macro/032008/perinc/new08_000.htm; calculations by New Strategist

Poverty Rate Is below Average for Older Americans

Only 9.2 percent of people aged 55 or older are poor compared with a larger 12.5 percent of all Americans.

Of the nation's 37 million poor in 2007, just 17 percent were aged 55 or older. Older blacks are three times as likely to be poor as non-Hispanic whites, however. Among people aged 55 or older, only 10.4 percent of Asians and 7.0 percent of non-Hispanic whites are poor versus 16.3 percent of Hispanics and 20.8 percent of blacks.

Among Americans of all ages, non-Hispanic whites account for a 43 percent minority of the poor. Among Americans aged 55 or older, however, non-Hispanic whites account for the 59 percent majority of the poor. Blacks account for 21 percent of the poor in the age group and Hispanics for 14 percent.

■ The black and Hispanic share of poor people aged 55 or older will rise as more diverse younger generations enter the 55-or-older age groups.

Among older Americans, blacks are most likely to be poor

(percent of people aged 55 or older who live below poverty level, by race and Hispanic origin, 2007)

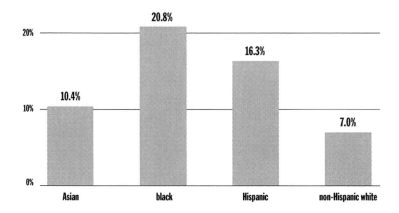

Table 5.35 People below Poverty Level by Age, Race, and Hispanic Origin, 2007

(number, percent, and percent distribution of people below poverty level by age, race, and Hispanic origin, 2007; people in thousands as of 2008)

	total	Asian	black	Hispanic	non-Hispanic white
NUMBER IN POVERTY					
Total people	**37,276**	**1,467**	**9,668**	**9,890**	**16,032**
Under age 55	30,852	1,193	8,290	9,019	12,218
Aged 55 or older	6,431	274	1,380	872	3,815
Aged 55 to 59	1,471	59	375	241	779
Aged 60 to 64	1,403	70	256	194	856
Aged 65 or older	3,557	145	749	437	2,180
Aged 65 to 74	1,727	71	442	252	929
Aged 75 to 84	1,272	57	234	134	837
Aged 85 or older	558	17	73	51	414
PERCENT IN POVERTY					
Total people	**12.5%**	**10.2%**	**24.4%**	**21.5%**	**8.2%**
Under age 55	13.5	10.1	25.2	22.2	8.6
Aged 55 or older	9.2	10.4	20.8	16.3	7.0
Aged 55 to 59	8.0	7.6	18.5	15.0	5.7
Aged 60 to 64	9.4	12.4	18.2	16.4	7.4
Aged 65 or older	9.7	11.2	23.3	17.1	7.4
Aged 65 to 74	8.8	9.2	23.6	16.5	6.1
Aged 75 to 84	9.9	16.8	22.5	16.9	7.9
Aged 85 or older	13.0	13.6	24.3	21.8	11.5
PERCENT DISTRIBUTION OF POOR BY AGE					
Total people	**100.0%**	**100.0%**	**100.0%**	**100.0%**	**100.0%**
Under age 55	82.8	81.3	85.7	91.2	76.2
Aged 55 or older	17.3	18.7	14.3	8.8	23.8
Aged 55 to 59	3.9	4.0	3.9	2.4	4.9
Aged 60 to 64	3.8	4.8	2.6	2.0	5.3
Aged 65 or older	9.5	9.9	7.7	4.4	13.6
Aged 65 to 74	4.6	4.8	4.6	2.5	5.8
Aged 75 to 84	3.4	3.9	2.4	1.4	5.2
Aged 85 or older	1.5	1.2	0.8	0.5	2.6
PERCENT DISTRIBUTION OF POOR BY RACE AND HISPANIC ORIGIN					
Total people	**100.0%**	**3.9%**	**25.9%**	**26.5%**	**43.0%**
Under age 55	100.0	3.9	26.9	29.2	39.6
Aged 55 or older	100.0	4.3	21.5	13.6	59.3
Aged 55 to 59	100.0	4.0	25.5	16.4	53.0
Aged 60 to 64	100.0	5.0	18.2	13.8	61.0
Aged 65 or older	100.0	4.1	21.1	12.3	61.3
Aged 65 to 74	100.0	4.1	25.6	14.6	53.8
Aged 75 to 84	100.0	4.5	18.4	10.5	65.8
Aged 85 or older	100.0	3.0	13.1	9.1	74.2

Note: Numbers do not add to total because Asians and blacks include those who identify themselves as being of the race alone and those who identify themselves as being of the race in combination with other races, because Hispanics may be of any race, and because not all races are shown. Non-Hispanic whites are those who identify themselves as being white alone and not Hispanic.
Source: Bureau of the Census, 2008 Current Population Survey Annual Social and Economic Supplement, Internet site http://www.census.gov/hhes/www/macro/032008/pov/new34_100.htm; calculations by New Strategist

6

Labor Force

■ The end of early retirement can be seen in labor force participation trends among older Americans. Since 2000, the percentage of men aged 55 or older in the labor force has grown.

■ The sixties is a time of transition for most Americans, when their roles change from worker to retiree. The labor force participation rate drops sharply for men and women as they age through their sixties.

■ The proportion of couples in which neither husband nor wife works becomes the majority in the 65-to-74 age group.

■ Only 12 percent of all men in the labor force work part-time, but the proportion is a higher 16 percent among men aged 55 or older.

■ Men and women aged 55 or older account for 31 percent of the self-employed, a much greater proportion than their share of all workers.

■ Older workers are staying on the job rather than face retirement with diminished resources. The percentage of men aged 65 or older who have been with their current employer for at least 10 years increased from 49 percent in 2000 to 59 percent in 2008.

■ Among men aged 65 or older, the Bureau of Labor Statistics projects a rise in labor force participation of 6.8 percentage points, to 27.1 percent by 2016. The increase is likely to be even greater because these projections were made before the economic turmoil of 2008.

Older Men Are More Likely to Work

The increase in participation has been especially sharp for men aged 60 to 69.

The end of early retirement can be seen clearly in labor force participation trends among older Americans. Since 2000—and despite (or perhaps because of) the weak economy—the percentage of men aged 55 or older in the labor force has grown, in some age groups substantially. The labor force participation rate of men aged 60 to 64, the age of early retirement, grew 5.0 percentage points between 2000 and 2008—to 59.9 percent. Among men aged 65 to 69, labor force participation increased 5.3 percentage points between 2000 and 2008—to 35.6 percent, the highest rate in more than two decades.

Among older women, labor force participation rose substantially as well. Much of the increase is a consequence of the entry of a more career-oriented generation into the age group. Nevertheless, some of the rise is also due to the loss of retirement wealth in the financial collapse of 2008, which drives older Americans back to work to supplement their dwindling retirement income.

■ As the Baby-Boom generation fills the 55-or-older age groups, the labor force participation rate of older Americans will continue to rise as early retirement becomes less common.

A growing share of older men are in the labor force

(percent of men aged 60 to 74 in the labor force, by age, 2000 and 2008)

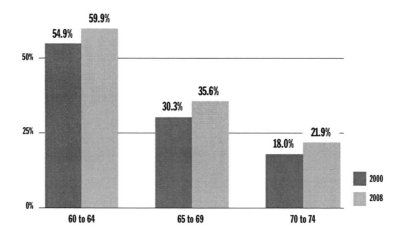

Table 6.1 Labor Force Participation Rate of People Aged 55 or Older by Sex, 2000 and 2008

(civilian labor force participation rate of people aged 16 or older and aged 55 or older by sex and age, 2000 and 2008; percentage point change, 2000–08)

	2008	2000	percentage point change
Men aged 16 or older	**73.0%**	**74.8%**	**−1.8**
Aged 16 to 19	40.1	52.8	−12.7
Aged 20 to 24	78.7	82.6	−3.9
Aged 25 to 54	90.5	91.6	−1.1
Aged 55 or older	46.0	39.8	6.2
Aged 55 to 64	70.4	67.3	3.1
Aged 55 to 59	78.8	77.0	1.8
Aged 60 to 64	59.9	54.9	5.0
Aged 65 or older	21.5	17.7	3.8
Aged 65 to 69	35.6	30.3	5.3
Aged 70 to 74	21.9	18.0	3.9
Aged 75 or older	10.4	8.1	2.3
Women aged 16 or older	**59.5**	**59.9**	**−0.4**
Aged 16 to 19	40.2	51.2	−11.0
Aged 20 to 24	70.0	73.1	−3.1
Aged 25 to 54	75.8	76.8	−1.0
Aged 55 or older	33.9	26.2	7.7
Aged 55 to 64	59.1	51.9	7.2
Aged 55 to 59	67.7	61.4	6.3
Aged 60 to 64	48.7	40.2	8.5
Aged 65 or older	13.3	9.4	3.9
Aged 65 to 69	26.4	19.5	6.9
Aged 70 to 74	14.3	10.0	4.3
Aged 75 or older	5.2	3.6	1.6

Source: Bureau of Labor Statistics, Public Query Data Tool, Internet site http://www.bls.gov/data; and 2008 Current Population Survey, Internet site http://www.bls.gov/cps/tables.htm#empstat; calculations by New Strategist

Labor Force Participation Rate Drops Sharply after Age 55

Most men aged 60 to 64 are in the labor force, but a minority of those aged 65 to 69 are still working.

The sixties is a time of transition for most Americans, when their role changes from worker to retiree. The labor force participation rate drops sharply with age. Among men aged 55 to 59, fully 78.8 percent are in the labor force. The figure falls to 59.9 percent among those aged 60 to 64, then drops to 35.6 percent among those aged 65 to 69. Only 10.4 percent of men aged 75 or older are in the labor force.

The 67.7 percent majority of women aged 55 to 59 are in the labor force, a figure that falls to a 48.7 percent minority among women aged 60 to 64. Only 26.4 percent of women aged 65 to 69 and 5.2 percent of those aged 75 or older are in the labor force.

■ The labor force participation rate of older Americans will rise in the coming decades as Baby Boomers postpone retirement.

Labor force participation falls with age

(percent of people aged 55 or older in the labor force, by sex, 2008)

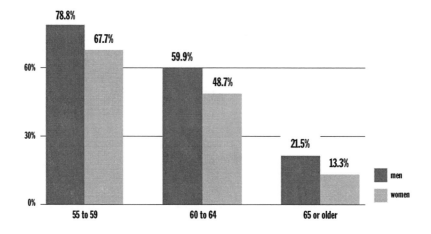

Table 6.2 Employment Status by Sex and Age, 2008

(number and percent of people aged 16 or older in the civilian labor force by sex and age, 2008; numbers in thousands)

	civilian noninstitutional population	civilian labor force			unemployed	
		total	percent of population	employed	number	percent of labor force
Total, aged 16 or older	**233,788**	**154,287**	**66.0%**	**145,362**	**8,924**	**5.8%**
Under age 55	163,136	126,429	77.5	118,571	7,857	6.2
Aged 55 or older	70,652	27,858	39.4	26,791	1,067	3.8
Aged 55 to 59	18,444	13,480	73.1	12,969	511	3.8
Aged 60 to 64	15,047	8,135	54.1	7,843	292	3.6
Aged 65 or older	37,161	6,243	16.8	5,979	264	4.2
Aged 65 to 69	11,242	3,451	30.7	3,307	144	4.2
Aged 70 to 74	8,639	1,534	17.8	1,462	72	4.7
Aged 75 or older	17,281	1,258	7.3	1,211	48	3.8
Men, aged 16 or older	**113,113**	**82,520**	**73.0**	**77,486**	**5,033**	**6.1**
Under age 55	80,988	67,739	83.6	63,285	4,455	6.6
Aged 55 or older	32,125	14,781	46.0	14,201	578	3.9
Aged 55 to 59	8,929	7,035	78.8	6,770	265	3.8
Aged 60 to 64	7,194	4,310	59.9	4,149	160	3.7
Aged 65 or older	16,002	3,436	21.5	3,282	153	4.5
Aged 65 to 69	5,246	1,866	35.6	1,779	87	4.7
Aged 70 to 74	3,912	858	21.9	818	40	4.7
Aged 75 or older	6,844	711	10.4	685	26	3.6
Women, aged 16 or older	**120,675**	**71,767**	**59.5**	**67,876**	**3,891**	**5.4**
Under age 55	82,148	58,689	71.4	55,286	3,402	5.8
Aged 55 or older	38,527	13,078	33.9	12,590	489	3.7
Aged 55 to 59	9,515	6,445	67.7	6,199	246	3.8
Aged 60 to 64	7,852	3,825	48.7	3,694	132	3.4
Aged 65 or older	21,160	2,808	13.3	2,697	111	3.9
Aged 65 to 69	5,995	1,585	26.4	1,528	57	3.6
Aged 70 to 74	4,728	676	14.3	644	32	4.7
Aged 75 or older	10,437	547	5.2	525	22	4.0

Source: Bureau of Labor Statistics, 2008 Current Population Survey, Internet site http://www.bls.gov/cps/tables.htm#empstat; calculations by New Strategist

Older Americans Are about Equally Likely to Work

Labor force participation rate does not differ much by race or Hispanic origin among men and women aged 65 or older.

The labor force participation rate declines with advancing age, and with increasing age there are fewer differences in rates by race and Hispanic origin. Among men aged 55 to 59, fully 80.5 percent of Asians and whites are in the labor force. The figure is a smaller 78.3 percent among Hispanic men and just 65.7 percent among black men. Among women in the age group, labor force participation ranges from a low of 57.0 percent among Hispanics to a high of 68.6 percent among whites.

Among men and women aged 65 or older, the differences in labor force participation are much less. Among men in the age group, the figure ranges from 18.1 percent among blacks to 21.8 percent among Asians and whites. Among women in the age group, the figure ranges from 11.7 percent among Hispanics to 13.4 percent among Asians.

■ The labor force participation rate of older workers in every racial and ethnic group will rise as Baby Boomers fill the 65-or-older age group and postpone retirement in the years ahead.

Among men aged 65 or older, about one in five is in the labor force

(percent of men aged 65 or older in the labor force, by race and Hispanic origin, 2008)

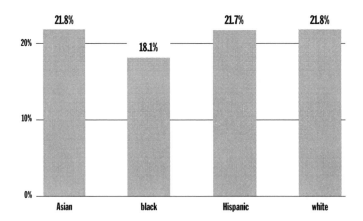

Table 6.3 Employment Status of Men by Race, Hispanic Origin, and Age, 2008

(number and percent of men aged 16 or older in the civilian labor force by race, Hispanic origin, and age, 2008; numbers in thousands)

	civilian noninstitutional population	civilian labor force			unemployed	
		total	percent of population	employed	number	percent of labor force
ASIAN MEN						
Total, aged 16 or older	5,112	3,852	75.3%	3,692	160	4.1%
Under age 55	3,943	3,275	83.1	3,140	134	4.1
Aged 55 or older	1,169	577	49.4	552	26	4.5
Aged 55 to 59	360	290	80.5	276	14	4.8
Aged 60 to 64	256	167	65.4	162	6	3.4
Aged 65 or older	553	120	21.8	114	6	5.1
Aged 65 to 69	201	74	36.9	70	4	5.2
Aged 70 to 74	157	26	16.4	24	–	–
Aged 75 or older	196	20	10.4	20	–	–
BLACK MEN						
Total, aged 16 or older	12,516	8,347	66.7	7,398	949	11.4
Under age 55	9,752	7,270	74.5	6,403	867	11.9
Aged 55 or older	2,764	1,077	39.0	995	82	7.6
Aged 55 to 59	876	575	65.7	536	39	6.8
Aged 60 to 64	643	277	43.1	255	22	7.9
Aged 65 or older	1,245	225	18.1	204	21	9.5
Aged 65 to 69	441	115	26.0	103	11	9.8
Aged 70 to 74	332	60	18.1	54	6	9.6
Aged 75 or older	471	50	10.6	46	4	8.5
HISPANIC MEN						
Total, aged 16 or older	16,524	13,255	80.2	12,248	1,007	7.6
Under age 55	14,038	12,033	85.7	11,095	938	7.8
Aged 55 or older	2,486	1,222	49.2	1,153	69	5.6
Aged 55 to 59	786	615	78.3	580	35	5.7
Aged 60 to 64	579	364	62.7	349	15	4.0
Aged 65 or older	1,121	243	21.7	224	19	7.8
Aged 65 to 69	387	128	33.0	118	10	7.8
Aged 70 to 74	291	55	18.8	50	5	8.7
Aged 75 or older	443	61	13.7	56	4	6.9
WHITE MEN						
Total, aged 16 or older	92,725	68,351	73.7	64,624	3,727	5.5
Under age 55	65,055	55,450	85.2	52,184	3,266	5.9
Aged 55 or older	27,670	12,901	46.6	12,440	461	3.6
Aged 55 to 59	7,528	6,060	80.5	5,853	207	3.4
Aged 60 to 64	6,170	3,795	61.5	3,665	130	3.4
Aged 65 or older	13,972	3,046	21.8	2,922	124	4.1
Aged 65 to 69	4,513	1,646	36.5	1,574	72	4.4
Aged 70 to 74	3,365	766	22.8	735	32	4.1
Aged 75 or older	6,094	634	10.4	613	21	3.3

Note: Race is shown only for those selecting that race group only. People who selected more than one race are not included. Hispanics may be of any race. "–" means sample is too small to make a reliable estimate.
Source: Bureau of Labor Statistics, 2008 Current Population Survey, Internet site http://www.bls.gov/cps/tables.htm#empstat; calculations by New Strategist

Table 6.4 Employment Status of Women by Race, Hispanic Origin, and Age, 2008

(number and percent of women aged 16 or older in the civilian labor force by race, Hispanic origin, and age, 2008; numbers in thousands)

| | civilian noninstitutional population | civilian labor force | | | unemployed | |
		total	percent of population	employed	number	percent of labor force
ASIAN WOMEN						
Total, aged 16 or older	5,639	3,350	59.4%	3,225	125	3.7%
Under age 55	4,175	2,818	67.5	2,710	108	3.8
Aged 55 or older	1,464	532	36.3	515	17	3.2
Aged 55 to 59	431	289	67.1	278	11	3.8
Aged 60 to 64	295	144	48.9	140	4	3.0
Aged 65 or older	738	99	13.4	97	2	2.2
Aged 65 to 69	238	53	22.5	51	2	3.8
Aged 70 to 74	160	29	18.4	29	–	–
Aged 75 or older	340	16	4.7	16	–	–
BLACK WOMEN						
Total, aged 16 or older	15,328	9,393	61.3	8,554	839	8.9
Under age 55	11,481	8,086	70.4	7,318	768	9.5
Aged 55 or older	3,847	1,307	34.0	1,236	71	5.4
Aged 55 to 59	1,088	681	62.6	644	37	5.5
Aged 60 to 64	822	375	45.6	356	19	5.0
Aged 65 or older	1,937	251	13.0	236	15	5.8
Aged 65 to 69	607	138	22.8	133	6	4.2
Aged 70 to 74	481	61	12.7	56	5	8.4
Aged 75 or older	849	51	6.1	48	4	7.3
HISPANIC WOMEN						
Total, aged 16 or older	15,616	8,769	56.2	8,098	672	7.7
Under age 55	12,654	7,873	62.2	7,246	628	8.0
Aged 55 or older	2,962	896	30.2	852	44	4.9
Aged 55 to 59	838	478	57.0	452	26	5.5
Aged 60 to 64	636	244	38.3	239	5	2.1
Aged 65 or older	1,488	174	11.7	161	13	7.7
Aged 65 to 69	505	105	20.8	97	8	7.8
Aged 70 to 74	372	40	10.7	37	3	6.8
Aged 75 or older	611	29	4.8	27	–	–
WHITE WOMEN						
Total, aged 16 or older	96,814	57,284	59.2	54,501	2,782	4.9
Under age 55	64,210	46,258	72.0	43,865	2,392	5.2
Aged 55 or older	32,604	11,026	33.8	10,636	390	3.5
Aged 55 to 59	7,829	5,368	68.6	5,175	193	3.6
Aged 60 to 64	6,582	3,241	49.2	3,136	105	3.2
Aged 65 or older	18,193	2,417	13.3	2,325	92	3.8
Aged 65 to 69	5,048	1,368	27.1	1,319	49	3.6
Aged 70 to 74	4,006	575	14.3	549	25	4.4
Aged 75 or older	9,139	475	5.2	457	18	3.7

Note: Race is shown only for those selecting that race group only. People who selected more than one race are not included. Hispanics may be of any race. "–" means sample is too small to make a reliable estimate.
Source: Bureau of Labor Statistics, 2008 Current Population Survey, Internet site http://www.bls.gov/cps/tables.htm#empstat; calculations by New Strategist

Few Older Couples Are Dual Earners

Nearly half of couples in the 55-to-64 age group are dual earners, however.

Dual incomes are by far the norm among married couples. Both husband and wife are in the labor force in 55 percent of the nation's couples. In another 22 percent, the husband is the only worker. Not far behind are the 16 percent of couples in which neither spouse is in the labor force. The wife is the sole worker among 7 percent of couples.

The 68 percent majority of couples under age 55 are dual earners. Among those aged 55 or older, however, both spouses are in the labor force in only 31 percent. The figure is a much higher 49 percent among couples aged 55 to 64. The wife is the only one employed in a substantial 13 percent of couples in the 55-to-64 age group. In these homes, typically, the older husband is retired while the younger wife is still at work. For 67 percent of couples aged 65 or older, neither husband nor wife is working.

■ Look for the percentage of dual-income older couples to rise as Boomers age and postpone retirement.

Dual earners account for nearly half of couples aged 55 to 64

(percent of married couples in which both husband and wife are in the labor force, by age, 2008)

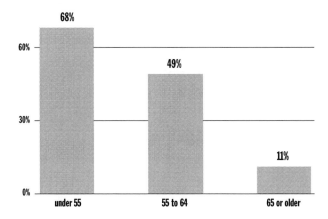

Table 6.5 Labor Force Status of Married-Couple Family Groups by Age, 2008

(number and percent distribution of married-couple family groups by age of reference person and labor force status of husband and wife, 2008; numbers in thousands)

	total	husband and wife in labor force	husband only in labor force	wife only in labor force	neither husband nor wife in labor force
Total married-couple family groups	**60,129**	**32,988**	**13,141**	**4,118**	**9,882**
Under age 55	38,284	26,212	9,539	1,570	960
Aged 55 or older	21,845	6,776	3,602	2,548	8,922
Aged 55 to 64	11,399	5,613	2,426	1,446	1,915
Aged 65 or older	10,446	1,163	1,176	1,102	7,007
Aged 65 to 74	6,542	986	901	916	3,740
Aged 75 or older	3,904	177	275	186	3,267
PERCENT DISTRIBUTION					
Total married-couple family groups	**100.0%**	**54.9%**	**21.9%**	**6.8%**	**16.4%**
Under age 55	100.0	68.5	24.9	4.1	2.5
Aged 55 or older	100.0	31.0	16.5	11.7	40.8
Aged 55 to 64	100.0	49.2	21.3	12.7	16.8
Aged 65 or older	100.0	11.1	11.3	10.5	67.1
Aged 65 to 74	100.0	15.1	13.8	14.0	57.2
Aged 75 or older	100.0	4.5	7.0	4.8	83.7

Source: Bureau of the Census, America's Families and Living Arrangements: 2008, Internet site http://www.census.gov/population/www/socdemo/hh-fam/cps2008.html; calculations by New Strategist

Few Working Americans Are Aged 55 or Older

Only 18 percent of the nation's 145 million employed are aged 55 or older.

The share of workers aged 55 or older varies by occupation. Only 8 percent of computer software engineers are aged 55 or older, for example, because of the rapid technological change that has occurred since older Americans began their career. Only 5 percent of firefighters and 8 percent of police are aged 55 or older, in part because of the physical requirements of the job and also because of early retirement options in those careers.

Workers aged 55 or older account for a disproportionate share of some occupations, however. They are 48 percent of all legislators, for example. They are 52 percent of farmers and ranchers, 33 percent of real estate agents, and 31 percent of artists.

■ As Boomers age, expect to see a growing share of older workers in technical jobs.

People aged 55 or older account for few workers in technical occupations

(percent of workers aged 55 or older, by occupation, 2008)

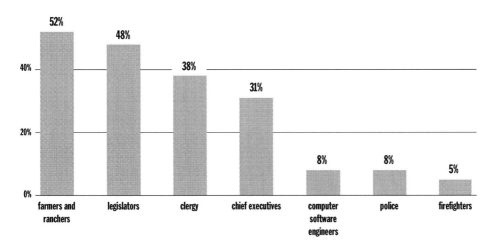

Table 6.6 Occupation of Workers Aged 55 or Older, 2008

(number of employed workers aged 16 or older, median age of workers, and number of workers aged 55 or older, by occupation, 2008; numbers in thousands)

	total	median age	aged 55 or older total	55 to 64	65 or older
TOTAL WORKERS	**145,362**	**41.3**	**26,791**	**20,812**	**5,979**
Management and professional occupations	**52,761**	**43.5**	**10,897**	**8,659**	**2,238**
Management, business and financial operations	22,059	44.8	4,978	3,896	1,082
Management	15,852	45.6	3,750	2,910	840
Business and financial operations	6,207	42.8	1,228	986	242
Professional and related occupations	30,702	42.5	5,920	4,764	1,156
Computer and mathematical	3,676	39.9	389	345	44
Architecture and engineering	2,931	43.1	552	441	111
Life, physical, and social sciences	1,307	41.4	237	186	51
Community and social services	2,293	44.1	563	430	133
Legal	1,671	44.7	381	288	93
Education, training, and library	8,605	42.8	1,855	1,518	337
Arts, design, entertainment, sports, and media	2,820	40.5	526	382	144
Health care practitioner and technician	7,399	43.3	1,418	1,175	243
Service occupations	**24,451**	**37.1**	**3,730**	**2,730**	**1,000**
Health care support	3,212	38.5	489	390	99
Protective service	3,047	40.6	492	353	139
Food preparation and serving	7,824	28.9	698	515	183
Building and grounds cleaning and maintenance	5,445	42.4	1,129	829	300
Personal care and service	4,923	39.0	923	643	280
Sales and office occupations	**35,544**	**40.6**	**6,840**	**5,170**	**1,670**
Sales and related occupations	16,295	39.5	3,111	2,239	872
Office and administrative support	19,249	41.4	3,729	2,932	797
Natural resources, construction, maintenance occupations	**14,806**	**39.9**	**2,059**	**1,706**	**353**
Farming, fishing, and forestry	988	37.7	160	120	40
Construction and extraction	8,667	39.0	1,072	901	171
Installation, maintenance, and repair	5,152	41.7	826	685	141
Production, transportation, material-moving occupations	**17,800**	**41.9**	**3,265**	**2,546**	**719**
Production	8,973	42.3	1,618	1,322	296
Transportation and material moving	8,827	41.4	1,647	1,224	423

Source: Bureau of Labor Statistics, unpublished data from the 2008 Current Population Survey; calculations by New Strategist

Table 6.7 Share of Workers Aged 55 or Older by Occupation, 2008

(percent distribution of employed people aged 16 or older and aged 55 or older by occupation, 2008)

	total	aged 55 or older		
		total	55 to 64	65 or older
TOTAL WORKERS	**100.0%**	**18.4%**	**14.3%**	**4.1%**
Management and professional occupations	**100.0**	**20.7**	**16.4**	**4.2**
Management, business and financial operations	100.0	22.6	17.7	4.9
Management	100.0	23.7	18.4	5.3
Business and financial operations	100.0	19.8	15.9	3.9
Professional and related occupations	100.0	19.3	15.5	3.8
Computer and mathematical	100.0	10.6	9.4	1.2
Architecture and engineering	100.0	18.8	15.0	3.8
Life, physical, and social sciences	100.0	18.1	14.2	3.9
Community and social services	100.0	24.6	18.8	5.8
Legal	100.0	22.8	17.2	5.6
Education, training, and library	100.0	21.6	17.6	3.9
Arts, design, entertainment, sports, and media	100.0	18.7	13.5	5.1
Health care practitioner and technician	100.0	19.2	15.9	3.3
Service occupations	**100.0**	**15.3**	**11.2**	**4.1**
Health care support	100.0	15.2	12.1	3.1
Protective service	100.0	16.1	11.6	4.6
Food preparation and serving	100.0	8.9	6.6	2.3
Building and grounds cleaning and maintenance	100.0	20.7	15.2	5.5
Personal care and service	100.0	18.7	13.1	5.7
Sales and office occupations	**100.0**	**19.2**	**14.5**	**4.7**
Sales and related occupations	100.0	19.1	13.7	5.4
Office and administrative support	100.0	19.4	15.2	4.1
Natural resources, construction, maintenance occupations	**100.0**	**13.9**	**11.5**	**2.4**
Farming, fishing, and forestry	100.0	16.2	12.1	4.0
Construction and extraction	100.0	12.4	10.4	2.0
Installation, maintenance, and repair	100.0	16.0	13.3	2.7
Production, transportation, material-moving occupations	**100.0**	**18.3**	**14.3**	**4.0**
Production	100.0	18.0	14.7	3.3
Transportation and material moving	100.0	18.7	13.9	4.8

Source: Calculations by New Strategist based on Bureau of Labor Statistics' unpublished data from the 2008 Current Population Survey

Table 6.8 Distribution of Workers Aged 55 or Older by Occupation, 2008

(percent distribution of total employed and employed aged 55 or older, by occupation, 2008)

	total	aged 55 or older		
		total	55 to 64	65 or older
TOTAL WORKERS	100.0%	100.0%	100.0%	100.0%
Management and professional occupations	**36.3**	**40.7**	**41.6**	**37.4**
Management, business and financial operations	15.2	18.6	18.7	18.1
Management	10.9	14.0	14.0	14.0
Business and financial operations	4.3	4.6	4.7	4.0
Professional and related occupations	21.1	22.1	22.9	19.3
Computer and mathematical	2.5	1.5	1.7	0.7
Architecture and engineering	2.0	2.1	2.1	1.9
Life, physical, and social sciences	0.9	0.9	0.9	0.9
Community and social services	1.6	2.1	2.1	2.2
Legal	1.1	1.4	1.4	1.6
Education, training, and library	5.9	6.9	7.3	5.6
Arts, design, entertainment, sports, and media	1.9	2.0	1.8	2.4
Health care practitioner and technician	5.1	5.3	5.6	4.1
Service occupations	**16.8**	**13.9**	**13.1**	**16.7**
Health care support	2.2	1.8	1.9	1.7
Protective service	2.1	1.8	1.7	2.3
Food preparation and serving	5.4	2.6	2.5	3.1
Building and grounds cleaning and maintenance	3.7	4.2	4.0	5.0
Personal care and service	3.4	3.4	3.1	4.7
Sales and office occupations	**24.5**	**25.5**	**24.8**	**27.9**
Sales and related occupations	11.2	11.6	10.8	14.6
Office and administrative support	13.2	13.9	14.1	13.3
Natural resources, construction, maintenance occupations	**10.2**	**7.7**	**8.2**	**5.9**
Farming, fishing, and forestry	0.7	0.6	0.6	0.7
Construction and extraction	6.0	4.0	4.3	2.9
Installation, maintenance, and repair	3.5	3.1	3.3	2.4
Production, transportation, material-moving occupations	**12.2**	**12.2**	**12.2**	**12.0**
Production	6.2	6.0	6.4	5.0
Transportation and material moving	6.1	6.1	5.9	7.1

Source: Calculations by New Strategist based on Bureau of Labor Statistics' unpublished 2008 Current Population Survey data

Table 6.9 Workers Aged 55 or Older by Detailed Occupation, 2008

(number of employed workers aged 16 or older, median age, and number and percent aged 55 or older, by selected detailed occupation, 2008; numbers in thousands)

	total workers	median age	total aged 55 or older		aged 55 to 64		aged 65 or older	
			number	percent of total	number	percent of total	number	percent of total
TOTAL WORKERS	**145,362**	**41.3**	**26,791**	**18.4%**	**20,812**	**14.3%**	**5,979**	**4.1%**
Chief executives	1,655	49.9	519	31.4	403	24.4	116	7.0
Legislators	23	54.5	11	47.8	7	30.4	4	17.4
Marketing and sales managers	922	41.5	125	13.6	108	11.7	17	1.8
Computer and information systems managers	475	42.5	57	12.0	51	10.7	6	1.3
Financial managers	1,168	42.9	207	17.7	180	15.4	27	2.3
Human resources managers	293	44.1	64	21.8	57	19.5	7	2.4
Farmers and ranchers	751	55.5	390	51.9	194	25.8	196	26.1
Construction managers	1,244	44.7	254	20.4	203	16.3	51	4.1
Education administrators	829	47.7	237	28.6	197	23.8	40	4.8
Food service managers	1,039	40.0	148	14.2	113	10.9	35	3.4
Medical and health services managers	561	46.8	135	24.1	118	21.0	17	3.0
Accountants and auditors	1,762	41.6	306	17.4	237	13.5	69	3.9
Computer scientists and systems analysts	837	41.0	114	13.6	100	11.9	14	1.7
Computer programmers	534	40.3	66	12.4	56	10.5	10	1.9
Computer software engineers	1,034	39.5	84	8.1	75	7.3	9	0.9
Architects	233	44.2	56	24.0	34	14.6	22	9.4
Civil engineers	346	42.9	72	20.8	55	15.9	17	4.9
Electrical engineers	350	44.7	71	20.3	60	17.1	11	3.1
Mechanical engineers	318	43.6	62	19.5	51	16.0	11	3.5
Medical scientists	132	39.7	18	13.6	14	10.6	4	3.0
Economists	19	47.3	5	26.3	5	26.3	0	0.0
Market researchers	134	38.8	13	9.7	10	7.5	3	2.2
Psychologists	176	48.9	66	37.5	46	26.1	20	11.4
Social workers	729	42.3	135	18.5	115	15.8	20	2.7
Clergy	441	51.3	168	38.1	112	25.4	56	12.7
Lawyers	1,014	45.8	242	23.9	177	17.5	65	6.4
Postsecondary teachers	1,218	43.7	318	26.1	225	18.5	93	7.6
Preschool and kindergarten teachers	685	39.2	97	14.2	84	12.3	13	1.9
Elementary and middle school teachers	2,958	42.6	602	20.4	524	17.7	78	2.6
Secondary school teachers	1,210	43.4	277	22.9	239	19.8	38	3.1
Librarians	197	51.2	74	37.6	61	31.0	13	6.6
Teacher assistants	1,020	43.1	196	19.2	164	16.1	32	3.1
Artists	213	46.2	67	31.5	45	21.1	22	10.3
Designers	834	40.8	144	17.3	107	12.8	37	4.4
Actors	30	32.6	4	13.3	2	6.7	2	6.7
Athletes, coaches, umpires	252	31.4	23	9.1	18	7.1	5	2.0
Musicians	186	44.0	43	23.1	27	14.5	16	8.6
Editors	171	40.9	30	17.5	23	13.5	7	4.1
Writers and authors	186	46.9	54	29.0	32	17.2	22	11.8
Dentists	152	48.2	44	28.9	32	21.1	12	7.9
Pharmacists	243	42.2	46	18.9	34	14.0	12	4.9

	total workers	median age	total aged 55 or older		aged 55 to 64		aged 65 or older	
			number	percent of total	number	percent of total	number	percent of total
Physicians and surgeons	877	45.7	222	25.3%	161	18.4%	61	7.0%
Registered nurses	2,778	45.0	558	20.1	480	17.3	78	2.8
Physical therapists	197	40.9	25	12.7	21	10.7	4	2.0
Emergency medical technicians, paramedics	138	32.8	10	7.2	6	4.3	4	2.9
Licensed practical nurses	566	43.7	117	20.7	100	17.7	17	3.0
Nursing, psychiatric, home health aides	1,889	39.8	328	17.4	256	13.6	72	3.8
Firefighters	293	39.3	15	5.1	12	4.1	3	1.0
Police and sheriff's patrol officers	674	38.7	51	7.6	44	6.5	7	1.0
Security guards, gaming surveillance officers	867	42.0	208	24.0	140	16.1	68	7.8
Chefs and head cooks	351	37.3	33	9.4	28	8.0	5	1.4
Cooks	1,997	32.2	197	9.9	150	7.5	47	2.4
Food preparation workers	724	27.9	80	11.0	57	7.9	23	3.2
Waiters and waitresses	2,010	24.8	102	5.1	74	3.7	28	1.4
Janitors and building cleaners	2,125	45.5	561	26.4	405	19.1	156	7.3
Maids and housekeeping cleaners	1,434	43.6	310	21.6	232	16.2	78	5.4
Grounds maintenance workers	1,262	35.5	151	12.0	106	8.4	45	3.6
Hairdressers, hair stylists, cosmetologists	773	39.0	128	16.6	96	12.4	32	4.1
Child care workers	1,314	36.3	206	15.7	148	11.3	58	4.4
Cashiers	3,031	27.1	367	12.1	257	8.5	110	3.6
Retail salespersons	3,416	34.9	651	19.1	425	12.4	226	6.6
Insurance sales agents	573	44.8	144	25.1	100	17.5	44	7.7
Securities, commodities, and financial services sales agents	388	40.0	54	13.9	44	11.3	10	2.6
Sales representatives, wholesale and manufacturing	1,343	42.8	251	18.7	193	14.4	58	4.3
Real estate brokers and sales agents	962	47.9	317	33.0	230	23.9	87	9.0
Bookkeeping, accounting, auditing clerks	1,434	46.5	400	27.9	304	21.2	96	6.7
Customer service representatives	1,908	35.3	223	11.7	186	9.7	37	1.9
Receptionists and information clerks	1,413	37.2	275	19.5	189	13.4	86	6.1
Stock clerks and order fillers	1,481	33.0	190	12.8	141	9.5	49	3.3
Secretaries and administrative assistants	3,296	45.7	829	25.2	666	20.2	163	4.9
Miscellaneous agricultural workers	723	34.1	94	13.0	68	9.4	26	3.6
Carpenters	1,562	39.4	193	12.4	163	10.4	30	1.9
Construction laborers	1,651	35.9	153	9.3	125	7.6	28	1.7
Automotive service technicians, mechanics	852	38.8	113	13.3	89	10.4	24	2.8
Miscellaneous assemblers and fabricators	1,050	40.8	148	14.1	125	11.9	23	2.2
Machinists	409	44.8	82	20.0	67	16.4	15	3.7
Aircraft pilots and flight engineers	141	43.6	23	16.3	20	14.2	3	2.1
Driver/sales workers and truck drivers	3,388	43.5	698	20.6	524	15.5	174	5.1
Laborers and freight, stock, material movers	1,889	34.3	210	11.1	163	8.6	47	2.5

Source: Bureau of Labor Statistics, unpublished tables from the 2008 Current Population Survey; calculations by New Strategist

Part-Time Work Appeals to Some Older Workers

Workers aged 55 or older are more likely than average to work part-time.

While only 12 percent of all employed men work part-time, the proportion is 16 percent among men aged 55 or older. Among employed women aged 55 or older, 28 percent work part-time, a somewhat greater share than the 24 percent of all women who have part-time jobs.

Men and women aged 55 or older who work part-time are more likely than middle-aged workers to be doing so voluntarily. Among men aged 55 or older who work part-time, only 20 percent say they are doing so because they cannot find a full-time job. In contrast, among men aged 25 to 54 who work part-time, the 57 percent majority say they have a part-time job because they cannot find a full-time position.

■ Expect to see a growing number of older Americans with part-time jobs as aging Boomers try to supplement their retirement income.

Among older men who work part-time, most are doing so by choice

(percent of men with part-time jobs who work part-time because they cannot find a full-time job, by age, 2008)

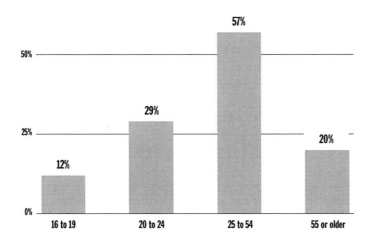

Table 6.10 Full-Time and Part-Time Workers by Age and Sex, 2008

(number and percent distribution of people aged 16 or older at work in nonagricultural industries by age, employment status, and sex, 2008; numbers in thousands)

	total			men			women		
	total	full-time	part-time	total	full-time	part-time	total	full-time	part-time
Total at work	**137,739**	**112,961**	**24,778**	**73,471**	**64,375**	**9,095**	**64,268**	**48,586**	**15,682**
Aged 16 to 19	5,252	1,526	3,727	2,556	875	1,681	2,696	650	2,046
Aged 20 to 24	13,091	9,058	4,033	6,866	5,067	1,798	6,225	3,990	2,235
Aged 25 to 54	94,577	82,960	11,617	50,972	47,468	3,504	43,605	35,492	8,112
Aged 55 or older	24,819	19,418	5,401	13,077	10,964	2,112	11,742	8,454	3,288

PERCENT DISTRIBUTION BY EMPLOYMENT STATUS

	total			men			women		
Total at work	**100.0%**	**82.0%**	**18.0%**	**100.0%**	**87.6%**	**12.4%**	**100.0%**	**75.6%**	**24.4%**
Aged 16 to 19	100.0	29.1	71.0	100.0	34.2	65.8	100.0	24.1	75.9
Aged 20 to 24	100.0	69.2	30.8	100.0	73.8	26.2	100.0	64.1	35.9
Aged 25 to 54	100.0	87.7	12.3	100.0	93.1	6.9	100.0	81.4	18.6
Aged 55 or older	100.0	78.2	21.8	100.0	83.8	16.2	100.0	72.0	28.0

PERCENT DISTRIBUTION BY AGE

	total			men			women		
Total at work	**100.0%**	**100.0%**	**100.0%**	**100.0%**	**100.0%**	**100.0%**	**100.0%**	**100.0%**	**100.0%**
Aged 16 to 19	3.8	1.4	15.0	3.5	1.4	18.5	4.2	1.3	13.0
Aged 20 to 24	9.5	8.0	16.3	9.3	7.9	19.8	9.7	8.2	14.3
Aged 25 to 54	68.7	73.4	46.9	69.4	73.7	38.5	67.8	73.0	51.7
Aged 55 or older	18.0	17.2	21.8	17.8	17.0	23.2	18.3	17.4	21.0

Note: Part-time work is less than 35 hours per week. Part-time workers exclude those who worked less than 35 hours in the previous week because of vacation, holidays, child care problems, weather issues, and other temporary, noneconomic reasons. Source: Bureau of Labor Statistics, Current Population Survey, Internet site http://www.bls.gov/cps/tables.htm#empstat; calculations by New Strategist

Table 6.11 Part-Time Workers by Sex, Age, and Reason, 2008

(total number of people aged 16 or older who work in nonagricultural industries part-time, and number and percent working part-time for economic reasons, by sex and age, 2008; numbers in thousands)

		working part-time for economic reasons	
	total	number	share of total
Men working part-time	**9,095**	**3,162**	**34.8%**
Aged 16 to 19	1,681	209	12.4
Aged 20 to 24	1,798	526	29.3
Aged 25 to 54	3,504	2,014	57.5
Aged 55 or older	2,112	412	19.5
Women working part-time	**15,682**	**2,611**	**16.6**
Aged 16 to 19	2,046	173	8.5
Aged 20 to 24	2,235	412	18.4
Aged 25 to 54	8,112	1,637	20.2
Aged 55 or older	3,288	388	11.8

Note: Part-time work is less than 35 hours per week. Part-time workers exclude those who worked less than 35 hours in the previous week because of vacation, holidays, child care problems, weather issues, and other temporary, noneconomic reasons. "Economic reasons" means a worker's hours have been reduced or workers cannot find full-time employment.
Source: Bureau of Labor Statistics, Current Population Survey, Internet site http://www.bls.gov/cps/tables.htm#empstat; calculations by New Strategist

Self-Employment Is Highest among Older Americans

Men and women aged 65 or older are more likely than average to work for themselves.

While only 7 percent of all employed workers aged 16 or older are self-employed, 17 percent of workers aged 65 or older work for themselves. Self-employment usually requires specialized skills, and those most likely to have such skills are older workers with decades of experience. Men and women aged 55 or older account for 31 percent of the self-employed, a much greater proportion than their share of all workers.

Older men are more likely to be self-employed than older women. While 9 percent of employed women aged 55 or older work for themselves, the proportion is 14 percent among men. Twenty percent of working men aged 65 or older are self-employed versus 13 percent of their female counterparts.

■ When Boomers enter the 65-or-older age group, the number of self-employed Americans may rise.

Self-employment is common among older working men

(percent of employed men aged 16 or older and aged 55 or older who are self-employed, 2008)

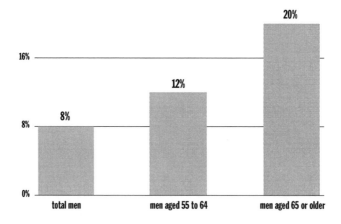

Table 6.12 Self-Employed Workers by Sex and Age, 2008

(number of employed workers aged 16 or older, number and percent who are self-employed, and percent distribution of self-employed, by age, 2008; numbers in thousands)

	total	self-employed number	self-employed percent	percent distribution of self-employed by age
Total aged 16 or older	**145,362**	**10,079**	**6.9%**	**100.0%**
Under age 45	84,042	4,119	4.9	40.9
Aged 45 to 54	34,529	2,832	8.2	28.1
Aged 55 or older	26,791	3,129	11.7	31.0
Aged 55 to 64	20,812	2,120	10.2	21.0
Aged 65 or older	5,979	1,009	16.9	10.0
Total men	**77,486**	**6,373**	**8.2**	**100.0**
Under age 45	45,161	2,592	5.7	40.7
Aged 45 to 54	18,124	1,769	9.8	27.8
Aged 55 or older	14,202	2,011	14.2	31.6
Aged 55 to 64	10,919	1,341	12.3	21.0
Aged 65 or older	3,283	670	20.4	10.5
Total women	**67,876**	**3,707**	**5.5**	**100.0**
Under age 45	38,880	1,522	3.9	41.1
Aged 45 to 54	16,405	1,063	6.5	28.7
Aged 55 or older	12,590	1,119	8.9	30.2
Aged 55 to 64	9,893	779	7.9	21.0
Aged 65 or older	2,697	340	12.6	9.2

Source: Bureau of Labor Statistics, Current Population Survey, Internet site http://www.bls.gov/cps/tables.htm#empstat; calculations by New Strategist

Among the Oldest Men, Job Tenure Has Increased

Women's job tenure has changed little.

Job tenure has not changed much for men overall since 2000, but tenure among men aged 65 or older has grown by more than one year as a growing share of older men postpone retirement. In 2008, male workers aged 65 or older had been with their current employer for a median of 10.4 years, up from 9.0 years in 2000. Among women aged 65 or older, median job tenure increased by just 0.2 years during that time.

The percentage of older men and women with long-term jobs—those who have been with their current employer for at least 10years—has been climbing. Older workers are staying on the job rather than face retirement with diminished resources. The percentage of men aged 65 or older who have been with their current employer for at least 10 years increased from 49 percent in 2000 to 59 percent in 2008. Among their female counterparts, the figure climbed from 51 to 54 percent.

■ Long-term employment among older workers is likely to continue to rise as Boomers try to recoup lost retirement savings by staying on the job longer.

More men aged 65 or older have long-term jobs

(percent of men aged 65 or older who have worked for their current employer for 10 or more years, 2000 and 2008)

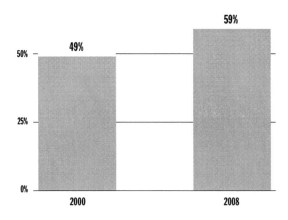

Table 6.13 Job Tenure by Sex and Age, 2000 and 2008

(median number of years workers aged 25 or older have been with their current employer by sex and age, and change in years, 2000 and 2008)

	2008	2000	change in years 2000–08
Total aged 25 or older	**5.1**	**4.7**	**0.4**
Aged 25 to 34	2.7	2.6	0.1
Aged 35 to 44	4.9	4.8	0.1
Aged 45 to 54	7.6	8.2	−0.6
Aged 55 to 64	9.9	10.0	−0.1
Aged 65 or older	10.2	9.4	0.8
Men aged 25 or older	**5.2**	**4.9**	**0.3**
Aged 25 to 34	2.8	2.7	0.1
Aged 35 to 44	5.2	5.3	−0.1
Aged 45 to 54	8.2	9.5	−1.3
Aged 55 to 64	10.1	10.2	−0.1
Aged 65 or older	10.4	9.0	1.4
Women aged 25 or older	**4.9**	**4.4**	**0.5**
Aged 25 to 34	2.6	2.5	0.1
Aged 35 to 44	4.7	4.3	0.4
Aged 45 to 54	7.0	7.3	−0.3
Aged 55 to 64	9.8	9.9	−0.1
Aged 65 or older	9.9	9.7	0.2

Source: Bureau of Labor Statistics, Employee Tenure, Internet site http://www.bls.gov/news.release/tenure.toc.htm; calculations by New Strategist

Table 6.14 Long-Term Employment by Sex and Age, 2000 and 2008

(percent of employed wage and salary workers aged 25 or older who have been with their current employer for 10 or more years, by sex and age, 2000 and 2008; percentage point change in share, 2000–08)

	2008	2000	percentage point change 2000–08
TOTAL AGED 25 OR OLDER	**31.5%**	**31.5%**	**0.0**
Men aged 25 or older	**32.9**	**33.4**	**−0.5**
Aged 25 to 29	2.4	3.0	−0.6
Aged 30 to 34	11.3	15.1	−3.8
Aged 35 to 39	25.4	29.4	−4.0
Aged 40 to 44	35.8	40.2	−4.4
Aged 45 to 49	43.5	49.0	−5.5
Aged 50 to 54	50.4	51.6	−1.2
Aged 55 to 59	54.9	53.7	1.2
Aged 60 to 64	52.4	52.4	0.0
Aged 65 or older	58.9	48.6	10.3
Women aged 25 or older	**30.0**	**29.5**	**0.5**
Aged 25 to 29	2.1	1.9	0.2
Aged 30 to 34	8.7	12.5	−3.8
Aged 35 to 39	20.3	22.3	−2.0
Aged 40 to 44	29.9	31.2	−1.3
Aged 45 to 49	36.7	41.4	−4.7
Aged 50 to 54	45.0	45.8	−0.8
Aged 55 to 59	50.0	52.5	−2.5
Aged 60 to 64	54.8	53.6	1.2
Aged 65 or older	53.8	51.0	2.8

Source: Bureau of Labor Statistics, Employee Tenure, Internet site http://www.bls.gov/news.release/tenure.toc.htm; calculations by New Strategist

Independent Contracting Appeals to Older Workers

Nearly one in four workers aged 65 or older has an alternative work arrangement.

Older workers are most likely to have alternative work arrangements. According to the Bureau of Labor Statistics, alternative workers are defined as independent contractors, on-call workers (such as substitute teachers), temporary-help agency workers, and people who work for contract firms (such as lawn or janitorial service companies).

The most popular alternative work arrangement is independent contracting—which includes most of the self-employed. Among the 15 million alternative workers, 10 million are independent contractors—or 70 percent. Among alternative workers aged 65 or older, 80 percent are independent contractors, accounting for 18 percent of all workers in the 65-or-older age group. This age group is also more likely than average to do on-call work, such as substitute teaching.

■ Many older workers opt for self-employment because it gives them more control over their work schedule, and their government-provided health insurance coverage allows them the freedom to strike out on their own.

Older workers are most likely to be independent contractors

(percent of employed workers who are independent contractors, by age, 2005)

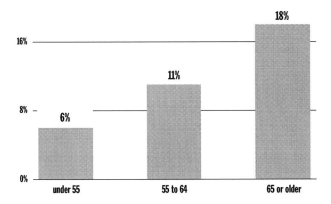

Table 6.15 Alternative Work Arrangements by Age, 2005

(number and percent distribution of employed people aged 16 or older by age and work arrangement, 2005; numbers in thousands)

	total employed	traditional arrangements	alternative workers total	independent contractors	on-call workers	temporary-help agency workers	workers provided by contract firms
Total people	**138,952**	**123,843**	**14,826**	**10,342**	**2,454**	**1,217**	**813**
Under age 55	116,155	104,646	11,260	7,518	2,011	1,050	681
Aged 55 to 64	17,980	15,496	2,459	1,943	267	135	114
Aged 65 or older	4,817	3,701	1,107	881	175	33	18
PERCENT DISTRIBUTION BY ALTERNATIVE WORK STATUS							
Total people	**100.0%**	**89.1%**	**10.7%**	**7.4%**	**1.8%**	**0.9%**	**0.6%**
Under age 55	100.0	90.1	9.7	6.5	1.7	0.9	0.6
Aged 55 to 64	100.0	86.2	13.7	10.8	1.5	0.8	0.6
Aged 65 or older	100.0	76.8	23.0	18.3	3.6	0.7	0.4
PERCENT DISTRIBUTION BY AGE							
Total people	**100.0%**	**100.0%**	**100.0%**	**100.0%**	**100.0%**	**100.0%**	**100.0%**
Under age 55	83.6	84.5	75.9	72.7	81.9	86.3	83.8
Aged 55 to 64	12.9	12.5	16.6	18.8	10.9	11.1	14.0
Aged 65 or older	3.5	3.0	7.5	8.5	7.1	2.7	2.2

Note: Numbers may not add to total because "total employed" includes day laborers, an alternative arrangement not shown separately, and a small number of workers were both on call and provided by contract firms. Independent contractors are workers who obtain customers on their own to provide a product or service, and includes the self-employed. On-call workers are in a pool of workers who are called to work only as needed, such as substitute teachers and construction workers supplied by a union hiring hall. Temporary-help agency workers are those who said they are paid by a temporary-help agency. Workers provided by contract firms are those employed by a company that provides employees or their services under contract, such as security, landscaping, and computer programming.
Source: Bureau of Labor Statistics, Contingent and Alternative Employment Arrangements, February 2005, Internet site http:// www.bls.gov/news.release/conemp.t05.htm; calculations by New Strategist

Most Minimum-Wage Workers Are Young Adults

The percentage of workers earning minimum wage or less rises in old age, however.

Among the nation's 75 million workers who were paid hourly rates in 2008, only 2.2 million (3 percent) made minimum wage or less, according to the Bureau of Labor Statistics. Fully 92 percent of minimum-wage workers are under age 55, and only 8 percent are aged 55 or older.

Among the 11.6 million workers aged 55 or older who are paid hourly rates, only 178,000 make no more than minimum wage—or 1.5 percent. The percentage of older workers who make minimum wage is as low as 1.2 percent among 55-to-64-year-olds and rises as high as 3.0 percent among workers aged 70 or older.

■ Older workers are more likely to earn minimum wage than the middle aged because many are part-timers supplementing their retirement income.

Few workers aged 55 to 64 make minimum wage

(percent of workers making minimum wage or less, by age, 2008)

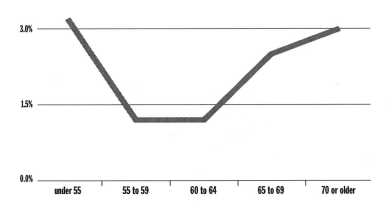

Table 6.16 Workers Earning Minimum Wage by Age, 2008

(number, percent, and percent distribution of workers aged 16 or older paid hourly rates at or below minimum wage, by age, 2008; numbers in thousands)

	total paid hourly rates	at or below minimum wage		
		number	share of total	percent distribution
Total aged 16 or older	**75,305**	**2,226**	**3.0%**	**100.0%**
Under age 55	63,676	2,048	3.2	92.0
Aged 55 or older	11,629	178	1.5	8.0
Aged 55 to 64	8,987	106	1.2	4.8
Aged 55 to 59	5,660	67	1.2	3.0
Aged 60 to 64	3,327	40	1.2	1.8
Aged 65 or older	2,642	72	2.7	3.2
Aged 65 to 69	1,465	37	2.5	1.7
Aged 70 or older	1,177	35	3.0	1.6

Source: Bureau of Labor Statistics, Characteristics of Minimum Wage Workers, 2008, Internet site http://www.bls.gov/cps/minwage2008.htm; calculations by New Strategist

Union Representation Peaks among Workers Aged 55 to 64

Men are more likely than women to be represented by a union.

Union representation has fallen sharply over the past few decades. In 2008, only 14 percent of workers were represented by a union.

The percentage of workers who are represented by a union peaks among men and women in the 55-to-64 age group at 19 and 17 percent, respectively. Men are more likely than women to be represented by a union because men are more likely to work in manufacturing—the traditional stronghold of labor unions. In fact, the decline of labor unions is partly the result of the shift in jobs from manufacturing to services.

■ Union representation may rise along with workers' concerns about job security and the cost of health care coverage.

Few workers are represented by a union

(percent of employed wage and salary workers who are represented by unions, by age, 2008)

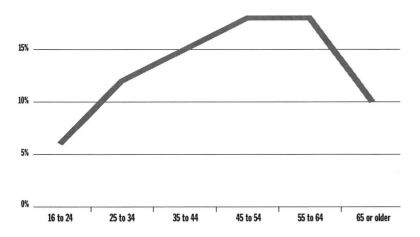

Table 6.17 Union Representation by Sex and Age, 2008

(number and percent of employed wage and salary workers aged 16 or older by union representation status, sex, and age, 2008; numbers in thousands)

	total employed	represented by unions	
		number	percent
Total aged 16 or older	**129,377**	**17,761**	**13.7%**
Aged 16 to 24	18,705	1,062	5.7
Aged 25 to 34	29,276	3,443	11.8
Aged 35 to 44	29,708	4,365	14.7
Aged 45 to 54	29,787	5,228	17.6
Aged 55 to 64	17,430	3,209	18.4
Aged 65 or older	4,471	454	10.2
Men aged 16 or older	**66,846**	**9,724**	**14.5**
Aged 16 to 24	9,537	617	6.5
Aged 25 to 34	15,780	1,909	12.1
Aged 35 to 44	15,653	2,491	15.9
Aged 45 to 54	14,988	2,812	18.8
Aged 55 to 64	8,657	1,682	19.4
Aged 65 or older	2,230	213	9.6
Women aged 16 or older	**62,532**	**8,036**	**12.9**
Aged 16 to 24	9,168	445	4.8
Aged 25 to 34	13,496	1,534	11.4
Aged 35 to 44	14,055	1,874	13.3
Aged 45 to 54	14,799	2,416	16.3
Aged 55 to 64	8,773	1,527	17.4
Aged 65 or older	2,241	241	10.7

Note: Workers represented by unions are either members of a labor union or similar employee association or workers who report no union affiliation but whose jobs are covered by a union or an employee association contract.
Source: Bureau of Labor Statistics, 2008 Current Population Survey, Internet site http://www.bls.gov/cps/tables.htm#empstat; calculations by New Strategist

More Older Americans Will Work

These projections, produced before the economic downturn of 2008, are probably conservative.

The Bureau of Labor Statistics projected that the labor force participation rate of older Americans would rise substantially between 2006 and 2016—and that was before the economic turmoil of 2008, which decimated retirement savings. Among men aged 65 or older, labor force participation was projected to rise by 6.8 percentage points to 27.1 percent. Among women in the age group, participation was projected to increase by 5.8 percentage points to 17.5 percent.

Behind the increased participation rates of older workers is the postponement of retirement as the Baby-Boom generation enters its late sixties with a much smaller nest egg than it had anticipated. The number of workers aged 65 or older is projected to climb by an enormous 78 percent among men and 91 percent among women between 2006 and 2016.

■ Expect to see the number of older workers increase even more than these projections.

Expect more older workers in the labor force

(number of people aged 65 or older in the labor force, 2006 and 2016)

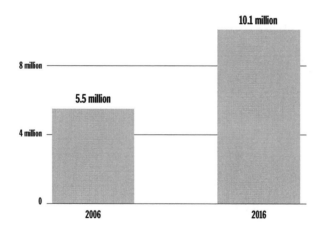

Table 6.18 Projections of the Labor Force by Sex and Age, 2006 and 2016

(number and percent of people aged 16 or older in the civilian labor force by sex and age, 2006 and 2016; percent change in number and percentage point change in participation rate, 2006–16; numbers in thousands)

	number			participation rate		
	2006	2016	percent change 2006–16	2006	2016	percentage point change 2006–16
TOTAL LABOR FORCE	**151,428**	**164,232**	**8.5%**	**66.2%**	**65.5%**	**–0.7**
Total men in labor force	**81,255**	**87,781**	**8.0**	**73.5**	**72.3**	**–1.2**
Under age 25	11,810	10,915	–7.6	63.3	59.3	–4.0
Aged 25 to 54	55,840	57,491	3.0	90.6	91.3	0.7
Aged 55 or older	13,605	19,376	42.4	44.9	48.3	3.4
Aged 55 to 64	10,509	13,865	31.9	69.6	70.1	0.5
Aged 65 or older	3,096	5,511	78.0	20.3	27.1	6.8
Aged 65 to 74	2,466	4,387	77.9	28.8	34.6	5.8
Aged 75 or older	630	1,124	78.4	9.5	14.7	5.2
Total women in labor force	**70,173**	**76,450**	**8.9**	**59.4**	**59.2**	**–0.2**
Under age 25	10,584	9,937	–6.1	57.9	54.8	–3.1
Aged 25 to 54	47,726	48,534	1.7	75.5	76.0	0.5
Aged 55 or older	11,863	17,979	51.6	32.3	38.1	5.8
Aged 55 to 64	9,475	13,423	41.7	58.2	63.5	5.3
Aged 65 or older	2,388	4,556	90.8	11.7	17.5	5.8
Aged 65 to 74	1,937	3,689	90.4	19.2	25.1	5.9
Aged 75 or older	451	867	92.2	4.4	7.6	3.2

Source: Bureau of Labor Statistics, Labor Force Projections to 2016: More Workers in Their Golden Years, Monthly Labor Review, November 2007, Internet site http://www.bls.gov/opub/mlr/2007/11/contents.htm; calculations by New Strategist

Living Arrangements

■ Among the 24 million households headed by people aged 65 or older, a 42 percent minority are married couples.

■ Among older Americans, married couples are a much larger share of Asian, Hispanic, and non-Hispanic white households than of black households.

■ Average household size is just over two people in the 60-to-64 age group. It falls below two in the 65-to-74 age group.

■ Among householders aged 55 to 64, a substantial 23 percent have children of any age living with them. The figure falls to 12 percent among householders aged 65 or older.

■ Half of women aged 75 or older live alone versus only 21 percent of their male counterparts.

■ Among people aged 85 or older, fully 76 percent of women but only 38 percent of men are currently widowed.

Married Couples Lose Ground with Age

Only 42 percent of householders aged 65 or older are married couples.

Of the nation's 117 million households in 2008, half were headed by married couples. But among the 24 million households headed by people aged 65 or older, a 42 percent minority are couples. Older people are less likely than the average American to live with their spouse because an important transition in living arrangements occurs among people in their seventies. While married couples account for the majority of households headed by 65-to-69-year-olds, the proportion falls just below 50 percent among householders aged 70 to 74, and drops to 32 percent among those aged 75 or older.

The married-couple share of older households falls as women become widowed and begin to live alone. Women who live alone account for 27 percent of all households headed by people aged 55 or older, ranging from 16 percent of households headed by 55-to-59-year-olds to 44 percent of those headed by people aged 75 or older. In the oldest age group, the most common household type is women who live alone.

■ American women must prepare themselves emotionally and financially for lone living in old age.

The married-couple share of households falls in the older age groups

(percent of households headed by married couples, by age, 2008)

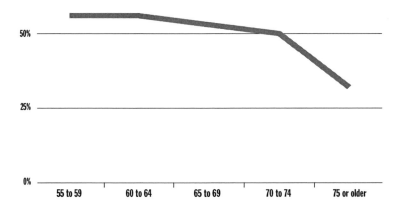

Table 7.1 Households Headed by People Aged 55 or Older by Household Type, 2008: Total Households

(number and percent distribution of total households and households headed by people aged 55 or older, by household type, 2008; numbers in thousands)

	total	aged 55 or older						
		total	55 to 59	60 to 64	aged 65 or older			
					total	65 to 69	70 to 74	75 or older
TOTAL HOUSEHOLDS	116,783	44,022	10,813	9,096	24,113	6,990	5,293	11,829
Family households	77,873	25,711	7,269	5,949	12,493	4,393	3,110	4,990
Married couples	58,370	21,322	6,049	5,095	10,178	3,726	2,639	3,813
Female householder, no spouse present	14,404	3,428	920	642	1,866	547	393	925
Male householder, no spouse present	5,100	962	301	212	449	119	78	252
Nonfamily households	38,910	18,310	3,543	3,147	11,620	2,598	2,183	6,839
Female householder	21,038	12,246	1,878	1,868	8,500	1,689	1,524	5,287
Living alone	18,297	11,731	1,703	1,731	8,297	1,620	1,463	5,213
Male householder	17,872	6,064	1,666	1,279	3,120	908	659	1,552
Living alone	13,870	5,478	1,448	1,112	2,917	856	603	1,458
Percent distribution by type								
TOTAL HOUSEHOLDS	100.0%	100.0%	100.0%	100.0%	100.0%	100.0%	100.0%	100.0%
Family households	66.7	58.4	67.2	65.4	51.8	62.8	58.8	42.2
Married couples	50.0	48.4	55.9	56.0	42.2	53.3	49.9	32.2
Female householder, no spouse present	12.3	7.8	8.5	7.1	7.7	7.8	7.4	7.8
Male householder, no spouse present	4.4	2.2	2.8	2.3	1.9	1.7	1.5	2.1
Nonfamily households	33.3	41.6	32.8	34.6	48.2	37.2	41.2	57.8
Female householder	18.0	27.8	17.4	20.5	35.3	24.2	28.8	44.7
Living alone	15.7	26.6	15.7	19.0	34.4	23.2	27.6	44.1
Male householder	15.3	13.8	15.4	14.1	12.9	13.0	12.5	13.1
Living alone	11.9	12.4	13.4	12.2	12.1	12.2	11.4	12.3
Percent distribution by age								
TOTAL HOUSEHOLDS	100.0%	37.7%	9.3%	7.8%	20.6%	6.0%	4.5%	10.1%
Family households	100.0	33.0	9.3	7.6	16.0	5.6	4.0	6.4
Married couples	100.0	36.5	10.4	8.7	17.4	6.4	4.5	6.5
Female householder, no spouse present	100.0	23.8	6.4	4.5	13.0	3.8	2.7	6.4
Male householder, no spouse present	100.0	18.9	5.9	4.2	8.8	2.3	1.5	4.9
Nonfamily households	100.0	47.1	9.1	8.1	29.9	6.7	5.6	17.6
Female householder	100.0	58.2	8.9	8.9	40.4	8.0	7.2	25.1
Living alone	100.0	64.1	9.3	9.5	45.3	8.9	8.0	28.5
Male householder	100.0	33.9	9.3	7.2	17.5	5.1	3.7	8.7
Living alone	100.0	39.5	10.4	8.0	21.0	6.2	4.3	10.5

Source: Bureau of the Census, 2008 Current Population Survey, Annual Social and Economic Supplement, Internet site http://www.census.gov/hhes/www/macro/032008/hhinc/new02_000.htm; calculations by New Strategist

Households of Older Americans Differ by Race and Hispanic Origin

Among older households, married couples are a much larger share of Asian, Hispanic, and non-Hispanic white households than of black households.

There are sharp differences in household composition among older people by race and Hispanic origin. Among householders aged 55 or older, 60 percent of Asians, 50 percent of non-Hispanic whites, and 48 percent of Hispanics are married couples. In contrast, married couples head only 31 percent of black households in the age group. Female-headed families are common among older blacks, accounting for nearly one in five households headed by blacks aged 55 or older. The comparable figure for non-Hispanic whites is just 6 percent.

Regardless of race or Hispanic origin, women who live alone account for a large share of the oldest householders. Among householders aged 75 or older, the proportion of households headed by women who live alone ranges from a low of 35 percent among Hispanics to a high of 45 percent among non-Hispanic whites.

■ Lone living is likely for many women in old age, regardless of race or Hispanic origin.

The married-couple share of households varies by race and Hispanic origin

(married-couple share of households headed by people aged 55 or older, by race and Hispanic origin, 2008)

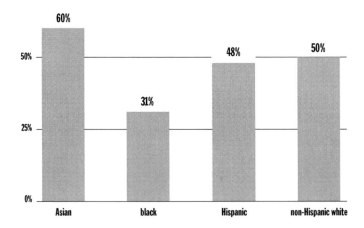

Table 7.2 Households Headed by People Aged 55 or Older by Household Type, 2008: Asian Households

(number and percent distribution of total households headed by Asians and households headed by Asians aged 55 or older, by household type, 2008; numbers in thousands)

	total	aged 55 or older						
		total	55 to 59	60 to 64	aged 65 or older			
					total	65 to 69	70 to 74	75 or older
TOTAL ASIAN HOUSEHOLDS	4,715	1,267	385	278	604	235	129	239
Family households	3,451	893	314	210	370	168	80	122
Married couples	2,757	759	268	186	305	142	68	95
Female householder, no spouse present	452	104	36	19	49	16	10	23
Male householder, no spouse present	242	30	9	5	16	10	2	4
Nonfamily households	1,265	374	71	69	234	67	50	117
Female householder	662	252	45	40	167	47	32	88
Living alone	545	239	39	37	163	46	31	85
Male householder	602	121	27	29	66	20	18	28
Living alone	420	106	25	23	58	14	18	27
Percent distribution by type								
TOTAL ASIAN HOUSEHOLDS	100.0%	100.0%	100.0%	100.0%	100.0%	100.0%	100.0%	100.0%
Family households	73.2	70.5	81.6	75.5	61.3	71.5	62.0	51.0
Married couples	58.5	59.9	69.6	66.9	50.5	60.4	52.7	39.7
Female householder, no spouse present	9.6	8.2	9.4	6.8	8.1	6.8	7.8	9.6
Male householder, no spouse present	5.1	2.4	2.3	1.8	2.6	4.3	1.6	1.7
Nonfamily households	26.8	29.5	18.4	24.8	38.7	28.5	38.8	49.0
Female householder	14.0	19.9	11.7	14.4	27.6	20.0	24.8	36.8
Living alone	11.6	18.9	10.1	13.3	27.0	19.6	24.0	35.6
Male householder	12.8	9.6	7.0	10.4	10.9	8.5	14.0	11.7
Living alone	8.9	8.4	6.5	8.3	9.6	6.0	14.0	11.3
Percent distribution by age								
TOTAL ASIAN HOUSEHOLDS	100.0%	26.9%	8.2%	5.9%	12.8%	5.0%	2.7%	5.1%
Family households	100.0	25.9	9.1	6.1	10.7	4.9	2.3	3.5
Married couples	100.0	27.5	9.7	6.7	11.1	5.2	2.5	3.4
Female householder, no spouse present	100.0	23.0	8.0	4.2	10.8	3.5	2.2	5.1
Male householder, no spouse present	100.0	12.4	3.7	2.1	6.6	4.1	0.8	1.7
Nonfamily households	100.0	29.6	5.6	5.5	18.5	5.3	4.0	9.2
Female householder	100.0	38.1	6.8	6.0	25.2	7.1	4.8	13.3
Living alone	100.0	43.9	7.2	6.8	29.9	8.4	5.7	15.6
Male householder	100.0	20.1	4.5	4.8	11.0	3.3	3.0	4.7
Living alone	100.0	25.2	6.0	5.5	13.8	3.3	4.3	6.4

Note: Asians include those who identify themselves as being of the race alone and those who identify themselves as being of the race in combination with other races.
Source: Bureau of the Census, 2008 Current Population Survey, Annual Social and Economic Supplement, Internet site http:// www.census.gov/hhes/www/macro/032008/hhinc/new02_000.htm; calculations by New Strategist

Table 7.3 Households Headed by People Aged 55 or Older by Household Type, 2008: Black Households

(number and percent distribution of total black households and black households headed by people aged 55 or older, by household type, 2008; numbers in thousands)

| | | aged 55 or older | | | | | | |
| | | | | | aged 65 or older | | | |
	total	total	55 to 59	60 to 64	total	65 to 69	70 to 74	75 or older
TOTAL BLACK HOUSEHOLDS	**14,976**	**4,580**	**1,344**	**964**	**2,272**	**736**	**583**	**953**
Family households	**9,503**	**2,367**	**793**	**543**	**1,031**	**370**	**290**	**372**
Married couples	4,461	1,407	490	333	584	220	176	188
Female householder, no spouse present	4,218	807	256	170	381	128	96	157
Male householder, no spouse present	824	154	47	40	67	22	18	27
Nonfamily households	**5,474**	**2,212**	**551**	**421**	**1,241**	**367**	**293**	**582**
Female householder	3,064	1,430	308	279	843	218	206	420
Living alone	2,748	1,376	290	270	817	208	197	412
Male householder	2,410	783	243	142	398	149	87	162
Living alone	2,012	711	209	129	373	143	85	145
Percent distribution by type								
TOTAL BLACK HOUSEHOLDS	**100.0%**	**100.0%**	**100.0%**	**100.0%**	**100.0%**	**100.0%**	**100.0%**	**100.0%**
Family households	**63.5**	**51.7**	**59.0**	**56.3**	**45.4**	**50.3**	**49.7**	**39.0**
Married couples	29.8	30.7	36.5	34.5	25.7	29.9	30.2	19.7
Female householder, no spouse present	28.2	17.6	19.0	17.6	16.8	17.4	16.5	16.5
Male householder, no spouse present	5.5	3.4	3.5	4.1	2.9	3.0	3.1	2.8
Nonfamily households	**36.6**	**48.3**	**41.0**	**43.7**	**54.6**	**49.9**	**50.3**	**61.1**
Female householder	20.5	31.2	22.9	28.9	37.1	29.6	35.3	44.1
Living alone	18.3	30.0	21.6	28.0	36.0	28.3	33.8	43.2
Male householder	16.1	17.1	18.1	14.7	17.5	20.2	14.9	17.0
Living alone	13.4	15.5	15.6	13.4	16.4	19.4	14.6	15.2
Percent distribution by age								
TOTAL BLACK HOUSEHOLDS	**100.0%**	**30.6%**	**9.0%**	**6.4%**	**15.2%**	**4.9%**	**3.9%**	**6.4%**
Family households	**100.0**	**24.9**	**8.3**	**5.7**	**10.8**	**3.9**	**3.1**	**3.9**
Married couples	100.0	31.5	11.0	7.5	13.1	4.9	3.9	4.2
Female householder, no spouse present	100.0	19.1	6.1	4.0	9.0	3.0	2.3	3.7
Male householder, no spouse present	100.0	18.7	5.7	4.9	8.1	2.7	2.2	3.3
Nonfamily households	**100.0**	**40.4**	**10.1**	**7.7**	**22.7**	**6.7**	**5.4**	**10.6**
Female householder	100.0	46.7	10.1	9.1	27.5	7.1	6.7	13.7
Living alone	100.0	50.1	10.6	9.8	29.7	7.6	7.2	15.0
Male householder	100.0	32.5	10.1	5.9	16.5	6.2	3.6	6.7
Living alone	100.0	35.3	10.4	6.4	18.5	7.1	4.2	7.2

Note: Blacks include those who identify themselves as being of the race alone and those who identify themselves as being of the race in combination with other races.
Source: Bureau of the Census, 2008 Current Population Survey, Annual Social and Economic Supplement, Internet site http://www.census.gov/hhes/www/macro/032008/hhinc/new02_000.htm; calculations by New Strategist

Table 7.4 Households Headed by People Aged 55 or Older by Household Type, 2008: Hispanic Households

(number and percent distribution of total Hispanic households and Hispanic households headed by people aged 55 or older, by household type, 2008; numbers in thousands)

	total	aged 55 or older			aged 65 or older			
		total	55 to 59	60 to 64	total	65 to 69	70 to 74	75 or older
TOTAL HISPANIC HOUSEHOLDS	13,339	2,891	868	629	1,394	499	330	564
Family households	10,394	1,904	624	455	825	330	194	301
Married couples	6,888	1,384	446	335	603	253	148	202
Female householder, no spouse present	2,522	420	139	102	179	76	34	69
Male householder, no spouse present	983	102	39	18	44	2	12	30
Nonfamily households	2,945	987	245	174	569	169	136	264
Female householder	1,291	616	110	104	402	112	89	201
Living alone	1,065	595	104	101	390	108	85	196
Male householder	1,654	372	135	70	168	58	47	63
Living alone	1,138	305	112	53	140	53	38	49
Percent distribution by type								
TOTAL HISPANIC HOUSEHOLDS	100.0%	100.0%	100.0%	100.0%	100.0%	100.0%	100.0%	100.0%
Family households	77.9	65.9	71.9	72.3	59.2	66.1	58.8	53.4
Married couples	51.6	47.9	51.4	53.3	43.3	50.7	44.8	35.8
Female householder, no spouse present	18.9	14.5	16.0	16.2	12.8	15.2	10.3	12.2
Male householder, no spouse present	7.4	3.5	4.5	2.9	3.2	0.4	3.6	5.3
Nonfamily households	22.1	34.1	28.2	27.7	40.8	33.9	41.2	46.8
Female householder	9.7	21.3	12.7	16.5	28.8	22.4	27.0	35.6
Living alone	8.0	20.6	12.0	16.1	28.0	21.6	25.8	34.8
Male householder	12.4	12.9	15.6	11.1	12.1	11.6	14.2	11.2
Living alone	8.5	10.5	12.9	8.4	10.0	10.6	11.5	8.7
Percent distribution by age								
TOTAL HISPANIC HOUSEHOLDS	100.0%	21.7%	6.5%	4.7%	10.5%	3.7%	2.5%	4.2%
Family households	100.0	18.3	6.0	4.4	7.9	3.2	1.9	2.9
Married couples	100.0	20.1	6.5	4.9	8.8	3.7	2.1	2.9
Female householder, no spouse present	100.0	16.7	5.5	4.0	7.1	3.0	1.3	2.7
Male householder, no spouse present	100.0	10.4	4.0	1.8	4.5	0.2	1.2	3.1
Nonfamily households	100.0	33.5	8.3	5.9	19.3	5.7	4.6	9.0
Female householder	100.0	47.7	8.5	8.1	31.1	8.7	6.9	15.6
Living alone	100.0	55.9	9.8	9.5	36.6	10.1	8.0	18.4
Male householder	100.0	22.5	8.2	4.2	10.2	3.5	2.8	3.8
Living alone	100.0	26.8	9.8	4.7	12.3	4.7	3.3	4.3

Source: Bureau of the Census, 2008 Current Population Survey, Annual Social and Economic Supplement, Internet site http:// www.census.gov/hhes/www/macro/032008/hhinc/new02_000.htm; calculations by New Strategist

Table 7.5 Households Headed by People Aged 55 or Older by Household Type, 2008: Non-Hispanic White Households

(number and percent distribution of total non-Hispanic white households and non-Hispanic white households headed by people aged 55 or older, by household type, 2008; numbers in thousands)

		aged 55 or older						
					aged 65 or older			
	total	total	55 to 59	60 to 64	total	65 to 69	70 to 74	75 or older
TOTAL NON-HISPANIC WHITE HOUSEHOLDS	**82,765**	**34,863**	**8,126**	**7,112**	**19,625**	**5,446**	**4,181**	**9,998**
Family households	**53,902**	**20,296**	**5,478**	**4,673**	**10,146**	**3,487**	**2,500**	**4,158**
Married couples	43,739	17,575	4,791	4,185	8,599	3,083	2,208	3,309
Female householder, no spouse present	7,171	2,067	488	344	1,235	322	248	665
Male householder, no spouse present	2,991	654	199	143	312	83	45	185
Nonfamily households	**28,863**	**14,567**	**2,648**	**2,439**	**9,479**	**1,958**	**1,681**	**5,840**
Female householder	15,844	9,857	1,408	1,417	7,032	1,293	1,183	4,556
Living alone	13,771	9,434	1,265	1,298	6,871	1,237	1,136	4,498
Male householder	13,019	4,709	1,240	1,023	2,446	666	497	1,283
Living alone	10,151	4,279	1,079	892	2,308	631	453	1,224
Percent distribution by type								
TOTAL NON-HISPANIC WHITE HOUSEHOLDS	**100.0%**	**100.0%**	**100.0%**	**100.0%**	**100.0%**	**100.0%**	**100.0%**	**100.0%**
Family households	**65.1**	**58.2**	**67.4**	**65.7**	**51.7**	**64.0**	**59.8**	**41.6**
Married couples	52.8	50.4	59.0	58.8	43.8	56.6	52.8	33.1
Female householder, no spouse present	8.7	5.9	6.0	4.8	6.3	5.9	5.9	6.7
Male householder, no spouse present	3.6	1.9	2.4	2.0	1.6	1.5	1.1	1.9
Nonfamily households	**34.9**	**41.8**	**32.6**	**34.3**	**48.3**	**36.0**	**40.2**	**58.4**
Female householder	19.1	28.3	17.3	19.9	35.8	23.7	28.3	45.6
Living alone	16.6	27.1	15.6	18.3	35.0	22.7	27.2	45.0
Male householder	15.7	13.5	15.3	14.4	12.5	12.2	11.9	12.8
Living alone	12.3	12.3	13.3	12.5	11.8	11.6	10.8	12.2
Percent distribution by age								
TOTAL NON-HISPANIC WHITE HOUSEHOLDS	**100.0%**	**42.1%**	**9.8%**	**8.6%**	**23.7%**	**6.6%**	**5.1%**	**12.1%**
Family households	**100.0**	**37.7**	**10.2**	**8.7**	**18.8**	**6.5**	**4.6**	**7.7**
Married couples	100.0	40.2	11.0	9.6	19.7	7.0	5.0	7.6
Female householder, no spouse present	100.0	28.8	6.8	4.8	17.2	4.5	3.5	9.3
Male householder, no spouse present	100.0	21.9	6.7	4.8	10.4	2.8	1.5	6.2
Nonfamily households	**100.0**	**50.5**	**9.2**	**8.5**	**32.8**	**6.8**	**5.8**	**20.2**
Female householder	100.0	62.2	8.9	8.9	44.4	8.2	7.5	28.8
Living alone	100.0	68.5	9.2	9.4	49.9	9.0	8.2	32.7
Male householder	100.0	36.2	9.5	7.9	18.8	5.1	3.8	9.9
Living alone	100.0	42.2	10.6	8.8	22.7	6.2	4.5	12.1

Note: Non-Hispanic whites are those who identify themselves as being white alone and not Hispanic.
Source: Bureau of the Census, 2008 Current Population Survey, Annual Social and Economic Supplement, Internet site http://www.census.gov/hhes/www/macro/032008/hhinc/new02_000.htm; calculations by New Strategist

Household Size Shrinks in the Older Age Groups

Average household size falls below two in the 65-to-74 age group.

The average American household was home to 2.56 people in 2008. Household size peaks among householders aged 35 to 39, who are most likely to have at least one child at home. As householders age through their forties and fifties, the nest empties. The average number of children per household falls below one in the 45-to-49 age group.

Average household size is just over two people in the 60-to-64 age group. It falls below two, to 1.91, in the 65-to-74 age group as (usually) women become widows. For households headed by people aged 75 or older, average household size is just 1.59 people.

■ Most older householders are either empty-nesters or people living alone. Few have children at home.

Household size shrinks rapidly after age 50

(average household size by age of householder, 2008)

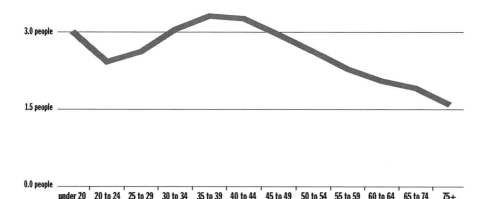

Table 7.6 Average Size of Household by Age of Householder, 2008

(number of households, average number of people per household, and average number of people under age 18 per household, by age of householder, 2008; number of households in thousands)

	number	average number of people	average number of people under age 18
Total households	**116,783**	**2.56**	**0.64**
Under age 20	862	3.01	0.84
Aged 20 to 24	5,691	2.42	0.51
Aged 25 to 29	9,400	2.62	0.80
Aged 30 to 34	9,825	3.05	1.25
Aged 35 to 39	10,900	3.31	1.43
Aged 40 to 44	11,548	3.26	1.25
Aged 45 to 49	12,685	2.95	0.81
Aged 50 to 54	11,851	2.62	0.44
Aged 55 to 59	10,813	2.28	0.23
Aged 60 to 64	9,096	2.05	0.14
Aged 65 to 74	12,284	1.91	0.09
Aged 75 or older	11,829	1.59	0.04

Source: Bureau of the Census, Current Population Survey Annual Social and Economic Supplement, America's Families and Living Arrangements: 2008, detailed tables, Internet site http://www.census.gov/population/www/socdemo/hh-fam/cps2008.html

Few Older Americans Have Children under Age 18 at Home

Many householders aged 55 to 64 have adult children at home, however.

Among householders aged 55 to 64, a substantial 23 percent have children living with them, although only 7 percent have children under age 18 at home. Many of the children living in the homes of 55-to-64-year-olds are students in college dormitories, since the Census Bureau regards children in dorms as living at home. Among householders aged 65 or older, 12 percent have children at home, almost all of them adults.

The percentage of older householders with children at home varies sharply by race and Hispanic origin. Among Asian and Hispanic householders aged 55 to 64, a substantial 41 percent have children at home, and 11 to 13 percent have children under age 18. Among non-Hispanic whites, only 20 percent have children of any age at home and just 6 percent have children under age 18.

■ The presence of children in the home creates lifestyle differences among older Americans by race and Hispanic origin.

The nest is slow to empty for Asians and Hispanics

(percent of householders aged 55 to 64 with children of any age at home, by race and Hispanic origin, 2008)

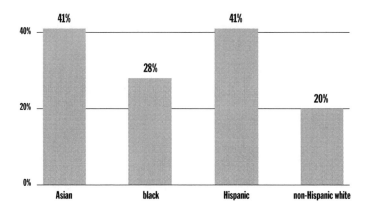

Table 7.7 Households by Presence and Age of Children at Home, 2008: Total Households

(number and percent distribution of households by presence and age of own children at home, by age of children and age of householder, 2008; numbers in thousands)

| | | | aged 55 or older | | | | |
| | | | | | aged 65 or older | | |
	total	under 55	total	55 to 64	total	65 to 74	75 or older
Total households	**116,783**	**72,761**	**44,022**	**19,909**	**24,113**	**12,283**	**11,829**
With children of any age	46,995	39,385	7,609	4,643	2,966	1,688	1,278
Under age 25	41,647	38,408	3,238	2,765	473	388	85
Under age 18	35,709	34,122	1,588	1,316	272	216	56
PERCENT DISTRIBUTION							
Total households	**100.0%**	**100.0%**	**100.0%**	**100.0%**	**100.0%**	**100.0%**	**100.0%**
With children of any age	40.2	54.1	17.3	23.3	12.3	13.7	10.8
Under age 25	35.7	52.8	7.4	13.9	2.0	3.2	0.7
Under age 18	30.6	46.9	3.6	6.6	1.1	1.8	0.5

Source: Bureau of the Census, Current Population Survey Annual Social and Economic Supplement, America's Families and Living Arrangements: 2008, detailed tables, Internet site http://www.census.gov/population/www/socdemo/hh-fam/cps2008 .html; calculations by New Strategist

Table 7.8 Households by Presence and Age of Children at Home, 2008: Asian Households

(number and percent distribution of Asian households by presence and age of own children at home, by age of children and age of householder, 2008; numbers in thousands)

| | | | aged 55 or older | | | | |
| | | | | | aged 65 or older | | |
	total	under 55	total	55 to 64	total	65 to 74	75 or older
Total Asian households	**4,715**	**3,448**	**1,267**	**663**	**604**	**364**	**239**
With children of any age	2,287	1,861	426	272	154	113	41
Under age 25	2,024	1,820	204	169	35	34	1
Under age 18	1,743	1,653	89	73	16	15	1
PERCENT DISTRIBUTION							
Total Asian households	**100.0%**	**100.0%**	**100.0%**	**100.0%**	**100.0%**	**100.0%**	**100.0%**
With children of any age	48.5	54.0	33.6	41.0	25.5	31.0	17.2
Under age 25	42.9	52.8	16.1	25.5	5.8	9.3	0.4
Under age 18	37.0	47.9	7.0	11.0	2.6	4.1	0.4

Note: Asians include those who identify themselves as being of the race alone and those who identify themselves as being of the race in combination with other races.
Source: Bureau of the Census, Current Population Survey Annual Social and Economic Supplement, America's Families and Living Arrangements: 2008, detailed tables, Internet site http://www.census.gov/population/www/socdemo/hh-fam/cps2008 .html; calculations by New Strategist

Table 7.9 Households by Presence and Age of Children at Home, 2008: Black Households

(number and percent distribution of black households by presence and age of own children at home, by age of children and age of householder, 2008; numbers in thousands)

| | | | aged 55 or older | | | | |
| | | | | | aged 65 or older | | |
	total	under 55	total	55 to 64	total	65 to 74	75 or older
Total black households	**14,976**	**10,396**	**4,580**	**2,308**	**2,272**	**1,319**	**953**
With children of any age	6,750	5,663	1,086	643	443	268	175
Under age 25	5,948	5,480	468	378	90	71	19
Under age 18	5,078	4,813	266	204	62	47	15
PERCENT DISTRIBUTION							
Total black households	**100.0%**	**100.0%**	**100.0%**	**100.0%**	**100.0%**	**100.0%**	**100.0%**
With children of any age	45.1	54.5	23.7	27.9	19.5	20.3	18.4
Under age 25	39.7	52.7	10.2	16.4	4.0	5.4	2.0
Under age 18	33.9	46.3	5.8	8.8	2.7	3.6	1.6

Note: Blacks include those who identify themselves as being of the race alone and those who identify themselves as being of the race in combination with other races.
Source: Bureau of the Census, Current Population Survey Annual Social and Economic Supplement, America's Families and Living Arrangements: 2008, detailed tables, Internet site http://www.census.gov/population/www/socdemo/hh-fam/cps2008 .html; calculations by New Strategist

Table 7.10 Households by Presence and Age of Children at Home, 2008: Hispanic Households

(number and percent distribution of Hispanic households by presence of own children at home, by age of children and age of householder, 2008; numbers in thousands)

| | | | aged 55 or older | | | | |
| | | | | | aged 65 or older | | |
	total	under 55	total	55 to 64	total	65 to 74	75 or older
Total Hispanic households	**13,339**	**10,448**	**2,891**	**1,497**	**1,394**	**829**	**564**
With children of any age	7,823	6,892	931	607	324	205	119
Under age 25	7,156	6,739	418	348	70	58	12
Under age 18	6,431	6,197	235	189	46	35	11
PERCENT DISTRIBUTION							
Total Hispanic households	**100.0%**	**100.0%**	**100.0%**	**100.0%**	**100.0%**	**100.0%**	**100.0%**
With children of any age	58.6	66.0	32.2	40.5	23.2	24.7	21.1
Under age 25	53.6	64.5	14.5	23.2	5.0	7.0	2.1
Under age 18	48.2	59.3	8.1	12.6	3.3	4.2	2.0

Source: Bureau of the Census, Current Population Survey Annual Social and Economic Supplement, America's Families and Living Arrangements: 2008, detailed tables, Internet site http://www.census.gov/population/www/socdemo/hh-fam/cps2008 .html; calculations by New Strategist

Table 7.11 Households by Presence and Age of Children at Home, 2008: Non-Hispanic White Households

(number and percent distribution of non-Hispanic white households by presence and age of own children at home, by age of children and age of householder, 2008; numbers in thousands)

| | | | aged 55 or older | | | | |
| | | | | | aged 65 or older | | |
	total	under 55	total	55 to 64	total	65 to 74	75 or older
Total non-Hispanic white households	**82,765**	**47,902**	**34,863**	**15,238**	**19,625**	**9,627**	**9,998**
With children of any age	29,805	24,701	5,104	3,086	2,018	1,083	935
Under age 25	26,236	24,105	2,130	1,859	271	218	53
Under age 18	22,221	21,226	995	850	145	115	30
PERCENT DISTRIBUTION							
Total non-Hispanic white households	**100.0%**	**100.0%**	**100.0%**	**100.0%**	**100.0%**	**100.0%**	**100.0%**
With children of any age	36.0	51.6	14.6	20.3	10.3	11.2	9.4
Under age 25	31.7	50.3	6.1	12.2	1.4	2.3	0.5
Under age 18	26.8	44.3	2.9	5.6	0.7	1.2	0.3

Note: Non-Hispanic whites are those who identify themselves as being white alone and not Hispanic.
Source: Bureau of the Census, Current Population Survey Annual Social and Economic Supplement, America's Families and Living Arrangements: 2008, detailed tables, Internet site http://www.census.gov/population/www/socdemo/hh-fam/cps2008 .html; calculations by New Strategist

Most People Who Live Alone Are Aged 55 or Older

The percentage of women who live alone rises steadily with age.

Among the 32 million Americans who live alone, people aged 55 or older account for the 53 percent majority. In 2008, nearly one in four people aged 55 or older lived by themselves.

Older women are much more likely than older men to live alone, and this becomes increasingly so with age. Among 55-to-59-year-olds, 16 percent of men and 18 percent of women live alone. In the 75-or-older age group, 21 percent of men and fully 50 percent of women head single-person households.

■ Because of the higher mortality rate of men, a growing share of women become widows and live by themselves as they age into their sixties and seventies.

Women are increasingly likely to live alone as they age

(percent of women aged 55 or older who live alone, by age, 2008)

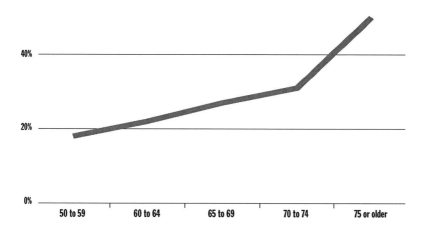

Table 7.12 People Who Live Alone by Sex and Age, 2008

(number of people aged 15 or older and number, percent, and percent distribution of people who live alone by sex and age, 2008; numbers in thousands)

		living alone		
	total	number	percent	percent distribution
TOTAL PEOPLE	**238,148**	**32,167**	**13.5%**	**100.0%**
Under age 55	**168,056**	**14,958**	**8.9**	**46.5**
Aged 55 or older	**70,092**	**17,209**	**24.6**	**53.5**
Aged 55 to 59	18,371	3,151	17.2	9.8
Aged 60 to 64	14,931	2,843	19.0	8.8
Aged 65 or older	36,790	11,214	30.5	34.9
Aged 65 to 69	11,166	2,476	22.2	7.7
Aged 70 to 74	8,423	2,066	24.5	6.4
Aged 75 or older	17,202	6,671	38.8	20.7
TOTAL MEN	**115,678**	**13,870**	**12.0**	**100.0**
Under age 55	**83,837**	**8,392**	**10.0**	**60.5**
Aged 55 or older	**31,841**	**5,478**	**17.2**	**39.5**
Aged 55 to 59	8,929	1,448	16.2	10.4
Aged 60 to 64	7,150	1,112	15.6	8.0
Aged 65 or older	15,762	2,917	18.5	21.0
Aged 65 to 69	5,238	856	16.3	6.2
Aged 70 to 74	3,740	603	16.1	4.3
Aged 75 or older	6,785	1,458	21.5	10.5
TOTAL WOMEN	**122,470**	**18,297**	**14.9**	**100.0**
Under age 55	**84,219**	**6,566**	**7.8**	**35.9**
Aged 55 or older	**38,251**	**11,731**	**30.7**	**64.1**
Aged 55 to 59	9,442	1,703	18.0	9.3
Aged 60 to 64	7,781	1,731	22.2	9.5
Aged 65 or older	21,028	8,297	39.5	45.3
Aged 65 to 69	5,928	1,620	27.3	8.9
Aged 70 to 74	4,683	1,463	31.2	8.0
Aged 75 or older	10,417	5,213	50.0	28.5

Source: Bureau of the Census, 2008 Current Population Survey, Annual Social and Economic Supplement, Internet sites http:// www.census.gov/hhes/www/macro/032008/perinc/new01_000.htm and http://www.census.gov/hhes/www/macro/032008/hhinc/ new02_000.htm; calculations by New Strategist

The Widowed Population Rises Sharply in Old Age

Fewer than half of women aged 75 or older are currently married.

Among all women aged 15 or older, only 9 percent are currently widowed. The figure stands at 42 percent among women aged 65 or older. The proportion rises from a 25 percent minority among women aged 65 to 74 to the 76 percent majority of women aged 85 or older. Women are far more likely to be currently widowed than men, since they tend to marry slightly older men and widowed men are more likely to remarry. Among men aged 85 or older, only 38 percent are currently widowed.

Women are more likely than men to be widowed in old age regardless of race or Hispanic origin. Among Hispanics, 40 percent of men and a larger 65 percent of women aged 85 or older are currently widowed. For blacks the figures are 30 and 72 percent, respectively. For non-Hispanic whites, the incidence of widowhood is 39 percent among men and 77 percent among women.

■ A growing number of women live alone as they become widows in old age.

Older women are more likely to be currently widowed

(percent of people aged 85 or older who are currently married or widowed, by sex, 2008)

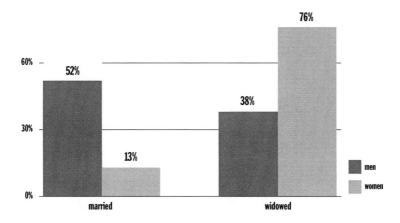

Table 7.13 Marital Status by Sex and Age, 2008: Total People

(number and percent distribution of people aged 15 or older by sex, age, and current marital status, 2008; numbers in thousands)

	total	never married	married spouse present	married spouse absent	separated	divorced	widowed
NUMBER							
Total men	**115,599**	**38,685**	**60,129**	**1,944**	**2,144**	**9,782**	**2,916**
Under age 55	83,774	36,818	37,132	1,517	1,613	6,345	350
Aged 55 or older	31,826	1,867	22,997	427	531	3,439	2,566
Aged 55 to 64	16,072	1,213	11,663	215	333	2,250	398
Aged 65 or older	15,754	653	11,334	212	199	1,189	2,168
Aged 65 to 74	8,973	399	6,853	104	147	851	619
Aged 75 to 84	5,302	186	3,715	73	42	295	992
Aged 85 or older	1,479	69	766	35	9	43	557
Total women	**122,394**	**32,794**	**60,129**	**1,470**	**3,039**	**13,564**	**11,398**
Under age 55	84,166	30,778	40,563	1,043	2,460	8,189	1,134
Aged 55 or older	38,228	2,017	19,567	428	579	5,375	10,263
Aged 55 to 64	17,215	1,181	10,812	179	355	3,225	1,464
Aged 65 or older	21,013	836	8,756	248	224	2,150	8,799
Aged 65 to 74	10,602	444	5,739	127	157	1,472	2,662
Aged 75 to 84	7,605	280	2,642	81	62	544	3,996
Aged 85 or older	2,806	112	374	41	5	134	2,141
PERCENT DISTRIBUTION							
Total men	**100.0%**	**33.5%**	**52.0%**	**1.7%**	**1.9%**	**8.5%**	**2.5%**
Under age 55	100.0	43.9	44.3	1.8	1.9	7.6	0.4
Aged 55 or older	100.0	5.9	72.3	1.3	1.7	10.8	8.1
Aged 55 to 64	100.0	7.5	72.6	1.3	2.1	14.0	2.5
Aged 65 or older	100.0	4.1	71.9	1.3	1.3	7.5	13.8
Aged 65 to 74	100.0	4.4	76.4	1.2	1.6	9.5	6.9
Aged 75 to 84	100.0	3.5	70.1	1.4	0.8	5.6	18.7
Aged 85 or older	100.0	4.7	51.8	2.4	0.6	2.9	37.7
Total women	**100.0**	**26.8**	**49.1**	**1.2**	**2.5**	**11.1**	**9.3**
Under age 55	100.0	36.6	48.2	1.2	2.9	9.7	1.3
Aged 55 or older	100.0	5.3	51.2	1.1	1.5	14.1	26.8
Aged 55 to 64	100.0	6.9	62.8	1.0	2.1	18.7	8.5
Aged 65 or older	100.0	4.0	41.7	1.2	1.1	10.2	41.9
Aged 65 to 74	100.0	4.2	54.1	1.2	1.5	13.9	25.1
Aged 75 to 84	100.0	3.7	34.7	1.1	0.8	7.2	52.5
Aged 85 or older	100.0	4.0	13.3	1.5	0.2	4.8	76.3

Source: Bureau of the Census, Current Population Survey Annual Social and Economic Supplement, America's Families and Living Arrangements: 2008, detailed tables, Internet site http://www.census.gov/population/www/socdemo/hh-fam/cps2008 .html; calculations by New Strategist

Table 7.14 Marital Status by Sex and Age, 2008: Asians

(number and percent distribution of total Asians aged 15 or older by sex, age, and current marital status, 2008; numbers in thousands)

	total	never married	married spouse present	married spouse absent	separated	divorced	widowed
NUMBER							
Total Asian men	**5,408**	**1,922**	**2,968**	**202**	**79**	**155**	**83**
Under age 55	4,245	1,856	2,044	163	60	108	14
Aged 55 or older	1161	65	924	38	20	45	69
Aged 55 to 64	604	34	494	24	13	30	9
Aged 65 or older	558	31	430	14	7	16	60
Total Asian women	**6,022**	**1,596**	**3,413**	**158**	**105**	**325**	**424**
Under age 55	4,554	1,537	2,565	119	74	211	50
Aged 55 or older	1,467	59	849	38	32	117	374
Aged 55 to 64	732	35	523	24	16	75	60
Aged 65 or older	735	25	326	14	16	41	313
PERCENT DISTRIBUTION							
Total Asian men	**100.0%**	**35.5%**	**54.9%**	**3.7%**	**1.5%**	**2.9%**	**1.5%**
Under age 55	100.0	43.7	48.2	3.8	1.4	2.5	0.3
Aged 55 or older	100.0	5.6	79.6	3.3	1.7	3.9	5.9
Aged 55 to 64	100.0	5.6	81.8	4.0	2.2	5.0	1.5
Aged 65 or older	100.0	5.6	77.1	2.5	1.3	2.9	10.8
Total Asian women	**100.0**	**26.5**	**56.7**	**2.6**	**1.7**	**5.4**	**7.0**
Under age 55	100.0	33.8	56.3	2.6	1.6	4.6	1.1
Aged 55 or older	100.0	4.0	57.9	2.6	2.2	8.0	25.5
Aged 55 to 64	100.0	4.8	71.4	3.3	2.2	10.2	8.2
Aged 65 or older	100.0	3.4	44.4	1.9	2.2	5.6	42.6

Note: Asians include those who identify themselves as being of the race alone and those who identify themselves as being of the race in combination with other races.
Source: Bureau of the Census, Current Population Survey Annual Social and Economic Supplement, America's Families and Living Arrangements: 2008, detailed tables, Internet site http://www.census.gov/population/www/socdemo/hh-fam/cps2008 .html; calculations by New Strategist

Table 7.15 Marital Status by Sex and Age, 2008: Blacks

(number and percent distribution of blacks aged 15 or older by sex, age, and current marital status, 2008; numbers in thousands)

	total	never married	married spouse present	married spouse absent	separated	divorced	widowed
NUMBER							
Total black men	**13,360**	**6,412**	**4,636**	**241**	**517**	**1,219**	**335**
Under age 55	10,592	6,106	3,072	191	361	815	46
Aged 55 or older	2,767	306	1,563	51	156	404	289
Aged 55 to 64	1,509	213	873	19	88	242	74
Aged 65 or older	1,258	93	689	32	68	162	214
Aged 65 to 74	789	54	444	13	56	129	93
Aged 75 to 84	372	31	199	12	8	29	93
Aged 85 or older	97	8	47	7	4	4	29
Total black women	**16,094**	**7,136**	**4,439**	**261**	**820**	**2,034**	**1,404**
Under age 55	12,212	6,681	3,206	193	659	1,269	205
Aged 55 or older	3,884	455	1,234	68	161	766	1,199
Aged 55 to 64	1,926	311	752	29	102	476	254
Aged 65 or older	1,957	144	481	38	58	290	945
Aged 65 to 74	1,085	92	335	14	47	218	380
Aged 75 to 84	669	43	131	17	12	47	419
Aged 85 or older	204	9	16	8	–	25	146
PERCENT DISTRIBUTION							
Total black men	**100.0%**	**48.0%**	**34.7%**	**1.8%**	**3.9%**	**9.1%**	**2.5%**
Under age 55	100.0	57.6	29.0	1.8	3.4	7.7	0.4
Aged 55 or older	100.0	11.1	56.5	1.8	5.6	14.6	10.4
Aged 55 to 64	100.0	14.1	57.9	1.3	5.8	16.0	4.9
Aged 65 or older	100.0	7.4	54.8	2.5	5.4	12.9	17.0
Aged 65 to 74	100.0	6.8	56.3	1.6	7.1	16.3	11.8
Aged 75 to 84	100.0	8.3	53.5	3.2	2.2	7.8	25.0
Aged 85 or older	100.0	8.2	48.5	7.2	4.1	4.1	29.9
Total black women	**100.0**	**44.3**	**27.6**	**1.6**	**5.1**	**12.6**	**8.7**
Under age 55	100.0	54.7	26.3	1.6	5.4	10.4	1.7
Aged 55 or older	100.0	11.7	31.8	1.8	4.1	19.7	30.9
Aged 55 to 64	100.0	16.1	39.0	1.5	5.3	24.7	13.2
Aged 65 or older	100.0	7.4	24.6	1.9	3.0	14.8	48.3
Aged 65 to 74	100.0	8.5	30.9	1.3	4.3	20.1	35.0
Aged 75 to 84	100.0	6.4	19.6	2.5	1.8	7.0	62.6
Aged 85 or older	100.0	4.4	7.8	3.9	–	12.3	71.6

Note: Blacks include those who identify themselves as being of the race alone and those who identify themselves as being of the race in combination with other races. "–" means number is less than 500 or sample is too small to make a reliable estimate.
Source: Bureau of the Census, Current Population Survey Annual Social and Economic Supplement, America's Families and Living Arrangements: 2008, detailed tables, Internet site http://www.census.gov/population/www/socdemo/hh-fam/cps2008 .html; calculations by New Strategist

Table 7.16 Marital Status by Sex and Age, 2008: Hispanics

(number and percent distribution of Hispanics aged 15 or older by sex, age, and current marital status, 2008; numbers in thousands)

	total	never married	married spouse present	married spouse absent	separated	divorced	widowed
NUMBER							
Total Hispanic men	**16,832**	**6,955**	**7,445**	**820**	**438**	**945**	**228**
Under age 55	14,397	6,772	5,780	743	358	709	36
Aged 55 or older	2,435	183	1,666	77	81	236	191
Aged 55 to 64	1,341	123	929	43	54	168	23
Aged 65 or older	1,094	60	737	34	27	67	168
Aged 65 to 74	665	48	471	24	20	52	51
Aged 75 to 84	344	7	228	10	3	12	83
Aged 85 or older	85	5	38	–	4	4	34
Total Hispanic women	**15,845**	**5,066**	**7,557**	**288**	**709**	**1,385**	**839**
Under age 55	12,936	4,855	6,173	239	579	930	160
Aged 55 or older	2,909	212	1,384	49	130	454	679
Aged 55 to 64	1,448	126	792	31	68	272	158
Aged 65 or older	1,461	85	593	18	61	182	521
Aged 65 to 74	865	57	426	14	45	117	205
Aged 75 to 84	447	26	137	4	17	45	219
Aged 85 or older	149	3	29	–	–	20	97
PERCENT DISTRIBUTION							
Total Hispanic men	**100.0%**	**41.3%**	**44.2%**	**4.9%**	**2.6%**	**5.6%**	**1.4%**
Under age 55	100.0	47.0	40.1	5.2	2.5	4.9	0.3
Aged 55 or older	100.0	7.5	68.4	3.2	3.3	9.7	7.8
Aged 55 to 64	100.0	9.2	69.3	3.2	4.0	12.5	1.7
Aged 65 or older	100.0	5.5	67.4	3.1	2.5	6.1	15.4
Aged 65 to 74	100.0	7.2	70.8	3.6	3.0	7.8	7.7
Aged 75 to 84	100.0	2.0	66.3	2.9	0.9	3.5	24.1
Aged 85 or older	100.0	5.9	44.7	–	4.7	4.7	40.0
Total Hispanic women	**100.0**	**32.0**	**47.7**	**1.8**	**4.5**	**8.7**	**5.3**
Under age 55	100.0	37.5	47.7	1.8	4.5	7.2	1.2
Aged 55 or older	100.0	7.3	47.6	1.7	4.5	15.6	23.3
Aged 55 to 64	100.0	8.7	54.7	2.1	4.7	18.8	10.9
Aged 65 or older	100.0	5.8	40.6	1.2	4.2	12.5	35.7
Aged 65 to 74	100.0	6.6	49.2	1.6	5.2	13.5	23.7
Aged 75 to 84	100.0	5.8	30.6	0.9	3.8	10.1	49.0
Aged 85 or older	100.0	2.0	19.5	–	–	13.4	65.1

Note: "–" means number is less than 500 or sample is too small to make a reliable estimate.
Source: Bureau of the Census, Current Population Survey Annual Social and Economic Supplement, America's Families and Living Arrangements: 2008, detailed tables, Internet site http://www.census.gov/population/www/socdemo/hh-fam/cps2008 .html; calculations by New Strategist

Table 7.17 Marital Status by Sex and Age, 2008: Non-Hispanic Whites

(number and percent distribution of non-Hispanic whites aged 15 or older by sex, age, and current marital status, 2008; numbers in thousands)

	total	never married	married spouse present	married spouse absent	separated	divorced	widowed
NUMBER							
Total non-Hispanic white men	**79043**	**23,142**	**44,570**	**681**	**1,099**	**7,309**	**2,242**
Under age 55	53,891	21,845	25,926	424	826	4,625	246
Aged 55 or older	25,152	1,298	18,644	257	273	2,684	1,996
Aged 55 to 64	12,446	832	9,260	125	177	1,764	289
Aged 65 or older	12,706	466	9,384	132	96	920	1,707
Aged 65 to 74	7,058	279	5,576	55	63	637	448
Aged 75 to 84	4,428	136	3,175	49	31	249	787
Aged 85 or older	1,220	51	633	28	2	34	472
Total non-Hispanic white women	**83,479**	**18,794**	**44,246**	**757**	**1,404**	**9,642**	**8,639**
Under age 55	53,816	17,507	28,313	488	1,149	5,652	708
Aged 55 or older	29,664	1,289	15,934	270	253	3,989	7,930
Aged 55 to 64	12,950	711	8,641	95	161	2,371	971
Aged 65 or older	16,714	577	7,293	175	91	1,618	6,959
Aged 65 to 74	8,154	277	4,717	87	60	1,086	1,927
Aged 75 to 84	6,183	201	2,263	55	27	446	3,191
Aged 85 or older	2,377	100	313	33	5	86	1,841
PERCENT DISTRIBUTION							
Total non-Hispanic white men	**100.0%**	**29.3%**	**56.4%**	**0.9%**	**1.4%**	**9.2%**	**2.8%**
Under age 55	100.0	40.5	48.1	0.8	1.5	8.6	0.5
Aged 55 or older	100.0	5.2	74.1	1.0	1.1	10.7	7.9
Aged 55 to 64	100.0	6.7	74.4	1.0	1.4	14.2	2.3
Aged 65 or older	100.0	3.7	73.9	1.0	0.8	7.2	13.4
Aged 65 to 74	100.0	4.0	79.0	0.8	0.9	9.0	6.3
Aged 75 to 84	100.0	3.1	71.7	1.1	0.7	5.6	17.8
Aged 85 or older	100.0	4.2	51.9	2.3	0.2	2.8	38.7
Total non-Hispanic white women	**100.0**	**22.5**	**53.0**	**0.9**	**1.7**	**11.6**	**10.3**
Under age 55	100.0	32.5	52.6	0.9	2.1	10.5	1.3
Aged 55 or older	100.0	4.3	53.7	0.9	0.9	13.4	26.7
Aged 55 to 64	100.0	5.5	66.7	0.7	1.2	18.3	7.5
Aged 65 or older	100.0	3.5	43.6	1.0	0.5	9.7	41.6
Aged 65 to 74	100.0	3.4	57.8	1.1	0.7	13.3	23.6
Aged 75 to 84	100.0	3.3	36.6	0.9	0.4	7.2	51.6
Aged 85 or older	100.0	4.2	13.2	1.4	0.2	3.6	77.5

Note: Non-Hispanic whites are those who identify themselves as being white alone and not Hispanic.
Source: Bureau of the Census, Current Population Survey Annual Social and Economic Supplement, America's Families and Living Arrangements: 2008, detailed tables, Internet site http://www.census.gov/population/www/socdemo/hh-fam/cps2008 .html; calculations by New Strategist

Divorce Is Highest among Men and Women in Their Fifties

The oldest Boomers are most likely to have gone through a divorce.

The experience of divorce is most common among men and women aged 50 to 59. Among men in the age group in 2004, 37.5 percent had ever divorced, according to a Census Bureau study of marriage and divorce. Among women in the age group, the ever-divorced percentage was an even higher 40.7 percent.

Among all Americans aged 15 or older, 41 percent of women and 44 percent of men had married once and were still married. The figure topped 50 percent for men aged 30 or older and for women aged 30 to 39.

■ Government studies have suggested that the Vietnam War and women's changing roles are factors in the higher divorce rates of Boomers.

More than one in five adults have experienced divorce

(percent of people aged 15 or older, by selected marital history and sex, 2004)

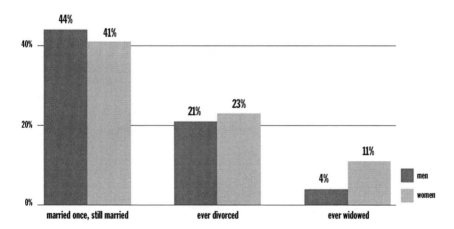

Table 7.18 Marital History of Men by Age, 2004

(number of men aged 15 or older and percent distribution by marital history and age, 2004; numbers in thousands)

	total	15–19	20–24	25–29	30–34	35–39	40–49	50–59	60–69	70+
TOTAL MEN, NUMBER	109,830	10,473	10,022	9,511	9,848	10,121	21,857	17,352	10,571	10,075
TOTAL MEN, PERCENT	100.0%	100.0%	100.0%	100.0%	100.0%	100.0%	100.0%	100.0%	100.0%	100.0%
Never married	31.2	98.1	84.0	53.6	30.3	20.2	14.1	8.7	4.8	3.2
Ever married	68.8	1.9	16.0	46.4	69.7	79.8	85.9	91.3	95.2	96.8
Married once	54.0	1.9	15.9	44.3	62.4	68.1	66.8	63.4	66.8	74.9
Still married	43.8	1.5	14.4	39.7	54.4	56.6	52.8	50.3	54.7	55.1
Married twice	11.8	0.0	0.1	2.0	6.7	10.3	15.7	21.3	20.6	17.0
Still married	9.2	0.0	0.1	1.9	6.0	8.5	12.5	16.1	16.1	12.6
Married three or more times	3.1	0.0	0.0	0.1	0.6	1.4	3.3	6.6	7.7	4.9
Still married	2.3	0.0	0.0	0.0	0.4	1.2	2.7	5.1	5.6	3.1
Ever divorced	20.7	0.1	0.8	5.1	13.1	20.7	30.3	37.5	34.1	20.6
Currently divorced	9.3	0.1	0.7	3.2	6.6	10.9	14.7	16.2	13.0	6.2
Ever widowed	3.6	0.2	0.0	0.1	0.1	0.6	1.1	2.8	7.1	23.8
Currently widowed	2.5	0.2	0.0	0.0	0.1	0.4	0.6	1.4	4.2	18.9

Source: Bureau of the Census, Number, Timing, and Duration of Marriages and Divorces: 2004, Detailed Tables, Internet site http://www.census.gov/population/www/socdemo/marr-div/2004detailed_tables.html

Table 7.19 Marital History of Women by Age, 2004

(number of women aged 15 or older and percent distribution by marital history and age, 2004; numbers in thousands)

	total	15–19	20–24	25–29	30–34	35–39	40–49	50–59	60–69	70+
TOTAL WOMEN, NUMBER	117,677	10,082	10,027	9,484	10,097	10,319	22,818	18,412	11,852	14,586
TOTAL WOMEN, PERCENT	100.0%	100.0%	100.0%	100.0%	100.0%	100.0%	100.0%	100.0%	100.0%	100.0%
Never married	25.8	97.3	73.3	41.3	22.3	16.2	11.9	7.6	4.3	4.9
Ever married	74.2	2.7	26.7	58.7	77.7	83.8	88.1	92.4	95.7	95.1
Married once	57.9	2.7	25.8	55.5	68.4	67.5	65.3	62.8	71.1	77.4
Still married	40.6	2.4	23.0	48.6	57.6	54.6	49.7	44.4	46.2	29.0
Married twice	13.2	0.1	0.8	3.1	8.2	14.1	18.9	22.6	18.7	14.9
Still married	8.8	0.0	0.7	2.8	6.6	11.3	14.0	15.5	11.3	5.3
Married three or more times	3.1	0.0	0.0	0.1	1.2	2.2	3.9	7.0	5.9	2.8
Still married	1.9	0.0	0.0	0.1	0.8	1.6	2.8	4.4	3.6	1.0
Ever divorced	22.9	0.2	2.5	7.0	17.1	25.6	33.9	40.7	32.3	17.8
Currently divorced	10.9	0.1	1.7	4.1	9.1	11.7	16.4	19.4	15.0	7.2
Ever widowed	10.8	0.1	0.1	0.3	0.7	1.1	2.5	7.8	21.2	54.5
Currently widowed	9.6	0.1	0.1	0.2	0.5	0.9	1.6	5.7	18.0	51.6

Source: Bureau of the Census, Number, Timing, and Duration of Marriages and Divorces: 2004, Detailed Tables, Internet site http://www.census.gov/population/www/socdemo/marr-div/2004detailed_tables.html

Population

■ The number of Americans aged 55 or older stood at 73 million in 2008, accounting for 24 percent of the total population.

■ In the years between 2008 and 2025, the number of people aged 55 or older will expand to 106 million, a much greater 46 percent increase than the 18 percent gain projected for the U.S. population as a whole.

■ The number of people aged 65 or older will grow by an enormous 64 percent between 2008 and 2025—a gain of more than 25 million people.

■ Seventy-eight percent of people aged 55 or older are non-Hispanic white. This figure is much higher than the 67 percent non-Hispanic white share among all Americans.

■ The share of the nation's foreign-born who are from Europe falls from a high of 36 percent in the 75-or-older age group to just 8 percent among 18-to-24-year-olds.

■ The non-Hispanic white share of the 55-or-older population ranges from a low of 71 percent in the West to a high of 88 percent in the Midwest.

Rapid Growth in the Older Age Groups

The 65-or-older age group is projected to expand by more than 25 million during the next 17 years.

According to projections by the Census Bureau, the number of Americans aged 55 or older stood at 73 million in 2008, accounting for 24 percent of the population. The oldest members of the Baby-Boom generation had entirely filled the 55-to-59 age group by 2008, and they were beginning to fill the 60-to-64 age group (Boomers were aged 44 to 62 in that year). Because mortality rates are higher for males than females, most older Americans are women. The sex ratio falls from 94 men per 100 women in the 55-to-59 age group to just 48 men per 100 women among people aged 85 or older.

The number of people aged 55 or older will expand to 106 million by 2025, a much greater 46 percent increase than the 18 percent gain projected for the U.S. population as a whole. Behind the expansion is the entry of the Baby-Boom generation into the older age groups.

In the years between 2008 and 2025, the number of people aged 65 or older will grow by an enormous 64 percent—a gain of more than 25 million people. By 2025, the generations preceding the Baby Boom will account for a miniscule 4 percent of the nation's population—down from 15 percent today. Boomers will account for 18 percent of the population, down from 25 percent.

■ Many Baby-Boomers will postpone retirement until their late sixties or seventies because of the economic downturn.

The number of older Americans will expand rapidly

(number of people aged 65 or older, 2008 and 2025)

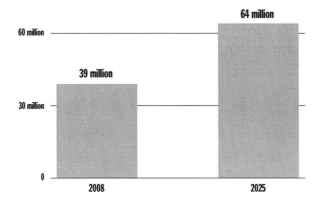

Table 8.1 Population by Age and Generation, 2008

(number and percent distribution of people by age and generation, 2008; numbers in thousands)

	number	percent distribution
Total people	**304,060**	**100.0%**
Under age 5	21,006	6.9
Aged 5 to 9	20,065	6.6
Aged 10 to 14	20,055	6.6
Aged 15 to 19	21,514	7.1
Aged 20 to 24	21,059	6.9
Aged 25 to 29	21,334	7.0
Aged 30 to 34	19,598	6.4
Aged 35 to 39	20,994	6.9
Aged 40 to 44	21,507	7.1
Aged 45 to 49	22,880	7.5
Aged 50 to 54	21,492	7.1
Aged 55 or older	72,556	23.9
Aged 55 to 59	18,583	6.1
Aged 60 to 64	15,103	5.0
Aged 65 or older	38,870	12.8
Aged 65 to 69	11,349	3.7
Aged 70 to 74	8,774	2.9
Aged 75 to 79	7,275	2.4
Aged 80 to 84	5,750	1.9
Aged 85 or older	5,722	1.9
Total people	**304,060**	**100.0**
iGeneration (under age 14)	57,115	18.8
Millennial (aged 14 to 31)	75,757	24.9
Generation X (aged 32 to 43)	49,958	16.4
Baby Boom (aged 44 to 62)	76,319	25.1
Older Americans (aged 63 or older)	44,911	14.8

Source: Bureau of the Census, Population Estimates, Internet site http://www.census.gov/popest/national/asrh/ NC-EST2008-sa.html; calculations by New Strategist

Table 8.2 Population by Age and Sex, 2008

(number of people by age and sex, and sex ratio by age, 2008; numbers in thousands)

	total	female	male	sex ratio
Total people	**304,060**	**154,135**	**149,925**	**97**
Under age 5	21,006	10,258	10,748	105
Aged 5 to 9	20,065	9,806	10,259	105
Aged 10 to 14	20,055	9,792	10,262	105
Aged 15 to 19	21,514	10,487	11,027	105
Aged 20 to 24	21,059	10,214	10,845	106
Aged 25 to 29	21,334	10,393	10,941	105
Aged 30 to 34	19,598	9,639	9,959	103
Aged 35 to 39	20,994	10,425	10,569	101
Aged 40 to 44	21,507	10,762	10,746	100
Aged 45 to 49	22,880	11,566	11,314	98
Aged 50 to 54	21,492	10,954	10,539	96
Aged 55 or older	72,556	39,840	32,715	82
Aged 55 to 59	18,583	9,569	9,015	94
Aged 60 to 64	15,103	7,867	7,236	92
Aged 65 or older	38,870	22,405	16,465	73
Aged 65 to 69	11,349	6,042	5,306	88
Aged 70 to 74	8,774	4,816	3,959	82
Aged 75 to 79	7,275	4,178	3,097	74
Aged 80 to 84	5,750	3,510	2,239	64
Aged 85 or older	5,722	3,858	1,864	48

Note: The sex ratio is the number of males per 100 females.
Source: Bureau of the Census, Population Estimates, Internet site http://www.census.gov/popest/national/asrh/ NC-EST2008-sa.html; calculations by New Strategist

Table 8.3 Population by Age, 2000 and 2008

(number of people by age, 2000 and 2008; percent change, 2000–08)

	2008	2000	percent change 2000–08
Total people	**304,060**	**281,422**	**8.0%**
Under age 5	21,006	19,176	9.5
Aged 5 to 9	20,065	20,550	–2.4
Aged 10 to 14	20,055	20,528	–2.3
Aged 15 to 19	21,514	20,220	6.4
Aged 20 to 24	21,059	18,964	11.0
Aged 25 to 29	21,334	19,381	10.1
Aged 30 to 34	19,598	20,510	–4.4
Aged 35 to 39	20,994	22,707	–7.5
Aged 40 to 44	21,507	22,442	–4.2
Aged 45 to 49	22,880	20,092	13.9
Aged 50 to 54	21,492	17,586	22.2
Aged 55 to 59	18,583	13,469	38.0
Aged 60 to 64	15,103	10,805	39.8
Aged 65 to 69	11,349	9,534	19.0
Aged 70 to 74	8,774	8,857	–0.9
Aged 75 to 79	7,275	7,416	–1.9
Aged 80 to 84	5,750	4,945	16.3
Aged 85 or older	5,722	4,240	35.0
Aged 18 to 24	29,757	27,143	9.6
Aged 18 or older	230,118	209,128	10.0
Aged 65 or older	38,870	34,992	11.1

Source: Bureau of the Census, National Population Estimates, Internet site http://www.census.gov/popest/national/asrh/ NC-EST2008-asrh.html; calculations by New Strategist

Table 8.4 Population by Age, 2008 to 2025

(number of people by age, 2008 to 2025; percent change for selected years; numbers in thousands)

	2008	2010	2015	2025	percent change 2008–10	percent change 2008–15	percent change 2008–25
Total people	**304,060**	**310,233**	**325,540**	**357,452**	**2.0%**	**7.1%**	**17.6%**
Under age 5	21,006	21,100	22,076	23,484	0.4	5.1	11.8
Aged 5 to 9	20,065	20,886	21,707	23,548	4.1	8.2	17.4
Aged 10 to 14	20,055	20,395	21,658	23,677	1.7	8.0	18.1
Aged 15 to 19	21,514	21,770	21,209	23,545	1.2	−1.4	9.4
Aged 20 to 24	21,059	21,779	22,342	23,168	3.4	6.1	10.0
Aged 25 to 29	21,334	21,418	22,400	22,417	0.4	5.0	5.1
Aged 30 to 34	19,598	20,400	22,099	23,699	4.1	12.8	20.9
Aged 35 to 39	20,994	20,267	20,841	23,645	−3.5	−0.7	12.6
Aged 40 to 44	21,507	21,010	20,460	22,851	−2.3	−4.9	6.2
Aged 45 to 49	22,880	22,596	21,001	21,154	−1.2	−8.2	−7.5
Aged 50 to 54	21,492	22,109	22,367	20,404	2.9	4.1	−5.1
Aged 55 or older	72,556	76,504	87,381	105,860	5.4	20.4	45.9
Aged 55 to 59	18,583	19,517	21,682	20,575	5.0	16.7	10.7
Aged 60 to 64	15,103	16,758	18,861	21,377	11.0	24.9	41.5
Aged 65 or older	38,870	40,229	46,837	63,907	3.5	20.5	64.4
Aged 65 to 69	11,349	12,261	15,812	19,957	8.0	39.3	75.9
Aged 70 to 74	8,774	9,202	11,155	16,399	4.9	27.1	86.9
Aged 75 to 79	7,275	7,282	7,901	12,598	0.1	8.6	73.2
Aged 80 to 84	5,750	5,733	5,676	7,715	−0.3	−1.3	34.2
Aged 85 or older	5,722	5,751	6,292	7,239	0.5	10.0	26.5

Source: Bureau of the Census, 2008 National Population Projections, Internet site http://www.census.gov/population/www/projections/2008projections.html; calculations by New Strategist

Table 8.5 Population by Generation, 2008 to 2025

(number and percent distribution of people by generation, 2008 to 2025; numbers in thousands)

	number	percent distribution
2008		
Total people	**304,060**	**100.0%**
iGeneration (under age 14)	57,115	18.8
Millennial (aged 14 to 31)	75,757	24.9
Generation X (aged 32 to 43)	49,958	16.4
Baby Boom (aged 44 to 62)	76,319	25.1
Older Americans (aged 63 or older)	44,911	14.8
2010		
Total people	**310,233**	**100.0**
iGeneration (under age 16)	66,594	21.5
Millennial (aged 16 to 33)	77,248	24.9
Generation X (aged 34 to 45)	49,651	16.0
Baby Boom (aged 46 to 64)	76,511	24.7
Older Americans (aged 65 or older)	40,229	13.0
2015		
Total people	**325,540**	**100.0**
iGeneration (under age 21)	91,002	28.0
Millennial (aged 21 to 38)	79,357	24.4
Generation X (aged 39 to 50)	49,872	15.3
Baby Boom (aged 51 to 69)	74,284	22.8
Older Americans (aged 70 or older)	31,025	9.5
2025		
Total people	**357,452**	**100.0**
iGeneration (under age 31)	144,444	40.4
Millennial (aged 31 to 48)	82,736	23.1
Generation X (aged 49 to 60)	49,278	13.8
Baby Boom (aged 61 to 79)	66,041	18.5
Older Americans (aged 80 or older)	14,953	4.2

Source: Bureau of the Census, 2008 National Population Projections, Internet site http://www.census.gov/population/www/projections/2008projections.html; calculations by New Strategist"

Older Americans Are Less Diverse than Younger Generations

Only one in five older Americans is black, Hispanic, or Asian.

Seventy-eight percent of U.S. residents aged 55 or older are non-Hispanic white, according to Census Bureau estimates for 2008. The figure peaks at 84 percent among the oldest Americans—aged 85 or older. Among children under age 5, only 53 percent are non-Hispanic white.

By generation, 80 percent of people in the generations that precede the Baby Boom (aged 63 or older in 2008) are non-Hispanic white. The figure is as low as 55 percent in the iGeneration (children under age 14). Only 7 percent of U.S. residents aged 63 or older are Hispanic compared with 23 percent of children under age 14.

■ The differences in the racial and ethnic composition of older and younger generations may create political problems in the years ahead.

Seventy-eight percent of the oldest Americans are non-Hispanic white

(percent distribution of people aged 55 or older by race and Hispanic origin, 2008)

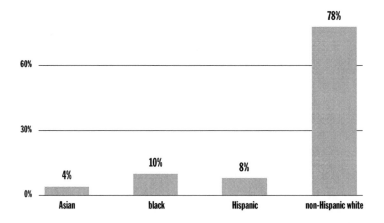

Table 8.6 Population by Age, Race, and Hispanic Origin, 2008

(number and percent distribution of people by age, race, and Hispanic origin, 2008; numbers in thousands)

	total	Asian	black	Hispanic	non-Hispanic white
Total people	**304,060**	**15,480**	**41,127**	**46,944**	**199,491**
Under age 5	21,006	1,242	3,573	5,288	11,065
Aged 5 to 9	20,065	1,107	3,298	4,464	11,222
Aged 10 to 14	20,055	1,033	3,363	3,989	11,660
Aged 15 to 19	21,514	1,018	3,667	3,850	12,903
Aged 20 to 24	21,059	1,027	3,307	3,663	12,949
Aged 25 to 29	21,334	1,206	3,166	4,141	12,740
Aged 30 to 34	19,598	1,334	2,724	4,041	11,456
Aged 35 to 39	20,994	1,404	2,823	3,730	12,981
Aged 40 to 44	21,507	1,210	2,847	3,279	14,085
Aged 45 to 49	22,880	1,107	2,882	2,795	15,964
Aged 50 to 54	21,492	986	2,563	2,187	15,615
Aged 55 or older	72,556	2,808	6,914	5,515	56,851
Aged 55 to 59	18,583	829	2,068	1,650	13,907
Aged 60 to 64	15,103	612	1,471	1,204	11,706
Aged 65 or older	38,870	1,367	3,375	2,661	31,238
Aged 65 to 69	11,349	443	1,075	853	8,899
Aged 70 to 74	8,774	339	829	653	6,899
Aged 75 to 79	7,275	255	614	496	5,871
Aged 80 to 84	5,750	176	438	346	4,763
Aged 85 or older	5,722	154	419	313	4,807

PERCENT DISTRIBUTION BY RACE AND HISPANIC ORIGIN

Total people	**100.0%**	**5.1%**	**13.5%**	**15.4%**	**65.6%**
Under age 5	100.0	5.9	17.0	25.2	52.7
Aged 5 to 9	100.0	5.5	16.4	22.2	55.9
Aged 10 to 14	100.0	5.1	16.8	19.9	58.1
Aged 15 to 19	100.0	4.7	17.0	17.9	60.0
Aged 20 to 24	100.0	4.9	15.7	17.4	61.5
Aged 25 to 29	100.0	5.7	14.8	19.4	59.7
Aged 30 to 34	100.0	6.8	13.9	20.6	58.5
Aged 35 to 39	100.0	6.7	13.4	17.8	61.8
Aged 40 to 44	100.0	5.6	13.2	15.2	65.5
Aged 45 to 49	100.0	4.8	12.6	12.2	69.8
Aged 50 to 54	100.0	4.6	11.9	10.2	72.7
Aged 55 or older	100.0	3.9	9.5	7.6	78.4
Aged 55 to 59	100.0	4.5	11.1	8.9	74.8
Aged 60 to 64	100.0	4.1	9.7	8.0	77.5
Aged 65 or older	100.0	3.5	8.7	6.8	80.4
Aged 65 to 69	100.0	3.9	9.5	7.5	78.4
Aged 70 to 74	100.0	3.9	9.5	7.4	78.6
Aged 75 to 79	100.0	3.5	8.4	6.8	80.7
Aged 80 to 84	100.0	3.1	7.6	6.0	82.8
Aged 85 or older	100.0	2.7	7.3	5.5	84.0

Note: Numbers do not add to total because Asians and blacks include those who identified themselves as being of the race alone and those who identified themselves as being of the race in combination with other races, and because Hispanics may be of any race. Non-Hispanic whites include those who identified themselves as being white alone and not Hispanic.
Source: Bureau of the Census, Population Estimates, Internet site http://www.census.gov/popest/national/asrh/ NC-EST2008-sa.html; calculations by New Strategist

Table 8.7 Population by Generation, Race, and Hispanic Origin, 2008

(number and percent distribution of people by generation, race, and Hispanic origin, 2008; numbers in thousands)

	total	Asian	black	Hispanic	non-Hispanic white
Total people	**304,060**	**15,480**	**41,127**	**46,944**	**199,491**
iGeneration (under age 14)	57,115	3,174	9,562	12,944	31,615
Millennial (aged 14 to 31)	75,757	3,991	11,902	14,068	45,506
Generation X (aged 32 to 43)	49,958	3,172	6,735	8,778	31,123
Baby Boom (aged 44 to 62)	76,319	3,531	8,965	8,011	55,326
Older Americans (aged 63 or older)	44,911	1,612	3,964	3,143	35,920
PERCENT DISTRIBUTION BY RACE AND HISPANIC ORIGIN					
Total people	**100.0%**	**5.1%**	**13.5%**	**15.4%**	**65.6%**
iGeneration (under age 14)	100.0	5.6	16.7	22.7	55.4
Millennial (aged 14 to 31)	100.0	5.3	15.7	18.6	60.1
Generation X (aged 32 to 43)	100.0	6.3	13.5	17.6	62.3
Baby Boom (aged 44 to 62)	100.0	4.6	11.7	10.5	72.5
Older Americans (aged 63 or older)	100.0	3.6	8.8	7.0	80.0
PERCENT DISTRIBUTION BY GENERATION					
Total people	**100.0%**	**100.0%**	**100.0%**	**100.0%**	**100.0%**
iGeneration (under age 14)	18.8	20.5	23.2	27.6	15.8
Millennial (aged 14 to 31)	24.9	25.8	28.9	30.0	22.8
Generation X (aged 32 to 43)	16.4	20.5	16.4	18.7	15.6
Baby Boom (aged 44 to 62)	25.1	22.8	21.8	17.1	27.7
Older Americans (aged 63 or older)	14.8	10.4	9.6	6.7	18.0

Note: Numbers do not add to total because Asians and blacks include those who identified themselves as being of the race alone and those who identified themselves as being of the race in combination with other races, and because Hispanics may be of any race. Non-Hispanic whites are those who identified themselves as being white alone and not Hispanic.
Source: Bureau of the Census, Population Estimates, Internet site http://www.census.gov/popest/national/asrh/ NC-EST2008-sa.html; calculations by New Strategist

Many Older Americans Live in Their State of Birth

One in eight is foreign-born.

According to the 2007 American Community Survey, 49 percent of people aged 55 or older were born in their current state of residence. Thirty-seven percent of older U.S. residents were born in the United States, but in a different state. Twelve percent were born in another country.

Among the foreign-born aged 55 or older, 39 percent were born in Latin America, 29 percent were born in Asia, and 25 percent are from Europe. The share of the nation's foreign-born who are from Europe falls from a high of 36 percent in the 75-or-older age group to just 8 percent among 18-to-24-year-olds.

■ The foreign-born population adds to the multicultural mix, which is becoming a significant factor in American business and politics.

One-fourth of the foreign-born in the 55-or-older age group are from Europe

(percent distribution of the foreign-born aged 55 or older by region of birth, 2008)

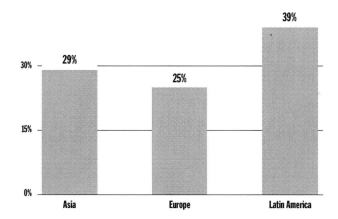

Table 8.8 Population by Age and Place of Birth, 2007

(number and percent distribution of people by age and place of birth, 2007; numbers in thousands)

| | | born in the United States | | | |
	total	in state of current residence	outside state of current residence	citizen born outside United states	foreign-born
Total people	**301,621**	**177,509**	**82,253**	**3,799**	**38,060**
Under age 18	73,908	59,667	10,643	625	2,973
Aged 18 to 24	29,821	18,880	7,062	395	3,484
Aged 25 to 34	39,987	20,889	10,532	611	7,955
Aged 35 to 44	43,410	21,083	13,067	692	8,569
Aged 45 to 54	43,925	22,275	14,527	669	6,455
Aged 55 or older	70,570	34,715	26,422	808	8,624
Aged 55 to 59	18,115	9,091	6,455	233	2,335
Aged 60 to 61	6,495	3,138	2,442	87	828
Aged 62 to 64	8,119	3,902	3,140	94	983
Aged 65 or older	37,841	18,584	14,385	394	4,478
Aged 65 to 74	19,397	9,364	7,315	225	2,494
Aged 75 or older	18,443	9,221	7,069	169	1,984
PERCENT DISTRIBUTION BY PLACE OF BIRTH					
Total people	**100.0%**	**58.9%**	**27.3%**	**1.3%**	**12.6%**
Under age 18	100.0	80.7	14.4	0.8	4.0
Aged 18 to 24	100.0	63.3	23.7	1.3	11.7
Aged 25 to 34	100.0	52.2	26.3	1.5	19.9
Aged 35 to 44	100.0	48.6	30.1	1.6	19.7
Aged 45 to 54	100.0	50.7	33.1	1.5	14.7
Aged 55 or older	100.0	49.2	37.4	1.1	12.2
Aged 55 to 59	100.0	50.2	35.6	1.3	12.9
Aged 60 to 61	100.0	48.3	37.6	1.3	12.8
Aged 62 to 64	100.0	48.1	38.7	1.2	12.1
Aged 65 or older	100.0	49.1	38.0	1.0	11.8
Aged 65 to 74	100.0	48.3	37.7	1.2	12.9
Aged 75 or older	100.0	50.0	38.3	0.9	10.8
PERCENT DISTRIBUTION BY AGE					
Total people	**100.0%**	**100.0%**	**100.0%**	**100.0%**	**100.0%**
Under age 18	24.5	33.6	12.9	16.4	7.8
Aged 18 to 24	9.9	10.6	8.6	10.4	9.2
Aged 25 to 34	13.3	11.8	12.8	16.1	20.9
Aged 35 to 44	14.4	11.9	15.9	18.2	22.5
Aged 45 to 54	14.6	12.5	17.7	17.6	17.0
Aged 55 or older	23.4	19.6	32.1	21.3	22.7
Aged 55 to 59	6.0	5.1	7.8	6.1	6.1
Aged 60 to 61	2.2	1.8	3.0	2.3	2.2
Aged 62 to 64	2.7	2.2	3.8	2.5	2.6
Aged 65 or older	12.5	10.5	17.5	10.4	11.8
Aged 65 to 74	6.4	5.3	8.9	5.9	6.6
Aged 75 or older	6.1	5.2	8.6	4.5	5.2

Source: Bureau of the Census, 2007 American Community Survey, Internet site http://factfinder.census.gov/home/saff/main
.html?_lang=en; calculations by New Strategist

Table 8.9 Foreign-Born Population by Age and World Region of Birth, 2007

(number and percent distribution of foreign-born by age and world region of birth, 2007; numbers in thousands)

	total	Asia	Europe	Latin America total	Mexico
Total people	**38,060**	**10,185**	**4,990**	**20,410**	**11,739**
Under age 18	2,973	713	329	1,694	1,103
Aged 18 to 24	3,484	744	284	2,225	1,456
Aged 25 to 44	16,524	4,308	1,382	9,858	6,104
Aged 45 to 54	6,455	1,915	808	3,286	1,655
Aged 55 or older	8,624	2,506	2,181	3,368	1,409
Aged 55 to 64	4,147	1,293	798	1,796	798
Aged 65 or older	4,478	1,212	1,382	1,572	610
Aged 65 to 74	2,494	744	669	939	376
Aged 75 or older	1,984	469	714	633	235
Median age (years)	40.2	42.0	50.8	37.4	35.1

PERCENT DISTRIBUTION OF FOREIGN-BORN BY REGION OF BIRTH

Total people	**100.0%**	**26.8%**	**13.1%**	**53.6%**	**30.8%**
Under age 18	100.0	24.0	11.1	57.0	37.1
Aged 18 to 24	100.0	21.3	8.2	63.9	41.8
Aged 25 to 44	100.0	26.1	8.4	59.7	36.9
Aged 45 to 54	100.0	29.7	12.5	50.9	25.6
Aged 55 or older	100.0	29.1	25.3	39.0	16.3
Aged 55 to 64	100.0	31.2	19.3	43.3	19.2
Aged 65 or older	100.0	27.1	30.9	35.1	13.6
Aged 65 to 74	100.0	29.8	26.8	37.6	15.1
Aged 75 or older	100.0	23.6	36.0	31.9	11.8

PERCENT DISTRIBUTION BY AGE

Total people	**100.0%**	**100.0%**	**100.0%**	**100.0%**	**100.0%**
Under age 18	7.8	7.0	6.6	8.3	9.4
Aged 18 to 24	9.2	7.3	5.7	10.9	12.4
Aged 25 to 44	43.4	42.3	27.7	48.3	52.0
Aged 45 to 54	17.0	18.8	16.2	16.1	14.1
Aged 55 or older	22.7	24.6	43.7	16.5	12.0
Aged 55 to 64	10.9	12.7	16.0	8.8	6.8
Aged 65 or older	11.8	11.9	27.7	7.7	5.2
Aged 65 to 74	6.6	7.3	13.4	4.6	3.2
Aged 75 or older	5.2	4.6	14.3	3.1	2.0

Note: Numbers do not add to total because "other" is not shown.
Source: Bureau of the Census, 2007 American Community Survey, Internet site http://factfinder.census.gov/home/saff/main
.html?_lang=en; calculations by New Strategist

Few Immigrants Are in the Older Age Groups

Only 13 percent of immigrants admitted in 2008 were aged 55 or older.

The number of legal immigrants admitted to the United States in 2008 numbered over 1 million. Only about 140,000 were aged 55 or older, accounting for 13 percent of the total. Most immigrants are young adults seeking economic opportunity for themselves and their families.

Within the 55-or-older age group, the immigrant share declines with age. Four percent of immigrants admitted to the United States in 2008 were aged 55 to 59, the figure falling to just 1 percent in the 75-or-older age group.

■ Because most immigrants are young adults, immigration has a much greater impact on the diversity of younger Americans than on the older population.

Most immigrants are under age 35

(percent distribution of immigrants by age, 2008)

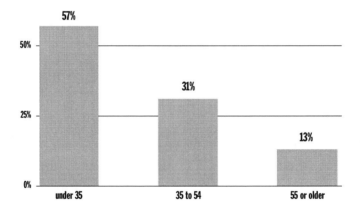

Table 8.10 Newly Arrived Immigrants by Age, 2008

(number and percent distribution of immigrants admitted in 2008, by age)

	number	percent distribution
Total immigrants	**1,107,126**	**100.0%**
Under age 1	8,280	0.7
Aged 1 to 4	29,998	2.7
Aged 5 to 9	52,993	4.8
Aged 10 to 14	74,608	6.7
Aged 15 to 19	94,697	8.6
Aged 20 to 24	104,332	9.4
Aged 25 to 29	121,416	11.0
Aged 30 to 34	140,132	12.7
Aged 35 to 39	124,341	11.2
Aged 40 to 44	92,627	8.4
Aged 45 to 49	69,868	6.3
Aged 50 to 54	53,848	4.9
Aged 55 or older	139,979	12.6
Aged 55 to 59	43,789	4.0
Aged 60 to 64	35,586	3.2
Aged 65 or older	60,604	5.5
Aged 65 to 74	45,399	4.1
Aged 75 or older	15,205	1.4

Note: Immigrants are those granted legal permanent residence in the United States. They either arrive in the United States with immigrant visas issued abroad or adjust their status in the United States from temporary to permanent residence. Numbers may not sum to total because "age not stated" is not shown.
Source: Department of Homeland Security, 2008 Yearbook of Immigration Statistics, Internet site http://www.uscis.gov/ graphics/shared/statistics/yearbook/index.htm

Many Older U.S. Residents Do Not Speak English at Home

The largest share speaks Spanish, and most do not speak English very well.

Fifty-five million residents of the United States speak a language other than English at home, according to the Census Bureau's 2007 American Community Survey—20 percent of the population aged 5 or older. Among those who do not speak English at home, 62 percent speak Spanish.

In the 65-plus age group, a smaller 14 percent speak a language other than English at home. Among those who speak a language other than English at home, only 44 percent speak Spanish while a substantial 34 percent speak another Indo-European language.

Many older U.S. residents who speak a language other than English at home do not speak English very well. The figure peaks at 73 percent among Asian language speakers. For those who speak Spanish at home, the 64 percent majority has trouble speaking English.

■ The language barrier is a bigger problem for adults than for children.

Many older people who speak Spanish at home cannot speak English very well

(percent of people aged 65 or older who speak a language other than English at home who speak English less than "very well," by language spoken at home, 2007

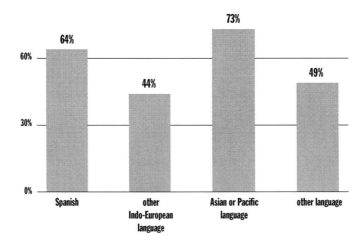

Table 8.11 Language Spoken at Home by People Aged 65 or Older, 2007

(number and percent distribution of people aged 5 or older and aged 65 or older who speak a language other than English at home by language spoken at home and ability to speak English very well, by age, 2007; numbers in thousands)

	total		aged 65 or older	
	number	percent distribution	number	percent distribution
Total, aged 5 or older	**280,950**	**100.0%**	**37,841**	**100.0%**
Speak only English at home	225,506	80.3	32,552	86.0
Speak a language other than English at home	55,444	19.7	5,288	14.0
Speak English less than very well	24,469	8.7	3,097	8.2
Total who speak a language other than English at home	**55,444**	**100.0**	**5,288**	**100.0**
Speak Spanish at home	34,547	62.3	2,342	44.3
Speak other Indo-European language at home	10,321	18.6	1,808	34.2
Speak Asian or Pacific Island language at home	8,316	15.0	941	17.8
Speak other language at home	2,260	4.1	197	3.7
Speak Spanish at home	34,547	100.0	2,342	100.0
Speak English less than very well	16,368	47.4	1,508	64.4
Speak other Indo-European language at home	10,321	100.0	1,808	100.0
Speak English less than very well	3,384	32.8	804	44.4
Speak Asian or Pacific Island language at home	8,316	100.0	941	100.0
Speak English less than very well	4,042	48.6	687	73.0
Speak other language at home	2,260	100.0	197	100.0
Speak English less than very well	676	29.9	97	49.4

Source: Bureau of the Census, 2007 American Community Survey, Internet site http://factfinder.census.gov/servlet/ DatasetMainPageServlet?_program=ACS&_submenuId=&_lang=en&_ts=; calculations by New Strategist

The Largest Share of Older Americans Lives in the South

People aged 55 or older account for 29 percent of the populations of Florida and West Virginia.

The South is home to the largest share of the population, and consequently to the largest share of older Americans. According to Census Bureau estimates for 2008, 36 percent of people aged 55 or older live in the South, where they accounted for 24 percent of the population.

The diversity of older Americans varies by region, but not nearly as much as it does among middle-aged and younger Americans. The non-Hispanic white share of the 55-or-older population ranges from a low of 71 percent in the West to a high of 88 percent in the Midwest.

By state, the smallest proportion of older Americans is found in Utah and Alaska—just 17 to 18 percent of residents of those states are aged 55 or older. Florida's warm climate has attracted many retirees, which is why the state ranks number one in the proportion of residents aged 55 or older.

■ The diversity of the older population will surge when Generation X enters the 55-or-older age group beginning in 2020.

The smallest share of older Americans lives in the Northeast

(percent distribution of people aged 55 or older by region, 2008)

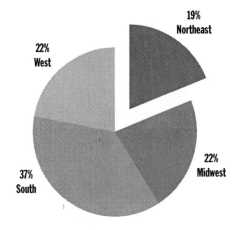

19%
Northeast

22%
West

22%
Midwest

37%
South

Table 8.12 Population by Age and Region, 2008

(number and percent distribution of people by age and region, 2008; numbers in thousands)

	total	Northeast	Midwest	South	West
Total people	**304,060**	**54,925**	**66,561**	**111,719**	**70,855**
Under age 55	231,504	40,924	50,341	85,055	55,184
Aged 55 or older	72,556	14,001	16,220	26,664	15,671
Aged 55 to 59	18,583	3,514	4,186	6,729	4,155
Aged 60 to 64	15,103	2,865	3,302	5,624	3,312
Aged 65 or older	38,870	7,622	8,733	14,311	8,204
Aged 65 to 69	11,349	2,140	2,511	4,269	2,428
Aged 70 to 74	8,774	1,673	1,946	3,289	1,866
Aged 75 to 79	7,275	1,436	1,626	2,686	1,527
Aged 80 to 84	5,750	1,175	1,310	2,067	1,197
Aged 85 or older	5,722	1,197	1,339	2,000	1,186
PERCENT DISTRIBUTION BY AGE					
Total people	**100.0%**	**100.0%**	**100.0%**	**100.0%**	**100.0%**
Under age 55	76.1	74.5	75.6	76.1	77.9
Total, aged 55 or older	23.9	25.5	24.4	23.9	22.1
Aged 55 to 59	6.1	6.4	6.3	6.0	5.9
Aged 60 to 64	5.0	5.2	5.0	5.0	4.7
Aged 65 or older	12.8	13.9	13.1	12.8	11.6
Aged 65 to 69	3.7	3.9	3.8	3.8	3.4
Aged 70 to 74	2.9	3.0	2.9	2.9	2.6
Aged 75 to 79	2.4	2.6	2.4	2.4	2.2
Aged 80 to 84	1.9	2.1	2.0	1.9	1.7
Aged 85 or older	1.9	2.2	2.0	1.8	1.7
PERCENT DISTRIBUTION BY REGION					
Total people	**100.0%**	**18.1%**	**21.9%**	**36.7%**	**23.3%**
Under age 55	100.0	17.7	21.7	36.7	23.8
Total, aged 55 or older	100.0	19.3	22.4	36.7	21.6
Aged 55 to 59	100.0	18.9	22.5	36.2	22.4
Aged 60 to 64	100.0	19.0	21.9	37.2	21.9
Aged 65 or older	100.0	19.6	22.5	36.8	21.1
Aged 65 to 69	100.0	18.9	22.1	37.6	21.4
Aged 70 to 74	100.0	19.1	22.2	37.5	21.3
Aged 75 to 79	100.0	19.7	22.4	36.9	21.0
Aged 80 to 84	100.0	20.4	22.8	36.0	20.8
Aged 85 or older	100.0	20.9	23.4	34.9	20.7

Source: Bureau of the Census, State Population Estimates, Internet site http://www.census.gov/popest/states/asrh/; calculations by New Strategist

Table 8.13 Population by Generation and Region, 2008

(number and percent distribution of people by generation and region, 2008; numbers in thousands)

	total	Northeast	Midwest	South	West
Total people	**304,060**	**54,925**	**66,561**	**111,719**	**70,855**
iGeneration (under age 14)	57,115	9,422	12,350	21,429	13,914
Millennial (aged 14 to 31)	75,757	13,150	16,497	27,709	18,401
Generation X (aged 32 to 43)	49,958	9,063	10,583	18,408	11,905
Baby Boom (aged 44 to 62)	76,319	14,522	17,078	27,612	17,106
Older Americans (aged 63 or older)	44,911	8,768	10,054	16,560	9,529
PERCENT DISTRIBUTION BY GENERATION					
Total people	**100.0%**	**100.0%**	**100.0%**	**100.0%**	**100.0%**
iGeneration (under age 14)	18.8	17.2	18.6	19.2	19.6
Millennial (aged 14 to 31)	24.9	23.9	24.8	24.8	26.0
Generation X (aged 32 to 43)	16.4	16.5	15.9	16.5	16.8
Baby Boom (aged 44 to 62)	25.1	26.4	25.7	24.7	24.1
Older Americans (aged 63 or older)	14.8	16.0	15.1	14.8	13.4
PERCENT DISTRIBUTION BY REGION					
Total people	**100.0%**	**18.1%**	**21.9%**	**36.7%**	**23.3%**
iGeneration (under age 14)	100.0	16.5	21.6	37.5	24.4
Millennial (aged 14 to 31)	100.0	17.4	21.8	36.6	24.3
Generation X (aged 32 to 43)	100.0	18.1	21.2	36.8	23.8
Baby Boom (aged 44 to 62)	100.0	19.0	22.4	36.2	22.4
Older Americans (aged 63 or older)	100.0	19.5	22.4	36.9	21.2

Source: Bureau of the Census, State Population Estimates, Internet site http://www.census.gov/popest/states/asrh/; calculations by New Strategist

Table 8.14 Population Aged 55 or Older by Region, Race, and Hispanic Origin, 2007

(number and percent distribution of people aged 55 or older by region, race, and Hispanic origin, 2007; numbers in thousands)

	total 55 or older	Asian	black	Hispanic	non-Hispanic white
United States	**70,570**	**2,530**	**6,438**	**5,158**	**55,538**
Northeast	13,713	472	1,156	823	11,178
Midwest	15,849	232	1,158	359	13,959
South	25,854	443	3,574	1,935	19,603
West	15,154	1,382	551	2,040	10,798
PERCENT DISTRIBUTION BY RACE AND HISPANIC ORIGIN					
United States	**100.0%**	**3.6%**	**9.1%**	**7.3%**	**78.7%**
Northeast	100.0	3.4	8.4	6.0	81.5
Midwest	100.0	1.5	7.3	2.3	88.1
South	100.0	1.7	13.8	7.5	75.8
West	100.0	9.1	3.6	13.5	71.3
PERCENT DISTRIBUTION BY REGION					
United States	**100.0%**	**100.0%**	**100.0%**	**100.0%**	**100.0%**
Northeast	19.4	18.7	18.0	16.0	20.1
Midwest	22.5	9.2	18.0	7.0	25.1
South	36.6	17.5	55.5	37.5	35.3
West	21.5	54.6	8.6	39.6	19.4

Note: Numbers do not add to total because Asians and blacks are only those who identified themselves as being of the race alone and because Hispanics may be of any race. Non-Hispanic whites are only those who identified themselves as being white alone and not Hispanic.
Source: Bureau of the Census, 2007 American Community Survey, Internet site http://factfinder.census.gov/home/saff/main .html?_lang=en; calculations by New Strategist

Table 8.15 State Populations by Age, 2008

(total number of people and number aged 55 or older by state and age, 2008; numbers in thousands)

	total population	aged 55 or older total	55 to 59	60 to 64	aged 65 or older total	65 to 69	70 to 74	75 to 79	80 to 84	85 or older
United States	304,060	72,556	18,583	15,103	38,870	11,349	8,774	7,275	5,750	5,722
Alabama	4,662	1,183	295	247	642	192	153	121	91	85
Alaska	686	125	45	30	50	19	12	9	6	5
Arizona	6,500	1,540	364	314	863	249	195	165	130	123
Arkansas	2,855	738	176	155	407	121	94	76	58	59
California	36,757	7,782	2,054	1,614	4,114	1,191	935	767	608	612
Colorado	4,939	1,058	310	237	511	161	118	94	70	67
Connecticut	3,501	886	223	186	478	135	102	88	74	79
Delaware	873	224	54	48	122	37	28	24	17	16
District of Columbia	592	134	35	28	71	21	16	13	10	11
Florida	18,328	5,325	1,125	1,013	3,188	846	690	619	511	521
Georgia	9,686	1,991	558	452	981	322	231	176	129	122
Hawaii	1,288	342	83	69	190	49	40	37	32	32
Idaho	1,524	349	92	75	182	56	42	33	26	26
Illinois	12,902	2,942	766	601	1,575	458	354	291	233	239
Indiana	6,377	1,523	395	314	814	240	183	151	120	119
Iowa	3,003	789	193	152	445	118	96	83	70	79
Kansas	2,802	672	171	135	367	100	79	68	56	62
Kentucky	4,269	1,068	276	226	566	175	133	105	79	75
Louisiana	4,411	1,030	272	217	540	163	126	102	77	72
Maine	1,316	378	98	81	199	58	45	38	29	29
Maryland	5,634	1,318	354	285	680	210	156	125	97	92
Massachusetts	6,498	1,620	412	336	871	241	188	163	136	143
Michigan	10,003	2,473	651	518	1,304	388	292	243	195	187
Minnesota	5,220	1,230	328	252	651	188	142	118	96	107
Mississippi	2,939	692	176	145	372	111	87	69	53	52
Missouri	5,912	1,478	368	305	805	235	181	149	118	122
Montana	967	263	71	55	137	41	31	25	20	20
Nebraska	1,783	436	110	85	241	64	53	46	37	41
Nevada	2,600	588	156	135	297	100	71	55	39	32
New Hampshire	1,316	335	91	74	170	51	38	32	25	24
New Jersey	8,683	2,127	536	441	1,151	331	254	217	174	175
New Mexico	1,984	484	124	100	260	77	61	50	37	36
New York	19,490	4,817	1,219	990	2,608	747	585	488	390	398
North Carolina	9,222	2,194	571	484	1,139	352	266	212	161	148
North Dakota	641	167	41	31	94	23	20	18	15	18
Ohio	11,486	2,903	745	588	1,571	452	355	296	239	229
Oklahoma	3,642	898	220	187	491	145	114	92	70	70
Oregon	3,790	980	264	212	504	151	111	91	75	76
Pennsylvania	12,448	3,399	822	666	1,911	511	410	367	312	310
Rhode Island	1,051	269	67	54	148	39	31	28	24	26
South Carolina	4,480	1,141	292	253	596	187	140	110	83	77

	total population	aged 55 or older								
		total	55 to 59	60 to 64	aged 65 or older					
					total	65 to 69	70 to 74	75 to 79	80 to 84	85 or older
South Dakota	804	209	52	41	116	31	25	22	18	21
Tennessee	6,215	1,554	398	336	820	255	194	152	113	106
Texas	24,327	4,829	1,314	1,043	2,472	754	579	462	345	333
Utah	2,736	472	127	99	246	74	57	47	35	33
Vermont	621	171	47	37	87	27	19	16	13	12
Virginia	7,769	1,817	480	396	941	295	219	174	131	122
Washington	6,549	1,556	429	343	784	240	176	142	111	115
West Virginia	1,814	526	133	108	285	83	66	54	43	39
Wisconsin	5,628	1,397	365	282	750	213	166	141	113	117
Wyoming	533	130	37	28	66	20	15	12	9	9

Source: Bureau of the Census, State Population Estimates, Internet site http://www.census.gov/popest/states/asrh/; calculations by New Strategist

Table 8.16 Distribution of State Populations by Age, 2008

(percent distribution of people aged 55 or older by state and age, 2008)

| | total population | aged 55 or older | | | | | | | | |
| | | total | 55 to 59 | 60 to 64 | aged 65 or older | | | | | |
					total	65 to 69	70 to 74	75 to 79	80 to 84	85 or older
United States	**100.0%**	**23.9%**	**6.1%**	**5.0%**	**12.8%**	**3.7%**	**2.9%**	**2.4%**	**1.9%**	**1.9%**
Alabama	100.0	25.4	6.3	5.3	13.8	4.1	3.3	2.6	1.9	1.8
Alaska	100.0	18.2	6.5	4.4	7.3	2.8	1.8	1.3	0.8	0.7
Arizona	100.0	23.7	5.6	4.8	13.3	3.8	3.0	2.5	2.0	1.9
Arkansas	100.0	25.9	6.2	5.4	14.3	4.2	3.3	2.6	2.0	2.1
California	100.0	21.2	5.6	4.4	11.2	3.2	2.5	2.1	1.7	1.7
Colorado	100.0	21.4	6.3	4.8	10.3	3.3	2.4	1.9	1.4	1.4
Connecticut	100.0	25.3	6.4	5.3	13.7	3.8	2.9	2.5	2.1	2.3
Delaware	100.0	25.7	6.2	5.5	13.9	4.2	3.2	2.7	2.0	1.8
District of Columbia	100.0	22.6	5.9	4.8	11.9	3.5	2.7	2.1	1.7	1.9
Florida	100.0	29.1	6.1	5.5	17.4	4.6	3.8	3.4	2.8	2.8
Georgia	100.0	20.6	5.8	4.7	10.1	3.3	2.4	1.8	1.3	1.3
Hawaii	100.0	26.6	6.5	5.3	14.8	3.8	3.1	2.9	2.5	2.5
Idaho	100.0	22.9	6.0	4.9	12.0	3.7	2.7	2.2	1.7	1.7
Illinois	100.0	22.8	5.9	4.7	12.2	3.6	2.7	2.3	1.8	1.9
Indiana	100.0	23.9	6.2	4.9	12.8	3.8	2.9	2.4	1.9	1.9
Iowa	100.0	26.3	6.4	5.0	14.8	3.9	3.2	2.8	2.3	2.6
Kansas	100.0	24.0	6.1	4.8	13.1	3.6	2.8	2.4	2.0	2.2
Kentucky	100.0	25.0	6.5	5.3	13.3	4.1	3.1	2.5	1.8	1.8
Louisiana	100.0	23.3	6.2	4.9	12.2	3.7	2.9	2.3	1.8	1.6
Maine	100.0	28.7	7.4	6.1	15.1	4.4	3.4	2.9	2.2	2.2
Maryland	100.0	23.4	6.3	5.1	12.1	3.7	2.8	2.2	1.7	1.6
Massachusetts	100.0	24.9	6.3	5.2	13.4	3.7	2.9	2.5	2.1	2.2
Michigan	100.0	24.7	6.5	5.2	13.0	3.9	2.9	2.4	1.9	1.9
Minnesota	100.0	23.6	6.3	4.8	12.5	3.6	2.7	2.3	1.8	2.0
Mississippi	100.0	23.5	6.0	4.9	12.6	3.8	3.0	2.4	1.8	1.8
Missouri	100.0	25.0	6.2	5.2	13.6	4.0	3.1	2.5	2.0	2.1
Montana	100.0	27.2	7.3	5.7	14.2	4.3	3.2	2.6	2.0	2.1
Nebraska	100.0	24.4	6.2	4.7	13.5	3.6	3.0	2.6	2.1	2.3
Nevada	100.0	22.6	6.0	5.2	11.4	3.8	2.7	2.1	1.5	1.2
New Hampshire	100.0	25.5	6.9	5.6	12.9	3.9	2.9	2.4	1.9	1.9
New Jersey	100.0	24.5	6.2	5.1	13.3	3.8	2.9	2.5	2.0	2.0
New Mexico	100.0	24.4	6.2	5.0	13.1	3.9	3.1	2.5	1.9	1.8
New York	100.0	24.7	6.3	5.1	13.4	3.8	3.0	2.5	2.0	2.0
North Carolina	100.0	23.8	6.2	5.3	12.4	3.8	2.9	2.3	1.7	1.6
North Dakota	100.0	26.0	6.4	4.9	14.7	3.7	3.1	2.8	2.3	2.8
Ohio	100.0	25.3	6.5	5.1	13.7	3.9	3.1	2.6	2.1	2.0
Oklahoma	100.0	24.6	6.0	5.1	13.5	4.0	3.1	2.5	1.9	1.9
Oregon	100.0	25.9	7.0	5.6	13.3	4.0	2.9	2.4	2.0	2.0
Pennsylvania	100.0	27.3	6.6	5.4	15.3	4.1	3.3	2.9	2.5	2.5
Rhode Island	100.0	25.6	6.3	5.2	14.1	3.7	2.9	2.6	2.3	2.5
South Carolina	100.0	25.5	6.5	5.6	13.3	4.2	3.1	2.5	1.8	1.7
South Dakota	100.0	26.0	6.4	5.1	14.4	3.9	3.1	2.7	2.2	2.6

	total population	aged 55 or older			aged 65 or older					
		total	55 to 59	60 to 64	total	65 to 69	70 to 74	75 to 79	80 to 84	85 or older
Tennessee	100.0%	25.0%	6.4%	5.4%	13.2%	4.1%	3.1%	2.4%	1.8%	1.7%
Texas	100.0	19.9	5.4	4.3	10.2	3.1	2.4	1.9	1.4	1.4
Utah	100.0	17.2	4.6	3.6	9.0	2.7	2.1	1.7	1.3	1.2
Vermont	100.0	27.6	7.6	6.0	13.9	4.3	3.1	2.6	2.0	2.0
Virginia	100.0	23.4	6.2	5.1	12.1	3.8	2.8	2.2	1.7	1.6
Washington	100.0	23.8	6.6	5.2	12.0	3.7	2.7	2.2	1.7	1.8
West Virginia	100.0	29.0	7.3	6.0	15.7	4.6	3.7	3.0	2.4	2.1
Wisconsin	100.0	24.8	6.5	5.0	13.3	3.8	2.9	2.5	2.0	2.1
Wyoming	100.0	24.5	6.9	5.3	12.3	3.8	2.8	2.3	1.7	1.7

Source: Bureau of the Census, State Population Estimates, Internet site http://www.census.gov/popest/states/asrh/; calculations by New Strategist

Table 8.17 State Populations by Generation, 2008

(number of people by state and generation, 2008; numbers in thousands)

	total population	iGeneration (under 14)	Millennial (14 to 31)	Generation X (32 to 43)	Baby Boom (44 to 62)	Older Americans (63 or older)
United States	**304,060**	**57,115**	**75,757**	**49,958**	**76,319**	**44,911**
Alabama	4,662	864	1,145	732	1,180	741
Alaska	686	138	192	113	181	62
Arizona	6,500	1,344	1,631	1,053	1,484	988
Arkansas	2,855	545	695	443	703	469
California	36,757	7,224	9,724	6,342	8,706	4,760
Colorado	4,939	946	1,258	863	1,266	606
Connecticut	3,501	617	806	577	949	552
Delaware	873	159	209	140	224	141
District of Columbia	592	87	180	106	137	82
Florida	18,328	3,087	4,164	2,887	4,597	3,593
Georgia	9,686	1,993	2,459	1,719	2,353	1,162
Hawaii	1,288	222	319	208	321	218
Idaho	1,524	323	391	233	364	212
Illinois	12,902	2,458	3,300	2,148	3,180	1,816
Indiana	6,377	1,225	1,574	1,028	1,610	940
Iowa	3,003	548	735	447	767	505
Kansas	2,802	545	714	426	696	421
Kentucky	4,269	779	1,031	699	1,104	656
Louisiana	4,411	855	1,160	669	1,100	627
Maine	1,316	206	287	207	385	231
Maryland	5,634	1,026	1,378	950	1,486	793
Massachusetts	6,498	1,088	1,595	1,093	1,717	1,006
Michigan	10,003	1,810	2,442	1,598	2,641	1,511
Minnesota	5,220	967	1,294	842	1,366	751
Mississippi	2,939	593	756	449	710	429
Missouri	5,912	1,092	1,455	924	1,513	927
Montana	967	168	235	137	268	159
Nebraska	1,783	348	453	267	441	275
Nevada	2,600	525	631	457	637	351
New Hampshire	1,316	220	299	218	379	200
New Jersey	8,683	1,572	1,985	1,502	2,296	1,327
New Mexico	1,984	391	509	298	487	300
New York	19,490	3,360	4,857	3,257	5,013	3,004
North Carolina	9,222	1,752	2,241	1,577	2,320	1,333
North Dakota	641	110	176	88	162	107
Ohio	11,486	2,088	2,774	1,810	3,008	1,806
Oklahoma	3,642	706	934	547	890	565
Oregon	3,790	668	918	614	1,002	589
Pennsylvania	12,448	2,091	2,913	1,943	3,324	2,177
Rhode Island	1,051	173	262	170	276	169
South Carolina	4,480	822	1,096	717	1,147	697

	total population	iGeneration (under 14)	Millennial (14 to 31)	Generation X (32 to 43)	Baby Boom (44 to 62)	Older Americans (63 or older)
South Dakota	804	153	201	114	204	132
Tennessee	6,215	1,143	1,489	1,028	1,600	954
Texas	24,327	5,307	6,426	4,130	5,575	2,890
Utah	2,736	680	828	413	530	286
Vermont	621	96	145	96	183	102
Virginia	7,769	1,413	1,935	1,332	1,990	1,099
Washington	6,549	1,185	1,630	1,096	1,718	921
West Virginia	1,814	296	412	283	496	328
Wisconsin	5,628	1,005	1,379	891	1,490	863
Wyoming	533	99	136	78	143	77

Source: Bureau of the Census, State Population Estimates, Internet site http://www.census.gov/popest/states/asrh/; calculations by New Strategist

Table 8.18 **Distribution of State Populations by Generation, 2008**

(percent distribution of people by state and generation, 2008)

	total population	iGeneration (under 14)	Millennial (14 to 31)	Generation X (32 to 43)	Baby Boom (44 to 62)	Older Americans (63 or older)
United States	**100.0%**	**18.8%**	**24.9%**	**16.4%**	**25.1%**	**14.8%**
Alabama	100.0	18.5	24.6	15.7	25.3	15.9
Alaska	100.0	20.1	28.0	16.5	26.3	9.1
Arizona	100.0	20.7	25.1	16.2	22.8	15.2
Arkansas	100.0	19.1	24.4	15.5	24.6	16.4
California	100.0	19.7	26.5	17.3	23.7	12.9
Colorado	100.0	19.2	25.5	17.5	25.6	12.3
Connecticut	100.0	17.6	23.0	16.5	27.1	15.8
Delaware	100.0	18.2	23.9	16.1	25.6	16.1
District of Columbia	100.0	14.7	30.4	17.8	23.1	13.9
Florida	100.0	16.8	22.7	15.8	25.1	19.6
Georgia	100.0	20.6	25.4	17.7	24.3	12.0
Hawaii	100.0	17.2	24.8	16.1	25.0	16.9
Idaho	100.0	21.2	25.7	15.3	23.9	13.9
Illinois	100.0	19.0	25.6	16.6	24.7	14.1
Indiana	100.0	19.2	24.7	16.1	25.3	14.7
Iowa	100.0	18.3	24.5	14.9	25.5	16.8
Kansas	100.0	19.5	25.5	15.2	24.8	15.0
Kentucky	100.0	18.2	24.1	16.4	25.9	15.4
Louisiana	100.0	19.4	26.3	15.2	24.9	14.2
Maine	100.0	15.6	21.8	15.7	29.3	17.6
Maryland	100.0	18.2	24.5	16.9	26.4	14.1
Massachusetts	100.0	16.7	24.5	16.8	26.4	15.5
Michigan	100.0	18.1	24.4	16.0	26.4	15.1
Minnesota	100.0	18.5	24.8	16.1	26.2	14.4
Mississippi	100.0	20.2	25.7	15.3	24.2	14.6
Missouri	100.0	18.5	24.6	15.6	25.6	15.7
Montana	100.0	17.3	24.3	14.1	27.7	16.5
Nebraska	100.0	19.5	25.4	15.0	24.7	15.4
Nevada	100.0	20.2	24.2	17.6	24.5	13.5
New Hampshire	100.0	16.7	22.7	16.5	28.8	15.2
New Jersey	100.0	18.1	22.9	17.3	26.4	15.3
New Mexico	100.0	19.7	25.6	15.0	24.5	15.1
New York	100.0	17.2	24.9	16.7	25.7	15.4
North Carolina	100.0	19.0	24.3	17.1	25.2	14.5
North Dakota	100.0	17.1	27.4	13.7	25.2	16.6
Ohio	100.0	18.2	24.1	15.8	26.2	15.7
Oklahoma	100.0	19.4	25.6	15.0	24.4	15.5
Oregon	100.0	17.6	24.2	16.2	26.4	15.5
Pennsylvania	100.0	16.8	23.4	15.6	26.7	17.5
Rhode Island	100.0	16.5	25.0	16.2	26.3	16.1
South Carolina	100.0	18.4	24.5	16.0	25.6	15.6

	total population	iGeneration (under 14)	Millennial (14 to 31)	Generation X (32 to 43)	Baby Boom (44 to 62)	Older Americans (63 or older)
South Dakota	100.0%	19.1%	25.0%	14.1%	25.3%	16.5%
Tennessee	100.0	18.4	24.0	16.5	25.7	15.4
Texas	100.0	21.8	26.4	17.0	22.9	11.9
Utah	100.0	24.9	30.2	15.1	19.4	10.4
Vermont	100.0	15.4	23.4	15.5	29.4	16.4
Virginia	100.0	18.2	24.9	17.1	25.6	14.1
Washington	100.0	18.1	24.9	16.7	26.2	14.1
West Virginia	100.0	16.3	22.7	15.6	27.3	18.1
Wisconsin	100.0	17.9	24.5	15.8	26.5	15.3
Wyoming	100.0	18.7	25.5	14.7	26.8	14.4

Source: Bureau of the Census, State Population Estimates, Internet site http://www.census.gov/popest/states/asrh/; calculations by New Strategist

Spending

■ Householders aged 55 to 64 spent 14 percent more in 2007 than in 2000, after adjusting for inflation. The age group's spending is growing because two-earner couples head a growing proportion of households and fewer are opting for early retirement.

■ The spending of householders aged 65 or older is becoming more like the spending of middle-aged householders as better-educated generations fill the older age groups. Spending on entertainment among householders aged 65 or older rose 53 percent between 2000 and 2007, after adjusting for inflation.

■ Older Americans are the most ardent travelers, and this is reflected in their spending. Householders aged 55 to 64 spend 68 percent more than average on other lodging (mostly hotels and motels) and 42 percent more than average on public transportation (mostly airfares).

■ Householders aged 65 to 74 spend 9 percent more than the average household on new cars and trucks and 6 percent more than average on public transportation (mostly airfares). They spend 28 percent more than average on reading material.

■ Retirees spent more in 2007 than in 2000 on many discretionary items. Their spending on entertainment climbed by a whopping 39 percent during those years, after adjusting for inflation.

Older Householders Open Their Wallets

Householders aged 55 and older boosted their spending between 2000 and 2007.

Householders aged 55 to 64 spent 14 percent more in 2007 than in 2000, after adjusting for infla-tion—almost double the 8 percent rise in spending by the average household during those years. Householders aged 65 to 74 boosted their spending by 14 percent, and those aged 75 or older spent an even greater 15 percent more. Rising labor force participation rates—and incomes—explain the increased spending of householders aged 55 to 64. Spending has grown for householders aged 65 or older because a more educated, affluent generation has moved into the age group.

Householders aged 55 to 64 are spending more not only on necessities, but also on discretionary items. Between 2000 and 2007, they spent 10 percent more on food away from home, 19 percent more on alcoholic beverages, and 16 percent more on entertainment. They also spent more on necessities: their spending on property taxes rose by 21 percent, vehicle insurance spending grew 27 percent, and out-of-pocket health insurance costs increased by 28 percent.

The spending of householders aged 65 or older is becoming more like the spending of middle-aged householders as better-educated generations fill the older age groups. Spending on food away from home grew 11 percent among householders aged 65 or older. Households in the age group spent 11 percent more on housekeeping supplies, 12 percent more on alcoholic beverages, and 53 percent more on entertainment.

■ The spending of older Americans will continue to rise as the labor force participation rates of older workers climb.

The 55-and-older age groups saw the biggest increases in spending

(percent change in average household spending by age of householder, 2000–07; in 2007 dollars)

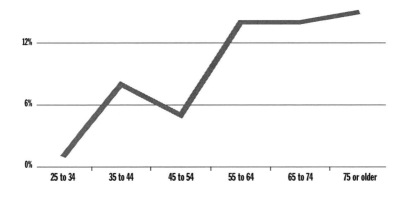

Table 9.1 Average Spending of Total Households, 2000 and 2007

(average annual spending of consumer units, 2000 and 2007; percent change, 2000–07; in 2007 dollars)

	2007	2000	percent change 2000–07
Number of consumer units (in 000s)	120,171	109,367	9.9%
Average annual spending	$49,638	$45,809	8.4
FOOD	6,133	6,211	−1.2
Food at home	3,465	3,638	−4.7
Cereals and bakery products	460	545	−15.7
Cereals and cereal products	143	188	−23.9
Bakery products	317	358	−11.4
Meats, poultry, fish, and eggs	777	957	−18.8
Beef	216	287	−24.6
Pork	150	201	−25.4
Other meats	104	122	−14.5
Poultry	142	175	−18.7
Fish and seafood	122	132	−7.9
Eggs	43	41	5.0
Dairy products	387	391	−1.1
Fresh milk and cream	154	158	−2.4
Other dairy products	234	232	0.7
Fruits and vegetables	600	627	−4.4
Fresh fruits	202	196	2.9
Fresh vegetables	190	191	−0.8
Processed fruits	112	138	−19.1
Processed vegetables	96	101	−5.1
Other food at home	1,241	1,116	11.2
Sugar and other sweets	124	141	−12.0
Fats and oils	91	100	−8.9
Miscellaneous foods	650	526	23.5
Nonalcoholic beverages	333	301	10.6
Food prepared by household on trips	43	48	−10.7
Food away from home	2,668	2,573	3.7
ALCOHOLIC BEVERAGES	457	448	2.0
HOUSING	16,920	14,833	14.1
Shelter	10,023	8,566	17.0
Owned dwellings	6,730	5,541	21.5
Mortgage interest and charges	3,890	3,178	22.4
Property taxes	1,709	1,371	24.6
Maintenance, repairs, insurance, other expenses	1,131	993	13.9
Rented dwellings	2,602	2,449	6.2
Other lodging	691	576	20.1

	2007	2000	percent change 2000–07
Utilities, fuels, public services	**$3,477**	**$2,997**	**16.0%**
Natural gas	480	370	29.9
Electricity	1,303	1,097	18.8
Fuel oil and other fuels	151	117	29.3
Telephone services	1,110	1,056	5.1
Water and other public services	434	356	21.8
Household services	**984**	**824**	**19.5**
Personal services	415	393	5.7
Other household services	569	431	32.0
Housekeeping suppplies	**639**	**580**	**10.1**
Laundry and cleaning supplies	140	158	–11.2
Other household products	347	272	27.5
Postage and stationery	152	152	0.2
Household furnishings and equipment	**1,797**	**1,865**	**–3.7**
Household textiles	133	128	4.2
Furniture	446	471	–5.3
Floor coverings	46	53	–13.2
Major appliances	231	228	1.5
Small appliances, miscellaneous housewares	101	105	–3.6
Miscellaneous household equipment	840	880	–4.6
APPAREL AND SERVICES	**1,881**	**2,235**	**–15.8**
Men and boys	**435**	**530**	**–17.9**
Men, aged 16 or older	351	414	–15.3
Boys, aged 2 to 15	84	116	–27.3
Women and girls	**749**	**873**	**–14.2**
Women, aged 16 or older	627	731	–14.2
Girls, aged 2 to 15	122	142	–14.1
Children under age 2	**93**	**99**	**–5.8**
Footwear	**327**	**413**	**–20.8**
Other apparel products and services	**276**	**320**	**–13.8**
TRANSPORTATION	**8,758**	**8,931**	**–1.9**
Vehicle purchases	3,244	4,116	–21.2
Cars and trucks, new	1,572	1,933	–18.7
Cars and trucks, used	1,567	2,131	–26.5
Other vehicles	105	52	102.8
Gasoline and motor oil	**2,384**	**1,554**	**53.4**
Other vehicle expenses	**2,592**	**2,746**	**–5.6**
Vehicle finance charges	305	395	–22.8
Maintenance and repairs	738	751	–1.8
Vehicle insurance	1,071	937	14.3
Vehicle rental, leases, licenses, other charges	478	663	–28.0
Public transportation	**538**	**514**	**4.6**

	2007	2000	percent change 2000–07
HEALTH CARE	**$2,853**	**$2,488**	**14.7%**
Health insurance	1,545	1,184	30.5
Medical services	709	684	3.7
Drugs	481	501	–4.0
Medical supplies	118	119	–1.0
ENTERTAINMENT	**2,698**	**2,243**	**20.3**
Fees and admissions	658	620	6.1
Audio and visual equipment and services	987	749	31.8
Pets, toys, hobbies, and playground equipment	560	402	39.2
Other entertainment supplies, services	493	473	4.2
PERSONAL CARE PRODUCTS, SERVICES	**588**	**679**	**–13.4**
READING	**118**	**176**	**–32.9**
EDUCATION	**945**	**761**	**24.2**
TOBACCO PRODUCTS, SMOKING SUPPLIES	**323**	**384**	**–15.9**
MISCELLANEOUS	**808**	**934**	**–13.5**
CASH CONTRIBUTIONS	**1,821**	**1,435**	**26.9**
PERSONAL INSURANCE AND PENSIONS	**5,336**	**4,052**	**31.7**
Life and other personal insurance	309	480	–35.7
Pensions and Social Security	5,027	–	–
PERSONAL TAXES	**2,233**	**3,753**	**–40.5**
Federal income taxes	1,569	2,901	–45.9
State and local income taxes	468	677	–30.8
Other taxes	196	176	11.5
GIFTS FOR PEOPLE IN OTHER HOUSEHOLDS	**1,198**	**1,304**	**–8.1**

Note: The Bureau of Labor Statistics uses consumer unit rather than household as the sampling unit in the Consumer Expenditure Survey. For the definition of consumer unit, see the glossary. Spending on gifts is also included in the preceding product and service categories. Average spending is rounded to the nearest dollar, but the percent change calculation is based on unrounded figures. "–" means comparable data are not available.
Source: Bureau of Labor Statistics, 2000 and 2007 Consumer Expenditure Survey, Internet site http://www.bls.gov/cex/; calculations by New Strategist

Table 9.2 Average Spending of Householders Aged 55 or Older, 2000 and 2007

(average annual spending of total consumer units and consumer units headed by people aged 55 or older, 2000 and 2007; percent change, 2000–07; in 2007 dollars)

	2007	2000	percent change 2000–07
Number of consumer units (in 000s)	42,862	36,316	18.0%
Average annual spending	$44,347	$37,995	16.7
FOOD	5,292	5,125	3.3
Food at home	3,153	3,246	−2.9
Cereals and bakery products	428	484	−11.6
Cereals and cereal products	122	157	−22.1
Bakery products	306	328	−6.6
Meats, poultry, fish, and eggs	690	852	−19.1
Beef	185	248	−25.4
Pork	141	193	−26.8
Other meats	94	105	−10.3
Poultry	115	148	−22.4
Fish and seafood	114	117	−2.4
Eggs	41	42	−2.7
Dairy products	356	353	0.9
Fresh milk and cream	133	141	−5.6
Other dairy products	222	212	4.8
Fruits and vegetables	594	626	−5.1
Fresh fruits	204	212	−3.7
Fresh vegetables	189	189	0.0
Processed fruits	109	134	−18.4
Processed vegetables	92	93	−0.8
Other food at home	1,085	931	16.6
Sugar and other sweets	119	123	−3.1
Fats and oils	91	98	−6.7
Miscellaneous foods	539	411	31.3
Nonalcoholic beverages	290	254	14.1
Food prepared by household on trips	47	46	2.7
Food away from home	2,139	1,877	13.9
ALCOHOLIC BEVERAGES	396	331	19.6
HOUSING	14,584	12,245	19.1
Shelter	8,067	6,470	24.7
Owned dwellings	5,617	4,480	25.4
Mortgage interest and charges	2,274	1,652	37.7
Property taxes	1,867	1,550	20.5
Maintenance, repairs, insurance, other expenses	1,476	1,278	15.5
Rented dwellings	1,594	1,364	16.8
Other lodging	857	625	37.1

	2007	2000	percent change 2000–07
Utilities, fuels, public services	**$3,406**	**$2,909**	**17.1%**
Natural gas	524	388	35.2
Electricity	1,279	1,105	15.7
Fuel oil and other fuels	191	153	24.9
Telephone services	956	883	8.3
Water and other public services	457	380	20.1
Household services	**841**	**739**	**13.8**
Personal services	184	201	–8.5
Other household services	657	538	22.1
Housekeeping supplies	**715**	**586**	**21.9**
Laundry and cleaning supplies	124	157	–20.8
Other household products	420	267	57.1
Postage and stationery	171	161	6.0
Household furnishings and equipment	**1,555**	**1,542**	**0.8**
Household textiles	141	113	24.6
Furniture	326	317	2.9
Floor coverings	48	54	–11.4
Major appliances	219	222	–1.2
Small appliances, miscellaneous housewares	95	90	5.2
Miscellaneous household equipment	726	747	–2.7
APPAREL AND SERVICES	**1,422**	**1,481**	**–4.0**
Men and boys	**296**	**331**	**–10.6**
Men, aged 16 or older	268	297	–9.9
Boys, aged 2 to 15	28	34	–16.9
Women and girls	**625**	**619**	**1.0**
Women, aged 16 or older	578	576	0.4
Girls, aged 2 to 15	47	43	8.4
Children under age 2	**38**	**40**	**–4.4**
Footwear	**246**	**260**	**–5.4**
Other apparel products and services	**217**	**231**	**–6.1**
TRANSPORTATION	**7,520**	**6,913**	**8.8**
Vehicle purchases	**2,600**	**3,099**	**–16.1**
Cars and trucks, new	1,432	1,775	–19.3
Cars and trucks, used	1,122	1,312	–14.5
Other vehicles	46	12	282.0
Gasoline and motor oil	**1,935**	**1,173**	**65.0**
Other vehicle expenses	**2,410**	**2,124**	**13.5**
Vehicle finance charges	214	248	–13.7
Maintenance and repairs	698	639	9.2
Vehicle insurance	1,083	783	38.4
Vehicle rental, leases, licenses, other charges	415	454	–8.6
Public transportation	**575**	**515**	**11.6**

	2007	2000	percent change 2000–07
HEALTH CARE	**$4,107**	**$3,562**	**15.3%**
Health insurance	2,307	1,721	34.1
Medical services	862	832	3.6
Drugs	775	856	–9.5
Medical supplies	163	153	6.6
ENTERTAINMENT	**2,311**	**1,705**	**35.5**
Fees and admissions	538	473	13.7
Audio and visual equipment and services	817	566	44.4
Pets, toys, hobbies, and playground equipment	480	306	56.9
Other entertainment supplies, services	476	359	32.7
PERSONAL CARE PRODUCTS, SERVICES	**575**	**582**	**–1.1**
READING	**147**	**193**	**–23.7**
EDUCATION	**581**	**258**	**125.5**
TOBACCO PRODUCTS, SMOKING SUPPLIES	**256**	**284**	**–9.9**
MISCELLANEOUS	**858**	**873**	**–1.7**
CASH CONTRIBUTIONS	**2,493**	**1,954**	**27.6**
PERSONAL INSURANCE AND PENSIONS	**3,805**	**2,491**	**52.7**
Life and other personal insurance	389	553	–29.6
Pensions and Social Security	3,416	–	–
PERSONAL TAXES	**2,015**	**2,797**	**–28.0**
Federal income taxes	1,430	2,113	–32.3
State and local income taxes	328	424	–22.6
Other taxes	257	260	–1.2
GIFTS FOR PEOPLE IN OTHER HOUSEHOLDS	**1,476**	**1,270**	**16.2**

Note: The Bureau of Labor Statistics uses consumer unit rather than household as the sampling unit in the Consumer Expenditure Survey. For the definition of consumer unit, see the glossary. Spending on gifts is also included in the preceding product and service categories. Average spending is rounded to the nearest dollar, but the percent change calculation is based on unrounded figures. "–" means comparable data are not available.
Source: Bureau of Labor Statistics, 2000 and 2007 Consumer Expenditure Survey, Internet site http://www.bls.gov/cex/; calculations by New Strategist

Table 9.3 Average Spending of Householders Aged 55 to 64, 2000 and 2007

(average annual spending of consumer units headed by people aged 55 to 64, 2000 and 2007; percent change, 2000–07; in 2007 dollars)

	2007	2000	percent change 2000–07
Number of consumer units (in 000s)	19,462	14,161	37.4%
Average annual spending	$53,786	$47,368	13.5
FOOD	6,241	6,223	0.3
Food at home	3,457	3,698	−6.5
Cereals and bakery products	456	531	−14.1
Cereals and cereal products	129	169	−23.5
Bakery products	327	362	−9.8
Meats, poultry, fish, and eggs	758	1,002	−24.3
Beef	200	293	−31.6
Pork	147	224	−34.4
Other meats	107	119	−10.2
Poultry	134	176	−23.8
Fish and seafood	127	138	−8.3
Eggs	44	52	−15.0
Dairy products	384	387	−0.6
Fresh milk and cream	142	152	−6.4
Other dairy products	242	235	3.1
Fruits and vegetables	640	672	−4.7
Fresh fruits	219	223	−1.7
Fresh vegetables	207	208	−0.6
Processed fruits	113	138	−18.4
Processed vegetables	102	105	−2.6
Other food at home	1,219	1,105	10.3
Sugar and other sweets	119	138	−14.1
Fats and oils	95	108	−12.3
Miscellaneous foods	599	479	25.0
Nonalcoholic beverages	343	317	8.3
Food prepared by household on trips	63	63	0.6
Food away from home	2,784	2,525	10.3
ALCOHOLIC BEVERAGES	533	447	19.3
HOUSING	17,223	14,885	15.7
Shelter	9,763	7,931	23.1
Owned dwellings	7,063	5,755	22.7
Mortgage interest and charges	3,421	2,743	24.7
Property taxes	2,127	1,760	20.8
Maintenance, repairs, insurance, other expenses	1,515	1,252	21.0
Rented dwellings	1,539	1,352	13.8
Other lodging	1,161	825	40.8

	2007	2000	percent change 2000–07
Utilities, fuels, public services	**$3,754**	**$3,318**	**13.1%**
Natural gas	557	411	35.7
Electricity	1,403	1,262	11.2
Fuel oil and other fuels	171	136	25.7
Telephone services	1,135	1,095	3.7
Water and other public services	488	415	17.5
Household services	**860**	**653**	**31.8**
Personal services	159	112	42.0
Other household services	701	541	29.7
Housekeeping supplies	**902**	**704**	**28.1**
Laundry and cleaning supplies	134	222	−39.5
Other household products	572	315	81.3
Postage and stationery	197	167	17.7
Household furnishings and equipment	**1,944**	**2,277**	**−14.6**
Household textiles	170	151	12.9
Furniture	437	435	0.5
Floor coverings	48	67	−28.8
Major appliances	266	266	0.0
Small appliances, miscellaneous housewares	92	128	−27.9
Miscellaneous household equipment	931	1,231	−24.3
APPAREL AND SERVICES	**1,888**	**2,040**	**−7.4**
Men and boys	**402**	**476**	**−15.5**
Men, aged 16 or older	367	424	−13.4
Boys, aged 2 to 15	35	51	−30.8
Women and girls	**793**	**827**	**−4.1**
Women, aged 16 or older	723	759	−4.7
Girls, aged 2 to 15	70	69	2.0
Children under age 2	**55**	**64**	**−13.8**
Footwear	**351**	**361**	**−2.8**
Other apparel products and services	**286**	**312**	**−8.3**
TRANSPORTATION	**9,608**	**9,442**	**1.8**
Vehicle purchases	**3,348**	**4,362**	**−23.3**
Cars and trucks, new	1,700	2,525	−32.7
Cars and trucks, used	1,582	1,816	−12.9
Other vehicles	66	22	204.5
Gasoline and motor oil	**2,504**	**1,624**	**54.2**
Other vehicle expenses	**2,993**	**2,860**	**4.7**
Vehicle finance charges	325	420	−22.7
Maintenance and repairs	885	809	9.4
Vehicle insurance	1,214	958	26.7
Vehicle rental, leases, licenses, other charges	569	673	−15.5
Public transportation	**763**	**596**	**28.0**

	2007	2000	percent change 2000–07
HEALTH CARE	**$3,476**	**$3,020**	**15.1%**
Health insurance	1,751	1,363	28.5
Medical services	883	868	1.7
Drugs	674	648	4.0
Medical supplies	168	141	19.3
ENTERTAINMENT	**2,730**	**2,354**	**16.0**
Fees and admissions	645	613	5.2
Audio and visual equipment and services	965	700	37.9
Pets, toys, hobbies, and playground equipment	653	431	51.5
Other entertainment supplies, services	468	610	–23.3
PERSONAL CARE PRODUCTS, SERVICES	**632**	**685**	**–7.8**
READING	**151**	**216**	**–29.9**
EDUCATION	**929**	**458**	**103.0**
TOBACCO PRODUCTS, SMOKING SUPPLIES	**353**	**420**	**–16.0**
MISCELLANEOUS	**1,084**	**992**	**9.3**
CASH CONTRIBUTIONS	**2,746**	**1,567**	**75.3**
PERSONAL INSURANCE AND PENSIONS	**6,193**	**4,621**	**34.0**
Life and other personal insurance	461	707	–34.8
Pensions and Social Security	5,732	3,916	46.4
PERSONAL TAXES	**3,083**	**4,815**	**–36.0**
Federal income taxes	2,234	3,687	–39.4
State and local income taxes	551	845	–34.8
Other taxes	298	283	5.3
GIFTS FOR PEOPLE IN OTHER HOUSEHOLDS	**1,948**	**1,619**	**20.3**

Note: The Bureau of Labor Statistics uses consumer unit rather than household as the sampling unit in the Consumer Expenditure Survey. For the definition of consumer unit, see the glossary. Spending on gifts is also included in the preceding product and service categories. Average spending is rounded to the nearest dollar, but the percent change calculation is based on unrounded figures. "–" means comparable data are not available.
Source: Bureau of Labor Statistics, 2000 and 2007 Consumer Expenditure Survey, Internet site http://www.bls.gov/cex/; calculations by New Strategist

Table 9.4 Average Spending of Householders Aged 65 or Older, 2000 and 2007

(average annual spending of consumer units headed by people aged 65 or older, 2000 and 2007; percent change, 2000–07; in 2007 dollars)

	2007	2000	percent change 2000–07
Number of consumer units (in 000s)	23,400	22,155	5.6%
Average annual spending	$36,530	$31,948	14.3
FOOD	**4,515**	**4,397**	**2.7**
Food at home	**2,905**	**2,948**	**–1.4**
Cereals and bakery products	405	453	–10.5
Cereals and cereal products	116	148	–21.7
Bakery products	289	305	–5.1
Meats, poultry, fish, and eggs	634	754	–15.9
Beef	174	219	–20.6
Pork	135	172	–21.6
Other meats	83	95	–12.7
Poultry	101	130	–22.3
Fish and seafood	103	101	1.8
Eggs	39	36	8.0
Dairy products	332	331	0.3
Fresh milk and cream	126	135	–6.6
Other dairy products	206	196	5.0
Fruits and vegetables	557	596	–6.5
Fresh fruits	193	203	–5.2
Fresh vegetables	175	176	–0.5
Processed fruits	106	131	–19.2
Processed vegetables	84	85	–1.7
Other food at home	976	814	19.9
Sugar and other sweets	118	112	5.4
Fats and oils	89	89	–0.1
Miscellaneous foods	489	366	33.6
Nonalcoholic beverages	247	212	16.6
Food prepared by household on trips	33	35	–5.5
Food away from home	**1,610**	**1,451**	**11.0**
ALCOHOLIC BEVERAGES	**285**	**254**	**12.2**
HOUSING	**12,396**	**10,547**	**17.5**
Shelter	**6,656**	**5,535**	**20.2**
Owned dwellings	4,414	3,664	20.5
Mortgage interest and charges	1,320	955	38.2
Property taxes	1,651	1,415	16.7
Maintenance, repairs, insurance, other expenses	1,443	1,294	11.5
Rented dwellings	1,639	1,373	19.4
Other lodging	604	497	21.5

	2007	2000	percent change 2000–07
Utilities, fuels, public services	**$3,117**	**$2,647**	**17.8%**
Natural gas	497	373	33.1
Electricity	1,175	1,004	17.0
Fuel oil and other fuels	208	165	26.1
Telephone services	806	747	8.0
Water and other public services	431	359	20.1
Household services	**825**	**796**	**3.7**
Personal services	205	259	−20.8
Other household services	620	537	15.5
Housekeeping supplies	**562**	**507**	**10.9**
Laundry and cleaning supplies	115	114	0.5
Other household products	296	236	25.4
Postage and stationery	150	157	−4.2
Household furnishings and equipment	**1,235**	**1,062**	**16.3**
Household textiles	117	88	33.1
Furniture	235	242	−2.9
Floor coverings	48	46	4.9
Major appliances	180	193	−6.6
Small appliances, miscellaneous housewares	98	65	50.7
Miscellaneous household equipment	558	429	30.2
APPAREL AND SERVICES	**1,040**	**1,114**	**−6.6**
Men and boys	**209**	**236**	**−11.4**
Men, aged 16 or older	187	213	−12.3
Boys, aged 2 to 15	22	23	−3.8
Women and girls	**487**	**482**	**1.1**
Women, aged 16 or older	460	455	1.1
Girls, aged 2 to 15	28	26	5.7
Children under age 2	**23**	**24**	**−4.5**
Footwear	**160**	**191**	**−16.4**
Other apparel products and services	**160**	**181**	**−11.4**
TRANSPORTATION	**5,785**	**5,294**	**9.3**
Vehicle purchases	**1,977**	**2,293**	**−13.8**
Cars and trucks, new	1,209	1,296	−6.7
Cars and trucks, used	740	991	−25.3
Other vehicles	29	6	381.7
Gasoline and motor oil	**1,461**	**885**	**65.1**
Other vehicle expenses	**1,928**	**1,654**	**16.5**
Vehicle finance charges	122	138	−11.9
Maintenance and repairs	543	531	2.3
Vehicle insurance	975	671	45.4
Vehicle rental, leases, licenses, other charges	287	313	−8.3
Public transportation	**420**	**464**	**−9.4**

	2007	2000	percent change 2000–07
HEALTH CARE	**$4,631**	**$3,910**	**18.5%**
Health insurance	2,770	1,949	42.1
Medical services	844	809	4.3
Drugs	859	990	–13.2
Medical supplies	159	160	–0.7
ENTERTAINMENT	**1,966**	**1,287**	**52.7**
Fees and admissions	450	384	17.2
Audio and visual equipment and services	694	480	44.5
Pets, toys, hobbies, and playground equipment	338	225	50.1
Other entertainment supplies, services	484	197	145.1
PERSONAL CARE PRODUCTS, SERVICES	**528**	**513**	**2.9**
READING	**143**	**178**	**–19.8**
EDUCATION	**292**	**130**	**124.5**
TOBACCO PRODUCTS, SMOKING SUPPLIES	**176**	**196**	**–10.3**
MISCELLANEOUS	**672**	**796**	**–15.6**
CASH CONTRIBUTIONS	**2,282**	**2,201**	**3.7**
PERSONAL INSURANCE AND PENSIONS	**1,819**	**1,131**	**60.9**
Life and other personal insurance	329	455	–27.7
Pensions and Social Security	1,491	–	–
PERSONAL TAXES	**1,126**	**1,601**	**–29.7**
Federal income taxes	760	1,179	–35.5
State and local income taxes	143	175	–18.1
Other taxes	223	247	–9.7
GIFTS FOR PEOPLE IN OTHER HOUSEHOLDS	**1,085**	**1,043**	**4.1**

Note: The Bureau of Labor Statistics uses consumer unit rather than household as the sampling unit in the Consumer Expenditure Survey. For the definition of consumer unit, see the glossary. Spending on gifts is also included in the preceding product and service categories. Average spending is rounded to the nearest dollar, but the percent change calculation is based on unrounded figures. "–" means comparable data are not available.
Source: Bureau of Labor Statistics, 2000 and 2007 Consumer Expenditure Survey, Internet site http://www.bls.gov/cex/; calculations by New Strategist

Table 9.5 Average Spending of Householders Aged 65 to 74, 2000 and 2007

(average annual spending of consumer units headed by people aged 65 to 74, 2000 and 2007; percent change, 2000–07; in 2007 dollars)

	2007	2000	percent change 2000–07
Number of consumer units (in 000s)	12,011	11,538	4.1%
Average annual spending	$42,262	$37,064	14.0
FOOD	5,226	5,031	3.9
Food at home	3,348	3,323	0.7
Cereals and bakery products	459	498	−7.9
Cereals and cereal products	137	160	−14.5
Bakery products	322	338	−4.8
Meats, poultry, fish, and eggs	738	875	−15.7
Beef	190	261	−27.3
Pork	166	202	−17.9
Other meats	93	104	−10.2
Poultry	125	157	−20.1
Fish and seafood	122	114	6.7
Eggs	42	39	9.0
Dairy products	376	373	0.7
Fresh milk and cream	136	142	−4.3
Other dairy products	240	231	3.8
Fruits and vegetables	628	637	−1.4
Fresh fruits	212	197	7.4
Fresh vegetables	205	195	5.1
Processed fruits	113	143	−21.1
Processed vegetables	99	101	−2.1
Other food at home	1,147	938	22.3
Sugar and other sweets	136	126	7.6
Fats and oils	97	105	−7.4
Miscellaneous foods	569	419	35.8
Nonalcoholic beverages	297	240	24.0
Food prepared by household on trips	49	48	1.7
Food away from home	1,878	1,707	10.0
ALCOHOLIC BEVERAGES	346	314	10.1
HOUSING	13,547	11,645	16.3
Shelter	7,271	6,158	18.1
Owned dwellings	5,329	4,358	22.3
Mortgage interest and charges	2,049	1,420	44.3
Property taxes	1,767	1,532	15.4
Maintenance, repairs, insurance, other expenses	1,513	1,406	7.6
Rented dwellings	1,277	1,146	11.4
Other lodging	664	654	1.6

	2007	2000	percent change 2000–07
Utilities, fuels, public services	**$3,392**	**$2,936**	**15.5%**
Natural gas	522	383	36.3
Electricity	1,289	1,109	16.2
Fuel oil and other fuels	185	182	1.8
Telephone services	946	867	9.1
Water and other public services	451	395	14.2
Household services	**715**	**600**	**19.2**
Personal services	83	119	−30.4
Other household services	632	480	31.5
Housekeeping supplies	**661**	**615**	**7.4**
Laundry and cleaning supplies	138	132	4.2
Other household products	348	290	19.9
Postage and stationery	175	193	−9.2
Household furnishings and equipment	**1,508**	**1,337**	**12.8**
Household textiles	145	122	19.2
Furniture	308	308	−0.1
Floor coverings	58	48	20.4
Major appliances	205	236	−13.1
Small appliances, miscellaneous housewares	115	82	40.5
Miscellaneous household equipment	678	542	25.1
APPAREL AND SERVICES	**1,323**	**1,361**	**−2.8**
Men and boys	**255**	**324**	**−21.3**
Men, aged 16 or older	220	289	−23.9
Boys, aged 2 to 15	36	35	3.1
Women and girls	**636**	**543**	**17.1**
Women, aged 16 or older	590	507	16.4
Girls, aged 2 to 15	46	37	23.2
Children under age 2	**32**	**37**	**−14.3**
Footwear	**209**	**224**	**−6.7**
Other apparel products and services	**190**	**231**	**−17.8**
TRANSPORTATION	**7,669**	**6,980**	**9.9**
Vehicle purchases	**2,701**	**3,168**	**−14.7**
Cars and trucks, new	1,721	1,742	−1.2
Cars and trucks, used	925	1,412	−34.5
Other vehicles	56	12	365.1
Gasoline and motor oil	**1,862**	**1,154**	**61.4**
Other vehicle expenses	**2,536**	**2,126**	**19.3**
Vehicle finance charges	197	219	−10.1
Maintenance and repairs	693	672	3.1
Vehicle insurance	1,321	810	63.0
Vehicle rental, leases, licenses, other charges	325	425	−23.5
Public transportation	**569**	**532**	**6.9**

	2007	2000	percent change 2000–07
HEALTH CARE	**$4,967**	**$3,808**	**30.4%**
Health insurance	2,821	1,936	45.7
Medical services	1,027	826	24.3
Drugs	935	896	4.4
Medical supplies	184	152	21.3
ENTERTAINMENT	**2,636**	**1,689**	**56.0**
Fees and admissions	575	501	14.8
Audio and visual equipment and services	812	564	44.1
Pets, toys, hobbies, and playground equipment	429	315	36.0
Other entertainment supplies, services	821	309	165.3
PERSONAL CARE PRODUCTS, SERVICES	**599**	**577**	**3.9**
READING	**151**	**200**	**–24.5**
EDUCATION	**245**	**179**	**36.6**
TOBACCO PRODUCTS, SMOKING SUPPLIES	**243**	**269**	**–9.5**
MISCELLANEOUS	**787**	**916**	**–14.1**
CASH CONTRIBUTIONS	**1,923**	**2,435**	**–21.0**
PERSONAL INSURANCE AND PENSIONS	**2,600**	**1,660**	**56.6**
Life and other personal insurance	375	619	–39.4
Pensions and Social Security	2,225	–	–
PERSONAL TAXES	**1,374**	**2,163**	**–36.5**
Federal income taxes	1,003	1,611	–37.7
State and local income taxes	139	241	–42.3
Other taxes	232	309	–25.0
GIFTS FOR PEOPLE IN OTHER HOUSEHOLDS	**1,265**	**1,166**	**8.5**

Note: The Bureau of Labor Statistics uses consumer unit rather than household as the sampling unit in the Consumer Expenditure Survey. For the definition of consumer unit, see the glossary. Spending on gifts is also included in the preceding product and service categories. Average spending is rounded to the nearest dollar, but the percent change calculation is based on unrounded figures. "–" means comparable data are not available.
Source: Bureau of Labor Statistics, 2000 and 2007 Consumer Expenditure Survey, Internet site http://www.bls.gov/cex/; calculations by New Strategist

Table 9.6 Average Spending of Householders Aged 75 or Older, 2000 and 2007

(average annual spending of consumer units headed by people aged 75 or older, 2000 and 2007; percent change, 2000–07; in 2007 dollars)

	2007	2000	percent change 2000–07
Number of consumer units (in 000s)	11,390	10,617	7.3%
Average annual spending	$30,414	$26,379	15.3
FOOD	3,738	3,705	0.9
Food at home	2,419	2,536	−4.6
Cereals and bakery products	346	402	−14.0
Cereals and cereal products	94	135	−30.3
Bakery products	252	267	−5.7
Meats, poultry, fish, and eggs	520	620	−16.1
Beef	156	173	−10.0
Pork	102	140	−27.0
Other meats	72	84	−14.6
Poultry	73	101	−27.8
Fish and seafood	81	88	−7.8
Eggs	36	34	6.8
Dairy products	284	284	−0.1
Fresh milk and cream	115	125	−8.2
Other dairy products	169	159	6.3
Fruits and vegetables	479	550	−13.0
Fresh fruits	172	211	−18.4
Fresh vegetables	142	154	−7.9
Processed fruits	99	117	−15.2
Processed vegetables	67	69	−2.4
Other food at home	789	678	16.4
Sugar and other sweets	99	96	2.8
Fats and oils	80	72	10.7
Miscellaneous foods	403	308	30.7
Nonalcoholic beverages	192	182	5.6
Food prepared by household on trips	16	20	−21.8
Food way from home	1,319	1,169	12.8
ALCOHOLIC BEVERAGES	218	187	16.8
HOUSING	11,173	9,351	19.5
Shelter	6,009	4,857	23.7
Owned dwellings	3,448	2,911	18.4
Mortgage interest and charges	550	452	21.8
Property taxes	1,529	1,288	18.7
Maintenance, repairs, insurance, other expenses	1,369	1,172	16.9
Rented dwellings	2,020	1,618	24.8
Other lodging	540	328	64.9

	2007	2000	percent change 2000–07
Utilities, fuels, public services	$2,828	$2,332	21.3%
Natural gas	470	362	29.7
Electricity	1,055	891	18.4
Fuel oil and other fuels	232	146	59.2
Telephone services	659	615	7.1
Water and other public services	411	318	29.3
Household services	**941**	**1,010**	**−6.9**
Personal services	334	409	−18.4
Other household services	607	600	1.2
Housekeeping supplies	**453**	**388**	**16.8**
Laundry and cleaning supplies	90	95	−5.4
Other household products	240	176	36.5
Postage and stationery	123	117	5.3
Household furnishings and equipment	**943**	**763**	**23.5**
Household textiles	86	52	66.1
Furniture	159	170	−6.3
Floor coverings	37	43	−14.6
Major appliances	152	147	3.5
Small appliances, miscellaneous housewares	79	47	68.2
Miscellaneous household equipment	429	306	40.3
APPAREL AND SERVICES	**732**	**844**	**−13.3**
Men and boys	**160**	**141**	**13.6**
Men, aged 16 or older	152	130	16.9
Boys, aged 2 to 15	8	11	−26.2
Women and girls	**325**	**413**	**−21.3**
Women, aged 16 or older	316	399	−20.7
Girls, aged 2 to 15	8	14	−44.6
Children under age 2	**14**	**10**	**45.3**
Footwear	**106**	**157**	**−32.3**
Other apparel products and services	**128**	**124**	**3.2**
TRANSPORTATION	**3,784**	**3,462**	**9.3**
Vehicle purchases	**1,213**	**1,341**	**−9.6**
Cars and trucks, new	668	810	−17.6
Cars and trucks, used	545	531	2.6
Other vehicles	–	–	–
Gasoline and motor oil	**1,039**	**591**	**75.7**
Other vehicle expenses	**1,270**	**1,140**	**11.4**
Vehicle finance charges	43	52	−16.9
Maintenance and repairs	384	378	1.6
Vehicle insurance	597	519	15.0
Vehicle rental, leases, licenses, other charges	247	191	29.0
Public transportation	**262**	**388**	**−32.4**

	2007	2000	percent change 2000–07
HEALTH CARE	**$4,275**	**$4,019**	**6.4%**
Health insurance	2,716	1,964	38.3
Medical services	651	792	−17.8
Drugs	777	1,093	−28.9
Medical supplies	132	170	−22.2
ENTERTAINMENT	**1,255**	**851**	**47.4**
Fees and admissions	318	258	23.4
Audio and visual equipment and services	570	391	45.7
Pets, toys, hobbies, and playground equipment	239	125	90.9
Other entertainment supplies, services	128	76	68.7
PERSONAL CARE PRODUCTS, SERVICES	**451**	**443**	**1.8**
READING	**136**	**154**	**−11.8**
EDUCATION	**341**	**76**	**349.5**
TOBACCO PRODUCTS, SMOKING SUPPLIES	**106**	**119**	**−11.1**
MISCELLANEOUS	**548**	**666**	**−17.7**
CASH CONTRIBUTIONS	**2,661**	**1,948**	**36.6**
PERSONAL INSURANCE AND PENSIONS	**996**	**554**	**79.8**
Life and other personal insurance	279	277	0.7
Pensions and Social Security	716	–	–
PERSONAL TAXES	**864**	**968**	**−10.8**
Federal income taxes	505	691	−26.9
State and local income taxes	147	100	47.1
Other taxes	212	177	19.8
GIFTS FOR PEOPLE IN OTHER HOUSEHOLDS	**889**	**909**	**−2.2**

Note: The Bureau of Labor Statistics uses consumer unit rather than household as the sampling unit in the Consumer Expenditure Survey. For the definition of consumer unit, see the glossary. Spending on gifts is also included in the preceding product and service categories. Average spending is rounded to the nearest dollar, but the percent change calculation is based on unrounded figures. "–" means sample is too small to make a reliable estimate or comparable data are not available.
Source: Bureau of Labor Statistics, 2000 and 2007 Consumer Expenditure Survey, Internet site http://www.bls.gov/cex/; calculations by New Strategist

The Spending of Householders Aged 55 to 64 Is above Average

As Boomers fill the age group, spending patterns are changing.

Households headed by 55-to-64-year-olds spent $53,786 in 2007—8 percent more than the average household. The age group's spending is growing because lifestyles are changing. Two-earner couples head a growing proportion of households, and many are postponing retirement. Rather than cope with reduced incomes in retirement, many 55-to-64-year-olds are continuing to enjoy peak earnings well into their sixties.

On many discretionary items, householders aged 55 to 64 spend well above average. People in this age group are the most ardent travelers, and this is reflected in their spending. Householders aged 55 to 64 spend 68 percent more than average on other lodging (mostly hotels and motels) and 42 percent more than average on public transportation (mostly airfares). They spend 15 percent more than average on women's clothes, 17 percent more on alcoholic beverages, and 51 percent more on cash contributions.

■ The spending patterns of householders aged 55 to 64 will continue to change as Boomers fill the age group.

Householders aged 55 to 64 spend more than average on women's clothes

(indexed spending of householders aged 55 to 64 on selected items, 2007)

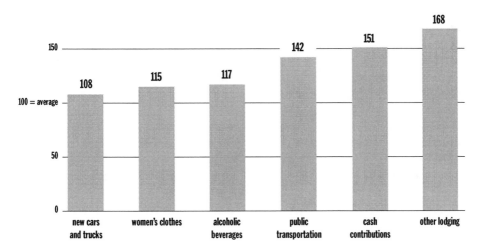

Table 9.7 Average, Indexed, and Market Share of Spending by Householders Aged 55 or Older, 2007

(average annual spending of total consumer units and average annual, indexed, and market share of spending by consumer units headed by people aged 55 or older, 2007)

	total consumer units	consumer units headed by householders aged 55 or older		
		average spending	indexed spending	market share
Number of consumer units (in 000s)	120,171	42,862	–	35.7%
Average annual spending	$49,638	$44,347	89	31.9
FOOD	6,133	5,292	86	30.8
Food at home	3,465	3,153	91	32.5
Cereals and bakery products	460	428	93	33.2
Cereals and cereal products	143	122	85	30.4
Bakery products	317	306	97	34.4
Meats, poultry, fish, and eggs	777	690	89	31.7
Beef	216	185	86	30.5
Pork	150	141	94	33.5
Other meats	104	94	90	32.2
Poultry	142	115	81	28.9
Fish and seafood	122	114	93	33.3
Eggs	43	41	95	34.0
Dairy products	387	356	92	32.8
Fresh milk and cream	154	133	86	30.8
Other dairy products	234	222	95	33.8
Fruits and vegetables	600	594	99	35.3
Fresh fruits	202	204	101	36.0
Fresh vegetables	190	189	99	35.5
Processed fruits	112	109	97	34.7
Processed vegetables	96	92	96	34.2
Other food at home	1,241	1,085	87	31.2
Sugar and other sweets	124	119	96	34.2
Fats and oils	91	91	100	35.7
Miscellaneous foods	650	539	83	29.6
Nonalcoholic beverages	333	290	87	31.1
Food prepared by household on trips	43	47	109	39.0
Food away from home	2,668	2,139	80	28.6
ALCOHOLIC BEVERAGES	457	396	87	30.9
HOUSING	16,920	14,584	86	30.7
Shelter	10,023	8,067	80	28.7
Owned dwellings	6,730	5,617	83	29.8
Mortgage interest and charges	3,890	2,274	58	20.9
Property taxes	1,709	1,867	109	39.0
Maintenance, repairs, insurance, other expenses	1,131	1,476	131	46.5
Rented dwellings	2,602	1,594	61	21.9
Other lodging	691	857	124	44.2

	total consumer units	consumer units headed by householders aged 55 or older		
		average spending	indexed spending	market share
Utilities, fuels, public services	**$3,477**	**$3,406**	**98**	**34.9%**
Natural gas	480	524	109	38.9
Electricity	1,303	1,279	98	35.0
Fuel oil and other fuels	151	191	126	45.1
Telephone services	1,110	956	86	30.7
Water and other public services	434	457	105	37.6
Household services	**984**	**841**	**85**	**30.5**
Personal services	415	184	44	15.8
Other household services	569	657	115	41.2
Housekeeping supplies	**639**	**715**	**112**	**39.9**
Laundry and cleaning supplies	140	124	89	31.6
Other household products	347	420	121	43.2
Postage and stationery	152	171	113	40.1
Household furnishings and equipment	**1,797**	**1,555**	**87**	**30.9**
Household textiles	133	141	106	37.8
Furniture	446	326	73	26.1
Floor coverings	46	48	104	37.2
Major appliances	231	219	95	33.8
Small appliances, miscellaneous housewares	101	95	94	33.5
Miscellaneous household equipment	840	726	86	30.8
APPAREL AND SERVICES	**1,881**	**1,422**	**76**	**27.0**
Men and boys	**435**	**296**	**68**	**24.3**
Men, aged 16 or older	351	268	76	27.2
Boys, aged 2 to 15	84	28	33	11.9
Women and girls	**749**	**625**	**83**	**29.8**
Women, aged 16 or older	627	578	92	32.9
Girls, aged 2 to 15	122	47	39	13.7
Children under age 2	**93**	**38**	**41**	**14.6**
Footwear	**327**	**246**	**75**	**26.8**
Other apparel products and services	**276**	**217**	**79**	**28.0**
TRANSPORTATION	8,758	7,520	86	30.6
Vehicle purchases	**3,244**	**2,600**	**80**	**28.6**
Cars and trucks, new	1,572	1,432	91	32.5
Cars and trucks, used	1,567	1,122	72	25.5
Other vehicles	105	46	44	15.6
Gasoline and motor oil	**2,384**	**1,935**	**81**	**28.9**
Other vehicle expenses	**2,592**	**2,410**	**93**	**33.2**
Vehicle finance charges	305	214	70	25.0
Maintenance and repairs	738	698	95	33.7
Vehicle insurance	1,071	1,083	101	36.1
Vehicle rental, leases, licenses, other charges	478	415	87	31.0
Public transportation	**538**	**575**	**107**	**38.1**

	total consumer units	consumer units headed by householders aged 55 or older		
		average spending	indexed spending	market share
HEALTH CARE	**$2,853**	**$4,107**	**144**	**51.3%**
Health insurance	1,545	2,307	149	53.3
Medical services	709	862	122	43.4
Drugs	481	775	161	57.5
Medical supplies	118	163	138	49.3
ENTERTAINMENT	**2,698**	**2,311**	**86**	**30.6**
Fees and admissions	658	538	82	29.2
Audio and visual equipment and services	987	817	83	29.5
Pets, toys, hobbies, and playground equipment	560	480	86	30.6
Other entertainment supplies, services	493	476	97	34.4
PERSONAL CARE PRODUCTS, SERVICES	**588**	**575**	**98**	**34.9**
READING	**118**	**147**	**125**	**44.4**
EDUCATION	**945**	**581**	**61**	**21.9**
TOBACCO PRODUCTS, SMOKING SUPPLIES	**323**	**256**	**79**	**28.3**
MISCELLANEOUS	**808**	**858**	**106**	**37.9**
CASH CONTRIBUTIONS	**1,821**	**2,493**	**137**	**48.8**
PERSONAL INSURANCE AND PENSIONS	**5,336**	**3,805**	**71**	**25.4**
Life and other personal insurance	309	389	126	44.9
Pensions and Social Security	5,027	3,416	68	24.2
PERSONAL TAXES	**2,233**	**2,015**	**90**	**32.2**
Federal income taxes	1,569	1,430	91	32.5
State and local income taxes	468	328	70	25.0
Other taxes	196	257	131	46.8
GIFTS FOR PEOPLE IN OTHER HOUSEHOLDS	**1,198**	**1,476**	**123**	**43.9**

Note: The Bureau of Labor Statistics uses consumer unit rather than household as the sampling unit in the Consumer Expenditure Survey. For the definition of consumer unit, see the glossary. Spending on gifts is also included in the preceding product and service categories. "–" means not applicable.
Source: Bureau of Labor Statistics, 2007 Consumer Expenditure Survey, Internet site http://www.bls.gov/cex/; calculations by New Strategist

Table 9.8 Average, Indexed, and Market Share of Spending by Householders Aged 55 to 64, 2007

(average annual spending of total consumer units and average annual, indexed, and market share of spending by consumer units headed by 55-to-64-year-olds, 2007)

	total consumer units	consumer units headed by 55-to-64-year-olds		
		average spending	indexed spending	market share
Number of consumer units (in 000s)	120,171	19,462	–	16.2%
Average annual spending	$49,638	$53,786	108	17.5
FOOD	6,133	6,241	102	16.5
Food at home	3,465	3,457	100	16.2
Cereals and bakery products	460	456	99	16.1
Cereals and cereal products	143	129	90	14.6
Bakery products	317	327	103	16.7
Meats, poultry, fish, and eggs	777	758	98	15.8
Beef	216	200	93	15.0
Pork	150	147	98	15.9
Other meats	104	107	103	16.7
Poultry	142	134	94	15.3
Fish and seafood	122	127	104	16.9
Eggs	43	44	102	16.6
Dairy products	387	384	99	16.1
Fresh milk and cream	154	142	92	14.9
Other dairy products	234	242	103	16.7
Fruits and vegetables	600	640	107	17.3
Fresh fruits	202	219	108	17.6
Fresh vegetables	190	207	109	17.6
Processed fruits	112	113	101	16.3
Processed vegetables	96	102	106	17.2
Other food at home	1,241	1,219	98	15.9
Sugar and other sweets	124	119	96	15.5
Fats and oils	91	95	104	16.9
Miscellaneous foods	650	599	92	14.9
Nonalcoholic beverages	333	343	103	16.7
Food prepared by household on trips	43	63	147	23.7
Food away from home	2,668	2,784	104	16.9
ALCOHOLIC BEVERAGES	457	533	117	18.9
HOUSING	16,920	17,223	102	16.5
Shelter	10,023	9,763	97	15.8
Owned dwellings	6,730	7,063	105	17.0
Mortgage interest and charges	3,890	3,421	88	14.2
Property taxes	1,709	2,127	124	20.2
Maintenance, repairs, insurance, other expenses	1,131	1,515	134	21.7
Rented dwellings	2,602	1,539	59	9.6
Other lodging	691	1,161	168	27.2

	total consumer units	consumer units headed by 55-to-64-year-olds		
		average spending	indexed spending	market share
Utilities, fuels, public services	**$3,477**	**$3,754**	**108**	**17.5%**
Natural gas	480	557	116	18.8
Electricity	1,303	1,403	108	17.4
Fuel oil and other fuels	151	171	113	18.3
Telephone services	1,110	1,135	102	16.6
Water and other public services	434	488	112	18.2
Household services	**984**	**860**	**87**	**14.2**
Personal services	415	159	38	6.2
Other household services	569	701	123	20.0
Housekeeping supplies	**639**	**902**	**141**	**22.9**
Laundry and cleaning supplies	140	134	96	15.5
Other household products	347	572	165	26.7
Postage and stationery	152	197	130	21.0
Household furnishings and equipment	**1,797**	**1,944**	**108**	**17.5**
Household textiles	133	170	128	20.7
Furniture	446	437	98	15.9
Floor coverings	46	48	104	16.9
Major appliances	231	266	115	18.6
Small appliances, miscellaneous housewares	101	92	91	14.8
Miscellaneous household equipment	840	931	111	17.9
APPAREL AND SERVICES	**1,881**	**1,888**	**100**	**16.3**
Men and boys	**435**	**402**	**92**	**15.0**
Men, aged 16 or older	351	367	105	16.9
Boys, aged 2 to 15	84	35	42	6.7
Women and girls	**749**	**793**	**106**	**17.1**
Women, aged 16 or older	627	723	115	18.7
Girls, aged 2 to 15	122	70	57	9.3
Children under age 2	**93**	**55**	**59**	**9.6**
Footwear	**327**	**351**	**107**	**17.4**
Other apparel products and services	**276**	**286**	**104**	**16.8**
TRANSPORTATION	**8,758**	**9,608**	**110**	**17.8**
Vehicle purchases	**3,244**	**3,348**	**103**	**16.7**
Cars and trucks, new	1,572	1,700	108	17.5
Cars and trucks, used	1,567	1,582	101	16.4
Other vehicles	105	66	63	10.2
Gasoline and motor oil	**2,384**	**2,504**	**105**	**17.0**
Other vehicle expenses	**2,592**	**2,993**	**115**	**18.7**
Vehicle finance charges	305	325	107	17.3
Maintenance and repairs	738	885	120	19.4
Vehicle insurance	1,071	1,214	113	18.4
Vehicle rental, leases, licenses, other charges	478	569	119	19.3
Public transportation	**538**	**763**	**142**	**23.0**

	total consumer units	consumer units headed by 55-to-64-year-olds		
		average spending	indexed spending	market share
HEALTH CARE	**$2,853**	**$3,476**	**122**	**19.7%**
Health insurance	1,545	1,751	113	18.4
Medical services	709	883	125	20.2
Drugs	481	674	140	22.7
Medical supplies	118	168	142	23.1
ENTERTAINMENT	**2,698**	**2,730**	**101**	**16.4**
Fees and admissions	658	645	98	15.9
Audio and visual equipment and services	987	965	98	15.8
Pets, toys, hobbies, and playground equipment	560	653	117	18.9
Other entertainment supplies, services	493	468	95	15.4
PERSONAL CARE PRODUCTS, SERVICES	**588**	**632**	**107**	**17.4**
READING	**118**	**151**	**128**	**20.7**
EDUCATION	**945**	**929**	**98**	**15.9**
TOBACCO PRODUCTS, SMOKING SUPPLIES	**323**	**353**	**109**	**17.7**
MISCELLANEOUS	**808**	**1,084**	**134**	**21.7**
CASH CONTRIBUTIONS	**1,821**	**2,746**	**151**	**24.4**
PERSONAL INSURANCE AND PENSIONS	**5,336**	**6,193**	**116**	**18.8**
Life and other personal insurance	309	461	149	24.2
Pensions and Social Security	5,027	5,732	114	18.5
PERSONAL TAXES	**2,233**	**3,083**	**138**	**22.4**
Federal income taxes	1,569	2,234	142	23.1
State and local income taxes	468	551	118	19.1
Other taxes	196	298	152	24.6
GIFTS FOR PEOPLE IN OTHER HOUSEHOLDS	**1,198**	**1,948**	**163**	**26.3**

Note: The Bureau of Labor Statistics uses consumer unit rather than household as the sampling unit in the Consumer Expenditure Survey. For the definition of consumer unit, see the glossary. Spending on gifts is also included in the preceding product and service categories; "–" means not applicable.
Source: Bureau of Labor Statistics, 2007 Consumer Expenditure Survey, Internet site http://www.bls.gov/cex/; calculations by New Strategist

Householders Aged 65 or Older Can Be Big Spenders

Despite their smaller household size, householders aged 65 to 74 spend 85 percent as much as the average household.

In 2007, householders aged 65 or older spent $36,530, only 74 percent of the $49,638 spent by the average household. The spending of older householders is below average because their households are small and most are retired.

Householders aged 65 to 74 spend more than those aged 75 or older. In 2007, householders aged 65 to 74 spent $42,262, while householders aged 75 or older spent $30,414. Together, the two age groups control 14 percent of household spending. They account for 24 percent of spending on reading material and 35 percent of out-of-pocket spending on drugs.

Despite their small household size, householders aged 65 to 74 spend just 4 percent less than the average household on other lodging, a category that includes hotel and motel expenses. They spend 6 percent more than average on public transportation, a category that includes airfares. They spend 28 percent more than the average household on reading material.

Householders aged 75 or older spend 61 percent as much as the average household. Their spending is above average only for health care, reading material, cash contributions, and other taxes.

■ As better-educated generations age into their sixties and seventies, older Americans are not acting so old anymore. The revolution in the older market will continue as Boomers enter the age group.

Many older Americans spend more than average on a variety of items

(indexed spending of householders aged 65 to 74, 2007)

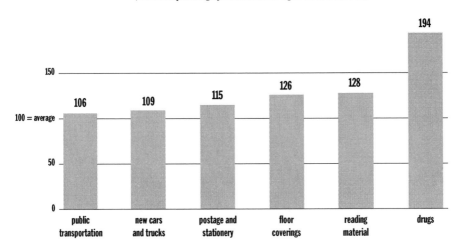

Table 9.9 Average, Indexed, and Market Share of Spending by Householders Aged 65 or Older, 2007

(average annual spending of total consumer units and average annual, indexed, and market share of spending by consumer units headed by people aged 65 or older, 2007)

	total consumer units	consumer units headed by people aged 65 or older		
		average spending	indexed spending	market share
Number of consumer units (in 000s)	120,171	23,400	–	19.5%
Average annual spending	$49,638	$36,530	74	14.3
FOOD	6,133	4,515	74	14.3
Food at home	3,465	2,905	84	16.3
Cereals and bakery products	460	405	88	17.1
Cereals and cereal products	143	116	81	15.8
Bakery products	317	289	91	17.8
Meats, poultry, fish, and eggs	777	634	82	15.9
Beef	216	174	81	15.7
Pork	150	135	90	17.5
Other meats	104	83	80	15.5
Poultry	142	101	71	13.8
Fish and seafood	122	103	84	16.4
Eggs	43	39	91	17.7
Dairy products	387	332	86	16.7
Fresh milk and cream	154	126	82	15.9
Other dairy products	234	206	88	17.1
Fruits and vegetables	600	557	93	18.1
Fresh fruits	202	193	96	18.6
Fresh vegetables	190	175	92	17.9
Processed fruits	112	106	95	18.4
Processed vegetables	96	84	88	17.0
Other food at home	1,241	976	79	15.3
Sugar and other sweets	124	118	95	18.5
Fats and oils	91	89	98	19.0
Miscellaneous foods	650	489	75	14.6
Nonalcoholic beverages	333	247	74	14.4
Food prepared by household on trips	43	33	77	14.9
Food away from home	2,668	1,610	60	11.8
ALCOHOLIC BEVERAGES	457	285	62	12.1
HOUSING	16,920	12,396	73	14.3
Shelter	10,023	6,656	66	12.9
Owned dwellings	6,730	4,414	66	12.8
Mortgage interest and charges	3,890	1,320	34	6.6
Property taxes	1,709	1,651	97	18.8
Maintenance, repairs, insurance, other expenses	1,131	1,443	128	24.8
Rented dwellings	2,602	1,639	63	12.3
Other lodging	691	604	87	17.0

	total consumer units	consumer units headed by people aged 65 or older		
		average spending	indexed spending	market share
Utilities, fuels, public services	**$3,477**	**$3,117**	**90**	**17.5%**
Natural gas	480	497	104	20.2
Electricity	1,303	1,175	90	17.6
Fuel oil and other fuels	151	208	138	26.8
Telephone services	1,110	806	73	14.1
Water and other public services	434	431	99	19.3
Household services	**984**	**825**	**84**	**16.3**
Personal services	415	205	49	9.6
Other household services	569	620	109	21.2
Housekeeping supplies	**639**	**562**	**88**	**17.1**
Laundry and cleaning supplies	140	115	82	16.0
Other household products	347	296	85	16.6
Postage and stationery	152	150	99	19.2
Household furnishings and equipment	**1,797**	**1,235**	**69**	**13.4**
Household textiles	133	117	88	17.1
Furniture	446	235	53	10.3
Floor coverings	46	48	104	20.3
Major appliances	231	180	78	15.2
Small appliances, miscellaneous housewares	101	98	97	18.9
Miscellaneous household equipment	840	558	66	12.9
APPAREL AND SERVICES	**1,881**	**1,040**	**55**	**10.8**
Men and boys	**435**	**209**	**48**	**9.4**
Men, aged 16 or older	351	187	53	10.4
Boys, aged 2 to 15	84	22	26	5.1
Women and girls	**749**	**487**	**65**	**12.7**
Women, aged 16 or older	627	460	73	14.3
Girls, aged 2 to 15	122	28	23	4.5
Children under age 2	**93**	**23**	**25**	**4.8**
Footwear	**327**	**160**	**49**	**9.5**
Other apparel products and services	**276**	**160**	**58**	**11.3**
TRANSPORTATION	**8,758**	**5,785**	**66**	**12.9**
Vehicle purchases	**3,244**	**1,977**	**61**	**11.9**
Cars and trucks, new	1,572	1,209	77	15.0
Cars and trucks, used	1,567	740	47	9.2
Other vehicles	105	29	28	5.4
Gasoline and motor oil	**2,384**	**1,461**	**61**	**11.9**
Other vehicle expenses	**2,592**	**1,928**	**74**	**14.5**
Vehicle finance charges	305	122	40	7.8
Maintenance and repairs	738	543	74	14.3
Vehicle insurance	1,071	975	91	17.7
Vehicle rental, leases, licenses, other charges	478	287	60	11.7
Public transportation	**538**	**420**	**78**	**15.2**

	total consumer units	consumer units headed by people aged 65 or older		
		average spending	indexed spending	market share
HEALTH CARE	**$2,853**	**$4,631**	**162**	**31.6%**
Health insurance	1,545	2,770	179	34.9
Medical services	709	844	119	23.2
Drugs	481	859	179	34.8
Medical supplies	118	159	135	26.2
ENTERTAINMENT	**2,698**	**1,966**	**73**	**14.2**
Fees and admissions	658	450	68	13.3
Audio and visual equipment and services	987	694	70	13.7
Pets, toys, hobbies, and playground equipment	560	338	60	11.8
Other entertainment supplies, services	493	484	98	19.1
PERSONAL CARE PRODUCTS, SERVICES	**588**	**528**	**90**	**17.5**
READING	**118**	**143**	**121**	**23.6**
EDUCATION	**945**	**292**	**31**	**6.0**
TOBACCO PRODUCTS, SMOKING SUPPLIES	**323**	**176**	**54**	**10.6**
MISCELLANEOUS	**808**	**672**	**83**	**16.2**
CASH CONTRIBUTIONS	**1,821**	**2,282**	**125**	**24.4**
PERSONAL INSURANCE AND PENSIONS	**5,336**	**1,819**	**34**	**6.6**
Life and other personal insurance	309	329	106	20.7
Pensions and Social Security	5,027	1,491	30	5.8
PERSONAL TAXES	**2,233**	**1,126**	**50**	**9.8**
Federal income taxes	1,569	760	48	9.4
State and local income taxes	468	143	31	5.9
Other taxes	196	223	114	22.2
GIFTS FOR PEOPLE IN OTHER HOUSEHOLDS	**1,198**	**1,085**	**91**	**17.6**

Note: The Bureau of Labor Statistics uses consumer unit rather than household as the sampling unit in the Consumer Expenditure Survey. For the definition of consumer unit, see the glossary. Spending on gifts is also included in the preceding product and service categories. "–" means not applicable.
Source: Bureau of Labor Statistics, 2007 Consumer Expenditure Survey, Internet site http://www.bls.gov/cex/; calculations by New Strategist

Table 9.10 Average, Indexed, and Market Share of Spending by Householders Aged 65 to 74, 2007

(average annual spending of total consumer units and average annual, indexed, and market share of spending by consumer units headed by people aged 65 to 74, 2007)

	total consumer units	consumer units headed by 65-to-74-year-olds average spending	indexed spending	market share
Number of consumer units (in 000s)	120,171	12,011	–	10.0%
Average annual spending	$49,638	$42,262	85	8.5
FOOD	**6,133**	**5,226**	**85**	**8.5**
Food at home	**3,465**	**3,348**	**97**	**9.7**
Cereals and bakery products	460	459	100	10.0
Cereals and cereal products	143	137	96	9.6
Bakery products	317	322	102	10.2
Meats, poultry, fish, and eggs	777	738	95	9.5
Beef	216	190	88	8.8
Pork	150	166	111	11.1
Other meats	104	93	89	8.9
Poultry	142	125	88	8.8
Fish and seafood	122	122	100	10.0
Eggs	43	42	98	9.8
Dairy products	387	376	97	9.7
Fresh milk and cream	154	136	88	8.8
Other dairy products	234	240	103	10.3
Fruits and vegetables	600	628	105	10.5
Fresh fruits	202	212	105	10.5
Fresh vegetables	190	205	108	10.8
Processed fruits	112	113	101	10.1
Processed vegetables	96	99	103	10.3
Other food at home	1,241	1,147	92	9.2
Sugar and other sweets	124	136	110	11.0
Fats and oils	91	97	107	10.7
Miscellaneous foods	650	569	88	8.7
Nonalcoholic beverages	333	297	89	8.9
Food prepared by household on trips	43	49	114	11.4
Food away from home	**2,668**	**1,878**	**70**	**7.0**
ALCOHOLIC BEVERAGES	**457**	**346**	**76**	**7.6**
HOUSING	**16,920**	**13,547**	**80**	**8.0**
Shelter	**10,023**	**7,271**	**73**	**7.3**
Owned dwellings	6,730	5,329	79	7.9
Mortgage interest and charges	3,890	2,049	53	5.3
Property taxes	1,709	1,767	103	10.3
Maintenance, repairs, insurance, other expenses	1,131	1,513	134	13.4
Rented dwellings	2,602	1,277	49	4.9
Other lodging	691	664	96	9.6

	total consumer units	consumer units headed by 65-to-74-year-olds		
		average spending	indexed spending	market share
Utilities, fuels, public services	**$3,477**	**$3,392**	**98**	**9.8%**
Natural gas	480	522	109	10.9
Electricity	1,303	1,289	99	9.9
Fuel oil and other fuels	151	185	123	12.2
Telephone services	1,110	946	85	8.5
Water and other public services	434	451	104	10.4
Household services	**984**	**715**	**73**	**7.3**
Personal services	415	83	20	2.0
Other household services	569	632	111	11.1
Housekeeping supplies	**639**	**661**	**103**	**10.3**
Laundry and cleaning supplies	140	138	99	9.9
Other household products	347	348	100	10.0
Postage and stationery	152	175	115	11.5
Household furnishings and equipment	**1,797**	**1,508**	**84**	**8.4**
Household textiles	133	145	109	10.9
Furniture	446	308	69	6.9
Floor coverings	46	58	126	12.6
Major appliances	231	205	89	8.9
Small appliances, miscellaneous housewares	101	115	114	11.4
Miscellaneous household equipment	840	678	81	8.1
APPAREL AND SERVICES	**1,881**	**1,323**	**70**	**7.0**
Men and boys	**435**	**255**	**59**	**5.9**
Men, aged 16 or older	351	220	63	6.3
Boys, aged 2 to 15	84	36	43	4.3
Women and girls	**749**	**636**	**85**	**8.5**
Women, aged 16 or older	627	590	94	9.4
Girls, aged 2 to 15	122	46	38	3.8
Children under age 2	**93**	**32**	**34**	**3.4**
Footwear	**327**	**209**	**64**	**6.4**
Other apparel products and services	**276**	**190**	**69**	**6.9**
TRANSPORTATION	**8,758**	**7,669**	**88**	**8.8**
Vehicle purchases	**3,244**	**2,701**	**83**	**8.3**
Cars and trucks, new	1,572	1,721	109	10.9
Cars and trucks, used	1,567	925	59	5.9
Other vehicles	105	56	53	5.3
Gasoline and motor oil	**2,384**	**1,862**	**78**	**7.8**
Other vehicle expenses	**2,592**	**2,536**	**98**	**9.8**
Vehicle finance charges	305	197	65	6.5
Maintenance and repairs	738	693	94	9.4
Vehicle insurance	1,071	1,321	123	12.3
Vehicle rental, leases, licenses, other charges	478	325	68	6.8
Public transportation	**538**	**569**	**106**	**10.6**

	total consumer units	consumer units headed by 65-to-74-year-olds		
		average spending	indexed spending	market share
HEALTH CARE	**$2,853**	**$4,967**	**174**	**17.4%**
Health insurance	1,545	2,821	183	18.2
Medical services	709	1,027	145	14.5
Drugs	481	935	194	19.4
Medical supplies	118	184	156	15.6
ENTERTAINMENT	**2,698**	**2,636**	**98**	**9.8**
Fees and admissions	658	575	87	8.7
Audio and visual equipment and services	987	812	82	8.2
Pets, toys, hobbies, and playground equipment	560	429	77	7.7
Other entertainment supplies, services	493	821	167	16.6
PERSONAL CARE PRODUCTS, SERVICES	**588**	**599**	**102**	**10.2**
READING	**118**	**151**	**128**	**12.8**
EDUCATION	**945**	**245**	**26**	**2.6**
TOBACCO PRODUCTS, SMOKING SUPPLIES	**323**	**243**	**75**	**7.5**
MISCELLANEOUS	**808**	**787**	**97**	**9.7**
CASH CONTRIBUTIONS	**1,821**	**1,923**	**106**	**10.6**
PERSONAL INSURANCE AND PENSIONS	**5,336**	**2,600**	**49**	**4.9**
Life and other personal insurance	309	375	121	12.1
Pensions and Social Security	5,027	2,225	44	4.4
PERSONAL TAXES	**2,233**	**1,374**	**62**	**6.2**
Federal income taxes	1,569	1,003	64	6.4
State and local income taxes	468	139	30	3.0
Other taxes	196	232	118	11.8
GIFTS FOR PEOPLE IN OTHER HOUSEHOLDS	**1,198**	**1,265**	**106**	**10.6**

Note: The Bureau of Labor Statistics uses consumer unit rather than household as the sampling unit in the Consumer Expenditure Survey. For the definition of consumer unit, see the glossary. Spending on gifts is also included in the preceding product and service categories. "–" means not applicable.
Source: Bureau of Labor Statistics, 2007 Consumer Expenditure Survey, Internet site http://www.bls.gov/cex/; calculations by New Strategist

Table 9.11 Average, Indexed, and Market Share of Spending by Householders Aged 75 or Older, 2007

(average annual spending of total consumer units and average annual, indexed, and market share of spending by consumer units headed by people aged 75 or older, 2007)

	total consumer units	consumer units headed by people aged 75 or older		
		average spending	indexed spending	market share
Number of consumer units (in 000s)	120,171	11,390	–	9.5%
Average annual spending	$49,638	$30,414	61	5.8
FOOD	6,133	3,738	61	5.8
Food at home	3,465	2,419	70	6.6
Cereals and bakery products	460	346	75	7.1
Cereals and cereal products	143	94	66	6.2
Bakery products	317	252	79	7.5
Meats, poultry, fish, and eggs	777	520	67	6.3
Beef	216	156	72	6.8
Pork	150	102	68	6.4
Other meats	104	72	69	6.6
Poultry	142	73	51	4.9
Fish and seafood	122	81	66	6.3
Eggs	43	36	84	7.9
Dairy products	387	284	73	7.0
Fresh milk and cream	154	115	75	7.1
Other dairy products	234	169	72	6.8
Fruits and vegetables	600	479	80	7.6
Fresh fruits	202	172	85	8.1
Fresh vegetables	190	142	75	7.1
Processed fruits	112	99	88	8.4
Processed vegetables	96	67	70	6.6
Other food at home	1,241	789	64	6.0
Sugar and other sweets	124	99	80	7.6
Fats and oils	91	80	88	8.3
Miscellaneous foods	650	403	62	5.9
Nonalcoholic beverages	333	192	58	5.5
Food prepared by household on trips	43	16	37	3.5
Food away from home	2,668	1,319	49	4.7
ALCOHOLIC BEVERAGES	457	218	48	4.5
HOUSING	16,920	11,173	66	6.3
Shelter	10,023	6,009	60	5.7
Owned dwellings	6,730	3,448	51	4.9
Mortgage interest and charges	3,890	550	14	1.3
Property taxes	1,709	1,529	89	8.5
Maintenance, repairs, insurance, other expenses	1,131	1,369	121	11.5
Rented dwellings	2,602	2,020	78	7.4
Other lodging	691	540	78	7.4

	total consumer units	consumer units headed by people aged 75 or older		
		average spending	indexed spending	market share
Utilities, fuels, public services	$3,477	$2,828	81	7.7%
Natural gas	480	470	98	9.3
Electricity	1,303	1,055	81	7.7
Fuel oil and other fuels	151	232	154	14.6
Telephone services	1,110	659	59	5.6
Water and other public services	434	411	95	9.0
Household services	984	941	96	9.1
Personal services	415	334	80	7.6
Other household services	569	607	107	10.1
Housekeeping supplies	639	453	71	6.7
Laundry and cleaning supplies	140	90	64	6.1
Other household products	347	240	69	6.6
Postage and stationery	152	123	81	7.7
Household furnishings and equipment	1,797	943	52	5.0
Household textiles	133	86	65	6.1
Furniture	446	159	36	3.4
Floor coverings	46	37	80	7.6
Major appliances	231	152	66	6.2
Small appliances, miscellaneous housewares	101	79	78	7.4
Miscellaneous household equipment	840	429	51	4.8
APPAREL AND SERVICES	1,881	732	39	3.7
Men and boys	435	160	37	3.5
Men, aged 16 or older	351	152	43	4.1
Boys, aged 2 to 15	84	8	10	0.9
Women and girls	749	325	43	4.1
Women, aged 16 or older	627	316	50	4.8
Girls, aged 2 to 15	122	8	7	0.6
Children under age 2	93	14	15	1.4
Footwear	327	106	32	3.1
Other apparel products and services	276	128	46	4.4
TRANSPORTATION	8,758	3,784	43	4.1
Vehicle purchases	3,244	1,213	37	3.5
Cars and trucks, new	1,572	668	42	4.0
Cars and trucks, used	1,567	545	35	3.3
Other vehicles	105	–	–	–
Gasoline and motor oil	2,384	1,039	44	4.1
Other vehicle expenses	2,592	1,270	49	4.6
Vehicle finance charges	305	43	14	1.3
Maintenance and repairs	738	384	52	4.9
Vehicle insurance	1,071	597	56	5.3
Vehicle rental, leases, licenses, other charges	478	247	52	4.9
Public transportation	538	262	49	4.6

	total consumer units	consumer units headed by people aged 75 or older		
		average spending	indexed spending	market share
HEALTH CARE	**$2,853**	**$4,275**	**150**	**14.2%**
Health insurance	1,545	2,716	176	16.7
Medical services	709	651	92	8.7
Drugs	481	777	162	15.3
Medical supplies	118	132	112	10.6
ENTERTAINMENT	**2,698**	**1,255**	**47**	**4.4**
Fees and admissions	658	318	48	4.6
Audio and visual equipment and services	987	570	58	5.5
Pets, toys, hobbies, and playground equipment	560	239	43	4.0
Other entertainment supplies, services	493	128	26	2.5
PERSONAL CARE PRODUCTS, SERVICES	**588**	**451**	**77**	**7.3**
READING	**118**	**136**	**115**	**10.9**
EDUCATION	**945**	**341**	**36**	**3.4**
TOBACCO PRODUCTS, SMOKING SUPPLIES	**323**	**106**	**33**	**3.1**
MISCELLANEOUS	**808**	**548**	**68**	**6.4**
CASH CONTRIBUTIONS	**1,821**	**2,661**	**146**	**13.9**
PERSONAL INSURANCE AND PENSIONS	**5,336**	**996**	**19**	**1.8**
Life and other personal insurance	309	279	90	8.6
Pensions and Social Security	5,027	716	14	1.3
PERSONAL TAXES	**2,233**	**864**	**39**	**3.7**
Federal income taxes	1,569	505	32	3.1
State and local income taxes	468	147	31	3.0
Other taxes	196	212	108	10.3
GIFTS FOR PEOPLE IN OTHER HOUSEHOLDS	**1,198**	**889**	**74**	**7.0**

Note: The Bureau of Labor Statistics uses consumer unit rather than household as the sampling unit in the Consumer Expenditure Survey. For the definition of consumer unit, see the glossary. Spending on gifts is also included in the preceding product and service categories. "–" means not applicable or sample is too small to make a reliable estimate.
Source: Bureau of Labor Statistics, 2007 Consumer Expenditure Survey, Internet site http://www.bls.gov/cex/; calculations by New Strategist

Retirees Are Spending More

The spending of retirees grew substantially between 2000 and 2007.

The average household headed by a retiree spent $35,424 in 2007—13 percent more than in 2000, after adjusting for inflation. This spending gain was greater than the 8 percent increase in spending by the average household.

Retirees spent more in 2007 than in 2000 on many discretionary items. Their spending on food away from home rose 8 percent during those years. Spending on alcoholic beverages increased 11 percent, and spending on entertainment climbed by 39 percent. They boosted their spending on education by 88 percent, many helping to pay for their grandchildren's college costs.

Retirees spent only 71 percent as much as the average household in 2007 because their households are relatively small. On most products and services, retirees spend less than the average household, but they spend more on some products and services such as health care, reading material, cash contributions, and postage and stationery.

■ As Baby Boomers begin to retire, the spending patterns of retirees are likely to change.

Retirees boosted their spending on many items between 2000 and 2007

(percent change in spending by retirees on selected items, 2000 to 2007; in 2007 dollars)

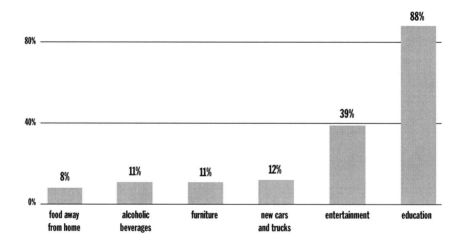

Table 9.12 Average Spending of Retirees, 2000 and 2007

(average annual spending of consumer units headed by retirees, 2000 and 2007; percent change, 2000–07; in 2007 dollars)

	2007	2000	percent change 2000–07
Number of consumer units (in 000s)	20,658	19,499	5.9%
Average annual spending	$35,424	$31,231	13.4
FOOD	**4,420**	**4,438**	**−0.4**
Food at home	**2,813**	**2,954**	**−4.8**
Cereals and bakery products	382	450	−15.2
Cereals and cereal products	110	144	−23.9
Bakery products	272	306	−11.1
Meats, poultry, fish, and eggs	629	766	−17.9
Beef	171	223	−23.2
Pork	138	175	−21.0
Other meats	79	95	−16.9
Poultry	101	130	−22.3
Fish and seafood	100	105	−4.5
Eggs	39	37	4.5
Dairy products	315	334	−5.6
Fresh milk and cream	123	136	−9.6
Other dairy products	192	197	−2.8
Fruits and vegetables	537	586	−8.4
Fresh fruits	187	196	−4.7
Fresh vegetables	170	176	−3.3
Processed fruits	101	129	−21.6
Processed vegetables	80	83	−3.7
Other food at home	950	819	16.0
Sugar and other sweets	105	116	−9.2
Fats and oils	88	88	0.1
Miscellaneous foods	470	365	28.8
Nonalcoholic beverages	251	213	17.8
Food prepared by household on trips	37	36	2.4
Food away from home	**1,607**	**1,485**	**8.2**
ALCOHOLIC BEVERAGES	**303**	**272**	**11.3**
HOUSING	**12,274**	**10,431**	**17.7**
Shelter	**6,455**	**5,314**	**21.5**
Owned dwellings	4,277	3,536	20.9
Mortgage interest and charges	1,179	908	29.9
Property taxes	1,622	1,368	18.6
Maintenance, repairs, insurance, other expenses	1,476	1,261	17.1
Rented dwellings	1,635	1,322	23.7
Other lodging	543	456	19.0

	2007	2000	percent change 2000–07
Utilities, fuels, public services	**$3,022**	**$2,624**	**15.2%**
Natural gas	476	372	27.9
Electricity	1,142	1,005	13.6
Fuel oil and other fuels	182	149	21.9
Telephone services	791	738	7.2
Water and other public services	431	358	20.5
Household services	**726**	**691**	**5.0**
Personal services	143	234	–38.8
Other household services	583	458	27.4
Housekeeping supplies	**791**	**525**	**50.7**
Laundry and cleaning supplies	118	118	0.0
Other household products	510	240	112.8
Postage and stationery	163	167	–2.6
Household furnishings and equipment	**1,280**	**1,276**	**0.3**
Household textiles	111	98	13.8
Furniture	272	246	10.7
Floor coverings	34	40	–14.4
Major appliances	161	213	–24.5
Small appliances, miscellaneous housewares	88	69	28.2
Miscellaneous household equipment	614	612	0.4
APPAREL AND SERVICES	**1,044**	**1,115**	**–6.4**
Men and boys	**208**	**217**	**–4.0**
Men, aged 16 or older	193	194	–0.4
Boys, aged 2 to 15	16	23	–30.1
Women and girls	**473**	**521**	**–9.3**
Women, aged 16 or older	446	484	–7.9
Girls, aged 2 to 15	26	36	–28.0
Children under age 2	**28**	**28**	**1.1**
Footwear	**188**	**190**	**–1.2**
Other apparel products and services	**146**	**159**	**–8.1**
TRANSPORTATION	**5,970**	**5,297**	**12.7**
Vehicle purchases	**2,169**	**2,247**	**–3.5**
Cars and trucks, new	1,319	1,182	11.6
Cars and trucks, used	826	1,064	–22.4
Other vehicles	25	–	–
Gasoline and motor oil	**1,432**	**916**	**56.3**
Other vehicle expenses	**1,969**	**1,691**	**16.5**
Vehicle finance charges	115	157	–26.5
Maintenance and repairs	549	544	0.9
Vehicle insurance	1,052	690	52.5
Vehicle rental, leases, licenses, other charges	253	300	–15.6
Public transportation	**399**	**443**	**–10.0**

	2007	2000	percent change 2000–07
HEALTH CARE	**$4,380**	**$3,819**	**14.7%**
Health insurance	2,664	1,902	40.0
Medical services	751	804	−6.6
Drugs	823	955	−13.8
Medical supplies	143	157	−8.6
ENTERTAINMENT	**1,852**	**1,331**	**39.2**
Fees and admissions	441	409	7.7
Audio and visual equipment and services	716	479	49.4
Pets, toys, hobbies, and playground equipment	333	230	44.8
Other entertainment supplies, services	361	212	70.3
PERSONAL CARE PRODUCTS, SERVICES	**514**	**514**	**0.0**
READING	**141**	**171**	**−17.5**
EDUCATION	**279**	**148**	**88.4**
TOBACCO PRODUCTS, SMOKING SUPPLIES	**187**	**216**	**−13.2**
MISCELLANEOUS	**647**	**733**	**−11.8**
CASH CONTRIBUTIONS	**2,167**	**2,024**	**7.1**
PERSONAL INSURANCE AND PENSIONS	**1,246**	**722**	**72.5**
Life and other personal insurance	305	407	−25.1
Pensions and Social Security	941	–	–
PERSONAL TAXES	**1,029**	**1,066**	**−3.4**
Federal income taxes	687	695	−1.1
State and local income taxes	144	118	22.0
Other taxes	198	252	−21.3
GIFTS FOR PEOPLE IN OTHER HOUSEHOLDS	**1,039**	**964**	**7.7**

Note: The Bureau of Labor Statistics uses consumer unit rather than household as the sampling unit in the Consumer Expenditure Survey. For the definition of consumer unit, see the glossary. Spending on gifts is also included in the preceding product and service categories. "–" means sample is too small to make a reliable estimate or comparable data are not available.
Source: Bureau of Labor Statistics, 2000 and 2007 Consumer Expenditure Survey, Internet site http://www.bls.gov/cex/; calculations by New Strategist

Table 9.13 Average, Indexed, and Market Share of Spending by Retirees, 2007

(average annual spending of total consumer units, and average annual, indexed, and market share of spending by consumer units headed by retirees, 2007)

	total consumer units	consumer units headed by retirees		
		average spending	indexed spending	market share
Number of consumer units (in 000s)	120,171	20,658	–	17.2%
Average annual spending	$49,638	$35,424	71	12.3
FOOD	6,133	4,420	72	12.4
Food at home	3,465	2,813	81	14.0
Cereals and bakery products	460	382	83	14.3
Cereals and cereal products	143	110	77	13.2
Bakery products	317	272	86	14.8
Meats, poultry, fish, and eggs	777	629	81	13.9
Beef	216	171	79	13.6
Pork	150	138	92	15.8
Other meats	104	79	76	13.1
Poultry	142	101	71	12.2
Fish and seafood	122	100	82	14.1
Eggs	43	39	91	15.6
Dairy products	387	315	81	14.0
Fresh milk and cream	154	123	80	13.7
Other dairy products	234	192	82	14.1
Fruits and vegetables	600	537	90	15.4
Fresh fruits	202	187	93	15.9
Fresh vegetables	190	170	89	15.4
Processed fruits	112	101	90	15.5
Processed vegetables	96	80	83	14.3
Other food at home	1,241	950	77	13.2
Sugar and other sweets	124	105	85	14.6
Fats and oils	91	88	97	16.6
Miscellaneous foods	650	470	72	12.4
Nonalcoholic beverages	333	251	75	13.0
Food prepared by household on trips	43	37	86	14.8
Food away from home	2,668	1,607	60	10.4
ALCOHOLIC BEVERAGES	457	303	66	11.4
HOUSING	16,920	12,274	73	12.5
Shelter	10,023	6,455	64	11.1
Owned dwellings	6,730	4,277	64	10.9
Mortgage interest and charges	3,890	1,179	30	5.2
Property taxes	1,709	1,622	95	16.3
Maintenance, repairs, insurance, other expenses	1,131	1,476	131	22.4
Rented dwellings	2,602	1,635	63	10.8
Other lodging	691	543	79	13.5

	total consumer units	consumer units headed by retirees		
		average spending	indexed spending	market share
Utilities, fuels, public services	**$3,477**	**$3,022**	**87**	**14.9%**
Natural gas	480	476	99	17.0
Electricity	1,303	1,142	88	15.1
Fuel oil and other fuels	151	182	121	20.7
Telephone services	1,110	791	71	12.3
Water and other public services	434	431	99	17.1
Household services	**984**	**726**	**74**	**12.7**
Personal services	415	143	34	5.9
Other household services	569	583	102	17.6
Housekeeping supplies	**639**	**791**	**124**	**21.3**
Laundry and cleaning supplies	140	118	84	14.5
Other household products	347	510	147	25.3
Postage and stationery	152	163	107	18.4
Household furnishings and equipment	**1,797**	**1,280**	**71**	**12.2**
Household textiles	133	111	83	14.3
Furniture	446	272	61	10.5
Floor coverings	46	34	74	12.7
Major appliances	231	161	70	12.0
Small appliances, miscellaneous housewares	101	88	87	15.0
Miscellaneous household equipment	840	614	73	12.6
APPAREL AND SERVICES	**1,881**	**1,044**	**56**	**9.5**
Men and boys	**435**	**208**	**48**	**8.2**
Men, aged 16 or older	351	193	55	9.5
Boys, aged 2 to 15	84	16	19	3.3
Women and girls	**749**	**473**	**63**	**10.9**
Women, aged 16 or older	627	446	71	12.2
Girls, aged 2 to 15	122	26	21	3.7
Children under age 2	**93**	**28**	**30**	**5.2**
Footwear	**327**	**188**	**57**	**9.9**
Other apparel products and services	**276**	**146**	**53**	**9.1**
TRANSPORTATION	**8,758**	**5,970**	**68**	**11.7**
Vehicle purchases	**3,244**	**2,169**	**67**	**11.5**
Cars and trucks, new	1,572	1,319	84	14.4
Cars and trucks, used	1,567	826	53	9.1
Other vehicles	105	25	24	4.1
Gasoline and motor oil	**2,384**	**1,432**	**60**	**10.3**
Other vehicle expenses	**2,592**	**1,969**	**76**	**13.1**
Vehicle finance charges	305	115	38	6.5
Maintenance and repairs	738	549	74	12.8
Vehicle insurance	1,071	1,052	98	16.9
Vehicle rental, leases, licenses, other charges	478	253	53	9.1
Public transportation	**538**	**399**	**74**	**12.7**

	total consumer units	consumer units headed by retirees		
		average spending	indexed spending	market share
HEALTH CARE	**$2,853**	**$4,380**	**154**	**26.4%**
Health insurance	1,545	2,664	172	29.6
Medical services	709	751	106	18.2
Drugs	481	823	171	29.4
Medical supplies	118	143	121	20.8
ENTERTAINMENT	**2,698**	**1,852**	**69**	**11.8**
Fees and admissions	658	441	67	11.5
Audio and visual equipment and services	987	716	73	12.5
Pets, toys, hobbies, and playground equipment	560	333	59	10.2
Other entertainment supplies, services	493	361	73	12.6
PERSONAL CARE PRODUCTS, SERVICES	**588**	**514**	**87**	**15.0**
READING	**118**	**141**	**119**	**20.5**
EDUCATION	**945**	**279**	**30**	**5.1**
TOBACCO PRODUCTS, SMOKING SUPPLIES	**323**	**187**	**58**	**10.0**
MISCELLANEOUS	**808**	**647**	**80**	**13.8**
CASH CONTRIBUTIONS	**1,821**	**2,167**	**119**	**20.5**
PERSONAL INSURANCE AND PENSIONS	**5,336**	**1,246**	**23**	**4.0**
Life and other personal insurance	309	305	99	17.0
Pensions and Social Security	5,027	941	19	3.2
PERSONAL TAXES	**2,233**	**1,029**	**46**	**7.9**
Federal income taxes	1,569	687	44	7.5
State and local income taxes	468	144	31	5.3
Other taxes	196	198	101	17.4
GIFTS FOR PEOPLE IN OTHER HOUSEHOLDS	**1,198**	**1,039**	**87**	**14.9**

Note: The Bureau of Labor Statistics uses consumer unit rather than household as the sampling unit in the Consumer Expenditure Survey. For the definition of consumer unit, see the glossary. Spending on gifts is also included in the preceding product and service categories. "–" means not applicable.
Source: Bureau of Labor Statistics, 2007 Consumer Expenditure Survey, Internet site http://www.bls.gov/cex/; calculations by New Strategist

Time Use

■ Leisure time expands as people age into their sixties and seventies. Time at work drops to near zero among those aged 75 or older.

■ Men aged 65 or older spend 7.18 hours a day in leisure activities, including more than four hours a day spent watching TV.

■ Women aged 65 or older spend 6.51 hours a day in leisure activities, including 3.61 hours in front of the TV.

Leisure Time Expands Greatly in the Older Age Groups

People aged 65 or older have 50 percent more leisure time than the average person.

Time use varies sharply by age. Leisure time expands as people age into their sixties. Time at work drops below one hour per day, on average, among people aged 65 or older.

Men aged 65 or older spend 7.18 hours a day in leisure activities, including more than four hours a day spent watching TV. In fact, they spend 56 percent more time than the average man in front of the television set. They spend 90 percent more time than the average man caring for their lawn and garden and 33 percent more time caring for animals and pets.

Women aged 65 or older spend 6.51 hours a day in leisure activities, including 3.61 hours in front of the TV. They spend more than twice as much time as the average woman reading and 56 percent more time caring for children in other households—primarily their grandchildren.

■ As Boomers age, the nation's elderly will have less leisure time because many Boomers will have to postpone retirement.

Time at work drops sharply in the older age groups

(average number of hours per day spent working, by age, 2007)

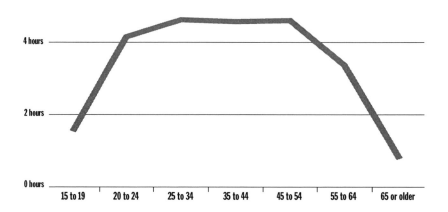

Table 10.1 Detailed Time Use of People Aged 55 to 64, 2007

(hours per day spent in primary activities by total people aged 15 or older and people aged 55 to 64, and index of age group to total, 2007)

	hours per day for total people	hours per day for people aged 55 to 64	index, 55 to 64 to total
TOTAL, ALL ACTIVITIES	**24.00**	**24.00**	**100**
Personal care activities	**9.31**	**9.02**	**97**
Sleeping	8.57	8.26	96
Grooming	0.67	0.65	97
Health-related self-care	0.07	0.11	157
Household activities	**1.87**	**2.41**	**129**
Housework	0.64	0.77	120
Food preparation and cleanup	0.52	0.59	113
Lawn, garden, and houseplants	0.21	0.34	162
Animals and pets	0.09	0.14	156
Vehicles	0.04	0.05	125
Household management	0.22	0.28	127
Household and personal mail and messages (except email)	0.02	0.03	150
Household and personal email and messages	0.05	0.06	120
Caring for and helping household members	**0.45**	**0.13**	**29**
Caring for and helping household children	0.38	0.05	13
Caring for household adults	0.03	0.06	200
Helping household adults	0.01	0.01	100
Caring for and helping people in other households	**0.14**	**0.24**	**171**
Caring for and helping children in other households	0.06	0.13	217
Caring for adults in other households	0.01	0.04	400
Helping adults in other households	0.06	0.08	133
Working and work-related activities	**3.53**	**3.37**	**95**
Working	3.47	3.33	96
Educational activities	**0.40**	**0.03**	**8**
Attending class	0.26	0.01	4
Homework and research	0.14	0.01	7
Consumer purchases	**0.39**	**0.49**	**126**
Shopping (store, telephone, Internet)	0.39	0.49	126
Grocery shopping	0.10	0.11	110
Shopping (except groceries, food, and gas)	0.27	0.35	130
Professional and personal care services	**0.09**	**0.11**	**122**
Medical and care services	0.05	0.07	140
Eating and drinking	**1.11**	**1.19**	**107**
Socializing, relaxing, and leisure	**4.52**	**4.83**	**107**
Socializing and communicating	0.64	0.55	86
Attending or hosting social events	0.09	0.05	56
Relaxing and leisure	3.70	4.14	112
Television and movies	2.62	2.91	111
Playing games	0.19	0.12	63
Computer use for leisure (except games)	0.14	0.12	86
Reading for personal interest	0.35	0.54	154
Arts and entertainment (other than sports)	0.09	0.09	100
Attending movies	0.03	0.02	67

	hours per day for total people	hours per day for people aged 55 to 64	index, 55 to 64 to total
Sports, exercise, and recreation	**0.35**	**0.28**	**80**
Participating in sports, exercise, and recreation	0.32	0.26	81
Attending sporting or recreational events	0.03	0.02	67
Religious and spiritual activities	**0.15**	**0.18**	**120**
Volunteer activities	**0.16**	**0.21**	**131**
Telephone calls	**0.11**	**0.10**	**91**
Traveling	**1.23**	**1.21**	**98**

Note: Primary activities are those respondents identified as their main activity. Other activities done simultaneously are not included. Travel related to activities is reported separately. Numbers do not sum to total because not all activities are shown. The index is calculated by dividing time spent by age group by time spent by average person and multiplying by 100.
Source: Bureau of Labor Statistics, unpublished tables from the 2007 American Time Use Survey, Internet site http://www.bls.gov/tus/home.htm

Table 10.2 Detailed Time Use of Men Aged 55 to 64, 2007

(hours per day spent in primary activities by total men aged 15 or older and men aged 55 to 64, and index of age group to total, 2007)

	hours per day for total men	hours per day for men aged 55 to 64	index, 55 to 64 to total
TOTAL, ALL ACTIVITIES	**24.00**	**24.00**	**100**
Personal care activities	**9.12**	**8.96**	**98**
Sleeping	8.52	8.32	98
Grooming	0.54	0.51	94
Health-related self-care	0.05	0.13	260
Household activities	**1.45**	**2.02**	**139**
Housework	0.29	0.30	103
Food preparation and cleanup	0.28	0.38	136
Lawn, garden, and houseplants	0.30	0.51	170
Animals and pets	0.09	0.14	156
Vehicles	0.07	0.09	129
Household management	0.19	0.27	142
Household and personal mail and messages (except email)	0.02	0.02	100
Household and personal email and messages	0.05	0.06	120
Caring for and helping household members	**0.27**	**0.10**	**37**
Caring for and helping household children	0.22	0.03	14
Caring for household adults	0.02	0.04	200
Helping household adults	0.01	0.01	100
Caring for and helping people in other households	**0.11**	**0.14**	**127**
Caring for and helping children in other households	0.04	0.06	150
Caring for adults in other households	0.01	0.01	100
Helping adults in other households	0.06	0.08	133
Working and work-related activities	**4.16**	**3.82**	**92**
Working	4.09	3.77	92
Educational activities	**0.38**	**0.03**	**8**
Attending class	0.26	0.02	8
Homework and research	0.12	0.01	8
Consumer purchases	**0.31**	**0.35**	**113**
Shopping (store, telephone, Internet)	0.31	0.35	113
Grocery shopping	0.07	0.08	114
Shopping (except groceries, food, and gas)	0.21	0.24	114
Professional and personal care services	**0.06**	**0.06**	**100**
Medical and care services	0.04	0.05	125
Eating and drinking	**1.14**	**1.23**	**108**
Socializing, relaxing, and leisure	**4.77**	**5.13**	**108**
Socializing and communicating	0.59	0.54	92
Attending or hosting social events	0.08	0.04	50
Relaxing and leisure	4.02	4.48	111
Television and movies	2.88	3.22	112
Playing games	0.24	0.14	58
Computer use for leisure (except games)	0.17	0.14	82
Reading for personal interest	0.28	0.51	182
Arts and entertainment (other than sports)	0.09	0.07	78
Attending movies	0.03	0.01	33

	hours per day for total men	hours per day for men aged 55 to 64	index, 55 to 64 to total
Sports, exercise, and recreation	**0.45**	**0.39**	**87**
Participating in sports, exercise, and recreation	0.42	0.36	86
Attending sporting or recreational events	0.03	0.03	100
Religious and spiritual activities	**0.11**	**0.16**	**145**
Volunteer activities	**0.13**	**0.18**	**138**
Telephone calls	**0.06**	**0.05**	**83**
Traveling	**1.28**	**1.18**	**92**

Note: Primary activities are those respondents identified as their main activity. Other activities done simultaneously are not included. Travel related to activities is reported separately. Numbers do not sum to total because not all activities are shown. The index is calculated by dividing time spent by age group by time spent by average man and multiplying by 100.
Source: Bureau of Labor Statistics, unpublished tables from the 2007 American Time Use Survey, Internet site http://www.bls.gov/tus/home.htm

Table 10.3 Detailed Time Use of Women Aged 55 to 64, 2007

(hours per day spent in primary activities by total women aged 15 or older and women aged 55 to 64, and index of age group to total, 2007)

	hours per day for total women	hours per day for women aged 55 to 64	index, 55 to 64 to total
TOTAL, ALL ACTIVITIES	**24.00**	**24.00**	**100**
Personal care activities	**9.50**	**9.08**	**96**
Sleeping	8.63	8.20	95
Grooming	0.79	0.78	99
Health-related self-care	0.08	0.09	113
Household activities	**2.27**	**2.77**	**122**
Housework	0.97	1.21	125
Food preparation and cleanup	0.74	0.80	108
Lawn, garden, and houseplants	0.12	0.18	150
Animals and pets	0.10	0.14	140
Vehicles	0.01	0.01	100
Household management	0.24	0.28	117
Household and personal mail and messages (except email)	0.03	0.05	167
Household and personal email and messages	0.05	0.06	120
Caring for and helping household members	**0.62**	**0.15**	**24**
Caring for and helping household children	0.52	0.06	12
Caring for household adults	0.03	0.07	233
Helping household adults	0.01	0.01	100
Caring for and helping people in other households	**0.16**	**0.34**	**213**
Caring for and helping children in other households	0.09	0.19	211
Caring for adults in other households	0.02	0.06	300
Helping adults in other households	0.05	0.08	160
Working and work-related activities	**2.93**	**2.95**	**101**
Working	2.89	2.92	101
Educational activities	**0.42**	**0.02**	**5**
Attending class	0.25	0.01	4
Homework and research	0.15	0.01	7
Consumer purchases	**0.48**	**0.63**	**131**
Shopping (store, telephone, Internet)	0.48	0.63	131
Grocery shopping	0.12	0.13	108
Shopping (except groceries, food, and gas)	0.33	0.46	139
Professional and personal care services	**0.12**	**0.16**	**133**
Medical and care services	0.06	0.09	150
Eating and drinking	**1.09**	**1.16**	**106**
Socializing, relaxing, and leisure	**4.29**	**4.54**	**106**
Socializing and communicating	0.69	0.56	81
Attending or hosting social events	0.10	0.05	50
Relaxing and leisure	3.40	3.81	112
Television and movies	2.38	2.61	110
Playing games	0.14	0.10	71
Computer use for leisure (except games)	0.11	0.10	91
Reading for personal interest	0.42	0.58	138
Arts and entertainment (other than sports)	0.10	0.11	110
Attending movies	0.03	0.03	100

	hours per day for total women	hours per day for women aged 55 to 64	index, 55 to 64 to total
Sports, exercise, and recreation	**0.25**	**0.19**	**76**
Participating in sports, exercise, and recreation	0.22	0.17	77
Attending sporting or recreational events	0.03	0.01	33
Religious and spiritual activities	**0.18**	**0.20**	**111**
Volunteer activities	**0.18**	**0.24**	**133**
Telephone calls	**0.15**	**0.15**	**100**
Traveling	**1.18**	**1.24**	**105**

Note: Primary activities are those respondents identified as their main activity. Other activities done simultaneously are not included. Travel related to activities is reported separately. Numbers do not sum to total because not all activities are shown. The index is calculated by dividing time spent by age group by time spent by average woman and multiplying by 100.
Source: Bureau of Labor Statistics, unpublished tables from the 2007 American Time Use Survey, Internet site http://www.bls .gov/tus/home.htm

Table 10.4 Detailed Time Use of People Aged 65 or Older, 2007

(hours per day spent in primary activities by total people aged 15 or older and people aged 65 or older, and index of age group to total, 2007)

	hours per day for total people	hours per day for people aged 65 or older	index, 65 or older to total
TOTAL, ALL ACTIVITIES	**24.00**	**24.00**	**100**
Personal care activities	**9.31**	**9.64**	**104**
Sleeping	8.57	8.91	104
Grooming	0.67	0.62	93
Health-related self-care	0.07	0.11	157
Household activities	**1.87**	**2.51**	**134**
Housework	0.64	0.80	125
Food preparation and cleanup	0.52	0.69	133
Lawn, garden, and houseplants	0.21	0.38	181
Animals and pets	0.09	0.11	122
Vehicles	0.04	0.03	75
Household management	0.22	0.33	150
Household and personal mail and messages (except email)	0.02	0.07	350
Household and personal email and messages	0.05	0.06	120
Caring for and helping household members	**0.45**	**0.08**	**18**
Caring for and helping household children	0.38	0.02	5
Caring for household adults	0.03	0.05	167
Helping household adults	0.01	0.01	100
Caring for and helping people in other households	**0.14**	**0.17**	**121**
Caring for and helping children in other households	0.06	0.10	167
Caring for adults in other households	0.01	0.02	200
Helping adults in other households	0.06	0.05	83
Working and work-related activities	**3.53**	**0.78**	**22**
Working	3.47	0.74	21
Educational activities	**0.40**	**0.02**	**5**
Attending class	0.26	0.02	8
Homework and research	0.14	–	–
Consumer purchases	**0.39**	**0.40**	**103**
Shopping (store, telephone, Internet)	0.39	0.39	100
Grocery shopping	0.10	0.12	120
Shopping (except groceries, food, and gas)	0.27	0.26	96
Professional and personal care services	**0.09**	**0.13**	**144**
Medical and care services	0.05	0.09	180
Eating and drinking	**1.11**	**1.35**	**122**
Socializing, relaxing, and leisure	**4.52**	**6.79**	**150**
Socializing and communicating	0.64	0.68	106
Attending or hosting social events	0.09	0.07	78
Relaxing and leisure	3.70	5.98	162
Television and movies	2.62	3.98	152
Playing games	0.19	0.24	126
Computer use for leisure (except games)	0.14	0.10	71
Reading for personal interest	0.35	0.91	260
Arts and entertainment (other than sports)	0.09	0.06	67
Attending movies	0.03	0.01	33

	hours per day for total people	hours per day for people aged 65 or older	index, 65 or older to total
Sports, exercise, and recreation	**0.35**	**0.28**	**80**
Participating in sports, exercise, and recreation	0.32	0.27	84
Attending sporting or recreational events	0.03	0.01	33
Religious and spiritual activities	**0.15**	**0.25**	**167**
Volunteer activities	**0.16**	**0.22**	**138**
Telephone calls	**0.11**	**0.14**	**127**
Traveling	**1.23**	**0.92**	**75**

Note: Primary activities are those respondents identified as their main activity. Other activities done simultaneously are not included. Travel related to activities is reported separately. Numbers do not sum to total because not all activities are shown. The index is calculated by dividing time spent by age group by time spent by average person and multiplying by 100. "–" means sample is too small to make a reliable estimate.

Source: Bureau of Labor Statistics, unpublished tables from the 2007 American Time Use Survey, Internet site http://www.bls .gov/tus/home.htm

Table 10.5 Detailed Time Use of Men Aged 65 or Older, 2007

(hours per day spent in primary activities by total men aged 15 or older and men aged 65 or older, and index of age group to total, 2007)

	hours per day for total men	hours per day for men aged 65 or older	index, 65 or older to total
TOTAL, ALL ACTIVITIES	**24.00**	**24.00**	**100**
Personal care activities	**9.12**	**9.47**	**104**
Sleeping	8.52	8.91	105
Grooming	0.54	0.47	87
Health-related self-care	0.05	0.08	160
Household activities	**1.45**	**1.98**	**137**
Housework	0.29	0.29	100
Food preparation and cleanup	0.28	0.34	121
Lawn, garden, and houseplants	0.30	0.57	190
Animals and pets	0.09	0.12	133
Vehicles	0.07	0.07	100
Household management	0.19	0.30	158
Household and personal mail and messages (except email)	0.02	0.06	300
Household and personal email and messages	0.05	0.08	160
Caring for and helping household members	**0.27**	**0.06**	**22**
Caring for and helping household children	0.22	0.01	5
Caring for household adults	0.02	0.04	200
Helping household adults	0.01	0.01	100
Caring for and helping people in other households	**0.11**	**0.09**	**82**
Caring for and helping children in other households	0.04	0.05	125
Caring for adults in other households	0.01	0.01	100
Helping adults in other households	0.06	0.03	50
Working and work-related activities	**4.16**	**1.21**	**29**
Working	4.09	1.13	28
Educational activities	**0.38**	**0.01**	**3**
Attending class	0.26	0.01	4
Homework and research	0.12	0.01	8
Consumer purchases	**0.31**	**0.36**	**116**
Shopping (store, telephone, Internet)	0.31	0.36	116
Grocery shopping	0.07	0.10	143
Shopping (except groceries, food, and gas)	0.21	0.24	114
Professional and personal care services	**0.06**	**0.09**	**150**
Medical and care services	0.04	0.07	175
Eating and drinking	**1.14**	**1.42**	**125**
Socializing, relaxing, and leisure	**4.77**	**7.18**	**151**
Socializing and communicating	0.59	0.66	112
Attending or hosting social events	0.08	0.07	88
Relaxing and leisure	4.02	6.38	159
Television and movies	2.88	4.48	156
Playing games	0.24	0.17	71
Computer use for leisure (except games)	0.17	0.14	82
Reading for personal interest	0.28	0.79	282
Arts and entertainment (other than sports)	0.09	0.07	78
Attending movies	0.03	0.01	33

	hours per day for total men	hours per day for men aged 65 or older	index, 65 or older to total
Sports, exercise, and recreation	**0.45**	**0.37**	**82**
Participating in sports, exercise, and recreation	0.42	0.37	88
Attending sporting or recreational events	0.03	–	–
Religious and spiritual activities	**0.11**	**0.18**	**164**
Volunteer activities	**0.13**	**0.16**	**123**
Telephone calls	**0.06**	**0.06**	**100**
Traveling	**1.28**	**1.01**	**79**

Note: Primary activities are those respondents identified as their main activity. Other activities done simultaneously are not included. Travel related to activities is reported separately. Numbers do not sum to total because not all activities are shown. The index is calculated by dividing time spent by age group by time spent by average man and multiplying by 100. "–" means sample is too small to make a reliable estimate.

Source: Bureau of Labor Statistics, unpublished tables from the 2007 American Time Use Survey, Internet site http://www.bls .gov/tus/home.htm

Table 10.6 Detailed Time Use of Women Aged 65 or Older, 2007

(hours per day spent in primary activities by total women aged 15 or older and women aged 65 or older, and index of age group to total, 2007)

	hours per day for total women	hours per day for women aged 65 or older	index, 65 or older to total
TOTAL, ALL ACTIVITIES	**24.00**	**24.00**	**100**
Personal care activities	**9.50**	**9.78**	**103**
Sleeping	8.63	8.91	103
Grooming	0.79	0.72	91
Health-related self-care	0.08	0.14	175
Household activities	**2.27**	**2.90**	**128**
Housework	0.97	1.19	123
Food preparation and cleanup	0.74	0.95	128
Lawn, garden, and houseplants	0.12	0.23	192
Animals and pets	0.10	0.10	100
Vehicles	0.01	–	–
Household management	0.24	0.35	146
Household and personal mail and messages (except email)	0.03	0.09	300
Household and personal email and messages	0.05	0.05	100
Caring for and helping household members	**0.62**	**0.10**	**16**
Caring for and helping household children	0.52	0.04	8
Caring for household adults	0.03	0.06	200
Helping household adults	0.01	0.01	100
Caring for and helping people in other households	**0.16**	**0.24**	**150**
Caring for and helping children in other households	0.09	0.14	156
Caring for adults in other households	0.02	0.04	200
Helping adults in other households	0.05	0.06	120
Working and work-related activities	**2.93**	**0.46**	**16**
Working	2.89	0.44	15
Educational activities	**0.42**	**0.03**	**7**
Attending class	0.25	0.03	12
Homework and research	0.15	–	–
Consumer purchases	**0.48**	**0.42**	**88**
Shopping (store, telephone, Internet)	0.48	0.42	88
Grocery shopping	0.12	–	–
Shopping (except groceries, food, and gas)	0.33	0.27	82
Professional and personal care services	**0.12**	**0.17**	**142**
Medical and care services	0.06	0.10	167
Eating and drinking	**1.09**	**1.30**	**119**
Socializing, relaxing, and leisure	**4.29**	**6.51**	**152**
Socializing and communicating	0.69	0.70	101
Attending or hosting social events	0.10	0.08	80
Relaxing and leisure	3.40	5.68	167
Television and movies	2.38	3.61	152
Playing games	0.14	0.29	207
Computer use for leisure (except games)	0.11	0.07	64
Reading for personal interest	0.42	1.00	238
Arts and entertainment (other than sports)	0.10	0.05	50
Attending movies	0.03	0.01	33

	hours per day for total women	hours per day for women aged 65 or older	index, 65 or older to total
Sports, exercise, and recreation	**0.25**	**0.21**	**84**
Participating in sports, exercise, and recreation	0.22	0.20	91
Attending sporting or recreational events	0.03	0.02	67
Religious and spiritual activities	**0.18**	**0.31**	**172**
Volunteer activities	**0.18**	**0.27**	**150**
Telephone calls	**0.15**	**0.20**	**133**
Traveling	**1.18**	**0.85**	**72**

Note: Primary activities are those respondents identified as their main activity. Other activities done simultaneously are not included. Travel related to activities is reported separately. Numbers do not sum to total because not all activities are shown. The index is calculated by dividing time spent by age group by time spent by average woman and multiplying by 100. "–" means sample is too small to make a reliable estimate.

Source: Bureau of Labor Statistics, unpublished tables from the 2007 American Time Use Survey, Internet site http://www.bls .gov/tus/home.htm

Wealth

■ Householders aged 55 to 64 saw their net worth decline between 2004 and 2007, after adjusting for inflation. Nevertheless, they still had the highest median net worth of any age group, at $253,700.

■ Householders aged 65 to 74 saw the median value of their financial assets climb by an enormous 72 percent between 2004 and 2007. The age groups on either side saw their financial assets decline, however.

■ The nonfinancial assets owned by householders aged 55 to 64 fell 6 percent between 2004 and 2007 after adjusting for inflation, to $233,100. Householders aged 65 or older saw their nonfinancial assets grow during those years.

■ Among householders aged 55 to 64, debt rose by 14 percent between 2004 and 2007, after adjusting for inflation—slightly faster than the increase recorded by the average household. Those aged 65 to 74 saw their median debt increase by a much larger 46 percent, while householders aged 75 or older were able to shrink their debt by 23 percent.

■ Only 13 percent of workers aged 55 or older are "very confident" they will have enough money to live comfortably throughout retirement, according to the Employee Benefit Research Institute's Retirement Confidence Survey, down from 18 percent in 1999.

The Net Worth of the Oldest Americans Has Grown

Net worth declined among 55-to-64-year-olds, however.

Net worth is one of the most important measures of wealth. It is the amount that remains after a household's debts are subtracted from its assets. During this decade's housing bubble, housing values rose faster than mortgage debt. Consequently, net worth grew substantially—up 18 percent for the average household between 2004 and 2007, after adjusting for inflation. The gain did not last, however. The Federal Reserve Board estimates that by October 2008, median net worth for the average household had fallen to $99,000—3 percent less than in 2004.

The net worth of householders aged 65 or older grew 15 to 19 percent between 2004 and 2007 after adjusting for inflation. The net worth of this age group is probably much lower today because of the ongoing decline in housing values and stock prices. Householders aged 55 to 64 saw their net worth decline even before the financial meltdown, the median falling by 7 percent between 2004 and 2007—to $253,700. The figure is probably much lower today.

■ Although the net worth of 55-to-64-year-olds fell between 2004 and 2007, the age group continues to have a greater net worth than any other.

Net worth of householders aged 65 or older grew between 2004 and 2007

(percent change in net worth of households by age of householder, 2004 to 2007; in 2007 dollars)

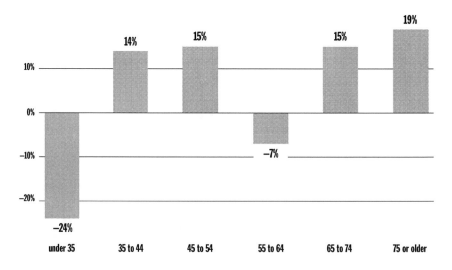

Table 11.1 Net Worth of Households by Age of Householder, 2004 to 2007

(median net worth of households by age of householder, 2004 to 2007; percent change, 2004–07; in 2007 dollars)

	2007	2004	percent change 2004–07
Total households	**$120,300**	**$102,200**	**17.7%**
Under age 35	11,800	15,600	−24.4
Aged 35 to 44	86,600	76,200	13.6
Aged 45 to 54	182,500	158,900	14.9
Aged 55 to 64	253,700	273,100	−7.1
Aged 65 to 74	239,400	208,800	14.7
Aged 75 or older	213,500	179,100	19.2

Source: Federal Reserve Board, Changes in U.S. Family Finances from 2004 to 2007: Evidence from the Survey of Consumer Finances, Federal Reserve Bulletin, February 2009, Internet site http://www.federalreserve.gov/pubs/oss/oss2/2007/scf2007home.html; calculations by New Strategist

Oldest Householders Are Most Likely to Own Stock

Their stock holdings lost more than half their value between 2004 and 2007.

Between 2004 and 2007, the value of the financial assets owned by the average American household rose 14 percent after adjusting for inflation—to a median of $28,800, according to the Federal Reserve Board's Survey of Consumer Finances. The median financial assets of householders aged 55 to 64, however, declined by 15 percent during those years (to $72,400), while the assets of those aged 75 or older declined by 3 percent. Householders aged 65 to 74, on the other hand, saw their financial assets climb by a substantial 72 percent. Householders aged 55 to 64 have more financial assets (a median of $72,400) than any other age group, but those aged 65 to 74 are closing in rapidly ($68,100).

Slightly more than half of all households (51 percent) owned stocks directly or indirectly in 2007, up slightly from the 50 percent of 2004. Stock ownership among householders aged 55 to 64 declined by 4 percentage points (to 59 percent), but it increased by 5 percentage points among those aged 65 or older. The median value of stock holdings did not change for owners aged 55 to 64, but older stockholders incurred heavy losses. The median value of stock owned by 65-to-74-year-olds fell 26 percent between 2004 and 2007, and that of owners aged 75 or older plummeted 56 percent.

Only 53 percent of households owned a retirement account in 2007, but among householders aged 55 to 64 the figure is 61 percent. The median value of the retirement accounts owned by house-holders in the age group was $98,000. Retirement account ownership drops to 52 percent among 65-to-74-year-olds and to 30 percent among those aged 75 or older, while the median value declines to $77,000 and then $35,000, respectively.

■ The value of retirement accounts has plunged since these figures were collected by the Survey of Consumer Finances.

Financial assets are modest for most householders regardless of age

(median value of financial assets of households, by age of householder, 2007)

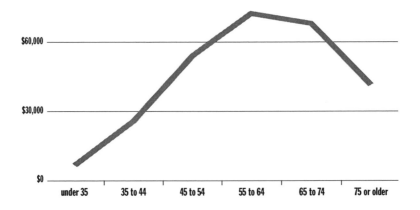

under 35	35 to 44	45 to 54	55 to 64	65 to 74	75 or older

Table 11.2 Financial Assets of Households by Age of Householder, 2004 and 2007

(percentage of households owning financial assets and median value of assets for owners, by age of householder, 2004 and 2007; percentage point change in ownership and percent change in value of asset, 2004–07; in 2007 dollars)

	2007	2004	percentage point change
PERCENT OWNING ANY FINANCIAL ASSET			
Total households	**93.9%**	**93.8%**	**0.1**
Under age 35	89.2	90.1	−0.9
Aged 35 to 44	93.1	93.6	−0.5
Aged 45 to 54	93.3	93.6	−0.3
Aged 55 to 64	97.8	95.2	2.6
Aged 65 to 74	96.1	96.5	−0.4
Aged 75 or older	97.4	97.6	−0.2

	2007	2004	percent change
MEDIAN VALUE OF FINANCIAL ASSETS			
Total households	**$28,800**	**$25,300**	**13.8%**
Under age 35	6,800	5,700	19.3
Aged 35 to 44	25,800	20,900	23.4
Aged 45 to 54	54,000	42,400	27.4
Aged 55 to 64	72,400	85,700	−15.5
Aged 65 to 74	68,100	39,600	72.0
Aged 75 or older	41,500	42,600	−2.6

Source: Federal Reserve Board, Changes in U.S. Family Finances from 2004 to 2007: Evidence from the Survey of Consumer Finances, Federal Reserve Bulletin, February 2009, Internet site http://www.federalreserve.gov/pubs/oss/oss2/2007/scf2007home.html; calculations by New Strategist

Table 11.3 Financial Assets of Households by Type of Asset and Age of Householder, 2007

(percentage of households owning financial assets, and median value of asset for owners, by type of asset and age of householder, 2007)

	total	under 35	35 to 44	45 to 54	55 to 64	65 to 74	75 or older
PERCENT OWNING ASSET							
Any financial asset	**93.9%**	**89.2%**	**93.1%**	**93.3%**	**97.8%**	**96.1%**	**97.4%**
Transaction accounts	92.1	87.3	91.2	91.7	96.4	94.6	95.3
Certificates of deposit	16.1	6.7	9.0	14.3	20.5	24.2	37.0
Savings bonds	14.9	13.7	16.8	19.0	16.2	10.3	7.9
Bonds	1.6	–	0.7	1.1	2.1	4.2	3.5
Stocks	17.9	13.7	17.0	18.6	21.3	19.1	30.2
Pooled investment funds	11.4	5.3	11.6	12.6	14.3	14.6	13.2
Retirement accounts	52.6	41.6	57.5	64.7	60.9	51.7	30.0
Cash value life insurance	23.0	11.4	17.5	22.3	35.2	34.3	27.6
Other managed assets	5.8	–	2.2	5.1	7.7	13.2	14.0
Other financial assets	9.3	10.0	9.6	10.5	9.2	9.4	5.3
MEDIAN VALUE OF ASSET							
Any financial asset	**$28,800**	**$6,800**	**$25,800**	**$54,000**	**$72,400**	**$68,100**	**$41,500**
Transaction accounts	4,000	2,400	3,400	5,000	5,200	7,700	6,100
Certificates of deposit	20,000	5,000	5,000	15,000	23,000	23,200	30,000
Savings bonds	1,000	700	1,000	1,000	1,900	1,000	20,000
Bonds	80,000	–	9,700	200,000	90,800	50,000	100,000
Stocks	17,000	3,000	15,000	18,500	24,000	38,000	40,000
Pooled investment funds	56,000	18,000	22,500	50,000	112,000	86,000	75,000
Retirement accounts	45,000	10,000	36,000	67,000	98,000	77,000	35,000
Cash value life insurance	8,000	2,800	8,300	10,000	10,000	10,000	5,000
Other managed assets	70,000	–	24,000	45,000	59,000	70,000	100,000
Other financial assets	6,000	1,500	8,000	6,000	20,000	10,000	15,000

Note: "–" means sample is too small to make a reliable estimate.
Source: Federal Reserve Board, Changes in U.S. Family Finances from 2004 to 2007: Evidence from the Survey of Consumer Finances, Federal Reserve Bulletin, February 2009, Internet site http://www.federalreserve.gov/pubs/oss/oss2/2007/scf2007home.html; calculations by New Strategist

Table 11.4 Stock Ownership of Households by Age of Householder, 2004 and 2007

(percentage of households owning stock directly or indirectly, median value of stock for owners, and share of total household financial assets accounted for by stock holdings, by age of householder, 2004 and 2007; percent and percentage point change, 2004–07; in 2007 dollars)

	2007	2004	percentage point change
PERCENT OWNING STOCK			
Total households	**51.1%**	**50.2%**	**0.9**
Under age 35	38.6	40.8	–2.2
Aged 35 to 44	53.5	54.5	–1.0
Aged 45 to 54	60.4	56.5	3.9
Aged 55 to 64	58.9	62.8	–3.9
Aged 65 to 74	52.1	46.9	5.2
Aged 75 or older	40.1	34.8	5.3

	2007	2004	percent change
MEDIAN VALUE OF STOCK			
Total households	**$35,000**	**$35,700**	**–2.0%**
Under age 35	7,000	8,800	–20.5
Aged 35 to 44	26,000	22,000	18.2
Aged 45 to 54	45,000	54,900	–18.0
Aged 55 to 64	78,000	78,000	0.0
Aged 65 to 74	57,000	76,900	–25.9
Aged 75 or older	41,000	94,300	–56.5

	2007	2004	percentage point change
STOCK AS SHARE OF FINANCIAL ASSETS			
Total households	**53.3%**	**51.3%**	**2.0**
Under age 35	44.3	40.3	4.0
Aged 35 to 44	53.7	53.5	0.2
Aged 45 to 54	53.0	53.8	–0.8
Aged 55 to 64	55.0	55.0	0.0
Aged 65 to 74	55.3	51.5	3.8
Aged 75 or older	48.1	39.3	8.8

Source: Federal Reserve Board, Changes in U.S. Family Finances from 2004 to 2007: Evidence from the Survey of Consumer Finances, Federal Reserve Bulletin, February 2009, Internet site http://www.federalreserve.gov/pubs/oss/oss2/2007/scf2007home.html; calculations by New Strategist

The Nonfinancial Assets of Older Americans Have Grown

Householders aged 55 to 64 have lost ground, however.

The median value of the nonfinancial assets owned by the average American household stood at $177,400 in 2007—9 percent more than in 2004, after adjusting for inflation. All age groups did not see gains, however. Whereas the median value of the nonfinancial assets owned by householders aged 65 or older rose between 4 and 20 percent during those years, the median value of the nonfinancial assets owned by householders aged 55 to 64 declined 6 percent after adjusting for inflation, to $233,100.

Because housing equity accounts for the largest share of nonfinancial assets, the rise in home values was the biggest contributor to gains in this category. Among homeowners aged 55 to 64, however, median home value declined to $210,000—4 percent less than in 2004, after adjusting for inflation. Among homeowners aged 65 to 74, median home value soared by 21 percent during those years, to $200,000, and their homeownership rate rose 4 percentage points. The rate declined by 8 points among householders aged 75 or older, but the remaining homeowners saw a 9 percent increase in median home value, to $150,000.

Since 2007, housing values have plunged and the decline is ongoing. The Federal Reserve Board has estimated that the median value of the average home fell from $200,000 in 2007 to $181,600 in October 2008—a 9 percent decline. Housing values have continued to fall since then and are likely lower today than they were in 2004, after adjusting for inflation.

■ The drop in housing values since 2007 has greatly reduced household net worth.

Median housing value exceeded $200,000 for householders ranging in age from 35 to 74

(median value of the primary residence among homeowners, by age of householder, 2007)

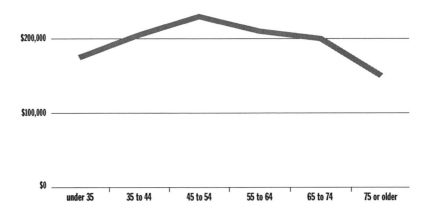

Table 11.5 Nonfinancial Assets of Households by Age of Householder, 2004 and 2007

(percentage of households owning nonfinancial assets and median value of assets for owners, by age of house-holder, 2004 and 2007; percentage point change in ownership and percent change in value of asset, 2004–07; in 2007 dollars)

	2007	2004	percentage point change
PERCENT OWNING ANY NONFINANCIAL ASSET			
Total households	**92.0%**	**92.5%**	**–0.5**
Under age 35	88.2	88.6	–0.4
Aged 35 to 44	91.3	93.0	–1.7
Aged 45 to 54	95.0	94.7	0.3
Aged 55 to 64	95.6	92.6	3.0
Aged 65 to 74	94.5	95.6	–1.1
Aged 75 or older	87.3	92.5	–5.2

	2007	2004	percent change
MEDIAN VALUE OF NONFINANCIAL ASSETS			
Total households	**$177,400**	**$162,300**	**9.3%**
Under age 35	30,900	35,500	–13.0
Aged 35 to 44	182,600	166,200	9.9
Aged 45 to 54	224,900	202,600	11.0
Aged 55 to 64	233,100	248,600	–6.2
Aged 65 to 74	212,200	177,000	19.9
Aged 75 or older	157,100	150,600	4.3

Source: Federal Reserve Board, Changes in U.S. Family Finances from 2004 to 2007: Evidence from the Survey of Consumer Finances, Federal Reserve Bulletin, February 2009, Internet site http://www.federalreserve.gov/pubs/oss/oss2/2007/scf2007home.html; calculations by New Strategist

Table 11.6 Nonfinancial Assets of Households by Type of Asset and Age of Householder, 2007

(percentage of households owning nonfinancial assets, and median value of asset for owners, by type of asset and age of householder, 2007)

	total	under 35	35 to 44	45 to 54	55 to 64	65 to 74	75 or older
PERCENT OWNING ASSET							
Any nonfinancial asset	**92.0%**	**88.2%**	**91.3%**	**95.0%**	**95.6%**	**94.5%**	**87.3%**
Vehicles	87.0	85.4	87.5	90.3	92.2	90.6	71.5
Primary residence	68.6	40.7	66.1	77.3	81.0	85.5	77.0
Other residential property	13.7	5.6	12.0	15.7	20.9	18.9	13.4
Equity in nonresidential property	8.1	3.2	7.5	9.5	11.5	12.3	6.8
Business equity	12.0	6.8	16.0	15.2	16.3	10.1	3.8
Other nonfinancial assets	7.2	5.9	5.5	8.7	8.5	9.1	5.8
MEDIAN VALUE OF ASSET							
Total nonfinancial assets	**$177,400**	**$30,900**	**$182,600**	**$224,900**	**$233,100**	**$212,200**	**$157,100**
Vehicles	15,500	13,300	17,400	18,700	17,400	14,600	9,400
Primary residence	200,000	175,000	205,000	230,000	210,000	200,000	150,000
Other residential property	146,000	85,000	150,000	150,000	157,000	150,000	100,000
Equity in nonresidential property	75,000	50,000	50,000	80,000	90,000	75,000	110,000
Business equity	100,500	59,900	86,000	100,000	116,300	415,000	250,000
Other nonfinancial assets	14,000	8,000	10,000	15,000	20,000	20,000	25,000

Source: Federal Reserve Board, Changes in U.S. Family Finances from 2004 to 2007: Evidence from the Survey of Consumer Finances, Federal Reserve Bulletin, February 2009, Internet site http://www.federalreserve.gov/pubs/oss/oss2/2007/scf2007home.html; calculations by New Strategist

Table 11.7 Household Ownership of Primary Residence by Age of Householder, 2004 and 2007

(percentage of households owning their primary residence, median value of asset for owners, and median value of home-secured debt for owners, by age of householder, 2004 and 2007; percentage point change in ownership and percent change in value of asset, 2004–07; in 2007 dollars)

	2007	2004	percentage point change
PERCENT OWNING PRIMARY RESIDENCE			
Total households	**68.6%**	**69.1%**	**–0.5**
Under age 35	40.7	41.6	–0.9
Aged 35 to 44	66.1	68.3	–2.2
Aged 45 to 54	77.3	77.3	0.0
Aged 55 to 64	81.0	79.1	1.9
Aged 65 to 74	85.5	81.3	4.2
Aged 75 or older	77.0	85.2	–8.2

	2007	2004	percent change
MEDIAN VALUE OF PRIMARY RESIDENCE			
Total households	**$200,000**	**$175,700**	**13.8%**
Under age 35	175,000	148,300	18.0
Aged 35 to 44	205,000	175,700	16.7
Aged 45 to 54	230,000	186,700	23.2
Aged 55 to 64	210,000	218,700	–4.0
Aged 65 to 74	200,000	164,700	21.4
Aged 75 or older	150,000	137,300	9.2

	2007	2004	percent change
MEDIAN VALUE OF HOME-SECURED DEBT			
Total households	**$100,000**	**$95,600**	**4.6%**
Under age 35	78,000	68,600	13.7
Aged 35 to 44	101,600	82,400	23.3
Aged 45 to 54	82,000	95,600	–14.2
Aged 55 to 64	130,000	119,500	8.8
Aged 65 to 74	125,000	109,800	13.8
Aged 75 or older	50,000	42,800	16.8

Source: Federal Reserve Board, Changes in U.S. Family Finances from 2004 to 2007: Evidence from the Survey of Consumer Finances, Federal Reserve Bulletin, February 2009, Internet site http://www.federalreserve.gov/pubs/oss/oss2/2007/scf2007home.html; calculations by New Strategist

Among the Oldest Americans, Debt Declined

Houses paid off, their debt is relatively modest.

The median debt of the average American household grew by 11 percent between 2004 and 2007 after adjusting for inflation—to $67,300. Among householders aged 55 to 64, median debt rose by a larger 14 percent during those years. Householders aged 65 to 74 saw their median debt increase by an enormous 46 percent, while householders aged 75 or older were able to shrink their debt by 23 percent. The median debt of the oldest householders now stands at $13,000. Those aged 65 to 74 owe a median of $40,100, and those aged 55 to 64 owe $60,300.

Home-secured debt accounts for the largest share of debt by far. Forty-nine percent of households have debt secured by their primary residence, and they owe a median of $107,000. Naturally such debt declines with age as householders pay off their mortgages. Householders aged 55 to 64 who have home-secured debt owe a median of $85,000, while those aged 65 to 74 owe a smaller $69,000. The few householders aged 75 or older who have home-secured debt owe a median of $40,000. Half the householders aged 55 to 64 carry a credit card balance, owing a median of $3,600. Both the percentage of householders with credit card debt and the outstanding balance decline with age, to 19 percent and just $800, respectively, among householders aged 75 or older. A similar pattern is true for installment loan debt (such as car loans).

■ By paying down their mortgage debt, older Americans build net worth.

Debt declines in the older age groups

(median amount of debt owed by households, by age of householder, 2007)

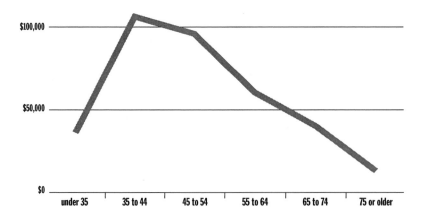

Table 11.8 Debt of Households by Age of Householder, 2004 and 2007

(percentage of households with debt and median amount of debt for debtors, by age of householder, 2004 and 2007; percentage point change in households with debt and percent change in amount of debt, 2004–07; in 2007 dollars)

	2007	2004	percentage point change
PERCENT WITH DEBT			
Total households	**77.0%**	**76.4%**	**0.6**
Under age 35	83.5	79.8	3.7
Aged 35 to 44	86.2	88.6	–2.4
Aged 45 to 54	86.8	88.4	–1.6
Aged 55 to 64	81.8	76.3	5.5
Aged 65 to 74	65.5	58.8	6.7
Aged 75 or older	31.4	40.3	–8.9

	2007	2004	percent change
MEDIAN AMOUNT OF DEBT			
Total households	**$67,300**	**$60,700**	**10.9%**
Under age 35	36,200	36,900	–1.9
Aged 35 to 44	106,200	95,800	10.9
Aged 45 to 54	95,900	91,400	4.9
Aged 55 to 64	60,300	52,700	14.4
Aged 65 to 74	40,100	27,500	45.8
Aged 75 or older	13,000	16,900	–23.1

Source: Federal Reserve Board, Changes in U.S. Family Finances from 2004 to 2007: Evidence from the Survey of Consumer Finances, Federal Reserve Bulletin, February 2009, Internet site http://www.federalreserve.gov/pubs/oss/oss2/2007/scf2007home.html; calculations by New Strategist

Table 11.9 Debt of Households by Type of Debt and Age of Householder, 2007

(percentage of households with debt, and median value of debt for those with debt, by type of debt and age of householder, 2007)

	total	under 35	35 to 44	45 to 54	55 to 64	65 to 74	75 or older
PERCENT WITH DEBT							
Any debt	**77.0%**	**83.5%**	**86.2%**	**86.8%**	**81.8%**	**65.5%**	**31.4%**
Secured by residential property							
Primary residence	48.7	37.3	59.5	65.5	55.3	42.9	13.9
Other	5.5	3.3	6.5	8.0	7.8	5.0	0.6
Lines of credit not secured by residential property	1.7	2.1	2.2	1.9	1.2	1.5	–
Installment loans	46.9	65.2	56.2	51.9	44.6	26.1	7.0
Credit card balances	46.1	48.5	51.7	53.6	49.9	37.0	18.8
Other debt	6.8	5.9	7.5	9.8	8.7	4.4	1.3
MEDIAN AMOUNT OF DEBT							
Any debt	**$67,300**	**$36,200**	**$106,200**	**$95,900**	**$60,300**	**$40,100**	**$13,000**
Secured by residential property							
Primary residence	107,000	135,300	128,000	110,000	85,000	69,000	40,000
Other	100,000	78,000	101,600	82,000	130,000	125,000	50,000
Lines of credit not secured by residential property	3,800	1,000	4,600	6,000	10,000	30,000	–
Installment loans	13,000	15,000	13,500	12,900	10,900	10,300	8,000
Credit card balances	3,000	1,800	3,500	3,600	3,600	3,000	800
Other debt	5,000	4,500	5,000	4,500	6,000	5,000	4,500

Note: "–" means sample is too small to make a reliable estimate.
Source: Federal Reserve Board, Changes in U.S. Family Finances from 2004 to 2007: Evidence from the Survey of Consumer Finances, Federal Reserve Bulletin, February 2009, Internet site http://www.federalreserve.gov/pubs/oss/oss2/2007/scf2007home.html; calculations by New Strategist

Slim Majority of Workers Aged 55 to 64 Participate in a Retirement Plan

Only 13 percent of older workers are confident in having enough money for retirement.

Fifty-two percent of American workers were offered an employer-sponsored retirement plan in 2007, but only 41.5 percent took advantage of the opportunity, according to an analysis by the Employee Benefit Research Institute (EBRI). Plan participation is highest among workers aged 45 to 64, at 52 to 53 percent. It falls to 29 percent among workers aged 65 or older.

Another EBRI study shows that only 52 percent of workers aged 55 to 64 own an IRA or participate in a 401(k)-type (defined-contribution) retirement plan. Among those aged 55 to 64 who participate in a 401(k)-type plan, only 13 percent made the maximum contribution in 2005.

Having little savings and being faced with a steep decline in stock values, it is no surprise that many older workers are worried about retirement. Only 13 percent of workers aged 55 or older are "very confident" they will have enough money to live comfortably throughout retirement, down from 18 percent in 1999.

■ The substitution of defined-contribution for defined-benefit pension plans puts the burden of retirement savings on workers rather than employers.

Among workers aged 55 to 64, just over half participate in an employer-sponsored retirement plan

(percent of workers who participate in an employer-sponsored retirement plan, by age, 2007)

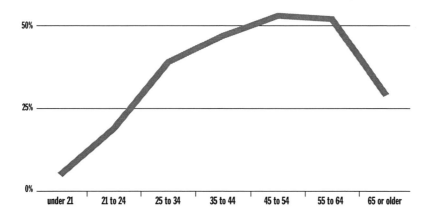

Table 11.10 Retirement Plan Coverage by Age, 2007

(total number of workers, percent whose employer offers a retirement plan, and percent participating in plan, by type of employment and age of worker, 2007; numbers in thousands)

	number of workers	percent with an employer who sponsors a retirement plan	percent participating in employer's retirement plan
Total workers	**158,099**	**51.8%**	**41.5%**
Under age 21	10,450	24.0	4.9
Aged 21 to 24	12,695	38.5	19.3
Aged 25 to 34	33,485	51.1	38.7
Aged 35 to 44	35,299	55.8	47.5
Aged 45 to 54	36,139	59.3	52.6
Aged 55 to 64	22,782	59.2	52.0
Aged 65 or older	7,249	39.1	28.7
PRIVATE WAGE AND SALARY WORKERS AGED 21 TO 64			
Total workers	**110,148**	**52.7**	**42.0**
Aged 21 to 24	11,397	37.3	17.9
Aged 25 to 34	27,816	48.9	35.7
Aged 35 to 44	27,788	54.5	45.3
Aged 45 to 54	27,068	58.1	50.7
Aged 55 to 64	16,079	57.7	49.9
PUBLIC WAGE AND SALARY WORKERS AGED 21 TO 64			
Total workers	**21,106**	**83.3**	**75.4**
Aged 21 to 24	1,035	58.5	38.9
Aged 25 to 34	4,250	80.1	69.5
Aged 35 to 44	5,183	84.3	77.7
Aged 45 to 54	6,179	85.7	79.9
Aged 55 to 64	4,459	87.9	80.7

Source: Employee Benefit Research Institute, Employment-Based Retirement Plan Participation: Geographic Differences and Trends, 2007, Issue Brief 322, October 2008, Internet site http://www.ebri.org/publications/ib/index.cfm?fa=ibDisp&content_id=3989

Table 11.11 Ownership of IRAs and 401(k)s by Age, 2005

(percentage of workers aged 21 to 64 owning IRAs and/or participating in a 401(k)-type plan, by age, 2005)

	IRA and/or 401(k)-type plan	IRA only	401(k)-type plan only	both IRA and 401(k)-type plan	neither IRA nor 401(k)-type plan
Total workers	**43.8%**	**10.7%**	**20.9%**	**12.2%**	**56.2%**
Aged 21 to 24	11.4	2.1	8.3	1.0	88.6
Aged 25 to 34	35.4	6.6	20.4	8.4	64.6
Aged 35 to 44	47.4	10.2	24.4	12.8	52.6
Aged 45 to 54	51.2	12.4	22.7	16.1	48.8
Aged 55 to 64	52.1	18.5	18.2	15.4	47.9

Source: Employee Benefit Research Institute, Ownership of Individual Retirement Accounts (IRAs) and 401(k)-Type Plans, by Craig Copeland, Notes, Vol. 29, No. 5, May 2008, Internet site http://www.ebri.org/publications/notes/index .cfm?fa=main&doc_type=2

Table 11.12 Participation in IRAs and 401(k)s by Age, 2005

(percent of workers aged 21 to 64 owning an IRA or participating in 401(k)-type plan, percent making a contribution to the IRA, and mean amount contributed and percent making maximum contribution among contributors, by age, 2005)

			among IRA contributors	
	has IRA in own name	made tax-deductible contribution to IRA	mean contribution	percent making maximum contribution
Total workers	**22.9%**	**6.2%**	**$2,540**	**26.8%**
Aged 21 to 24	3.2	0.6	1,149	0.0
Aged 25 to 34	15.0	4.3	2,089	20.5
Aged 35 to 44	23.0	6.4	2,497	31.3
Aged 45 to 54	28.5	7.4	2,527	25.0
Aged 55 to 64	33.9	9.2	2,943	29.3

		among 401(k) contributors	
	percent participating in 401(k)	mean contribution	percent making maximum contribution
Total workers	**33.1%**	**$4,274**	**8.9%**
Aged 21 to 24	9.3	1,597	0.0
Aged 25 to 34	28.8	3,353	5.0
Aged 35 to 44	37.2	4,226	8.4
Aged 45 to 54	38.8	1,695	10.3
Aged 55 to 64	33.5	4,993	13.2

Source: Employee Benefit Research Institute, Ownership of Individual Retirement Accounts (IRAs) and 401(k)-Type Plans, by Craig Copeland, Notes, Vol. 29, No. 5, May 2008; Internet site http://www.ebri.org/publications/notes/index .cfm?fa=main&doc_type=2

Table 11.13 Retirement Planning by Age, 2009

(percentage of workers aged 25 or older responding by age, 2009)

	total	25 to 34	35 to 44	45 to 54	55 or older
Very confident in having enough money to live comfortably throughout retirement	13%	18%	12%	10%	13%
Very confident in having enough money to take care of medical expenses in retirement	13	16	13	11	14
Worker and/or spouse have saved for retirement	75	66	78	78	79
Worker and/or spouse are currently saving for retirement	65	57	68	68	66
Contribute to a workplace retirement savings plan	64	52	72	65	64
Expected retirement age					
Before age 60	9	17	8	9	1
Aged 60 to 64	17	14	16	17	22
Aged 65	23	29	29	18	15
Aged 66 or older	31	22	33	35	34
Never retire	10	9	6	13	11
Don't know/refused	7	8	3	6	12
Total savings and investments (not including value of primary residence)					
Less than $25,000	53	73	53	43	36
$25,000 to $49,999	11	12	8	11	13
$50,000 to $99,999	12	9	14	14	10
$100,000 to $249,999	12	5	16	15	15
$250,000 or more	12	2	9	17	26

Source: Employee Benefit Research Institute, Retirement Confidence Surveys, Internet site http://www.ebri.org/surveys/rcs/2009/

Table 11.14 Changes in Retirement Confidence by Age, 1999 and 2009

(percentage of workers aged 25 or older responding by age, 1999 and 2009)

	total	25 to 34	35 to 44	45 to 54	55 or older
Very confident in having enough money to live comfortably throughout retirement					
2009	13%	18%	12%	10%	13%
1999	22	27	20	21	18
Very confident in having enough money to take care of medical expenses in retirement					
2009	13	16	13	11	14
1999	16	16	15	13	22
Say they are doing a good job of preparing financially for retirement					
2009	20	23	21	18	16
1999	23	22	22	24	29

Source: Employee Benefit Research Institute, Retirement Confidence Surveys, Internet site http://www.ebri.org/surveys/rcs/2009/

Glossary

adjusted for inflation Income or a change in income that has been adjusted for the rise in the cost of living, or the consumer price index (CPI-U-RS).

age Classification by age is based on the age of the person at his/her last birthday.

American Housing Survey The AHS collects national and metropolitan-level data on the nation's housing, including apartments, single-family homes, and mobile homes. The nationally representative survey, with a sample of 55,000 homes, is conducted by the Census Bureau for the Department of Housing and Urban Development every other year.

American Indians In this book, American Indians include Alaska Natives (Eskimos and Aleuts) unless those groups are shown separately.

American Time Use Survey Under contract with the Bureau of Labor Statistics, the Census Bureau collects ATUS information, which reveals how people spend their time. The ATUS sample is drawn from U.S. households that have completed their final month of interviews for the Current Population Survey. One individual from each selected household is chosen to participate in the ATUS. Respondents are interviewed by telephone only once about their time use on the previous day.

Asian Includes Native Hawaiians and other Pacific Islanders unless those groups are shown separately.

Baby Boom Americans born between 1946 and 1964.

Baby Bust Americans born between 1965 and 1976, also known as Generation X.

Behavioral Risk Factor Surveillance System A collaborative project of the Centers for Disease Control and Prevention and U.S. states and territories. It is an ongoing data collection program designed to measure behavioral risk factors in the adult population aged 18 or older. All 50 states, three territories, and the District of Columbia take part in the survey, making the BRFSS the primary source of information on the health-related behaviors of Americans.

black A racial category that includes those who identified themselves as "black" or "African American."

central cities The largest city in a metropolitan area. The balance of the metropolitan area outside the central city is regarded as the "suburbs."

Consumer Expenditure Survey An ongoing study of the day-to-day spending of American households administered by the Bureau of Labor Statistics. The CEX includes an interview survey and a diary survey. The average spending figures shown in this book are the integrated data from both the diary and interview components of the survey. Two separate, nationally representative samples are used for the interview and diary surveys. For the interview survey, about 7,500 consumer units are interviewed on a rotating panel basis each quarter for five consecutive quarters. For the diary survey, 7,500 consumer units keep weekly diaries of spending for two consecutive weeks.

consumer unit *(on spending tables only)* For convenience, the term consumer unit and households are used interchangeably in the spending section of this book, although consumer units are somewhat different from the Census Bureau's households. Consumer units are all related members of a household, or financially independent members of a household. A household may include more than one consumer unit.

Current Population Survey A nationally representative survey of the civilian noninstitutional population aged 15 or older. It is taken monthly by the Census Bureau for the Bureau of Labor Statistics, collecting information from more than 50,000 households on employment and unemployment. In March of each year, the survey includes the Annual Social and Economic Supplement (formerly called the Annual Demographic Survey), which is the source of most national data on the characteristics of Americans, such as educational attainment, living arrangements, and incomes.

disability As defined by the National Health Interview Survey, respondents aged 18 or older are asked whether they have difficulty in physical functioning, probing whether respondents can perform nine activities by themselves without using special equipment. The categories are walking a quarter mile; standing for two hours; sitting for two hours; walking up 10 steps without resting; stooping, bending, kneeling; reaching over one's head; grasping or handling small objects; carrying a 10-pound object; and pushing/pulling a large object. Adults who report that any of these activities is very difficult or they cannot do it at all are defined as having physical difficulties.

dual-earner couple A married couple in which both the householder and the householder's spouse are in the labor force.

earnings The amount of money a person receives from his or her job. *See also* Income.

employed All civilians who did any work as a paid employee or farmer/self-employed worker, or who worked 15 hours or more as an unpaid farm worker or in a family-owned business, during the reference period. All those who have jobs but who are temporarily absent from their jobs due to illness, bad weather, vacation, labor management dispute, or personal reasons are considered employed.

expenditure The transaction cost including excise and sales taxes of goods and services acquired during the survey period. The full cost of each purchase is recorded even though full payment may not have been made at the date of purchase. Average expenditure figures may be artificially low for infrequently purchased items such as cars because figures are calculated using all consumer units within a demographic segment rather than just purchasers. Expenditure estimates include money spent on gifts for others.

family A group of two or more people (one of whom is the householder) related by birth, marriage, or adoption and living in the same household.

family household A household maintained by a householder who lives with one or more people related to him or her by blood, marriage, or adoption.

female/male householder A woman or man who maintains a household without a spouse present. May head family or nonfamily households.

foreign-born population People who are not U.S. citizens at birth.

full-time employment Thirty-five or more hours of work per week during a majority of the weeks worked.

full-time, year-round Fifty or more weeks of full-time employment during the previous calendar year.

Generation X Americans born between 1965 and 1976, also known as the baby-bust generation.

Hispanic Because Hispanic is an ethnic origin rather than a race, Hispanics may be of any race. While most Hispanics are white, there are black, Asian, and American Indian Hispanics.

household All the persons who occupy a housing unit. A household includes the related family members and all the unrelated persons, if any, such as lodgers, foster children, wards, or employees who share the housing unit. A person living alone is counted as a household. A group of unrelated people who share a housing unit as roommates or unmarried partners is also counted as a household. Households do not include group quarters such as college dormitories, prisons, or nursing homes.

household, race/ethnicity of Households are categorized according to the race or ethnicity of the householder only.

householder The person (or one of the persons) in whose name the housing unit is owned or rented or, if there is no such person, any adult member. With married couples, the householder may be either the husband or wife. The householder is the reference person for the household.

householder, age of The age of the householder is used to categorize households into age groups such as those used in this book. Married couples, for example, are classified according to the age of either the husband or wife, depending on which one identified him or herself as the householder.

housing unit A house, an apartment, a group of rooms, or a single room occupied or intended for occupancy as separate living quarters. Separate living quarters are those in which the occupants do not live and eat with any other persons in the structure and that have direct access from the outside of the building or through a common hall that is used or intended for use by the occupants of another unit or by the general public. The occupants may be a single family, one person living alone, two or more families living together, or any other group of related or unrelated persons who share living arrangements.

Housing Vacancy Survey A supplement to the Current Population Survey, which provides quarterly and annual data on rental and homeowner vacancy rates, characteristics of units available for occupancy, and homeownership rates by age, household type, region, state, and metropolitan area. The Current Population Survey sample includes 51,000 occupied housing units and 9,000 vacant units.

housing value The respondent's estimate of how much his or her house and lot would sell for if it were for sale.

iGeneration Americans born from 1995 to the present.

immigration The relatively permanent movement (change of residence) of people into the country of reference.

income Money received in the preceding calendar year by each person aged 15 or older from each of the following sources: (1) earnings from longest job (or self-employment), (2) earnings from jobs other than longest job, (3) unemployment compensation, (4) workers' compensation, (5) Social Security, (6) Supplemental Security income, (7) public assistance, (8) veterans' payments, (9) survivor benefits, (10) disability benefits, (11) retirement pensions, (12) interest, (13) dividends, (14) rents and royalties or estates and trusts, (15) educational assistance, (16) alimony, (17) child support, (18) financial assistance from outside the household, and other periodic income. Income is reported in several ways in this book. Household income is the combined income of all household members. Income of persons is all income accruing to a person from all sources. Earnings are the money a person receives from his or her job.

industry The industry in which a person worked longest in the preceding calendar year.

job tenure The length of time a person has been employed continuously by the same employer.

labor force The labor force tables in this book show the civilian labor force only. The labor force includes both the employed and the unemployed (people who are looking for work). People are counted as in the labor force if they were working or looking for work during the reference week in which the Census Bureau fields the Current Population Survey.

labor force participation rate The percent of the civilian noninstitutional population that is in the civilian labor force, which includes both the employed and the unemployed.

married couples with or without children under age 18 Refers to married couples with or without own children under age 18 living in the same household. Couples without children under age 18 may be parents of grown children who live elsewhere, or they could be childless couples.

median The amount that divides the population or households into two equal portions: one below and one above the median. Medians can be calculated for income, age, and many other characteristics.

median income The amount that divides the income distribution into two equal groups, half having incomes above the median, half having incomes below the median. The medians for households or families are based on all households or families. The median for persons are based on all persons aged 15 or older with income.

Medical Expenditure Panel Survey A nationally representative survey that collects detailed information on the health status, access to care, health care use and expenses and health insurance coverage of the civilian noninstitutionalized population of the U.S. and nursing home residents. MEPS comprises four component surveys: the Household Component, the Medical Provider Component, the Insurance Component, and the Nursing Home Component. The Household Component is the core survey, is conducted each year, and includes 15,000 households and 37,000 people.

metropolitan statistical area A city with 50,000 or more inhabitants, or a Census Bureau-defined urbanized area of at least 50,000 inhabitants and a total metropolitan population of at least 100,000 (75,000 in New England). The county (or counties) that contains the largest city becomes the "central county" (counties), along with any adjacent counties that have at least 50 percent of their population in the urbanized area surrounding the largest city. Additional "outlying counties" are included in the MSA if they meet specified requirements of commuting to the central counties and other selected requirements of metropolitan character (such as population density and percent urban). In New England, MSAs are defined in terms of cities and towns rather than counties. For this reason, the concept of NECMA is used to define metropolitan areas in the New England division.

Millennial generation Americans born between 1977 and 1994.

mobility status People are classified according to their mobility status on the basis of a comparison between their place of residence at the time of the March Current Population Survey and their place of residence in March of the previous year. Nonmovers are people living in the same house at the end of the period as at the beginning of the period. Movers are people living in a different house at the end of the period than at the beginning of the period. Movers from abroad are either citizens or aliens whose place of residence is outside the United States at the beginning of the period, that is, in an outlying area under the jurisdiction of the United States or in a foreign country. The mobility status for children is fully allocated from the mother if she is in the household; otherwise it is allocated from the householder.

National Ambulatory Medical Care Survey An annual survey of visits to nonfederally employed office-based physicians who are primarily engaged in direct patient care. Data are collected from physicians rather than patients, with each physician assigned a one-week reporting period. During that week, a systematic random sample of visit characteristics are recorded by the physician or office staff.

National Health and Nutrition Examination Survey A continuous survey of a representative sample of the U.S. civilian noninstitutionalized population. Respondents are interviewed at home about their health and nutrition, and the interview is followed up by a physical examination that measures such things as height and weight in mobile examination centers.

National Health Interview Survey A continuing nationwide sample survey of the civilian noninstitutional population of the U.S. conducted by the Census

Bureau for the National Center for Health Statistics. Each year, data are collected from more than 100,000 people about their illnesses, injuries, impairments, chronic and acute conditions, activity limitations, and the use of health services.

National Hospital Ambulatory Medical Care Survey The NHAMCS, sponsored by the National Center for Health Statistics, is an annual national probability sample survey of visits to emergency departments and outpatient departments at non-Federal, short stay and general hospitals. Data are collected by hospital staff from patient records.

National Hospital Discharge Survey This survey has been conducted annually since 1965, sponsored by the National Center for Health Statistics, to collect nationally representative information on the characteristics of inpatients discharged from nonfederal, short-stay hospitals in the U.S. The survey collects data from a sample of approximately 270,000 inpatient records acquired from a national sample of about 500 hospitals.

National Household Education Survey The NHES, sponsored by the National Center for Education Statistics, provides descriptive data on the educational activities of the U.S. population, including after-school care and adult education. The NHES is a system of telephone surveys of a representative sample of 45,000 to 60,000 households in the U.S.

National Nursing Home Survey This is a series of national sample surveys of nursing homes, their residents, and staff conducted at various intervals since 1973-74 and sponsored by the National Center for Health Statistics. Data for the survey are obtained through personal interviews with administrators and staff, and occasionally with self-administered questionnaires, in a sample of about 1,500 facilities.

National Survey of Family Growth The 2002 NSFG, sponsored by the National Center for Health Statistics, is a nationally representative survey of the civilian noninstitutional population aged 15 to 44. In-person interviews were completed with 12,571 men and women, collecting data on marriage, divorce, contraception, and infertility. The 2002 survey updates previous NSFG surveys taken in 1973, 1976, 1988, and 1995.

National Survey on Drug Use and Health Formerly called the National Household Survey on Drug Abuse, this survey, sponsored by the Substance Abuse and Mental Health Services Administration, has been conducted since 1971. It is the primary source of information on the use of illegal drugs by the U.S. population. Each year, a nationally representative sample of about 70,000 individuals aged 12 or older are surveyed in the 50 states and the District of Columbia.

net worth The amount of money left over after a household's debts are subtracted from its assets.

nonfamily household A household maintained by a householder who lives alone or who lives with people to whom he or she is not related.

nonfamily householder A householder who lives alone or with nonrelatives.

non-Hispanic People who do not identify themselves as Hispanic are classified as non-Hispanic. Non-Hispanics may be of any race.

non-Hispanic white People who identify their race as white and who do not indicate a Hispanic origin.

nonmetropolitan area Counties that are not classified as metropolitan areas.

occupation Occupational classification is based on the kind of work a person did at his or her job during the previous calendar year. If a person changed jobs during the year, the data refer to the occupation of the job held the longest during that year.

occupied housing units A housing unit is classified as occupied if a person or group of people is living in it or if the occupants are only temporarily absent—on vacation, example. By definition, the count of occupied housing units is the same as the count of households.

outside central city The portion of a metropolitan county or counties that falls outside of the central city or cities; generally regarded as the suburbs.

own children Sons and daughters, including step-children and adopted children, of the householder. The totals include never-married children living away from home in college dormitories.

owner occupied A housing unit is "owner occupied" if the owner lives in the unit, even if it is mortgaged or not fully paid for. A cooperative or condominium unit is "owner occupied" only if the owner lives in it. All other occupied units are classified as "renter occupied."

part-time employment Less than 35 hours of work per week in a majority of the weeks worked during the year.

percent change The change (either positive or negative) in a measure that is expressed as a proportion of the starting measure. When median income changes from $20,000 to $25,000, for example, this is a 25 percent increase.

percentage point change The change (either positive or negative) in a value which is already expressed as a percentage. When a labor force participation rate changes from 70 percent of 75 percent, for example, this is a 5 percentage point increase.

poverty level The official income threshold below which families and people are classified as living in poverty. The threshold rises each year with inflation and varies depending on family size and age of householder.

primary activity In the time use tables, those activities that respondents identify as their main activity. Other activities done simultaneously are not included.

proportion or share The value of a part expressed as a percentage of the whole. If there are 4 million people aged 25 and 3 million of them are white, then the white proportion is 75 percent.

race Race is self-reported and can be defined in three ways. The "race alone" population comprises people who identify themselves as only one race. The "race in combination" population comprises people who identify themselves as more than one race, such as white and black. The "race, alone or in combination" population includes both those who identify themselves as one race and those who identify themselves as more than one race.

regions The four major regions and nine census divisions of the United States are the state groupings as shown below:

Northeast:
—New England: Connecticut, Maine, Massachusetts, New Hampshire, Rhode Island, and Vermont
—Middle Atlantic: New Jersey, New York, and Pennsylvania

Midwest:
—East North Central: Illinois, Indiana, Michigan, Ohio, and Wisconsin
—West North Central: Iowa, Kansas, Minnesota, Missouri, Nebraska, North Dakota, and South Dakota

South:
—South Atlantic: Delaware, District of Columbia, Florida, Georgia, Maryland, North Carolina, South Carolina, Virginia, and West Virginia
—East South Central: Alabama, Kentucky, Mississippi, and Tennessee
—West South Central: Arkansas, Louisiana, Oklahoma, and Texas

West:
—Mountain: Arizona, Colorado, Idaho, Montana, Nevada, New Mexico, Utah, and Wyoming
—Pacific: Alaska, California, Hawaii, Oregon, and Washington

renter occupied *See* Owner Occupied.

Retirement Confidence Survey An annual survey, sponsored by the Employee Benefit Research Institute, the American Savings Education Council, and Mathew Greenwald & Associates, of a nationally representative sample of 1,000 people aged 25 or older. Respondents are asked a core set of questions that have been asked since 1996, measuring attitudes and behavior towards retirement.

rounding Percentages are rounded to the nearest tenth of a percent; therefore, the percentages in a distribution do not always add exactly to 100.0 percent. The totals, however, are always shown as 100.0. Moreover, individual figures are rounded to the nearest thousand without being adjusted to group totals, which are independently rounded; percentages are based on the unrounded numbers.

self-employment A person is categorized as self-employed if he or she was self-employed in the job held longest during the reference period. Persons who report self-employment from a second job are excluded, but those who report wage-and-salary income from a second job are included. Unpaid workers in family businesses are excluded. Self-employment statistics include only nonagricultural workers and exclude people who work for themselves in incorporated business.

sex ratio The number of men per 100 women.

suburbs *See* Outside Central City.

Survey of Consumer Finances A triennial survey taken by the Federal Reserve Board. It collects data on the assets, debts, and net worth of American households. For the 2007 survey, the Federal Reserve Board interviewed more than 4,000 households.

unemployed Those who, during the survey period, had no employment but were available and looking for work. Those who were laid off from their jobs and were waiting to be recalled are also classified as unemployed.

white A racial category that includes many Hispanics (who may be of any race) unless the term "non-Hispanic white" is used.

Youth Risk Behavior Surveillance System Created by the Centers for Disease Control to monitor health risks being taken by young people at the national, state, and local level. The national survey is taken every two years based on a nationally representative sample of 16,000 students in 9th through 12th grade in public and private schools.

Bibliography

Agency for Healthcare Research and Quality
Internet site http://www.ahrq.gov/
—Medical Expenditure Panel Survey, Internet site http://www.meps.ahrq.gov/mepsweb/survey_comp/household.jsp

Bureau of Labor Statistics
Internet site http://www.bls.gov
—2000 and 2007 Consumer Expenditure Surveys, Internet site http://www.bls.gov/cex/
—2007 American Time Use Survey, Internet site http://www.bls.gov/tus/home.htm
—2007 American Time Use Survey, Summary Table 2. Number of persons and average hours per day by detailed activity classification (travel reported separately), 2007 annual averages, unpublished tables received upon special request
—Characteristics of Minimum Wage Workers, 2008, Internet site http://www.bls.gov/cps/minwage2008tbls.htm
—College Enrollment and Work Activity of 2008 High School Graduates, Internet site http://www.bls.gov/news.release/hsgec.toc.htm
—Contingent and Alternative Employment Arrangements, Internet site http://www.bls.gov/news.release/conemp.toc.htm
—Economic and Employment Projections, Internet site http://www.bls.gov/news.release/ecopro.toc.htm
—Employee Benefits Survey, Internet site http://www.bls.gov/ncs/ebs/benefits/2008/ownership_civilian.htm
—Employee Tenure, Internet site http://www.bls.gov/news.release/tenure.toc.htm
—Employment Characteristics of Families, Internet site http://www.bls.gov/news.release/famee.toc.htm
—Labor Force Statistics from the Current Population Survey, Internet site http://www.bls.gov/cps/tables.htm#empstat
—*Monthly Labor Review*, "Labor Force Projections to 2016: More Workers in Their Golden Years," November 2007, Internet site http://www.bls.gov/opub/mlr/2007/11/contents.htm
—*Monthly Labor Review*, "Youth enrollment and employment during the school year," February 2008, Internet site http://www.bls.gov/opub/mlr/2008/02/contents.htm
—Table 15. Employed persons by detailed occupation, sex, and age, Annual Average 2008 (Source: Current Population Survey), unpublished table received upon special request

Bureau of the Census
Internet site http://www.census.gov
—2007 American Community Survey, Internet site http://factfinder.census.gov/servlet/DatasetMainPageServlet?_program=ACS&_submenuId=&_lang=en&_ts=l
—2008 Current Population Survey Annual Social and Economic Supplement, Internet site http://www.census.gov/hhes/www/income/dinctabs.html

—2008 National Population Projections, Internet site http://www.census.gov/population/ www/projections/2008projections.html

—A Child's Day: 2006 (Selected Indicators of Child Well-Being), Detailed Tables, Internet site http://www.census.gov/population/www/socdemo/2006_detailedtables.html

—American Housing Survey for the United States in 2007, Internet site http://www.census .gov/hhes/www/housing/ahs/ahs07/ahs07.html

—America's Families and Living Arrangements, 2008 Current Population Survey Annual Social and Economic Supplement, Internet site http://www.census.gov/population/www/ socdemo/hh-fam/cps2008.html

—Educational Attainment, Historical Tables, Internet site http://www.census.gov/ population/www/socdemo/educ-attn.html

—Educational Attainment in the United States: 2008, Detailed Tables, Current Population Survey Annual Social and Economic Supplement, Internet site http://www.census.gov/ population/www/socdemo/education/cps2008.html

—Families and Living Arrangements, Historical Time Series, Current Population Survey Annual Social and Economic Supplements, Internet site http://www.census.gov/population/ www/socdemo/hh-fam.html

—Fertility of American Women, Current Population Survey—June 2006, Detailed Tables, Internet site http://www.census.gov/population/www/socdemo/fertility/cps2006.html

—Geographic Mobility: 2007 to 2008, Detailed Tables, Current Population Survey Annual Social and Economic Supplement, Internet site http://www.census.gov/population/www/ socdemo/migrate/cps2008.html

—Geographical Mobility/Migration, Current Population Survey Annual Social and Economic Supplements, Internet site http://www.census.gov/population/www/socdemo/migrate.html

—Health Insurance, Internet site http://pubdb3.census.gov/macro/032008/health/toc.htm

—Historical Health Insurance Tables, Internet site http://www.census.gov/hhes/www/ hlthins/historic/index.html

—Historical Income Tables, Current Population Survey Annual Social and Economic Supplements, Internet site http://www.census.gov/hhes/www/income/histinc/histinctb.html

—Housing Vacancy Surveys, Internet site http://www.census.gov/hhes/www/housing/hvs/ hvs.html

—National Population Estimates, Internet site http://www.census.gov/popest/national/asrh/ NC-EST2008-sa.html

—Number, Timing, and Duration of Marriages and Divorces: 2004, Detailed Tables, Internet site http://www.census.gov/population/www/socdemo/marr-div/2004detailed_tables.html

—School Enrollment, Historical Tables, Internet site http://www.census.gov/population/ www/socdemo/school.html

—School Enrollment—Social and Economic Characteristics of Students: October 2007, detailed tables, Internet site http://www.census.gov/population/www/socdemo/school/cps2007 .html

—State Population Estimates, Internet site http://www.census.gov/popest/states/asrh/

Centers for Disease Control and Prevention
>Internet site http://www.cdc.gov
>—Behavioral Risk Factor Surveillance System, Prevalence Data, Internet site http://apps
>.nccd.cdc.gov/brfss/
>—Cases of HIV/AIDS and AIDS, Internet site http://www.cdc.gov/hiv/topics/surveillance/
>resources/reports/2006report/table3.htm
>—"Youth Risk Behavior Surveillance–United States, 2007," *Mortality and Morbidity Weekly
>Report*, Vol. 57/SS-4, June 6, 2008; Internet site http://www.cdc.gov/HealthyYouth/yrbs/
>index.htm

Department of Homeland Security
>Internet site http://www.dhs.gov/index.shtm
>—Immigration, 2008 Yearbook of Immigration Statistics, Internet site http://www.uscis
>.gov/graphics/shared/statistics/yearbook/index.htm

Employee Benefit Research Institute
>Internet site http://www.ebri.org/
>—Retirement Confidence Surveys, Internet site http://www.ebri.org/surveys/rcs/
>—"Employment-Based Retirement Plan Participation: Geographic Differences and Trends,
>2007," *Issue Brief* 322, October 2008, Internet site http://www.ebri.org/publications/ib/
>index.cfm?fa=ibDisp&content_id=3989
>—"Ownership of Individual Accounts (IRAs) and 401(k)-Type Plans," by Craig Copeland,
>*Notes*, Vol. 29, No. 5, May 2008; Internet site http://www.ebri.org/publications/notes/index
>.cfm?fa=main&doc_type=2

Federal Interagency Forum on Child and Family Statistics
>Internet site http://childstats.gov
>—America's Children in Brief: Key National Indicators of Well-Being, 2008, Internet site
>http://childstats.gov/americaschildren/tables.asp

Federal Reserve Board
>Internet site http://www.federalreserve.gov/pubs/oss/oss2/scfindex.html
>—"Changes in U.S. Family Finance from 2004 to 2007: Evidence from the Survey of Con-
>sumer Finances," *Federal Reserve Bulletin*, February 2009, Internet site http://www
>.federalreserve.gov/pubs/oss/oss2/2007/scf2007home.html

National Center for Education Statistics
>Internet site http://nces.ed.gov
>—The Condition of Education, Internet site http://nces.ed.gov/programs/coe/
>—Digest of Education Statistics: 2008, Internet site http://nces.ed.gov/programs/digest/
>— National Household Education Surveys Program, Parent and Family Involvement in Edu-
>cation, 2006–07 School Year, Internet site http://nces.ed.gov/pubsearch/pubsinfo
>.asp?pubid=2008050

National Center for Health Statistics

Internet site http://www.cdc.gov/nchs

—*2006 National Hospital Discharge Survey,* National Health Statistics Report, No. 5, 2008, Internet site http://www.cdc.gov/nchs/about/major/hdasd/listpubs.htm

—*Ambulatory Medical Care Utilization Estimates for 2006*, National Health Statistics Reports, No. 8, 2008, Internet site http://www.cdc.gov/nchs/about/major/ahcd/adata .htm#CombinedReports

—*Anthropometric Reference Data for Children and Adults: United States, 2003–2006*, National Health Statistics Reports, Number 10, 2008, Internet site http://www.cdc.gov/nchs/ products/pubs/pubd/nhsr/nhsr.htm

—*Births: Final Data for 2006*, National Vital Statistics Reports, Vol. 57, No. 7, 2009, Internet site http://www.cdc.gov/nchs/products/nvsr.htm#57_12

—*Births: Preliminary Data for 2007*, National Vital Statistics Reports, Vol. 57, No. 12, 2009, Internet site http://www.cdc.gov/nchs/products/nvsr.htm#57_12

—*Complementary and Alternative Medicine Use Among Adults and Children: United States, 2007*, National Health Statistics Report, No. 12, 2008, Internet site http://nccam.nih.gov/ news/camstats/2007/index.htm

—*Deaths: Final Data for 2006*, National Vital Statistics Reports, Vol. 57, No. 14, 2009, Internet site http://www.cdc.gov/nchs/products/nvsr.htm#vol57

—*Fertility, Contraception, and Fatherhood: Data on Men and Women from Cycle 6 of the 2002 National Survey of Family Growth*, Vital and Health Statistics, Series 23, No. 26, 2006; Internet site http://www.cdc.gov/nchs/nsfg.htm

—*Fertility, Family Planning, and Reproductive Health of U.S. Women: Data from the 2002 National Survey of Family Growth*, Vital and Health Statistics, Series 23, No. 25, 2005; Internet site http://www.cdc.gov/nchs/nsfg.htm

—*Health Characteristics of Adults 55 Years of Age and Over: United States, 2000-2003, Advance Data, No. 370,* 2006, Internet site http://www.cdc.gov/nchs/nhis.htm

—*National Ambulatory Medical Care Survey: 2006 Summary,* National Health Statistics Report, No. 3, 2008, Internet site http://www.cdc.gov/nchs/about/major/ahcd/adata.htm

—National Center for Chronic Disease Prevention and Health Promotion, Prevalence Data, Internet site http://apps.nccd.cdc.gov/HRQOL/

—*National Hospital Ambulatory Medical Care Survey: 2006 Emergency Department Summary,* National Health Statistics Report, No. 4, 2007, Internet site http://www.cdc.gov/nchs/ about/major/ahcd/adata.htm

—*National Hospital Ambulatory Medical Care Survey: 2006 Outpatient Department Summary,* National Health Statistics Report, No. 4, 2008, Internet site http://www.cdc.gov/nchs/ about/major/ahcd/adata.htm

—*Health United States 2008,* Internet site http://www.cdc.gov/nchs/hus.htm

—*Sexual Behavior and Selected Health Measures: Men and Women 15-44 Years of Age, United States, 2002*, Advance Data, No. 362, 2005; Internet site http://www.cdc.gov/nchs/ nsfg.htm

—*Summary Health Statistics for U.S. Adults: National Health Interview Survey, 2007*, Series 10, No. 240, 2008, Internet site http://www.cdc.gov/nchs/nhis.htm

—*Summary Health Statistics for U.S. Children: National Health Interview Survey, 2007*, Series 10, No. 239, 2008, Internet site http://www.cdc.gov/nchs/nhis.htm

—*Summary Health Statistics for the U.S. Population: National Health Interview Survey, 2007*, Series 10, No. 238, 2008, Internet site http://www.cdc.gov/nchs/nhis.htm

National Sporting Goods Association

Internet site http://www.nsga.org

—Sports Participation, Internet site http://www.nsga.org

Substance Abuse and Mental Health Services Administration

Internet site http://www.samhsa.gov

—National Survey on Drug Use and Health, 2007, Internet site http://www.oas.samhsa.gov/nsduh.htm

Survey Documentation and Analysis, Computer-assisted Survey Methods Program, University of California, Berkeley

Internet site http://sda.berkeley.edu/

—General Social Surveys, 1972-2008 Cumulative Data Files, Internet site http://sda.berkeley.edu/cgi-bin32/hsda?harcsda+gss08

Index

401(k)s, 337, 339

abortion, attitude toward, 28, 30
accidents, as cause of death, 85–90
accounts, transaction, 326, 328
adult education, 48–49
air conditioning, houses with, 114–115
alcoholic beverages:
    consumption of, 58–59
    spending on, 265–308
alimony, as source of income, 172–176
alternative workers, 203–204
Alzheimer's disease, as cause of death, 85–88, 90
amenities in housing, 114–115
apartments:
    living in, 106–108
    nearby, 119–120
apparel, spending on, 265–308
arthritis, 68–71
Asia, place of birth, 245, 247
Asian Americans:
    by region, 252, 255
    educational attainment, 41–43
    employment status, 184–186
    full-time workers, 155, 157, 161, 163
    household income, 138–139
    household type, 214–215
    households with children, 221–222
    in poverty, 177–178
    marital status, 227, 229
    men's income, 155, 157
    population, 242–244, 252, 255
    women's income, 161, 163
Asian language speakers, 250–251
assets:
    financial, 326–329
    nonfinancial, 330–333
asthma, 68–71
attitudes:
    toward abortion, 28, 30
    toward Bible, 20, 23
    toward death penalty, 28–29
    toward euthanasia, 28, 30
    toward evolution, 20–21
    toward finances, 10–12
    toward government role in health care, 16, 19
    toward gun control, 28–29
    toward health, 52–54
    toward health care received, 80, 84
    toward home, 116–117
    toward life, 4, 6
    toward marriage, 4–5
    toward neighborhood, 116, 118
    toward politics, 26–27
    toward retirement, 337, 340–341
    toward science, 20–21
    toward sex roles, 16–18
    toward sexual behavior, 24–25
    toward social class membership, 10–11
    toward spanking, 16–17
    toward standard of living, 12–15
    toward work, 7–8
    toward working mothers, 16–18

back pain, 68–71
bathrooms, number of, 106, 109
bedrooms, number of, 106, 109
Bible, attitude toward, 20, 23
Black Americans:
    by region, 252, 255
    educational attainment, 41–43
    employment status, 184–186
    full-time workers, 155, 158, 161, 164
    homeownership of, 102–103
    household income, 138, 140
    household type, 214, 216
    households with children, 221, 223
    in poverty, 177–178
    marital status, 227, 230
    men's income, 155, 158
    population, 242–244, 252, 255
    women's income, 161, 164
blood pressure, high, 68–73
bonds, 326, 328
bronchitis, 68–71
business:
    equity, 330, 332
    ownership, 7, 9
    rooms used for, 106, 109

cancer:
    as cause of death, 85–90
    by type, 68–71
    hospital diagnosis, 83
carport, houses with, 114–115
cash contributions, spending on, 265–308
central cities, homeownership in, 104–105
cerebrovascular disease:
    as cause of death, 85–90
    hospital diagnosis, 83
certificates of deposit, 326, 328
child support, as source of income, 172–176

regions:
  homeownership by, 104–105
  population of, 252–255
religious: *See also* Bible.
  activities, time spent on, 310–322
  preference, 20, 22
renters: *See also* Shelter.
  amenities in housing unit, 114–115
  by heating fuel used, 112–113
  by metropolitan status, 104–105
  by opinion of home, 116–117
  by opinion of neighborhood, 116, 118
  by region, 104–105
  by size of housing unit, 106, 109
  by type of structure, 106–108
  housing cost of, 122–124
  in new housing, 110–111
  neighborhood characteristics, 119–120
  neighborhood problems, 119, 121
  number of, 98–99
respiratory disease:
  as cause of death, 85–90
  hospital diagnosis, 83
retirement:
  accounts, 326, 328, 337, 339–340
  age of, expected, 337, 340
  as reason for moving, 128, 130–131
  attitude toward, 337, 340–341
  income, 172–176
  plan coverage, 337–338
  savings, 337, 340
  spending in, 302–308
rooms, number of in housing, 106, 109

savings, 326, 328
savings bonds, 326, 328
school:
  attitude toward Bible in, 20, 23
  enrollment, 44–47
science, attitude toward, 20–21
self-employment:
  as alternative work arrangement, 203–204
  as source of income, 172–176
  by sex, 198–199
septicemia, as cause of death, 85–90
sex:
  homosexuality, attitude toward, 24–25
  premarital, attitude toward, 24–25
  roles, attitude toward, 16, 18
shelter, spending on, 265–308
shopping, time spent, 310–322
single-family homes:
  living in, 106–108
  nearby, 119–120
single-person households. *See* Households,
    single-person.

singles. *See* Never-married.
sinusitis, 68–71
skin diseases, hospital diagnosis, 83
sleeping, time spent, 310–322
smoking, 58–59
Social Security, as source of income, 172–176
Spanish language speakers, 250–251
spending: *See also* individual product categories.
  by category, 265–308
  of retirees, 302–308
  trends, 265–284
sports, time spent playing, 310–322
standard of living, 12–15
states:
  moving between, 128–131
  place of birth, 245–246
  population of, 252, 256–263
stock ownership, 326, 328–329
stroke, 68–71
suburbs, homeownership in, 104–105
suicide:
  as cause of death, 85–89
  doctor-assisted, attitude toward, 28, 30

taxes, personal, spending on, 265–308. *See also*
    Property taxes.
teeth, absence of, 68–72. *See also* Dental services.
telephone:
  houses with, 114–115
  time spent on, 310–322
television:
  as source of news, 26–27
  time spent watching, 310–322
temporary help workers, 203–204
tobacco products, spending on, 265–308
traffic, as neighborhood problem, 119, 121
transportation, spending on, 265–308
trash removal, monthly cost of, 122, 124. *See also*
    Utilities, fuels, and public services.
traveling, time spent, 310–322
trust in others, 4, 6

ulcers, 68–71
unemployment:
  compensation, as source of income, 172–176
  rate, 182–186
union representation, 207–208
utilities, fuels, and public services, spending on,
    122, 124, 265–308

vehicle purchases, spending on, 265–308
vehicles, as nonfinancial assets, 330, 332
veterans benefits, as source of income, 172–176
vision aids, spending on, 65, 67
visual impairments, 68–72
volunteering, time spent, 310–322